Assessment in Counseling

Assessment in Counseling

Practice and Applications

Richard S. Balkin
University of Mississippi

Gerald A. Juhnke
The University of Texas at San Antonio

Oxford University Press is a department of the University of Oxford. It furthers the University's objective of excellence in research, scholarship, and education by publishing worldwide. Oxford is a registered trade mark of Oxford University Press in the UK and certain other countries.

Published in the United States of America by Oxford University Press
198 Madison Avenue, New York, NY 10016, United States of America.

© Oxford University Press 2018

All rights reserved. No part of this publication may be reproduced, stored in a retrieval system, or transmitted, in any form or by any means, without the prior permission in writing of Oxford University Press, or as expressly permitted by law, by license, or under terms agreed with the appropriate reproduction rights organization. Inquiries concerning reproduction outside the scope of the above should be sent to the Rights Department, Oxford University Press, at the address above.

You must not circulate this work in any other form
and you must impose this same condition on any acquirer.

CIP data is on file at the Library of Congress
ISBN 978-0-19-067275-1

To the students who initially came in to my assessment class thinking "Ick!" and ended up loving it! —RSB

Contents

Preface ix
Acknowledgments xiii

1. The Role of Assessment in Counseling 1
2. Case Studies, Progress Notes, and Classification Systems 15
3. Fundamentals of Assessment 48
4. Current Standards for Validity 77
5. Current Standards for Reliability 88
6. How to Choose an Assessment Instrument 107
7. Conducting an Initial Interview 120
8. Multicultural and Special Population Assessment Issues in Counseling 138
9. Fundamentals of Ability Assessment 151
10. Fundamentals of Career Assessment 178
11. Marriage, Substance Abuse, and Suicide Assessment 191
12. Fundamentals of Interpretation in Assessment 219
13. Assessment of Accountability in Counseling 234

Appendix A 251
Appendix B 253
References 257
Index 267

Preface

Our approach to this book was to create a text that would emphasize assessment as a skill for professional counselors. When I teach assessment, as well as other courses that emphasize research methods and statistics, I often find students overwhelmed with the mathematical concepts and quite anxious about the coursework. Too often students experience assessment courses, and subsequently the textbooks used for the course, as a statistics-heavy class accompanied by an encyclopedia of a variety of assessments. We take a different approach. We emphasize the skills used in assessment and believe that once you understand the skills you can apply these skills across a broad range of assessment instruments and strategies. Assessment, like most core areas of counseling, has a theoretical basis and a pertinent, practical component. However, this practical component often gets lost in the application of the skills and use of instruments that heavily rely on psychometric properties.

Statistics are an influential component to assessment in counseling. If you are like many students and get mired in the mathematical concepts, I encourage you to take a step back and relax. Yes, there will be some math discussed and applied in this textbook, but we hope you will find that the explanation of the computations are provided to emphasize the process, as opposed to focusing on only the product. In my experience, most counseling students who express some intimidation with the statistical concepts do so as a result of past experience. My hope is that you will see these concepts expressed in a new or different light with focus on application, rather than the mere computation.

My coauthor and I worked hard to focus on the application of the theoretical and measurement concepts of assessment in counseling. We attempted to use a conversational style of writing and introduce three case studies that we follow throughout the text. This is different from other textbooks that also present similar principles but do not demonstrate the application of said principles. In addition, instead of introducing you to a plethora of instruments, we select seminal measures that you are likely to comes across and use in the profession. We do not focus on types of assessments typically not used by professional counselors, such as projective measures. The instruments we discuss are commonly used in professional counseling but by no means exhaustive. But through the use of this text and course content you will have the skills to search, select, and administer the type of assessment instruments that you deem helpful for your practice as a professional counselor, regardless of your specialization. Through this format, you will, we hope, see examples of assessment principles that may be applied to a variety of settings. Our goal is for this textbook to serve as a guide for administering, scoring, interpreting, and communicating assessment results.

Organization of This Book

We organized this book to provide a logical flow for the material we introduce. Chapters 1 through 5 represent foundational elements for assessment in counseling. In these chapters, you will learn about the background, history, and relevance of assessment and the properties of assessment instruments. Chapters 6 through 8 include practical issues related to selecting, administering, scoring, and interpreting assessment instruments. Chapters 9 through 13 include information on specific types of instruments, particularly for areas of specialization, fundamentals in interpreting and communicating results, and accountability issues. Each chapter ends with information related to applying the material presented in the chapter. We use the case studies from Chapter 2 to demonstrate how the material may be utilized in a counseling setting.

Chapter 1 We introduce assessment as a continuous process in counseling. Counselors have some choices with respect to the populations they serve and the modalities they employ, but assessment is an integral component to all populations and used within all models. Key terms are defined. We also cover the history of assessment, emphasizing past mistakes and connections to current practice. Ethical and legal issues are highlighted.

Chapter 2 We introduce three case studies that will be used throughout the text. We highlight the basic elements of an intake interview, which are addressed in detail in Chapter 7. The nature of diagnosis and an overview of common mental health disorders are presented in this chapter. We also provide information related to writing and maintaining progress notes and highlight common note-taking methods.

Chapter 3 This chapter is likely the most statistically focused chapter in the text. We cover basic concepts of measurement and address procedures in computing and conceptualizing scores on assessment instruments. Students will be able to differentiate between norm-referenced and criterion-referenced tests and compute and interpret measures of central tendency, variability, and correlation and convert the scores into meaningful information in order to make comparisons and formulate a conceptualization of the client.

Chapter 4 We provide the most up-to-date definitions of test validation with comparisons to previous iterations of test validity and how the concept evolved. The five types of validity evidence are emphasized and tied to the development of instruments. Students will learn how to evaluate validity in order to be informed consumers of instruments.

Chapter 5 We highlight reliability in this chapter. One important consideration is to understand reliability as a characteristic of test scores and not the test or scales. We focus on the various methods of evaluating reliability of scores, particularly as they relate to the normative sample. Applications of reliability estimates to the case study are provided.

Chapter 6 This chapter provides an opportunity to revisit the concepts in Chapters 1 through 5 and apply these concepts to selecting appropriate instruments. We emphasize the qualifications necessary to use specific instruments. We also highlight how counselors can obtain information on tests through the use of test reviews from various databases. We address information included in test reviews and keys to interpreting and using test reviews in order to be an informed consumer of assessment instruments.

Chapter 7 The clinical interview, initially addressed in Chapter 2, is presented in detail with emphasis on the psychosocial intake, using the CLISD-PA model, and the mental status exam. We emphasize different types of intake data and specifically address substance abuse intake. We also provide information on using basic counseling skills as an integral part of the intake interview. We apply the concepts of the clinical interview to the case studies.

Chapter 8 This chapter on multicultural issues in assessment is foundational in exploring such issues as test bias versus test fairness, assessment with special populations, and the limitations to generalizability from typical normative samples. We explore issues related to testing accommodations and how such accommodations may affect the interpretation of scores. Finally, we address how counselors can improve their cross-cultural competence as assessment professionals and explore multicultural implications in the case study.

Chapter 9 We discuss similarities and differences of intelligence, achievement, and aptitude tests and place these constructs into the context of ability testing. We introduce theories of intelligence and provide information related to instruments that were designed to measure intelligence, as well as the extent to which the instruments correspond to theories of intelligence. We also highlight research on emotional intelligence and some of the criticisms of emotional intelligence. We highlight common intelligence measures and address applications to a case study. We also discuss the development of achievement tests, how scores are reported, and the relationship of achievement and aptitude to general cognitive ability. Applications to a case study are addressed.

Chapter 10 In this chapter, we focus on how career assessment may provide valuable information to guide career counseling and overall wellness of clients served in multiple settings such as schools, agencies, organizations, and practices. Theories and elements of career assessment are presented, as well as an overview of common measures used in career assessment. We focus specifically on the O*NET system and applying career assessment to the case studies.

Chapter 11 This chapter is devoted to specialty areas of assessment, including assessment in marriage, couples, and family counseling; substance abuse counseling; and suicide assessment interventions. We provide information on scales related to these areas and apply them to our case studies. In addition, we provide a model for assessing suicide and an overview of instruments that may be used.

Chapter 12 Now that we have presented various types of assessment commonly used in counseling, we provide an overview of how to write an assessment report. We highlight both the structure and contents of the assessment report and provide clear examples, using the case studies, regarding how reports may be written for clients, referral agents, and stakeholders.

Chapter 13 We conclude this text with an overview of accountability in counseling and the role of assessment. We discuss standardized and nonstandardized measures of accountability and apply issues of accountability to our case studies.

Acknowledgments

I, first and foremost, thank my wife, Melissa, and my children, Abigail, Gabriela, and Isabel for their support during this writing endeavor. I also want to extend big thanks to my friend and colleague, Jerry Juhnke, for completing this journey with me and making such a wonderful contribution to the book. Finally, I wish to thank my publications editor, Dana Bliss, for his enthusiasm and optimism.

—Richard S. Balkin

I thank Deborah, Bryce, Brenna, Gerald, and Babe Juhnke for their love and support during this writing endeavor. As well, I thank my very good friend and professional colleague, Rick, for allowing me the privilege of co-authoring this text with him.

—Gerald A. Juhnke

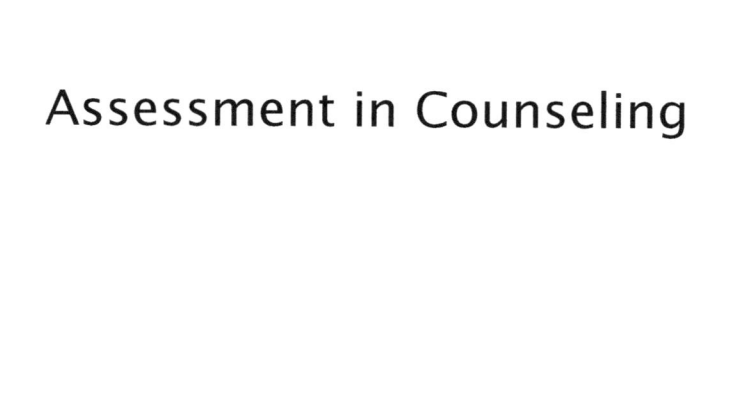

Assessment in Counseling

1

The Role of Assessment in Counseling

> ## Objectives
> 1. Understand the importance and role of assessment in counseling.
> 2. Identify psychological constructs and associated operational definitions.
> 3. Distinguish between standardized and nonstandardized assessments.
> 4. Identify relevant historical issues of assessment and the implications for assessment today.
> 5. Recognize the role and importance of professional organizations with respect to the practice of assessment.
> 6. Identify competencies related to assessment practices.
> 7. Identify ethical and legal codes affecting assessment.

Overview

In this chapter, we discuss why this book exists and why you might be interested in it! We discuss key terms related to assessment and the historical antecedents that address why we do what we do and why it is important. We also highlight important professional, ethical, and legal issues regarding assessment and accountability.

What Is Assessment?

If you are like most students we (Rick and Jerry) encounter in counseling programs, we would guess that you might not be too excited to be in this class. Most students in counseling programs do not aspire to be counselors dreaming of the day they will sit with clients and ask them to fill out some measures. There are a lot of reasons you chose to enter this field, but paperwork and reports are probably not one of those reasons.

However, assessment is not some obscure practice in counseling. Not only is assessment an essential tool in working with clients, but assessment is something you continually do in your own life. Maybe you have been to a party or bar recently, and you made eye contact with someone. What happened next? There was probably some nonverbal communication that could be interpreted somewhere between, "Come over here. I want to get to know you better" and "I am so far out of your league. Don't waste your time." There were probably a variety of social cues that transpired, which you used to interpret whether you should approach or walk away—you looked at the person's eyes, whether there was a smile, if the person sustained eye contact or turned away. As you observe these cues and decide your next move, you are engaged in *assessment*—the collection of information in order to identify, analyze, evaluate, and address the problems, issues, and circumstances of clients in the counseling relationship.

Assessment is used as a basis for identifying problems, planning interventions, evaluating and/or diagnosing clients, and informing clients and stakeholders. Many novice counselors may make the mistake of identifying assessment as a means to an end, such as providing a label or diagnosis to a client. In this text, assessment is viewed as a process essential to all elements of counseling. Whether practicing in a school, private practice, agency, or other healthcare setting, assessment plays an integral role. Assessment moves beyond the administration of measures. Assessment involves identifying statements, actions, and procedures to help individuals, groups, couples, and families make progress in the counseling environment. Although counselors have the opportunity to limit their scope of practice with respect to modalities, theories, and types of clients, a counselor cannot function without an understanding of the processes and procedures of assessment in counseling.

Some academics may discern between assessment and testing (Cohen, Swerdlik, & Sturman, 2013; Gladding, 2013). The focus of assessment is on gathering information; *testing* refers to the measurement of psychological constructs through instruments or specified procedures. In this sense, a *construct* refers to a phenomenon that exists but cannot be directly observed. For example, variables such as height and weight can be directly observed. Measurement systems for height and weight are available to minimize errors and guarantee accuracy of results. However, not all variables can be directly observed. Emotional states such as depression or happiness, or cognitive traits such as intelligence, or even psychological states such as stress, cannot be directly observed or measured. How often has a friend told you "I feel fine" rather than acknowledged something was wrong? Constructs may not be identified so easily. In addition, a construct may vary, depending on the *operational definition*—how the construct is measured. For example, Michael Jordan was labeled a *brilliant* basketball player. Does this imply that Michael Jordan was creative, had a high level of intelligence, or had superior analytic skills? Quite simply, an operational definition would need to be applied in order to measure the construct of brilliance, and this definition may vary depending on the instruments used or the experts' theoretical underpinnings of the measure.

The process of assessing, and sometimes testing, is necessary to understand a client. However, differentiating between assessment and testing may be viewed as an academic exercise. Often, these terms may be interchangeable, as the process of testing (i.e., administering, scoring, and interpreting an instrument) cannot be separated from the assessment process. Testing, therefore, is part of assessment. A distinction is made between standardized and nonstandardized assessment. *Standardized* assessment refers to a formal process in which a specific set of rules and guidelines related to administration, scoring, and interpretation are followed consistently to ensure accurate results over a period of time and across populations. Standardized assessments include instruments developed under a rigorous process and produce results that may be generalizable to a population or meaningful to an individual in the context of a population. Instruments such as achievement tests, aptitude tests, and personality tests fit this description. *Nonstandardized* assessment refers to a process of gathering information without adherence to a strict set of rules or guidelines. Nonstandardized assessments may include clinical interviews. Even when such interviews follow a formula or pattern, deviations in administrations occur because of the personal nature of the interactions and of addressing the client's personal needs. Such assessments may not adhere to a rigid administration, scoring, and interpretation process.

History of Assessment

The Council for Accreditation of Counseling and Related Educational Programs (2015) directs accredited counseling programs to address "historical perspectives concerning the nature and meaning of assessment" (p. 12). Such discussions may appear to lack relevance and come across as tedious and uninteresting when in fact the history of assessment and testing practices may shed light on how assessment practices evolved and why specific procedures, which may appear foreign or confusing, are used today (Gregory, 2014). More important, a review of assessment history may shed light on the past misuse of assessment instruments in order to ensure valid practice in the future.

Issues of testing and measurement are by no means new to the social sciences. As early as 2200 BCE, public officials in China were issued an examination every third year by the Chinese emperor (Cohen et al., 2013; Gregory, 2014). Although these examinations were nothing like the type of standardized measures given today—such exams throughout the Middle Ages emphasized archery, equestrian abilities (Cohen et al., 2013), poetry composition, handwriting, and elements of military, agriculture, and civil law—the exams were used for employment considerations (Gregory, 2014).

The foundation for modern testing began in the 19th century among biologists, particularly Charles Darwin (1809–1882) and Sir Francis Galton (1822–1911). Darwin's work had two important contributions to assessment. First, Darwin linked human development to animals, thereby influencing the use of animals to study human behavior. Second, Darwin identified the notion of individual differences when noting the relationship of children to parents, which led to increased studies in heredity (Cohen et al., 2013).

Francis Galton was a cousin of Darwin (Cohen et al., 2013), so the fact that he commenced studies in heredity and individual differences was not likely a coincidence. Interestingly, one area that Galton is known for turned out to be somewhat irrelevant to assessment by modern standards. Galton investigated the relationship between physical characteristics and mental capacities. For example, Galton would examine such physical characteristics as height, weight, arm span, head length, and finger length and make comparisons to such mental/behavioral characteristics as auditory and visual acuity, grip strength, and reaction time. Galton set up a laboratory at the 1884 International Exposition and charged individuals a minimal fee to take these tests (Anastasi & Urbina, 1997). One of Galton's primary interests was noting the individual differences in regard to perceptions of the senses. Galton noted that individuals with severe mental retardation were indifferent to sensory perceptions, such as hot, cold, or pain, which led to the investigation of how physical characteristics may be related to discerning sensory information (Anastasi & Urbina, 1997). Although biased sampling and the type of data may be criticized, three important contributions should be noted:

1. Galton believed anything could be measured. This belief is important to modern assessment practices, as counselors attempt to measure processes that are not directly observable, such as interests and emotional states.
2. Although Galton was not able to connect physical traits to mental capacities, the insignificant relationship is nevertheless important. Sometimes knowing where not to look for answers is as important as knowing where to find answers.
3. Galton devised a standardized method for gathering information and recording results (Gregory, 2014), which influenced modern practices of assessment.

Although the notion that physical characteristics relating to mental capacities may seem more closely aligned with the late 17th-century Salem witch trials, in which daily events were connected to unlikely phenomena—in this case, supernatural occurrences—the astute counselor may notice that society still searches for answers with overly simplistic explanations, such as attributing the achievement gap to differences in ethnicity. Many school districts across the country break down academic achievement levels across ethnicity. How different is that from identifying intellectual capacities based on arm length?

A contemporary of Galton was Wilhelm Wundt (1832–1920), who studied mental processes over 20 years prior to Galton's work at the 1884 International Exposition. In 1879, Wundt established the first psychological laboratory in Leipzig, Germany. Unlike Galton, who was interested in individual differences, Wundt was interested in similarities among humans, particularly with variables such as response time, perception, and attention (Cohen et al., 2013). Wundt used a calibrated pendulum to measure what he thought would be immediate thought processes (Gregory, 2014). As the pendulum swung back and forth, a bell was struck and participants were asked to identify the position of the pendulum when the bell was struck. Wundt ultimately concluded that the speed of thought varied among individuals. Wundt did not account for threats to experimental validity, such as variations in attention span or differences in the environment, so findings would be summarily dismissed using modern standards of assessment and research practices; however, studies by Wundt and Galton provided a foundation and interest in assessment practices (Gregory, 2014). These were initial attempts to measure mental processes.

James McKeen Cattell (1860–1944) studied the works of Galton and Wundt and was highly influenced by Galton's study of individual differences. Cattell coined the term *mental test*, and the focus of Cattell's work was to examine differences in reaction time for various mental tests, such as reaction time after hearing a sound, judgment of 10 seconds of time, and short-term memory. Similar to Galton, he also studied physical characteristics. One portion of a mental test included the strength of a hand squeeze and the degree of pressure needed to cause pain by pressing a rubber tip against the forehead (Cohen et al., 2013; Gregory, 2014). Once again, although some of these practices may appear preposterous today, keep in mind that many tests (e.g., American College Testing [ACT], Wechsler Intelligence Scale for Children—Fifth Edition [WISC-V], Test of Variables of Attention) that help counselors examine aptitude, achievement, intellectual functioning, and mental process are timed or have timed elements.

Not until 1901 did a student of Cattell, Clark Wissler, identify that the processes measured by Galton and Cattell had no correlation to academic achievement. Unfortunately, response times, not what criteria qualified as a mental test (e.g., grip strength), were summarily dismissed for about 70 years until researchers on intelligence readdressed the value of response time. Shortly thereafter, Alfred Binet (1857–1911) created what would become known as the first *intelligence test* in 1905 (Gregory, 2014).

Binet was influenced by the works of J. E. D. Esquirol (1772–1840) and Edouard Seguin (1812–1880), who spearheaded a modern approach for identifying and working with individuals with severe educational deficits. Gregory (2014) noted that Binet's intelligence tests were developed to identify children with severe educational deficits (at the time referred to as *mental retardation*) who would not benefit from the regular school environment. Binet's tests would be adopted internationally and would influence later works by David Wechsler, who would initially introduce intelligence tests specifically geared for adults (Cohen et al., 2013).

Unfortunately, the popularity of intelligence testing led to blatant misuse. Gregory (2014) described the misuse of intelligence testing by Henry Goddard (1866–1957), who translated Binet's scale from French to English in 1908. Goddard believed that individuals with low intellectual functioning should be segregated from society and that restrictions should be placed on such individuals in order to control procreation. Goddard was commissioned by Ellis Island to administer the Binet-Simon Intelligence Test to immigrants as they were arriving. Tests were administered by translators in various languages, such as

Yiddish, Russian, and Italian, and compared to the French norms established by Binet. The result, of course, was that over 80% of the immigrants tested were identified with low intellectual functioning.

Ultimately, the popularity of intelligence testing led to the construction and use of instruments to measure personality and aptitude. Freud and Jung developed theories of personality in the late 19th and early 20th centuries. Cohen et al. (2013) identified World War I (1914–1918) as the precursor to group testing. The military needed to identify individuals who may not be intellectually or emotionally fit for duty. The first self-report personality assessment, the Woodworth Personal Data Sheet, was not used until 1919–1920 by the U.S. Army (Butcher, 2010). The instrument consisted of 116 self-report items related to "physical problems, social behavior, and mental health symptoms" such as "Have you ever seen a vision?" "Do you have a great fear of fire?" "Do you feel tired most of the time?" "Is it easy to get you angry?" (Butcher, 2010, p. 5). The Personal Data Sheet was adapted for children in 1924. The Personal Data Sheet served as a precursor for the Minnesota Multiphasic Personality Inventory (MMPI). The MMPI revolutionized personality testing. Butcher indicated that large sets of items were developed and selected based on how homogeneous groups of psychiatric patients answered the items. Items that discriminated between diagnostic categories were retained. Items on the MMPI and MMPI-2 may seem to lack evidence based on test content. In other words, items may appear ambiguous, because the items may not have been developed to measure a particular symptom. For example, "I like mechanics magazines" may discriminate individuals with elevations on Scale 4, psychodeviance. Consider the implications—the MMPI and associated instruments (i.e., MMPI-2, MMPI–Restructured Form [MMPI-RF], and MMPI–Adolescent [MMPI-A]) are among the most widely used instruments with over 19,000 articles and books published in relation to these instruments (Butcher, 2010); yet the items were not created with a particular construct in mind to measure. Clearly, the lack of obvious connection between items and potential mental distress or disorders is a legitimate criticism.

The development of the MMPI and subsequent adaptations and revisions (i.e., MMPI-2 and MMPI-A) spawned additional diagnostic and personality measures, such as the Millon Clinical Mutiaxial Inventory (MCMI), which measures personality issues. Whereas the MMPI focused on the diagnosis of psychopathology (e.g., mood, anxiety, psychosis), the MCMI focused on personality disorders. In the 1950s, interest in general personality, as opposed to assessing clinical problems, spawned the emergence of the 16 Personality Factor Questionnaire and the California Psychological Inventory. These instruments served as predecessors to the NEO Personality Inventory (NEO-PI) in the 1980s. The NEO-PI assesses individuals on a five-factor model of personality, including openness, agreeableness, neuroticism, extraversion, and conscientiousness, also known as the "'Big Five' personality dimensions" (Butcher, 2010, p. 9).

In the 1960s to the present, measures were developed to focus on specific psychological constructs, such as depression, with the Beck Depression Inventory. Today, counselors may find instruments that measure a variety of constructs such as diagnostic categories, anxiety and trauma, suicide ideation, wellness, and substance abuse. Many instruments today are used less for diagnosis and more for identifying problem areas or strength-based areas. Many of these instruments continue to rely on self-report, which may be problematic in terms of producing a valid response from a client who may not be well. Therefore, the use of assessment instruments that focus on observations from parents, teachers, clinicians, and/or significant others was a natural progression. Such instruments as the Behavior Assessment System for Children and the Child Behavior Checklist were developed in the 1990s and include report forms for the client and observers (e.g., parent, teacher).

Refinement related to assessment and testing is ongoing, as are the issues. The standards for test construction are evolving continually. As a result, instruments constructed, normed, and validated in the 1980s may be out-of-date by today's standards. How instruments are used and individuals are compared is an ongoing debate. Issues related to educational placement, incarceration, job placement and promotion, and differential diagnoses permeate the counseling profession. Counselors need to be aware of the multicultural and social justice issues that emerge from testing and comparing populations.

The Development of Counselors as Assessment Professionals

As mentioned, assessment is an integral part of counseling practice, and therefore training in assessment is essential. The Council for Accreditation of Counseling and Related Educational Programs (2015) identified assessment as one of the "eight common core curricular areas" (p. 8) required for all students in accredited counseling programs. Although counselors receive training and practice in assessment, the right for counselors to practice assessment is not a given, as such rights are dictated by state licensing boards. However, in general, counselors may use a variety of instruments, with projective assessments being the least available. Many state licensing boards have rules that prevent professionals outside of psychology from using *projective tests*—tests in which the responses of individual are understood as an unconscious expression of personality.

The Association for Assessment and Research Counseling

The Association for Assessment and Research in Counseling (AARC; formerly known as the Association for Assessment in Counseling and Education [AACE] and the Association for Assessment in Counseling [AAC]) is a division of the American Counseling Association (ACA), whose mission is "to promote and recognize excellence in assessment, research, and evaluation in counseling in counseling" (AARC, 2016). The AARC and ACA produced statements with respect to counselors' use of standardized instruments. In addition to being a division of ACA, AARC represents counselors in a variety of work groups representing counselors' interests in assessment, measurement, evaluation, and diagnosis.

In terms of practicing assessment, counselors should be aware of guidelines in the *Responsibilities of Users of Standardized Tests* (RUST; Wall, Augustin, Eberly, Lungberg, & Vansickle, 2003), *Standards for Qualifications of Test Users* (Erford, Basham, Cashwell, Juhnke, & Wall, 2003), and the *ACA Code of Ethics* (ACA, 2014), as well as the qualification requirements for each test publisher.

Responsibilities of Users of Standardized Tests

The RUST statement (http://aarc-counseling.org/assets/cms/uploads/files/rust.pdf) was developed for the purposes of educating counselors and educators on ethical use of standardized tests. The AAC addressed guidelines across seven areas: (a) Qualifications of Test Users, (b) Technical Knowledge, (c) Test Selection, (d) Test Administration, (e) Test Scoring, (f) Interpreting Test Results, and (g) Communicating Test Results (Wall et al., 2003). Wall et al. indicated that the responsibility of ensuring appropriate test use lies with the counselor or educator administering the test. An understanding of measurement to select, score, and interpret results, as well as of protocols for administering and scoring tests, is pertinent. Efforts should be made to communicate test results to clients and stakeholders in a manner that is understandable and useful while also addressing any limitations to selected tests.

Standards for Qualifications of Test Users

The RUST statement was a precursor to the *Standards for Qualifications of Test Users*, a document that was adopted by the ACA (Erford et al., 2003; see http://aarc-counseling.org/assets/cms/uploads/files/standards.pdf) related to the training and skills necessary for counselors to use psychological tests. As noted previously, this document was developed, in part, to address concerns of legislative bodies that received pressure from outside organizations related to counselors' right to use psychological measures. Among the issues addressed in the document was that assessment is not a stand-alone practice. Assessment should be integrated along with counseling theory and never used with populations or issues outside the counselor's scope of practice. Similar to the RUST statement, counselors should have knowledge and skill in areas related to measurement, test development, administration, scoring, and communicating results. The ACA also addressed counselors' responsibility to promote fairness in assessment practices by understanding the role of diversity and the legal and ethical implications of assessment.

The *ACA Code of Ethics*

Section E of the *ACA Code of Ethics* (2014) covers evaluation, assessment, and interpretation. The ACA addressed ethics in both formal and informal assessments. The primary goal is to promote client welfare. This section of the *ACA Code of Ethics* (COE) is extensive and covers 13 areas. Some of the information in the COE is similar to the RUST statement and *Standards for Qualifications of Test Users*, particularly with respect to counselor competence, instrument selection, administration, scoring, interpretation, and attention to diversity. However, in addition to outlining the responsibilities of counselors, the COE also covers the rights of clients, including informed consent and release and security of assessment data. Clients have a right to know the nature of the assessment and how the assessment results may be used prior to administration. Clients also have the right to receive the results and identify qualified professionals, if any, with whom the results may be shared. Confidentiality may not be compromised, and this is an issue that needs to be addressed before administering an assessment, especially if the client is referred by an organization, agency, court, or other professional. For example, the U.S. Department of Transportation has policies and procedures related to who may administer substance abuse assessments for transportation employees and how the results should be communicated. Courts may order an individual for psychological testing and expect a report related to the results. Counselors, therefore, need to be proactive in addressing issues of informed consent and confidentiality, especially with regard to who will have access to the results and the implications of said results.

When administering assessments, counselors need to be aware of administration conditions, as tests should be administered under similar conditions in which the norms were established. However, accommodations may be necessary, especially if assessing individuals with any disability or impairment.

As mentioned, diagnosis is an aspect of assessment and perhaps represents an area that differs considerably from ethical codes in other mental health professions. As the counseling profession follows a developmental model, as opposed to a medical model focused on diagnosis and treatment, counselors need to be aware of the conditions and issues in providing a diagnosis. These issues include using multiple methods and data sources when providing a diagnosis and awareness of the impact that such a label may bring. The cultural context of the client should be considered with respect to providing a diagnosis. Perhaps an additional area in which counseling is unique is that the ACA (2014) indicated that "counselors may refrain from making and/or reporting a diagnosis if they believe it would cause harm to the client or others" (p. 11). Thus, when a diagnosis is not in the best interest of the client, the counselor may refrain from providing a diagnosis.

A growing area in the field of counseling is forensic evaluation. As in other types of assessment, the ACA addressed competency and consent, but one area of difference is the stipulation that counselors not evaluate their clients for forensic purposes and avoid relationships with individuals related to forensic evaluation, including the individual being evaluated and personal relationships associated with the individual.

The *ACA Code of Ethics* is used by licensure boards across the country. Assessment is an integral part of counseling and emphasized in the COE. Counselors need to implement the ethical codes into their practice and be particularly attentive to the manner in which assessments should be introduced, consent and assent procedures, rules regarding disclosures, issues of diversity, and the impact of diagnosis.

Fair Access to Tests

In the past, state psychology boards attempted to limit the use of psychological assessments to licensed psychologists (Naugle, 2009).

> While some professional groups are seeking to control and restrict the use of psychological tests, the American Counseling Association believes firmly that one's right to use tests in counseling practice is directly related to competence. This competence is achieved through education, training, and experience in the field of testing. Thus, professional counselors with a master's degree or higher and appropriate coursework in appraisal/assessment, supervision, and experience are qualified to use objective tests. With additional training and experience, professional counselors are also able to administer projective tests, individual intelligence tests, and clinical diagnostic test. (Erford et al., 2003, p. 1)

The right to use psychological tests is not a simple issue, as the debate includes licensing boards, professional organizations, and test publishers. Licensing boards address scope-of-practice issues. Turf battles ensue when licensing boards of one profession attempt to limit the scope of practice of another profession through legal wrangling. However, counselor licensure laws in most states clearly identify the right of counselors to use assessments, although the type of assessments may be limited, and such limitation vary from state to state. Professional organizations provide guidelines for training, practice, and ethics in assessment. Test publishers are responsible for "monitoring the competencies of those who purchase and utilize assessment instruments" (Naugle, 2009, p. 32). Note that these organizations have missions that may be aligned or have competing interests. As noted earlier, an effort to protect a professional turf may have an effect on individuals who purchase and use assessment instruments, which does not benefit test publishers. Although guidelines are necessary to protect the public from poor practice, the public does not benefit when professions duly qualified are limited in assessment practice.

The Fair Access Coalition on Testing (FACT), along with the ACA and the National Board of Certified Counselors who both serve on FACT, advocate for counselors and other qualified professionals for fair test use. FACT plays an important role in collaborating with other professionals who use standardized instruments and works to protect the rights of counselors and other associated professionals (e.g., school psychologists, speech–language pathologists).

In 1997, Indiana passed counselor licensure. This law was followed by legislation allowing the Indiana State Psychology Board to create a restricted test list. In 1998, the Indiana State Psychology Board submitted a list of 318 tests as restricted for sole use by psychologists. FACT, along with the ACA, AACE, and National Board for Certified Counselors, provided letters and testimony to the Indiana state legislature and governor. In 2007, the Indiana state legislature repealed the law allowing the Indiana State Psychology

Board to create a restricted test list. Other states (e.g., Maryland, Kentucky) have attempted to restrict use of assessment instruments (National Fair Access Coalition on Testing, n.d.). In addition, some states (e.g., Arkansas, Texas) included restrictions on using projective techniques in the counselor licensure laws (Naugle, 2009). Counselors should be aware of their rights as test users and stay abreast of legal challenges that attempt to limit said rights. The importance of joining and maintaining memberships to state and national counseling associations (e.g., ACA) cannot be overemphasized, as such organizations play a leading role in advocating for the rights of counselors.

Test Publisher Qualifications of Test Users

The Association of Test Publishers is also represented on FACT. As noted earlier, test publishers also monitor test use, by providing an application process or qualification process to administer assessment instruments. Some test companies use a tiered system. In the first tier, often referred to as *A level*, individuals with minimal training, a bachelor's degree, or certification may administer tests. In the second tier, often referred to as *B level*, individuals with a master's degree and/or membership in a professional organization (e.g., ACA) and/or professional licensure may administer tests. In the third tier, often referred to as *C level*, individuals with a doctoral degree and/or specialized training may administer tests.

Although this system appears to be the most common among test publishers, it is not the only system employed by test publishers. Some testing companies include an additional fourth tier, in which test users need to include a specific background related to the instrument (Naugle, 2009). Application procedures for other test companies may include information related to licensure, highest educational degree, specialized training, continuing education, certifications, and membership in professional associations.

Legal Issues

In addition to organizations that represent counselors' interests in assessment and ethical codes that address rights and responsibilities of counselors and clients, familiarity of legal and legislative issues that affect assessment practice in counseling are important. Laws that affect assessment practices may not necessarily be created with assessment in mind, but the practice of assessment may be affected in a variety of environments (Whiston, 2017), including healthcare, education, business, and public service.

Healthcare Legislation

The Health Insurance Portability and Accountability Act (HIPAA; 1996) is a complex law of regulations concerning the privacy of healthcare records. Counselors working in agencies and private practice need to be familiar with HIPAA guidelines. In essence, HIPAA provided clients with increased control and access to healthcare information (Erard, 2004). Clients have a right to their assessment results and reports and may decide who receives this information. HIPAA affects the manner in which counselors, agencies, and organizations operate, such as providing a privacy notice to all clients regarding their records and obtaining permission to release information to third-party payors for reimbursement. Counselors should also be aware of exceptions to HIPAA policies, such as laws related to being a mandated reporter in cases such as physical/sexual abuse of a minor. Counselors working in a private practice or agency setting should seek training regarding adherence to HIPAA guidelines and implementation.

Civil Rights Legislation

Civil rights legislation dates back to 1866 with the emancipation of slaves. Since that time, seven additional civil rights acts were passed. The 1964 and 1972 civil rights acts mandated discrimination-free workplaces. These laws affected employment-based testing, which led to disputes related to fair testing practices in the workplace, resulting in the Civil Rights Act of 1991. The Civil Rights Act of 1991 places the responsibility of appropriate test practices on the employer. In other words, employers must be able to demonstrate that employment testing relates to the duties of the job that are to be performed by employees. In addition, the use of separate norms based on race, ethnicity, sex, or religion was prohibited (Whiston, 2017).

In 2009, a lawsuit was filed against the city of New Haven, Connecticut, on behalf of firefighters who cited discrimination related to promotion. In *Ricci v. DeStafano*, an exam for the rank of lieutenant and captain was administered to 118 firefighters, in which the top scorers would be appointed to the vacant positions. None of the top scorers were African American, and only two Latino/a candidates were eligible for promotion. White candidates were eligible for all of the vacancies. The city of New Haven opted to disregard the test results on the notion that to use the results would be discriminatory. The lawsuit was filed by those who passed the test and were denied promotion. The U.S. Supreme Court ruled that the city acted wrongly in not accepting the results, as the test was created by a third party, I/O Solutions, and represented a reliable and valid result. In fact, testimony demonstrated the test items were related to the duties required for the jobs in question.

The Americans with Disabilities Act of 1990 required employers to provide reasonable accommodations related to employees with disabilities (Koch, 2000), and naturally this extends to testing. Note that this policy is in line with the *ACA Code of Ethics* (2014). Although the ACA indicated that assessments should be administered under the same conditions in which the instrument was standardized, it acknowledged that accommodations may be necessary, such as with individuals with disabilities, but the accommodations need to be addressed in the interpretations and the overall validity of the test. Koch's (2000) use of the term "reasonable accommodations" (p. 103) is in line with the wording from the Americans with Disabilities Act. Counselors should be cautious with respect to implementation, as the term *reasonable* is somewhat ambiguous and subject to interpretation.

Educational Legislation

Congress passed the Individuals with Disabilities Act (IDEA) in 1997 and reauthorized the act in 2004. IDEA was a reauthorization and extension of PL-94-142, the Education for All Handicapped Children Act in 1975. Telzrow and McNamara (2001) identified three new areas of IDEA that impacted assessment: "(a) increased parental involvement in educational decision-making; (b) greater emphasis on accountability and student results; and (c) the development of new assessment technologies" (p. 105). As IDEA mandated individualized education plans for children diagnosed with a disability, parental involvement was a core area, in which the parent/guardian has decision-making authority. Schools cannot evaluate a child for a disability without parental consent. Once parental consent is provided, the school has 60 days to conduct an evaluation on the student. School counselors may not be responsible for the educational evaluation, but they typically serve as a member of the committee developing the individualized educational plan in collaboration with the parent(s)/guardian(s). Parental consent for testing was not a new issue, as this right was also addressed in the Family Educational Rights and Privacy Act of 1974 (FERPA). FERPA also limited the release of educational records to parents/guardians and students over the age of 18. One issue that may be affected is counseling records, which are not generally part of the students' educational file but may be included. School counselors should be aware of district policy regarding counseling notes about students (Whiston, 2017).

Similar to IDEA, the No Child Left Behind legislation (NCLB; 2002) established accountability measures in educational settings. A major outcome of NCLB was the mandate for the implementation of high-stakes testing (Duffy, Giordano, Farrell, Paneque, & Crump, 2008). Schools became accountable through the implementation of minimal proficiency standards established by the state but approved by the U.S. Department of Education. The implementation of high-stakes testing resulted in increases in student testing, such as using preparatory testing procedures to increase performance on the state-mandated test. Additional criticisms include an overreliance on test scores to address educational shortcomings and the presence of increased anxiety over test performance among children.

In 2015 President Barack Obama requested Congress to overhaul NCLB, citing a high rate of school failure based on measures enacted by NCLB. The Every Student Succeeds Act (ESSA; enacted in 2015) maintained standardized testing requirements but reduced the role of the federal government, making accountability the responsibility of the states. The ESSA provides the following mandates (Klein, 2016):

1. States are required to submit accountability plans to the Department of Education and set goals related to exam scores, English-language proficiency, and graduation rates.
2. Participation rates in standardized testing must meet or exceed 95%.
3. States must identify and intervene in schools representing the bottom 5% and any school with graduation rates of 67% or less.

4. States must develop challenging academic standards.
5. Only 1% of students may be administered alternative tests.
6. States do not have to evaluate teachers based on testing outcomes.

Counselors need to stay aware of ongoing educational legislation, as such legislation affects clients and the advocacy efforts of counselors on behalf of their clients.

Summary

Assessment is used across all counseling settings in a variety of ways. Assessment is integral to the clinical interview. Assessment includes diagnosis and treatment planning. As counselors meet with their clients, they make decisions on what problems to address and what interventions to attempt. Hence, assessment permeates every aspect of the counseling process.

Assessment is also used for advocacy and placement. Through careful assessment, clients can be provided with needed services that otherwise may have been unattainable. When clients are active participants in the assessment process, they have the opportunity to learn something about themselves, including personal strengths, challenges, interests, and activities that promote growth and wellness.

Counselors, therefore, are both consumers and producers of assessment data. They need to be aware of the various types of assessment tools in order to select the best instruments for their clients. Counselors need to be well rounded in their delivery of services; application of both standardized and nonstandardized assessment strategies is integral to being a competent counselor. In addition to being aware and able to implement a variety of assessment tools, counselors need to be adept in administering, scoring, and interpreting assessment instruments. Counselors are not only accountable to their clients but also to the general public and stakeholders who demand accountability and effective practice.

2

Case Studies, Progress Notes, and Classification Systems

> ### Objectives
> 1. Describe the case studies of Ms. Eva Marie Garza, Mr. Robert Jones, and Ms. Ann Smith.
> 2. Recognize the basic elements contained within a typical clinical assessment intake interview—including but not limited to (a) general demographics, (b) client presentation and statements, (c) identified treatment goals, (d) marriages and significant other relationships, (e) family of origin and family history, (f) previous counseling and psychiatric hospitalization history, (g) substance use and addictive disorder history, (h) educational experiences, (i) work–career history, (j) legal history, (k) medical history, and (l) diagnosis.
> 3. Succinctly, describe the two primary mental health classification systems used in the United States (i.e., the *Diagnostic and Statistical Manual of Mental Disorders* [fifth edition] and the International Classification of Diseases-10) used by professional counselors and mental health professionals and succinctly describe how each is used.
> 4. Indicate the purpose of progress notes and the major components included within typical progress notes.
> 5. State the similarities and differences among SOAP, DART, and diagnostic-based progress notes.

Overview

The intent of this chapter is fivefold. First, the chapter provides three case studies. These case studies are used throughout the upcoming chapters. They will help readers understand how specific psychological assessment instruments can be used with persons presenting with concerns similar to the case study examples and how alike presenting persons may score on psychological assessment instruments. Second, the chapter succinctly describes the two primary diagnostic classification systems used by counselors in the United States. These include the *Diagnostic and Statistical Manual of Mental Disorders*, fifth edition (DSM-5) and the International Classification of Diseases-10 (ICD-10). Third, the chapter will help readers gain a general understanding of typical assessment intake interviews. Next, the authors describe the purpose and major components included within counseling progress notes. Finally, the chapter provides an overview of three common progress note-taking methods.

Case Studies

During our joint 55-plus years of clinical experience and teaching psychological assessment to doctoral and master's students as well as frontline-counseling professionals, we have learned many important and helpful teaching strategies. One strategy frequently cited as helpful by those we have trained is using one or two case study examples across the many different psychological assessment instruments. In other words, students and professionals alike find it helpful when we provide just two or three thorough case studies and then discuss how to use different psychological instruments with the same clients. Based on teaching evaluations and feedback, our adult learners report limiting case studies reduces confusion and the intermingling of client scenarios.

Thus, this chapter provides three fictional case studies. The case studies are continuously used throughout the book. The portrayed clients, although fictional, are based on an aggregate of clients previously treated or supervised by the authors. Names, circumstances, and potentially identifying characteristics have been changed to protect true client identities. However, the case studies are representative of clients frequently referred to and treated by counselors.

Anxiety and mood disorders (e.g., depression) are the most common mental health disorders diagnosed among American adults with more than 6.8 million Americans diagnosed with generalized anxiety disorder in 2005 (Kessler, Chiu, Demler, & Walter, 2005). Anxiety and mood disorders constitute the largest single portion of our clinical supervisees' caseloads. Many of the clients we have counseled fulfilled the complete diagnostic criteria necessary for such disorders. Thus, given the frequency of anxiety and mood disorders—especially from the robust increase in clients reporting "anxiety" as their chief presenting complaint since the onset of the reported double-dip housing recession, increased frequency of Islamic State in Iraq and Syria (ISIS) terror attacks, and police shootings —our first clinical vignette reflects a client presenting with generalized anxiety disorder.

Clients who experience severe anxiety suffer an especially debilitating mental illness that significantly interferes with daily living and greatly compromises life satisfaction. They are wracked with excessive, irrational, and uncontrollable worry; the vast majority of our supervisees' clients and the clients with whom we have counseled have experienced clinically significant anxiety throughout much of their lives. Ms. Eva Marie Garza is such a person.

Although most clients succinctly provide sufficient information to complete a clinical assessment intake interview in approximately 90 minutes, this was not the case with Eva Marie. Despite her above-average intelligence, she was remarkably nervous and distraught during the first 45 minutes of her initial assessment interview. At that time, her markedly elevated anxiety inhibited her ability to adequately focus and concentrate on counselor-asked questions or to respond in a succinct manner. Thus, until approximately halfway through the first session, her speech was noticeably tangential and pressured. Her responses to relatively simple, straightforward questions such as "Tell me how you arrived at my office today?" were loquacious, loosely associated to the asked question, and often somewhat difficult to follow or comprehend. Therefore, the clinical intake assessment interview required two separate intake interview sessions. During the latter half of the first session and following the first 10 minutes of her second session, Eva Marie's anxiety greatly diminished and it became evident via her more focused and detailed question responses that she was feeling far more comfortable and less nervous. Eva Marie's case study is presented next. You will want to become thoroughly familiar with Eva Marie because we refer to her throughout the remainder of the book.

Ms. Eva Marie Garza

The following psychosocial report is a summary of observations, client statements, and responses made by Ms. Eva Marie Garza during two clinical assessment intake interviews. The first interview occurred June 7, 2016, between 9:30 am and 11 am. The second occurred June 14, 2016, between 11 am and noon. Eva Marie was remarkably anxious during the first clinical assessment intake interview. Because of the severity of her anxiety, Eva Marie was unable to complete the standard initial clinical intake assessment in its entirety on June 7. The clinical intake was completed during our second interview, one week later on June 14. Both interviews were conducted by Gerald Juhnke, EdD, LPC, at his office located at 345 Colorado Street, San Antonio, Texas. No attempt was made to verify the veracity of Ms. Garza's statements or self-report. Exact quotations were used whenever possible to most accurately reflect Ms. Garza's responses.

Ms. Eva Marie Garza presents as a 40-year-old, married, Mexican American female. She was oriented to person, place, and time. Based on the complexity of language she used and the sophistication of the questions she asked within sessions, she appeared to have above-average intelligence. Her overall mood was anxious. Eva Marie's speech was noticeably pressured and rapid. During the first 45 minutes of her initial June 7 intake, her responses to counselor-asked questions were often tangential and only loosely associated with asked questions. During that time, she was especially loquacious, and she demonstrated slight to mild psychomotor agitation. Upon first entering the initial intake session, Eva Marie sat in the counseling office chair. She slowly rocked back and forth as she responded to verbal questions. Approximately halfway through the first session, she seemed to relax and discontinued her rocking. When she was more relaxed, her question responses became more focused, less tangential, and more succinct. However, she continued to demonstrate slight psychomotor agitation at times by tapping her feet, slightly bouncing her legs up and down, and tapping her fingers on the chair armrest.

Eva Marie was appropriately dressed wearing a clean, dark blue dress with matching dark blue pumps. Her dark red nail polish was unchipped and appeared recently applied. She wore no jewelry. Eva Marie's personal hygiene was appropriate and unremarkable. Eva Marie reports she is 5 feet, 1 inch tall and weighs 109 pounds. She looked healthy and was neither visibly overweight nor gaunt. Eva Marie works as an "assistant to the librarian" at Our Lady of Mercy Elementary School. When asked the reason for entering counseling, Eva Marie abruptly began to weep and reported "extreme anxiety" and "complete dissatisfaction" with her life. As her weeping slowed, Eva Marie stated, "I don't know what to do." Moments later she stated, "I'm so anxious and miserable. I've been this way all my life and want to change."

Identified Treatment Goals

When asked to identify the two most pressing concerns she would like to address in counseling, Eva Marie immediately responded, "I want to live without being anxious." Asked to clarify her response, Eva Marie reported significant levels of "anxiety and worry that have permeated my life forever." She reported, "I can't sleep. I can't concentrate. I feel like I'm constantly on edge—like something bad is going to happen." Marie reported her experienced anxiety is not limited to one behavior, a specific circumstance or place, or a single aspect of her life: "Worry and anxiety haunt me from the moment I awake until I finally fall asleep. . . . I can't even sleep the whole night because I'm so worried about everything." When asked about specific circumstances, events, persons, or places that promote, cause, or increase her anxiety, Eva Marie stated, "Everything." When queried about her statement "Everything," she responded, "I'm overwrought by worry, and it isn't limited to one specific thing." She continued by reporting that her mind "races" and claims to "worry about anything and everything I think about." Eva Marie reported "great fatigue" and "an inability to relax." She later stated, "I'm so nervous my head, neck, and shoulders constantly ache." She indicated that she often experienced "stress headaches" and complained of "stomach upsets" that frequently were correlated to "more stressful times." Eva Marie indicated difficulty performing daily tasks and a lack of concentration throughout the day from her "overwhelming" worry and anxiety: "My mother says I should 'stop worrying and enjoy life.' I can't. My mind races with worry. I constantly worry about what's going to go wrong next in my life." Eva Marie continued, "What I'd really like to do is simply go on a cruise and get away from Momma and my husband for about a year. However, they both need me, and as an only child, I have to take care of my mother. It would be a sin not to. It's like I'm taking care of two youngsters who need constant attention and care. Ugh!"

Asked about the second most pressing thing she would like to address via counseling, Eva Maria shook her head and said, "I'm too worried to think about a second thing [to address in counseling]." When asked to scale her degree of anxiety between zero or no anxiety and 10 or overwhelming anxiety, Eva Marie reported "11." She then stated, "Anxiety has ruined my life. I can't function because it [the anxiety] is so bad."

Marriages and Significant Other Relationships

Eva Marie is married to 55-year-old Ernest. The couple has been married for 21 years. This is Eva Marie's first marriage and Ernest's second. The couple has no children: "Ernest never wanted kids. His dad was an alcoholic. Kids were never his thing." Eva Marie continued by reporting she initially thought once she married Ernest her anxiety would diminish and her lonesomeness would "disappear." Immediately after making this statement, Eva Marie again began to weep and her chair rocking quickened. When asked what three words she would use to describe Ernest, Eva Marie quickly said "absent" and "emotionless." Eva Marie struggled to identify a third word to describe Ernest. After considerable thought, Eva Marie asked, "May I stop at two [two words to describe Ernest]?" When asked about Eva Marie's marital satisfaction level, she responded, "Can one be married and happy?" Later, Eva Marie reported "little marital satisfaction" and stated her marriage was one of "convenience." She quickly added that she was "jilted" by her "high school boyfriend . . . we [high school boyfriend and Eva Marie] had planned to marry during college." One week after being jilted, Ernest introduced himself to Eva Marie. This occurred at a parish social event where Eva Marie was working as food buffet server. The couple wed within two weeks. Eva Marie reported that the quick marriage ended her fears of being "forever lonesome and alone." She then stated, "I never realized one could be hopelessly lonesome and married. I can't wait for my mother to die so I can divorce Ernest without being told I'm a bad Catholic."

When asked about her dating history prior to Ernest, Eva Marie said, "My mother is Catholic. Dating before high school was absolutely forbidden." She reported her "only high school boyfriend" was Karl. He invited Eva Marie to the high school homecoming dance and later the prom her senior year. According to Eva Marie, she was "ecstatic. I had a huge crush on Karl." Eva Marie reported the high school homecoming occurred following a fall semester football game: "I was so anxious about going and had no idea what to wear." She described in great detail the events leading to the homecoming dance and the dance itself. When asked about anxiety when dating Karl, Eva Marie indicated, "Karl was almost as anxious as me." She indicated Karl's humor and frankness regarding his anxiety kept her from focusing on her own anxiety. According to Eva Marie, and unbeknownst to her mother, the couple exclusively dated each other throughout their senior year and into the following year. Eva Marie reported "the plan was" that she would complete her accounting associate's degree through Piedmont Community College. Given that Karl was attending Georgia Tech University, Eva Marie believed the couple would marry during Karl's junior year and live in married student housing: "I'd get a bookkeeping job downtown, and he'd complete his chemistry degree. It never happened." Eva Marie reported that Karl failed multiple classes and dropped out of college: "He interacted less and less with me until he just disappeared . . . not even a telephone call." Eva Marie said she was "devastated" and survived by focusing on her multiple jobs. A few weeks later, when it became evident Karl had "flown the coop," she met Ernest.

Eva Marie reported that the most important person in her life was her 56-year-old mother: "Momma is the center of my life." When asked to describe her mother in three words, Eva Maria stated, "nurturing, kind, and supportive, but ever since she has gotten elderly, she is often crotchety—I'd say 'bitchy' but good Catholics aren't supposed to swear."

Family of Origin and Family History

Eva Marie is an only child. She resides with her husband and mother at her mother's home located at 94213 South West Clark Road, San Antonio, Texas. Eva Marie's mother and father moved Eva Marie from Mission, Texas, in the Rio Grande River Valley to Atlanta, Georgia, when Eva Marie was seven years old. Eva Marie reported, "It was horrible. We were the only Mexican American family there [in Atlanta]" and "everybody made derogatory racial slurs about us." Eva Marie indicated that her mother and she wished to immediately return to "The Valley," but her father reported he could earn more money in Atlanta than in Texas. Eva Marie stated, "I cried myself to sleep almost every night when we moved to Atlanta." According to Eva Marie, she felt "ostracized" by others at her school because she was Mexican American: "No one befriended me." Despite ridicule and hardships, the family stayed in Atlanta while her father worked odd construction jobs. When Eva Marie was 11, her father was killed in a construction accident: "It was horrible. Momma tried to move us back to Mission [Texas], but we had no money or family to help."

Once Eva Marie and Ernest married, they moved in with Eva Marie's mother: "Ernest and I didn't have enough money for our own place." Two years ago, Eva Marie's grandmother passed away. Her grandmother left Eva Marie's mother the home where Eva Marie, her mother, and Ernest now reside in San Antonio: "Mother wanted to move back to Texas. So, with the help of our assistant parish priest and youth group, we packed up and here we are." Eva Marie reported that had it not been for her mother, she would have stayed in Atlanta, divorced Ernest, and never let her mother know that she had divorced Ernest.

Eva Marie described her mother as "strong willed and crotchety at times but very loving. And, she never means everything that she says—she is just getting elderly." When queried, Eva Marie smiled and stated, "Momma was the best momma in the whole world. But, as she has gotten a whole lot older, she has gotten a whole lot more cantankerous." When asked what three words she would use to describe her father, Eva Marie said, "Loving, genuine, the perfect father." Eva Marie described her father as "the most caring and kind man I ever met." Eva Marie reported her parents had a "perfect" marriage: "They constantly held hands and shared in each other's lives." When asked which parent Eva Marie is most similar, she stated, "I'm a blend of both. I look exactly like my mother; however, I have my father's sense of kindness toward others."

Eva Marie stated her first memory of her mother was singing a "church hymn": "She sang church hymns all the time." Her first memory of her father was of "him teaching me how to pray at our kitchen table. I must have been about three." She denies any corporal punishment or abuse within her family of origin experience. Eva Marie reported herself as "very religious" and indicated, "I grew up in a proud Catholic family with a proud Catholic tradition." When asked what this meant, Eva Marie reported that she had learned to "follow God's rules" and "God's way" from her parents and her involvement in the Catholic Church.

Previous Counseling and Psychiatric Hospitalizations

Eva Marie denies any previous counseling or psychiatric hospitalizations. She claims that she first noticed she was "nervous" when her father started praying that God would help her "relax" and "feel more comfortable" at elementary school. Eva Marie reported that in kindergarten and elementary school she often would awake early in the morning and "race" to her mother and father's bedroom: "I'd get them up at 5 am and demand my father immediately take me to school. I was worried I'd be late and fail the grade." According to Eva Marie, she would cry until father walked her to school. Reportedly, the two would sit on the school steps and wait until the janitors arrived at 6 am.

Substance Use and Addictive Disorders History

Eva Marie denies past or previous alcohol or other substance use. "I do drink coffee, which has caffeine, but I don't like the taste of alcohol. I have never even smoked a cigarette or used drugs; it wouldn't be very Catholic." When asked about potential addictive behaviors such as shopping, eating, running, gambling, or pornography, Eva Marie, denied each and stated, "I just live a boring life. I don't do any of those things."

Educational Experiences

Eva Marie reported being "an 'A' student." She stated, "I was always so nervous I would flunk classes that I studied very hard." She was inducted into the National Junior Honor Society in sixth grade and continued Honor Society until she graduated high school. According to Eva Marie, "I had four or five close friends [during her middle and high school years], and we stayed close friends from middle through high school." She proudly continued discussing how her friends and she would get together weekly until she moved her mother back to Texas two years ago. Eva Marie graduated from Downtown Central Catholic High School in Atlanta, Georgia, and completed her associate's degree in accounting from Piedmont Community College. When asked if she had considered entering a four-year college upon graduating from Piedmont Community College, Eva Marie stated, "Never. I was too nervous that I'd fail a class I had already passed, and I wanted to get a real job and earn money."

Work–Career History

Eva Marie reported, "I worked at home, cooking, canning, and cleaning, until high school." During her high school years, Eva Marie's mother required that Eva Marie work at their local Catholic parish, St. Patrick's Cathedral. Eva Marie reported that she was "good with numbers," so mother secured Eva Marie a job on the "Tithing Committee." Eva Marie smiled and her rate of speech significantly quickened as she described how she "worked my way up to bookkeeping [at the parish]." Eva Marie reported she "loved" bookkeeping: "It [bookkeeping at the parish] gave me a sense of purpose, and I was less nervous." She continued her work at the parish until she graduated from community college and began work as a bookkeeper at a local drug store. A fellow parish member owned the drug store: "Mr. Alexander knew I had just graduated from Piedmont and needed a job. He needed someone to get his books in order." Eva Marie took great pride in her perceptions that Mr. Alexander greatly valued her work. According to Eva Marie, Mr. Alexander put Eva Marie in charge of the pharmacy's local advertising campaign where she enjoyed making daily decisions about what items to advertise and what special sales would appear in the local newspaper advertisements: "It was great because I enjoyed telling others what to do and how to accomplish our advertising goals." She worked there "14 years" until her mother decided to move back to Texas: "I didn't want to move back to Texas, but I can't abandon my mother." Eva Marie went on to describe how a "good Catholic" would never abandon a parent who had been as dedicated to her child as Eva Marie's mother had: "God would strike me dead if I left her. And she needs me." Eva Marie continued, "It probably sounds bad, but I will feel so much freer when she passes." When asked to explain, Eva Marie described how her mother is aging and "crotchety," how overwhelming it is to take care of her given mother's declining self-care and "crabbiness," and how no matter what decisions Eva Marie makes, her mother finds fault with Eva Marie's decisions: "It is like I can never fully please her."

When Eva Marie moved to San Antonio she had a difficult time finding work: "I didn't know anyone, and I couldn't find a bookkeeping job." Ten months ago, Eva Marie "took" a position as "assistant to the chief librarian" at Our Lady of Mercy Elementary School: "I hate the job, but I get to work at the parish school, and it gets me out of the house and away from Ernest and my mother." She reports the things she likes most about working as the assistant to the librarian is "making decisions for the chief librarian" and "meeting and making new friends at work." When asked to clarifying her response, "making decisions for the chief librarian," Eva Marie indicated she had the ability to synthesize data and make rapid decisions regarding what books to purchase, how many books to purchase, and what to do to make the library more "user-friendly."

Eva Marie smiled when she discussed her work abilities and skills. When the counselor commented on Eva Marie's smile as she described her purchasing skills, Eva Marie responded, "I like to make sound business decisions, and I like it when people pay attention to me. Momma never lets me make decisions at home, and Ernest . . . I have to make every decision for him. It's like I'm married to an eight-year-old." She continued by reporting that although she "hates" her job, she likes being at work rather than at home because she could "take responsibility for myself" and "make new friends."

Legal History
Eva Marie denies any previous arrests or pending legal actions.

Medical History
Eva Marie reported having high blood pressure; temporomandibular joint disorder (TMJ) reportedly resulting from her "constant grinding and clinching of my teeth and jaw"; "chest pain, headaches, and nausea caused by my constant worrying"; and "sleep problems." She reported being under medical treatment for each of these disorders and taking the following medications as prescribed by either her general physician, Dr. Sylvia Torres, or her dentist, Dr. Robert Hartman:

> Lisinopril 20 mg per day prescribed by Dr. Torres (blood pressure)
>
> Xanax 5 mg per day (*Note:* This medication is jointly prescribed and monitored by both Drs. Torres [to reduce anxiety leading to chest pain and sleep disturbance] and Hartman [muscle relaxant for TMJ]). These doctors are working in unison with the prescription and thus the total amount of Xanax she is taking per day is 5 mg not 10 mg.

Eva Marie denies previous surgeries, head or spinal injuries, drug use, or medical conditions.

Diagnoses
See Table 2.1.

TABLE 2.1 Eva Marie's DSM-5 and ICD-10-CM Diagnoses

DSM-5	ICD-10-CM	Diagnose(s)	Contextual Factors
300.02	F41.1	Generalized Anxiety Disorder	Principal Diagnosis:
			Excessive anxiety and worry; fatigue; difficulty concentrating; muscle tension; sleep disturbance; constantly feeling "on edge"; restlessness; difficulty controlling worrying
			Anxiety and worrying are causing significant distress in relationship functioning
V61.10	Z63.0	Relationship Distress with Spouse or Intimate Partner	Marital issatisfaction
V62.89	Z60.0	Phase of Life Problem	Client living with husband in mother's home; job dissatisfaction
	I10	Essential (primary) hypertension	Self-report: Under the care of primary care physician
	M26.60	Temporomandibular joint disorder, unspecified	Self-report: Under the care of oral surgeon

Note: DSM-5 = *Diagnostic and Statistical Manual of Mental Disorders* (5th ed.); ICD-10-CM = International Classification of Diseases (10th revision, Clinical Modification).

Summary

This case study reflects the types of detailed information gathered during a typical counseling intake or psychosocial assessment. Chapters 7 and 12 describe in far greater detail both the face-to-face interview process and how to author psychological reports. Therefore, we do not go into great detail here. However, for the purposes of this chapter, it is important to note that the counselor documented Eva Marie's age, ethnicity, appearance, behaviors within session, mental status, and home address. Even the client's reported treatment goals are identified. Furthermore, the typical assessment process investigates the many complex domains of Eva Marie's life and reflects the synergy between these domains. Specifically, the counselor gathers information regarding marriages and significant other relationships, including Eva Marie's family of origin and family, as well as her perceptions of mother and father. In addition, Eva Marie's previous counseling and psychiatric hospitalization, substance use and addictive disorders history, education, work/career, legal, and medical histories are examined.

The intake assessment reveals Eva Marie's immediate anxiety symptoms are acute, problematic, unpleasant, and debilitating. It becomes strikingly evident that at least some of Eva Marie's poorer past decisions were made in an attempt to escape her anxiety. Unfortunately, these decisions have resulted in additional life problems and stressors. For example, in an attempt to lessen her anxiety and eliminate her lonesomeness, she married Ernest soon after being "jilted" by the man she wanted to marry. Unfortunately, her decision to quickly marry Ernest did not bring about her desired outcomes and now even magnifies Eva Marie's anxiety.

It is important to note that Eva Marie's overwhelming and expansive anxiety is her chief presenting concern. She likes making everyday decisions for herself without the need for excessive amounts of advice or reassurance from others. She also enjoys making work-related decisions—especially for her boss. Concomitantly, Eva Marie does not have an unrealistic fear of being left alone when her mother dies. Instead, Eva Marie wishes she could escape her mother and husband to enjoy personal "alone time." In addition, Eva Marie likes initiating and completing work specific projects without unrealistic needs for reassurance by others.

Like many clients, Eva Marie becomes more comfortable as she spends time with the counselor and the intake process becomes more familiar. This lessens her extreme anxiety and allows Eva Marie to use her precise language. The counselor recognizes Eva Marie's precise language and understands the correlation between such language and intelligence. Hence, the counselor can make a statement about her intelligence.

Our second case study highlights a male client fulfilling DSM-5 alcohol use disorder criteria. Like Eva Marie, the second-described client is fictional and based on an aggregate of clients counseled or supervised by the authors. Given the significant number of court-mandated clients who qualify for substance use disorder and counseled by our clinical supervisees, we believe this case is highly representative of clients served by professional counselors.

Mr. Robert Jones

The following psychosocial report is a summary of observations, client statements, and responses made by Mr. Robert Jones during an initial clinical intake interview. This September 29, 2016, interview was conducted between 1 pm and 2:51 pm at the counseling office of Gerald Juhnke, EdD, LPC, located at 345 Colorado Street, San Antonio, Texas. No attempt was made to verify the veracity of Mr. Jones's statements or self-report. Exact quotations are used whenever possible to reflect Mr. Jones's responses.

Robert Jones presented as a 37-year-old, married, Caucasian male. He was oriented to person, place, and time. He seemed of average intelligence. Although his face appeared flushed and unusually reddish, his speech was appropriate with average rate and volume. No slurring of his speech was noticed, and he had a friendly manner of interacting. Robert was appropriately dressed. He wore clean clothing, including navy blue trousers, an overly noticeable starched and pressed, white, button-down shirt; Sperry Topsider-type shoes; and no socks. His personal hygiene was appropriate and unremarkable except for the distinct and pungent aroma of Old Spice cologne mingled with the smell of alcohol and cigarettes about him. Robert presented as approximately 5 feet 10 inches tall, 175 pounds, with blue eyes and blonde hair. His appearance was trim but not gaunt. He reported being unemployed: "No big deal, I can always find work." In September of 2016, Robert was terminated from his most recent job as a "heavy-duty equipment and tractor salesman" for a large, national road equipment company. Robert reported his termination was the result of his being intoxicated on the job. When asked the reason for entering counseling, Robert stated, "Drinking has taken over my life." He remorsefully reported he has been terminated from nearly all of his jobs due to alcohol related violations: "I get a good job, swear I'll lay off the booze, but then get drunk while working." When asked if Robert had consumed alcohol prior to attending today's initial intake session, Robert stated, "I drank in my car before I came inside." When asked how much alcohol Robert had consumed immediately prior to coming to session he stated, "Two bombers and two shots." When asked, Robert confirmed bombers were 22 ounces of beer each: "It's not that much. I usually drink a couple bombers during lunch hour and have no problems at work."

Identified Treatment Goals

Robert reported his primary reason for coming to counseling is to "stop my drinking." He indicated his alcohol consumption has resulted in multiple car collisions, loss of multiple jobs, and court fines and brief incarcerations. Robert further reported that his wife of 20 years has threatened divorce if he does not discontinue his alcohol consumption: "I don't want to lose her."

Marriages and Significant Other Relationships

Robert reported he married his high school "sweetheart" Catherine 20 years ago. Robert stated he was a high school senior and 17 years old when they married: "We thought she was pregnant, but she wasn't." Robert stated, "She [Catherine] is the light of my world." When asked to explain, Robert indicated Catherine was "like a mother to me" and "pretty much runs our family." He continued by indicating that he "wouldn't be the man I am today without Catherine's support and love." When asked to rate his marital satisfaction on a scale between zero (meaning no marital satisfaction) and 10 (meaning superior marital satisfaction), he rated his marital satisfaction at an 8: "I'm pretty happy." Robert denied previous or current separations or significant problems such as infidelity: "Nah. Nothing like that—but she will leave me if I don't stop drinking." Robert stated, "The only problem we've got is my drinking." Robert described how his drinking has become progressively worse over the past 10 years: "I can't even hold down a job." Robert indicated Catherine has become increasingly "angry" at Robert for his alcohol consumption: "She says she's going to leave me if I don't stop drinking." When asked if he believes Catherine would actually leave him he stated, "She's so mad at me right now, I think she would leave me in a blink of an eye."

The couple has two children, Robert Jr. (19) and Catherine Ellen (16). Robert smiled when he spoke about his children. Robert Jr. is freshman at San Antonio University. He is studying business. Catherine Ellen is a junior at Witte High School and an honors student, "She takes after her momma." Both are reported to be healthy with no mental health, physical, substance use, or interpersonal concerns.

Family of Origin and Family History

Robert is the oldest of four siblings (Robert [37], Donny [36], Eddy [35], and Trish [34]). Robert's biological parents were Robert "Senior" and Martha Jones. Robert described Senior as "a good man with a bad drinking problem." Martha was described as a "saint with a temper." When queried, Robert stated his first memories of his father were "going fishing with dad; he was drunk the whole time." His first memories of Martha included her scolding Senior for his excessive drinking. When asked, Robert reported he looked "more like" Senior than Martha—"I've got his big nose, crooked smile, and small ears"—and had more of Senior's personality traits—"I drink like him." Robert indicated that despite his father's "drinking problems" his parents had a "loving" marriage. He described both his parents in mostly endearing terms such as "nurturing" and "loving."

When queried regarding his siblings, Robert stated, "We've always been close." Robert stated he and Donny had a "great relationship." Robert stated the two were "best friends" in middle and high school. Robert reported Donny joined the Army after high school and resides in Georgia near Fort Benning. According to Robert, the two call and text "all the time." Eddy, Robert's 35-year-old brother, is a computer technician and works for a local community college informational technology department. Robert reported, "He [Eddy] got the brains in the family." Robert indicated he frequently stops by Eddy's apartment and the two drink together: "We love to talk, drink, and laugh." Robert claimed Trish was "the angel-mother of the family." He stated when his mother and father died in a vehicular crash about 10 years ago Trish "took over the mom role for us boys." Robert reported he sometimes feels "sorry" for Trish for assuming the "angel- mother" role. According to Robert, Trish is a "nondrinker" who "tries to keep us boys from the evils of alcohol."

Previous Counseling and Psychiatric Hospitalizations

Robert reported counseling with Dr. Randal J. Watkins III, a Licensed Chemical Dependency Counselor following his first DUI on or about August 2007. According to Robert, "substance abuse counseling and AA attendance were mandated by the courts" following each of his DUI arrests and vehicular crashes. Each time Robert was court mandated to attend counseling, Robert discontinued treatment "one or two" sessions after starting "due to the costs." Robert further reported, "I never followed up on AA." Robert denied any other counseling services or inpatient or intensive outpatient treatment: "I probably could have used it [substance abuse counseling]." He further denied previous suicide attempts or harm toward others: "Nope, that's not me. If I have a problem with someone, I just leave 'em alone." Robert signed a confidential release of information requesting Dr. Watkins' clinical reports and a summary regarding those counseling sessions be forwarded to this counselor.

Substance Use and Addictive Disorders History

Robert stated he first remembers consuming alcohol about age 10: "I got some beer from the fridge. It tasted horrible." He reported he "really began drinking" on a regular basis during high school. In 2007, approximately 10 years ago, following the death of his mother and father, Robert reported daily drinking to a point of intoxication: "I don't know why it started getting bad then." Robert currently consumes seven or more beers a night and mixes his beer with whiskey shots "to get my buzz faster." He stated he used to get a faster buzz but now has to consume more beers and whiskey to experience the same degree of intoxication. Upon awakening in the mornings he often craves alcohol and frequently begins his day with "a beer or two to get my engine running." Robert further reported, "I usually drink a few beers before I go to bed; otherwise, I can't sleep."

Robert denied the use of other substance or drugs. When asked about his potential cannabis use, Robert stated, "Never. It makes me congested, like I'm having a cold or something. I hate that stuff." He further denies medical misuse of opioids or other prescribed medications: "Never!" Robert denied other potential process addictions such as gambling: "I hate gambling" or pornography: "My sex life with Catherine is fine, and I don't want anybody else."

Educational Experiences

Robert reported he was "mostly an 'A' student" during his elementary, middle, and high school years. He stated he enjoyed the sciences, math, and social sciences. Robert further reported he enjoyed school and had many friends: "I think I was friends with just about everybody in my school." When queried, Robert reported the thing he liked best about high school was "playing baseball." Robert discontinued playing baseball when he started dating Catherine. Robert graduated from John Greely Williams High School in San Antonio, Texas, with a "high school diploma." He initially wanted to attend the University of Texas in Austin but never enrolled because he married Catherine: "money was tight and I couldn't afford college for Catherine or me."

Work–Career History

Robert began working once he married Catherine. He started as a bagger at a local grocery store chain and worked his way up to assistant manager: "it was a really good job." Robert reported it was the only job he could get that had health insurance benefits to cover Catherine and the expected baby. According to Robert about two years into the job, he began consuming more and more alcohol in the parking lot with his subordinates after work: "I'd get so drunk, I would pass out in the store parking lot, and they would have to drive me home." This resulted in his termination. The next job he secured was at a furniture company as a mover. Again, Robert worked his way up from manual laborer to management. Within a year, Robert reported he was again drinking in the parking lot during breaks and lunch. He was later terminated for falling asleep in a showroom recliner: "It was humiliating." In 2014, Robert finally got a job he reportedly wanted, a heavy-duty equipment and tractor salesman for a national company located in San Antonio: "I muffed it again by drinking." Robert was terminated in September 2016 for driving a backhoe off a loading dock: "I was intoxicated."

Legal History

Robert denied legal problems until his first DUI arrest and incarceration in 2013. Since that arrest, Robert has had a checkered legal history. Robert reported four DUI arrests or vehicular crashes resulting from his intoxication. When queried about other arrests or incarcerations, he stated, "You can check my record. Those are the only charges against me." Robert denied any previous, pending charges or upcoming scheduled court dates or trials. He also denied arrests for battery, assault, larceny, burglary, or selling restricted substances: "You can ask Catherine. I don't do any of that."

Medical History

Robert denied any significant past or present medical issues. He reported his mother mentioned nothing remarkable regarding Robert's birth. He denied any head traumas or surgeries. Robert reported that his last medical evaluation occurred in March 2014 as part of a prehire screening physical required by a former employer Table 2.2.

Diagnoses

See Table 2.2.

TABLE 2.2 Robert's DSM-5 and ICD-10-CM Diagnoses

DSM-5	ICD-10-CM	Diagnose(s)	Contextual Factors
303.90	F10.20	Alcohol Use Disorder, Severe	Principal Diagnosis:
			Pharmacological Domain—Withdrawal and tolerance;
			Social Impairment Domain—Recurrent alcohol use resulting in a failure to fulfill major role obligations at work and home; Continued alcohol use despite recurrent interpersonal problems;
			Impaired Control Domain—History of unsuccessful efforts to cut down or control alcohol use; Significant time spent obtaining, using, and recovering from alcohol effects.
V61.10	Z63.0	Relationship Distress with Spouse or Intimate Partner	Marital dissatisfaction

Note: DSM-5 = *Diagnostic and Statistical Manual of Mental Disorders* (5th ed.); ICD-10-CM = International Classification of Diseases (10th revision, Clinical Modification).

Summary

Robert's intake assessment interview provides a clinical picture of a man struggling with alcohol use disorder. Alcohol problems have permeated his life. This is especially evident in Robert's marriage. Robert reports he wants to stop drinking and fears his wife will leave him if he does not stop his alcohol use.

Ms. Ann Smith

Unlike the previous case studies that describe adult clients, our third case study is specific to an adolescent. Similar to previous case studies, this case study is fictional and based on adolescent clients we have counseled or provided clinical supervision to in the past. This case study first includes information provided by the adolescent's mother and, later, in a separate, second interview, the adolescent. During the mother's interview, the daughter remained alone in the waiting room and did not participate. Likewise, the daughter was separately interviewed while the mother remained in the waiting room. Given the significant number of court-mandated adolescent clients required to participate in counseling and the number of adolescents who present with oppositional defiant disorder symptoms and self-injury-type behaviors, we believe this case is highly representative of adolescent clients served by professional counselors.

The following psychosocial report is a summary of statements made by Ms. Carlee Smith regarding her 16-year-old daughter, Ann Smith, as well as observations, client statements, and responses made by Ann Smith during an initial clinical intake interview. Ms. Carlee Smith met at the counseling office of Gerald Juhnke, EdD, LPC, located at 345 Colorado Street, San Antonio, Texas on November 1, 2016. That meeting was conducted between noon and 1 pm. During the meeting, the mother described her concerns about daughter and provided information regarding events at school that resulted in her contacting this counselor and arranging her daughter's counseling. Following the mother's one-hour meeting, the counselor met with the identified client, Ann Smith. No attempt was made to verify the veracity of either mother's or daughter's statements or self-report. Exact quotations are used whenever possible to reflect mother and client responses.

The mother (Ms. Carlee Smith) made initial contact with this counselor and scheduled her daughter's appointment. Immediately entering the counseling room, Mother stated, "Ann is a self-centered bitch. I want her in out of my house and in [juvenile] detention." Mother then said, "Ann ruined my marriage and my life." Mother continued, "She [Ann] got kicked out of school because of her pot smoking and attitude problems." When asked about mother's desired treatment goals for her daughter, Ann, mother indicated, "I want her fixed." When asked what "fixed" would look like, Mother stated, "She'd be living at juvie [juvenile detention], stop smoking [cannabis], stop arguing, and stop being a princess bitch." Later, Mother commented, "I'm scared Ann is borderline." When asked to explain the "borderline" term, Mother stated, "You know. Drinking, drugging, running away, and trying to kill yourself." Mother then reported she was diagnosed with borderline personality disorder at age 16 and was "scared she [Ann] is borderline like me." When asked what three words Mother would use to describe Ann, she replied "belligerent," "argumentative," and a "runaway." When queried regarding the onset of Ann's belligerent and argumentative symptoms, Mother stated, "She was born that way." When asked if Mother perceived Ann as suicidal or a danger to herself, Mother responded, "I can only hope." When asked for clarification, Mother indicated Ann had "ruined" Mother's life, by alleging Mother's husband (Ann's biological father) had sexually "molested" Ann. "He never molested her! But he couldn't live at home anymore. It's because of Ann that I lost him." We have included Mother's additional responses and comments specific to topic areas. Each is indicated as *Mother reported*.

Ann Smith presented as a 16-year-old, Caucasian female with shoulder length blonde hair and brown eyes. She appeared approximately 5 feet 4 inches tall and slightly overweight. Ann was oriented to person, place, time, and situation. She seemed somewhat above average in cognitive intelligence and intellectual functioning. Ann was age-appropriately dressed, wearing blue jeans, a red University of Arkansas Razorback t-shirt, and sandals. Ann's personal hygiene was unremarkable. No physical abnormalities were visibly noted, except scars on her left arm self-reported as a result of self-injurious behaviors: "cutting. The last time was six months ago when I was stressed." Ann's speech was appropriate with average rate, tone, and volume. Although Ann reported she is "often angry," her immediate mood appeared normal with neither psychomotor agitation nor slow behaviors. She reported her mother "made" her attend today's interview: "I don't get the point [of participating in counseling]; it won't work for me."

Identified Treatment Goals

Mother reported her desired treatment goals for Ann included (a) moving Ann out of Mother's home into juvenile detention, (b) stopping Ann's cannabis use and selling of cannabis, and (c) discontinuing Ann's arguing behaviors with Mother, teachers, and peers.

Ann reported she participated in today's psychosocial assessment interview because, "She [Mother] made me." When asked about treatment goals, Ann stated, "None. I don't want to be here." When asked about Ann's court-mandated participation in three to six counseling sessions due to her using and selling cannabis, Ann stated, "That's totally lame." When queried about potential goals, Ann indicated, "I just want to get my mother off my back. She makes me so angry." Ann reported daily feelings of "loneliness." When pressed to clarify, Ann stated, "I'm not like everyone else. I don't have friends." When asked if Ann would like to use counseling to help foster potential friendships she responded, "I could care less. If people don't want like me, that's their loss." Other goals identified by Ann's mother (i.e., stopping cannabis use, discontinuing arguing with mother, teachers, and peers, etc.) were discounted or denied: "Really? Stop smoking dope? Like I'm really going to do that?" She denied arguing with others: "I don't argue." By the conclusion of session Ann agreed to the following treatment goals: (a) reducing feelings of loneliness and anger; (b) stopping nonsuicidal, self-injury behaviors; (d) reducing intrusive sexual abuse memories and night terrors; and (e) reducing the frequency of her cannabis use.

Marriages and Significant Other Relationships

Mother reported Ann has no close friends and the peers she interacted typically were "from the wrong side of the tracks." According to Mother, Ann's "acquaintances" used cannabis and alcohol and frequently were under the influence: "They think I can't tell, but I know they're high." When asked the first names of Ann's three best friends, Mother stated, "Ann's so bitchy; no one wants be around her." Mother reported Ann recently attempted to join a church youth group near their home: "It won't work, 'cause she's not like them."

Ann reported she has limited friendships and denies having a "best friend." Within the past six months, Ann began attending "an evangelical recovery group" (ERG). According to Ann, she was drawn to the "friendliness" of the group members and reported, "They 'get' me and what I'm going through." Specifically, Ann reported most ERG group members were former drug and alcohol users, and many had struggled with depression, anxiety, self-injurious behaviors, and suicide. She indicated although her new acquaintances are friendly, she still feels as though she is not yet "really friends with anyone." When asked what would have to happen for Ann to feel as though she were friends with someone in the group, Ann reported, "I don't really know." When queried about her three closest friends, Ann reported she was in "transition." She indicated "Thomas" had been "somewhat close" the past three years. However, six months ago, Ann determined Thomas was more into "getting sex and drugs from me than really being my friend." Ann reported she started to "carve up my arm" to deal with her anger and resentment toward Thomas, "Then I found ERG. They helped me get over Thomas and stop hating myself." Ann reported she was "getting close to friendships" with ERG members "Kathy," "Shawn," and "Adam." However, Ann reported she did not want to get "burned again" by people who act like her friends but instead use her.

Family of Origin and Family History

Mother reported Ann as a "whiney, spoiled princess" who "refuses to treat me with respect." According to Mother, she and her husband decided against having additional children because "Ann demanded every ounce of our energy." Mother reported Ann and her mother have had a strained relationship since before Ann was four years old: "She was a horrible baby and has only gotten worse." Mother reported Ann told a teacher that Ann's biological father had sexually "molested" her between the ages of five and nine. According to Mother, the accusations resulted in her "losing" her husband. Mother further reports her former husband had a "drinking problem," which at times resulted in physical aggression and verbal arguments between the parents. When queried, Mother denied any physical or verbal abuse between Ann's biological father and Ann: "No. Never." The parents divorced when after Ann's father was incarcerated for sexual abuse.

Ann stated she was an "only child." She reported no fond memories of her childhood: "We weren't happy." Ann teared up and became emotional as she described being sexually fondled and sodomized between the ages of four and nine by her father. After a few moments, Ann stated, "What kind of person could do that to their own daughter?" Ann reported she continues to have intrusive memories and night terrors from the sexual abuse: "No one can understand unless they go through it." She reported she "hates" her father and indicated he was "lucky he went to prison, 'cause I knew where the shotgun was." When queried regarding the three favorite things Ann remembered as a child, Ann stated, "That perv [pervert] [her father] being carted off to jail"; "my mother going to the psych [psychiatric] hospital"; and "running away." Ann responded her first family memories were being "shaken" by her mother: "I remember crying while she shook me." Ann continued, "She [Mother] was an enforcer, not a mother." When queried about her father, Ann refused to comment: "He's gone. That's all I will say." Ann reported she "never knew any" uncles, aunts, or grandparents, "If they existed, they probably didn't want to be around them [her parents]."

Previous Counseling and Psychiatric Hospitalizations

Mother reported Child Protective Services (CPS) required Ann to participate in group counseling after their investigation of father's sexual abuse of Ann: "It didn't do any good, 'cause she was lying anyway." Mother denied Ann participating in any other counseling and denied any psychiatric or in-patient hospitalizations for Ann.

Ann reported she had participated in group counseling with other sexual abuse survivors. She did not remember how old she was at the time she participated in counseling and did not remember the counselor's name. However, she reported counseling had been required by CPS and was conducted at the Family Life Counseling Center on Durango Street in San Antonio. Ann did not recall how many sessions she participated—"not many." Ann further indicated, "It didn't do any good. I still have the memories." Ann denied other outpatient or inpatient counseling or substance abuse counseling.

Substance Use and Addictive Disorders History

Mother reported Ann frequently uses cannabis. Within the last year Ann has been court-mandated to participate in weekly drug testing. Mother reports Ann "tested positive" for cannabis during the last two drug tests. She denied Ann's use of other substances or process addictions: "We don't have money to shop."

Ann indicated she smokes "a couple [cannabis] joints a week." She reported the frequency of cannabis use depended on how much lunch money she could get from her mother and how much money she could find in her mother's purse. Ann indicated she "tried" to stop using cannabis many times but was unsuccessful: "Why fight it. I just use whenever I can now." Ann reported at least some degree of cannabis tolerance when she admitted, "I've gotta smoke more dope to get high than I used to." Ann admitted failing two recent drug tests and claimed the tests "just confirmed that I smoke dope." Ann denied the use of alcohol, opioids, and other drugs, "I'm not really into that." When asked to explain, Ann reported it was difficult to purchase alcohol: "I usually get carded and have to run." Ann reported her preference for cannabis was due to the drug's ability to "relax me." Ann's onset of cannabis misuse began when she was in middle school: "I liked it because it chilled me out and kept me from thinking about being molested." When queried, Ann denied any symptoms or risk factors commonly associated with process addictions.

Educational Experiences

Mother reported, "Ann is exceptionally smart. She could be an 'A' student if she didn't skip school." Mother indicated Ann was an "A" student throughout elementary school and became a "C" student in middle school.

Ann indicated she "hates" school. She indicated she "tolerates" math and science but "can't stand" the other courses. When asked why, Ann reported non-math and science courses required social interactions, whereas math and science were lectures and "I don't have to talk to anyone." Ann reported she wishes to attend San Antonio Community College to become a pharmacist technician.

Legal History

Mother reported Ann started to "running away" at age nine. According to Mother, Ann's running-away behaviors increased in frequency from "a couple times a month" to "nearly every day." Mother reported that, at approximately age 14, Ann ran away for three and four days at a time. Ann was arrested multiple times by police for her running-away behaviors. These arrests occurred when Ann was 15 and 16 and resulted in a two-week juvenile detention stay. Since then, Ann has been on probation. Her juvenile probation officer is Ms. Donna Rodriguez. Mother reported Ann was recently arrested for selling "pot" at her school and Ms. Rodriguez has scheduled weekly "in-home" meetings with Ann.

Ann reported a checkered history of running away, truancy, minor shoplifting, and selling cannabis. According to Ann, she started running away to escape her mother's perceived "constant nagging." Ann reported being arrested three weeks ago for selling cannabis to another student at her school. Due to the school's zero tolerance drug policy, Ann was

34 | Assessment in Counseling

suspended from school. Ann has an upcoming juvenile court arraignment in two weeks for charges of selling a controlled substance to minors on school property.

Medical History

Mother reported Ann had an unremarkable birth and medical history. Mother was unaware of any medical conditions or unusual illnesses.

Ann reported "stitches" on her left arm from "cutting." She indicated her cutting was in response to being used by Thomas, a former acquaintance. No other significant medical issues were noted by Ann.

Diagnoses
See Table 2.3.

TABLE 2.3 Ann's DSM-5 and ICD-10-CM Diagnoses

DSM-5	ICD-10-CM	Diagnose(s)	Contextual Factors
313.81	F91.3	Oppositional Defiant Disorder, Moderate	Principal Diagnosis:
			Frequent and persistent pattern of angry/irritable mode, argumentative/defiant behaviors, vindictiveness;
			Angry/Irritable Mood—Often loses temper, often touchy or easily annoyed, often angry and resentful;
			Argumentative/Deviant Behavior—Argues with authority figures, refuses to comply with requests from authority figures, ignores rules, blames others for her mistakes;
			Vindictive Behaviors—Has been spiteful or vindictive at least twice within the past six months.
292.90	F15.99	Cannabis-Use Disorder (Mild)	Cannabis taken in larger amounts to achieve desired effect.
			Previous unsuccessful efforts to stop cannabis use.
309.81	F43.10	Posttraumatic Stress Disorder	Long-term exposure to sexual abuse as child;
			Intrusive thoughts and memories of the sexual abuse commencing after sexual abuse occurred;
			Persistent avoidance of stimuli associated with the sexual abuse;
			Negative alterations in cognitions and mood associated with the sexual abuse after the sexual abuse occurred;
			Marked alteration in arousal and reactivity associated with the sexual abuse;
			Duration of disturbance is more than one month and has resulted in clinically significant impairment in academic, social, and relationship functioning;
			The disturbance is not attributable to the physiological effects of a substance (e.g., medication, alcohol) or another medication
V61.20	Z62.820	Parent–Child Relational Problem	Impaired functioning in behavioral, cognitive, and affective domains resulting from the negative quality of the parent–child relationship.

Note: DSM-5 = *Diagnostic and Statistical Manual of Mental Disorders* (5th ed.); ICD-10-CM = International Classification of Diseases (10th revision, Clinical Modification).

Assessment Report

These three case studies reflect interesting persons who will complete psychological assessment instruments in upcoming chapters. Their symptomatology and ways of behaving and thinking will become more apparent as we review their test results. Of course, clinical assessment intakes are not the only time we document what clients say and do. We next provide a general overview of progress notes and describe three common methods of recording such information.

DSM and ICD Classification Systems
What They Are and Potential Benefits

The two major classification systems used within the United States are the DSM and the ICD. The DSM was developed, authored, and published by the American Psychiatric Association (APA). It is specific to mental disorders (American Psychiatric Association, 2013). Unlike the DSM, the World Health Organization (WHO) created the ICD. The ICD is a broad spectrum internationally used and standardized classification system intended to report and define wide-ranging public health issues, "the universe of diseases, disorders, injuries, and other related health conditions" (WHO, 2016, para. 4). The ICD spans a far broader range of presenting health concerns ranging from insect bites (i.e., S30.860A: Insect bite [nonvenomous] of lower back and pelvis initial encounter) to surgeries (i.e.,T87.1X1: Complications of reattached [part of] right lower extremity [e.g., right leg]) and includes nearly every conceivable health symptom, disease, or illness known to humankind. Included as a sliver within the far broader ICD classification spectrum are mental health disorders (i.e., F34.8: Other persistent mood [affective] disorders, etc.). Conversely, the DSM covers only a limited range of disorders and symptoms, all of which are specific to mental disorders.

To improve clinical utility and scientific research, the APA and WHO worked to harmonize the most recent fifth version of the DSM (DSM-5) with the 10th and 11th version of the ICD (ICD-10 and ICD-11; APA, 2013, pp. 10-11). This forward thinking ensured DSM-5 diagnoses provide correlated IC-10 diagnoses. These correlated ICD diagnosis codes are visibly listed to the right of DSM-5 diagnostic codes. Thus, when counselors utilize the DSM-5 to diagnose and classify client-presenting concerns, the DSM-5 provides correlated ICD-10 classification codes. Therefore, counselors using the DSM-5 obtain both a DSM-5 diagnose and an ICD-10 classification code, which can be used for everything from clinical notes to insurance billing.

Students often do not understand the potential benefits of using the DSM-5 with corresponding ICD-10 code classifications. Many ask, "Why do I need to know the DSM?" They do not readily comprehend how accurate diagnoses are critically important when matching treatment goals and objectives to primary client diagnoses. Frequently, students voice concern they will be "spying on clients" via the assessment process or "labeling clients" and "overpathologizing" clients with DSM diagnoses. Instead, we have found careful assessment without voyeurism facilitates accurate DSM diagnoses. These key diagnoses then promote effective counseling practices that benefit clients.

Counselors skilled in assessment and DSM use comprehend their clients' presenting symptomatology and understand how to use diagnosis as a means to ensure treatment efficacy. This is accomplished via continuous assessment (Vacc, 1982). Here, counselors continually assess their clients' current symptom levels and compare the severity of these symptoms to previous levels as well as established DSM criteria. Hence, counselors constantly track clients' counseling progress. Should insufficient progress occur, counselors can investigate changing techniques or adding treatment options.

For example, a client diagnosed with major depressive disorder and failing to adequately respond to talk therapy may be referred to a psychiatrist to determine if psychotropic medications are warranted. If the client has been taking antidepressants and is actively invested in counseling, the counselor might obtain a release of confidential information. This will allow the counselor to speak with the prescribing psychiatrist and update the psychiatrist on the client's lack of improvement. The psychiatrist might then decide to reassess the client and determine the need to change either antidepressant dosage or medications. Concomitantly, the counselor may wish to investigate different treatment modalities (e.g., group or family counseling) and the use of different counseling theories (e.g., rational emotive behavioral therapy, cognitive-behavioral therapy) or techniques (e.g., the empty chair, visualizations, metaphors) to determine what works best to lessen or eliminate the client's depressive symptoms. None of this could occur without skilled and continuous counselor assessment and diagnosis.

When treatment is progressing well, counselors skilled in assessment ensure the continuation of counseling techniques noted as helpful by clients. Further, these same identified helpful techniques can be used by counselors to help clients affectively respond to stressors in other areas of their lives. In other words, if clients report the use of rational emotive behavioral therapy's "Activating Event, Beliefs, Consequences" (A-B-C) technique helpful in reducing depressed feelings, counselors will wish to replicate this technique in other areas noted by the client as stressful. Here, for example, the A-B-C technique could be used to help the client related to a job, interpersonal relationships, and parenting concerns.

Skilled DSM assessment and diagnosis also helps clients obtain necessary counseling services. Since the mid-1990s, managed care has used standardized treatment protocols. Clients experiencing similar symptoms are assigned to diagnostic-related groups (DRGs). DRGs cluster clients diagnosed with the same conditions (e.g., generalized anxiety disorder) and symptom severity levels (e.g., mild, moderate, or severe symptoms). Managed care typically uses DRGs to dictate the specific evidenced-based counseling theories counselors are required to use if they wish reimbursement from the managed care entity (e.g., cognitive-behavioral therapy, brief strategic family therapy) and the counseling modality (e.g., group counseling). In addition, the number of preauthorized treatment sessions is standardized by the client-assigned DRG. Counselors skilled in both assessment and DSM diagnosing increase the likelihood their clients will be included in the most appropriate DRG. This increases the probability that managed care will preauthorize an appropriate number of client-needed counseling sessions and increased treatment care levels for important services such as case management, inpatient psychiatric hospitalization, or medical detoxification. Correct DSM diagnoses ensure correct DRG assignment. This is especially important when clients present with severe symptomatology.

Clients who are inaccurately assessed and diagnosed often are assigned to less severe DRGs. Thus, they are preauthorized for fewer sessions and do not have access to many important services. The result? They may opt out of entering treatment because of projected out-of-pocket financial costs or discontinue counseling prematurely, because the DRG they were assigned has reduced benefits.

Correct DRG placement is not only important for clients but for counselors as well. Many counselors working in private practice settings petition to serve on local mental health provider panels. The benefits of serving on mental health provider panels include a steady flow of referred clients, a guaranteed per session charge (e.g., $80 per hour), and a set number of treatment sessions based on the client's DRG placement. However, these counselors often must agree to capitation clauses. Capitation clauses typically indicate that if clients require more treatment sessions than allotted within the client's corresponding DRG, the reimbursement charge will be less. Therefore, the counselor absorbs the additional financial costs. Given that the counselor's initial assessment and diagnosis determines the DRG the client is assigned, one quickly understands the importance of accurate assessment and diagnosis.

The DSM Assessment

The DSM-5 assessment identifies, incorporates, and succinctly lists all diagnostic clinical disorders and conditions, personality disorders, intellectual development disorders, medical conditions, and psychosocial and environment problems and concerns. The result is an encompassing, thorough, and accurate diagnostic presentation of the client and the client's presenting symptomatology and concerns. Such assessment and diagnostic presentation encourages investigation of potential interactions or synergy between the client's voiced concern(s) and major life areas such as the client's general medical condition and social interactions. Specifically, the assessment and diagnosis process promotes a thorough understanding of what contributes to or influences the client's voiced concerns. This understanding helps counselors develop accurate, thorough, and encompassing treatment plans that increase the probability of successful treatment. Although a complete description and overview of how to use the DSM-5 cannot be accomplished in this assessment-specific book, a number of essential DSM-5 fundamentals are mentioned.

In a case like Eva Marie's, clients voicing concerns specific to anxiety are assessed according to all DSM anxiety disorder diagnoses. These include anxiety-related disorders such as generalized anxiety disorder, panic disorder, agoraphobia, and posttraumatic stress disorder (APA, 2013). Concomitantly, anxiety is viewed within the synergistic context of other identified or potentially unacknowledged life areas. These may include (a) the presenting anxiety concerns or clinical disorders as well as other areas of concern that clients may not readily divulge such as addictive behaviors, marital problems, or depressive symptoms; (b) personality disorders or intellectual development disorders that may be related to or influencing presenting anxious concerns; (c) general medical conditions, especially medical factors that may contribute or influence voiced concerns; (d) psychosocial and environmental problems that may affect or engender stressors related to the client's noted anxiety concerns; and (e) overall functioning level. The intent is to secure the most complete and accurate picture of clients and their concerns via a thorough, complete, and accurate list of DSM diagnosis.

Some essential DSM features warrant discussion. One of the advantages of the DSM-5 is the use of five specifier types that enhance understanding of the client's diagnostic-related symptoms. These include (a) course (e.g., partial remission), (b) severity (e.g., mild, moderate, severe), (c) frequency (e.g., two times per week), (d) duration (e.g., minimum duration of six months), and (d) descriptive features (e.g., with poor insight) (Reichenberg, 2014). The use of these specifiers helps counselors describe idiosyncratic features of a client's presenting disorder. For example, in the case of Robert and his Alcohol Use Disorder 303.90, a severe specifier is used to indicate the severity of his alcohol use. This distinguishes Robert's drinking from others with the same alcohol use disorder but mild or moderate severity. Additionally, if Robert was in remission from his alcohol use, one of three other specifiers could be used to describe his remission (i.e., in early remission, in sustained remission, in a controlled environment).

Another essential DSM-5 feature is the use of "unspecified" disorders when an exact diagnosis cannot be determined. Here, for example, it is sometimes impossible to make an adequate diagnostic determination within a single 50-minute interview. This is especially true when clients present with one or more of the following: (a) severe symptoms such as anxiety, hallucinations, or depression; (b) overwhelming chaos in multiple life areas (e.g., interpersonal relationships, employment, finances); (c) limited intelligence; (d) acute physical needs (e.g., cancer, HIV); (e) substance use disorders; and (f) pressing legal issues that may either cause incarceration or influence sentencing determinations, terminate parental custody of children, or result in significant financial hardship.

If counselors are unable to make an immediate and exact disorder determination, they may utilize one of the many broader "unspecified" mental disorders such as 311 Unspecified Depressive Disorder. This diagnosis may be used to simply reflect inadequate information has thus far been obtained by the counselor to make a completely refined and final diagnostic determination (APA, 2017). Such was the case with Eva Marie during the first of her two initial intake sessions. As previously mentioned, Eva Marie was so anxious in the first assessment interview the counselor could not fully gather all the information needed to provide a thoroughly accurate diagnosis matching her presenting symptomatology. Thus, he denoted 399.0 Unspecified Anxiety Disorder on Eva Marie's initial diagnostic report following their first meeting. However, after his second meeting with Eva Marie, he was able to gather sufficient information to more accurately diagnosis her multiple presenting disorders and disorders (i.e., generalized anxiety disorder, relationship distress with spouse or intimate partner, phase of life problem, etc.).

When possible, such "unspecified diagnoses" should not continue indefinitely. The unspecified diagnosis is typically used early in the assessment and treatment process. As further client interactions occur and greater information is gained, the unspecified diagnosis should change to reflect this increased understanding of the client and the client's concerns. This most often will lead to a more accurately refined and specific diagnosis. In Eva Marie's case her 399.0 Unspecified Anxiety Disorder was changed to 300.02 Generalized Anxiety Disorder. In most cases, clearer and more accurately refined diagnoses will be noted within one to three clinical interview meetings.

Another essential DSM-5 feature is related to multiple diagnoses. Often clients fulfill criteria for more than one diagnosis. This was the case with both Eva Marie and Ann, both of whom were diagnosed with multiple disorders. When this occurs, diagnoses are presented in descending order. Thus, the most pressing diagnosis is reported first and the least pressing diagnosis is reported last (APA, 2013). For example, in Eva Marie's case her most pressing concern is the overwhelming anxiety she has experienced. This anxiety continues to negatively intrude on most every aspect of her life. Thus, her most pressing disorder (generalized anxiety disorder) is listed first. Her next most pressing disorder (relationship distress with spouse or intimate partner) is her marital dissatisfaction. It is listed second on the descending diagnosis disorder list. Moreover, her least pressing mental health concern (phase of life problem) is listed last.

The DSM-5 denotes six different personality disorders: (a) antisocial, (b) avoidant, (c) borderline, (d) narcissistic, (e) obsessive-compulsive, and (f) schizotypal. The DSM-5 further includes a category labeled personality disorder—trait specified. This personality disorder was created for clients who fulfill general personality disorder criteria but do not meet the necessary threshold to be included in one of the five personality disorders listed previously.

Personality disorders result from an individual's personality—a rigid, enduring, and inflexible way of interacting with others (Millon, 1981). O'Connor (2008) sums personality disorders best when he states personality disorders

> are more chronic, ingrained, resistant to change, and bearable by those who have them. People do not suddenly become ill with [personality disorders] and seek help. Rather, individuals with [personality disorders] feel normal and at home with their conditions because their disordered personalities and self-concepts are all they know and remember. They often value the very habits and features in themselves that are troublesome for others. (p. 438)

Personality-disordered persons usually create emotional distress for others. Typically, their maladaptive ways of behaving and interacting with others, as well as their dysfunctional ways of living and experiencing life, provoke and wear on others—especially over time within relationships (e.g., work, dating). This then results in sanctions toward or hardships on the personality-disordered persons and their maladaptive and enduring inner experiences.

WHO's Disability Assessment Schedule

The DSM-5 uses the newest World Health Organization's Disability Assessment Schedule 2.0 (WHODAS 2.0) (WHO, 25, January 2016) to measure client functioning within the preceding 30-day period and augment diagnostic code classifications. Thirty-six question stems are used to assess six broad WHODAS 2.0 domains. These domains include (a) cognition (point range 0 to 30), (b) mobility (point range 0 to 25), (c) self-care (point range 0 to 20), (d) getting along with people (point range 0 to 25), (e) life activities (this domain is broken into two subdomains each with a 0–20 point range [household and life activities, school/work]), and (f) participation in society (point range 0 to 40). Prescribed question stem responses for each question include: "none" (1 point), "mild" (2 points), "moderate" (3 points), "severe" (4 points), and "extreme or cannot do" (5 points). Counselors sum the domain scores for a corresponding domain subscore and then sum the subscores to generate a general disability score (total). The WHODAS is discussed at length in Section III of the DSM-5 (APA, 2013) and can be downloaded for free at http://www.who.int/classifications/icf/form_whodas_downloads/en/

Progress Notes

Progress notes are critically important. They establish a written summary of each counseling session, promote treatment efficacy and continuity, and potentially insulate counselors from wrongful liability. Counselors merely need to review previous session progress notes to remind them of pressing topics, themes, and assignments that require attention within the upcoming treatment session. Progress notes further provide documentation of what was said and done within the counseling session. Therefore, from a legal and reimbursement standpoint, progress notes are vitally important. They prove what services were rendered, what services should be reimbursed, and the ethical manner in which services were identified, determined, and provided.

Despite the potential importance and benefits of well-written progress notes, there exists wide variation among agencies regarding progress note-taking requirements and policies. Minimally, progress notes should describe (a) any significant changes in client symptoms or diagnoses, (b) changes in presenting concern severity, (c) the counseling modality used (e.g., individual, family, group), (d) the counseling theory or model used (e.g., motivational interviewing, cognitive-behavioral theory), (e) a summarization of interventions used to address each client presenting concern, and (f) any prescribed assignments or important communications within or outside the session. Should clients present with suicidal, homicidal, or violent ideation or verbalize or suggest harmful intent, progress notes must clearly report what the clients said or did to denote such ideation or intent, the interventions created to sufficiently neutralize the potential threat and ensure safety, consultations with professional peers and superiors to ensure adequate safety, and generated follow-up plans. Finally, given the importance of summarizing and documenting client sessions and to ensure the most accurate recall and reporting, we ask supervisees to complete progress notes immediately following each session. Therefore, we strongly encourage our charges to use 50 minutes of each treatment hour for counseling and the remaining 10 minutes to author corresponding session progress notes. In addition, we require progress note completion by the end of the treatment day. In other words, counselors complete all progress notes within their typical eight-hour work schedule, when memories and recall can adequately provide exact details regarding the session. It has been our experience that when counselors fail to complete multiple progress notes prior to the end of the treatment day, the later authored progress notes are void of important details. Concomitantly, the counselors often have a difficult time adequately describing session benefits and concerns.

Standardized Progress Note Formats
SOAP Progress Notes

Early in our education, we were trained to use SOAP Notes. SOAP is a mnemonic that uses the first letters of four words: *s*ubjective, *o*bjective, *a*ssessment, and *p*lan (J. Owen, personal communication, September 9, 1985; Shaw, 1997). Each letter and word corresponds to a specific component of the counselor-authored progress note. Thus, SOAP notes start with a subjective component, proceed through objective and assessment components, and end with a plan component. Typically, at the top of the first and following pages of the SOAP notes the client's name, the date and time of the session, and the counselor's name are prominently displayed. Counselors sign and date the notes after written content is added to the SOAP plan component. The signature is placed immediately under the last line of the plan component. This indicates the progress notes for that session are complete and whole. Furthermore, the signature placement helps ensure that others cannot add or delete written content. On the right-hand side next to the counselor's signature are the counselor's highest academic degree (e.g., MA, MS, PhD) and professional license and certification initials such as LPC (Licensed Professional Counselor), LMHC (Licensed Mental Health Counselor), or NCC (National Certified Counselor).

The SOAP notes subjective component includes client-provided information. Thus, the information is completely subjective. The information contained within the subjective component involves the client's perceptions of the chief presenting concerns or reasons for treatment. Here, the client describes symptoms including onset, duration, severity of the concern, and factors perceived by the client as influencing the concern. The SOAP notes objective component is intended to contain impartial and unbiased data from external information sources. Height and weight measurements, findings from physical examinations, or blood pressure measurements are the types of objective information contained in medical SOAP notes. However, within the realm of counseling, truly objective information is at best difficult to attain. Here, counselors may include direct client observations such as descriptions of clothing worn, predominate presenting affect, person hygiene, speech volume, rate, and tone, and eye contact. Yet we believe this information is typically far more subjective than implied by the SOAP term "objective." In general, the objective component contained within most SOAP notes we have read are typically scant of clinically useful or significant information. Thus, the clinical utility of the objective component for mental health treatment providers is questionable. The third SOAP component is assessment. Assessment typically includes a corresponding DSM diagnosis, counselor perceptions regarding client intelligence, cognitive functioning, emotional state, and behavioral symptoms, counselor-observed discrepancies between what the client states and does, and the identification of persons reported by the client as significant. Plan is the final SOAP notes component. Here, counselors indicate future treatment plans and recommendations, as well as client agreed upon assignments and treatment goals.

DART Progress Notes

DART notes and SOAP notes are similar. Like SOAP notes, DART notes use a four-letter mnemonic. Each letter represents a corresponding progress note component. These components include *d*ata, *a*ction, *r*esponse, and *t*eaching (Baird, 2008). However, unlike the previously described SOAP components, DART notes combine both subjective and objective information within a single progress note component. This component, data, is the first letter of the DART notes mnemonic. Data contains both the subjective client-reported symptoms and presenting concerns as well as the counselor's direct observations of the client. Action is the second DART component. Action describes the counseling interventions used within the treatment session. Thus, if the counselor used the familiar Solution Focused Miracle Question (Juhnke & Hagedorn, 2006) as the means for identifying client goals, this action is described. Client responses to these described actions are noted in the third DART notes component, response. Both favorable and unfavorable client responses to counselor-engendered intervention techniques are recorded. Thus, if the intervention was reported helpful by the client or perceived clinically useful by the counselor, the counselor would document the positive outcome. Teaching is the final DART component. Professional counselors often use psychoeducation and teaching within treatment sessions (Granello & Juhnke, 2009; Juhnke, 2002; Juhnke, Granello, & Granello, 2010; Kelly & Juhnke, 2005). For example, if the counselor provided psychoeducation about the addictive properties of cocaine to a substance-abusing client or taught a client how to identify triggering events that occur prior to arguing with a spouse, these would be documented within the DART notes' teaching component.

Diagnostic-Based Progress Notes

Over the years, we have found diagnostic-based progress notes provide the most comprehensive session documentation, greatest client treatment satisfaction, and increased insurance reimbursement probability. In addition, because diagnostic-based progress notes require each client-identified concern from the clinical intake assessment to be thoroughly assessed and ranked according to client-perceived importance, severity, and frequency, as well as counselor-noted clinical significance, clients and counselors collaborate to create treatment goals and objectives believed most helpful in reducing or eliminating diagnostic-related symptoms. Stated differently, it is impossible for clients to be dissatisfied with treatment, because they identify and rank order their concerns. Clients and counselors then jointly concrete treatment goals and objectives they believe will best alleviate the diagnoses corresponding to these concerns. These cocreated treatment goals and objectives are the core of diagnostic-based progress notes.

Diagnostic-based progress notes are far more structured than either SOAP or DART notes and use the standardized DSM-5 diagnoses within the clinical assessment intake. Hence, treatment goals and objectives specific to the client's chief and secondary presenting concerns are rank-ordered. At the conclusion of each counseling session, each corresponding component's goal is reported as "Addressed," "Partially Addressed," or "Not Addressed" and a description documenting how the goal or objective was addressed is entered.

The best way to demonstrate diagnostic-based progress notes is via example. Thus, we use our previous clinical vignette of 37-year-old Robert Jones. As you likely remember, Robert's chief presenting diagnosis is 303.90 Alcohol Use Disorder (Severe) with a secondary diagnosis of V61.10 Relationship Distress with Spouse or Intimate Partner. Using the previously described clinical vignette, the counselor would help Robert identify useful treatment goals and objectives for each concern. Thus, the counselor might say something like, "Robert, from the list of all concerns you want to address in counseling, which one item do you wish to address first?" Robert might reply, "I really want to stop drinking and get my wife back." Given the enormity of this goal, the counselor will help Robert identify stepping stones or objectives that will help him move toward accomplishing this significant goal. The following example shows how the counselor might do this and help Robert create his first goal and objectives that will be used in his progress notes.

COUNSELOR: "Stopping your drinking and getting your wife back are two excellent goals, Robert. However, they are big treatment goals and really interrelated. If I understand correctly, your wife indicated she will permanently leave you if you don't stop drinking. Thus, what would you think about first working on your drinking? If we make improvements in this area it may help your marriage."

ROBERT: "That makes sense. If I can stop my drinking then maybe my wife won't leave me."

COUNSELOR: "Although I can't guarantee your wife will come back if you stop drinking, you did tell me earlier the most important thing for you was to stop drinking and get your life back. So is that the primary goal you want to work on?"

ROBERT: "That is definitely what I want to do. That is my number one goal. I want to stop drinking."

COUNSELOR: "Like I said, Robert, that is an excellent goal. However, it is a big treatment goal. My clients often find it helpful to identify small stepping stones or objectives that will help them begin moving toward their larger treatment goals. What stepping stones could you use to start moving closer to your goal of stop drinking?"

ROBERT: "I don't know."

COUNSELOR: "Well, some of my clients who want to gain control over their alcohol use find attending AA meetings helpful. You had indicated in our intake session that you thought attending AA would have been helpful. Might finding an AA group that matches your needs and regularly attending AA at a convenient time be something you would like to do?"

ROBERT: "That really makes sense."

COUNSELOR: "So, let's make identifying a local AA group you want to attend our first stepping stone. Is that something you want to do, or do you want to make your first stepping stone toward stopping your alcohol use something else?"

ROBERT: "No, that would be a good first step. I could really use that."

COUNSELOR: "Okay, let's do that. For our second step, I think you will want to do more than simply identify an AA group that will meet at a convenient time for you. My guess is that you will want to regularly attend that group, right?"

ROBERT: (Laughs) "Yes, I certainly need to attend. I only went once or twice to AA before. It did help. But I stopped going."

COUNSELOR: "So, for our second stepping stone, I'm hearing you say that regularly attending AA is something you want. What other baby steps will help you move toward your goal of stopping your drinking, Robert?"

ROBERT: "Well, just about everyone know, other than my wife, drinks. I've got to make some nondrinking and nondrugging friends."

COUNSELOR: "So, am I hearing you saying another way to begin to stop your drinking is to make new friends who don't use alcohol or other drugs?"

ROBERT: "Yes."

COUNSELOR: "That all makes sense, and I believe those are some very good stepping stone goals to help us move toward your chief goal of stopping your drinking alcohol. How about if we use the behaviors you have just identified for our first treatment goal and objectives? Would those work for you?"

ROBERT: "Certainly."

COUNSELOR: "May I make one minor suggestion?"

ROBERT: "What's that?"

COUNSELOR: "Well, I have learned over the years that it is easier to achieve goals that add behaviors and ways of thinking rather than attempting to eliminate behaviors and thinking. Instead of saying our goal is to 'help Robert stop drinking alcohol,' would you mind if we slightly modify our goal? Maybe we could say Robert's number one goal is to 'increase the frequency of Robert's nonalcohol use times"? In other words, our goal will be to increase the time you are not drinking or using alcohol."

ROBERT: "That will work."

COUNSELOR: "So, our major goal will be to 'increase the frequency of Robert's nonalcohol using times.' The stepping stones or objectives you have identified as helpful in moving you closer to accomplishing that goal are to identify AA groups that would meet at a time and location convenient to you, regularly attending those AA meetings, and make new alcohol- and drug-free friends. How does that sound?"

ROBERT: "I think those are good places to start."

Diagnostic-based progress notes use these client-identified goals and objectives. Next to each written goal or objective, the counselor indicates "Addressed," "Partially Addressed," or "Not Addressed." Under each goal and objective is a succinct description of what occurred within the session related to the goal or objective. In this way, the progress notes exactly report what goals and objectives were addressed in session and how the goals and objectives were addressed. Thus, Robert's diagnostic-based progress notes are written as the following:

> Goal I: Increase the frequency of Robert's nonalcohol using times. (Addressed) During today's session, Robert identified his first treatment goal. That treatment goal is to increase the frequency of times when he is not using or consuming alcohol. According to Robert, he wishes to "stop" his alcohol consumption. Robert identified three stepping stones or objectives that he reports will help move him toward his treatment goal. These objectives are indicated below.
>
> Objective Number I: Robert will identify an AA group to attend. (Addressed.) During today's treatment session, Robert was given the national AA website. Robert used his iPhone to identify a local AA group that meets at a time and location near his home. He reports he will attend his first AA meeting today at 3 pm.
>
> Objective II: Robert will regularly attend AA meetings. (Partially Addressed.) During today's treatment session, Robert reported AA attendance would help increase the frequency of his nonalcohol using times. Robert identified an AA group he will attend this afternoon. When asked what Robert will need to do to actually fulfill this object for the day, Robert stated, "I have to make myself go to the meeting." When asked how he will do that, Robert reported, "I know if I want to get my wife back, I've got to stop drinking. When I drive to the meeting, I will be telling myself 'going to AA will help me get Catherine back.' That will make me go." He further reported he would tape a picture of Catherine, his wife, on the dashboard of his car, "Looking at her picture will ensure I attend [AA]."

Objective III: Robert will make new friends who do not consume alcohol or use other drugs. (Partially Addressed.)

During today's session, Robert indicated most of his close friends drink to the point of intoxication or use other drugs. Robert reported he believed it critically important to make new nondrinking and nondrugging friends. He indicated he would attend a 3 pm AA meeting today at Park Street Baptist Church. Robert stated he would "reach out" to others at the meeting to make new friendships with nondrinking/nondrugging people. When asked what "reach out" would look like, Robert responded, "I will simply say during the open meeting that I need some nondrugging friends for my wife and me to hang out with." Robert continued by indicating he had done this in the past and AA sponsors were helpful in connecting Robert with long-established nondrinking and nondrugging persons in the recovery community.

An important diagnostic-based progress note feature is that the client presenting concerns generates diagnoses and diagnoses encourage relevant and thoughtful treatment. Thus, all diagnoses require corresponding treatment goals and objectives. Therefore, unlike SOAP or DART progress notes where detailed goals and objectives are not required and progress notes may not document what specifically occurred within each treatment session to address client-identified goals or corresponding diagnoses, diagnostic-based progress notes ensure counselors document how all diagnoses were addressed via corresponding goals and objectives. Such documentation ensures treatment continuity and reduces the probability of overlooking important client-identified concerns. In addition, the documentation of each goal and objective enhances the probability of full insurance reimbursement.

Robert's goals and objectives are relatively simple and used for instructional purposes only. In most cases a minimum of three treatment goals with each goal having at least two objectives are used. In addition, all client-identified treatment goals should be noted at the onset of treatment. However, these goals should be rank-ordered by the client and counselor according to the most pressing and clinically significant concerns. Thus, issues specific to self-harm or potential harm to others (e.g., suicidal ideation suicide intent, domestic violence, homicide intent) or psychotic features are priority concerns and addressed first.

Summary

Chapter 2 has provided three thorough case studies that will be used throughout the upcoming chapters. Corresponding initial intake sessions were also described as well as a description regarding the two primary, U.S. diagnostic classification systems. Ms. Eva Marie Garza presents with five identified disorders. Generalized anxiety is the most predominant. Thus, generalized anxiety disorder is listed first. Mr. Robert Jones's chief presenting concern is his alcohol use disorder. Thus, this is ranked first and at the top of his diagnosis. Ann presents with four identified disorders. Oppositional defiant disorder is the most predominant. Thus, oppositional defiant disorder is listed first. These case studies demonstrate to readers the basic elements contained within typical clinical assessment intake interviews. This chapter has further indicated the general purpose and use of progress notes. Finally, the chapter has provided an overview of three different progress note-taking methods and described potential benefits of using diagnostic-based progress notes.

3

Fundamentals of Assessment

Objectives

1. Distinguish between norm-referenced tests and criterion-referenced tests.
2. Define the various types of scales of measurement.
3. Understand the basic elements of a frequency distribution.
4. Compute and interpret measures of central tendency and variability.
5. Understand the role of the normal curve and its purpose in norming assessments and interpreting scores.
6. Identify, define, and interpret various types of standard scores.
7. Compute and interpret correlation coefficients.

Chapter Overview

If you are like most graduate students, this will be your least favorite chapter, as it has more mathematical concepts than any other chapter in the book. However, not only are we getting this over with early in the book, but doing it now means you will have plenty of time and examples to use to master these concepts. We focus on the differences between criterion-referenced and norm-referenced test and then focus on the concept of norming and the mathematical properties associated with what these test results mean.

The Meanings of Test Scores

Scores on assessment results only have meaning based on the context in which the assessment was administered. A score, by itself, is essentially meaningless. However, when placed in proper context—that is, related to the purpose of the assessment, the nature of the administration, its interpretation, and the manner in which it will be used—a score can be quite meaningful. For example, a score on an achievement test is only meaningful when compared to an established criterion, past performance, or other individuals who completed the instrument. Each of these scenarios presents a way to understand and use test scores.

Criterion-Referenced Tests

Criterion-referenced tests refer to scores on instruments that are compared to a preestablished standard (Cohen et al., 2013). The standard for comparison could be defined in many different ways, such as a knowledge base or cut-score. Most exams given in a classroom are criterion-referenced exams—the teacher is testing a student's knowledge of information. The percentage correct, or score, is an estimate of the amount of knowledge a student can demonstrate. The score is a comparison to the total amount of information being evaluated by the exam. Often a *cut-score*, a score indicating a minimum for identifying a standard, is used to indicate sufficient mastery of material or passing an exam or as a diagnostic label. For example, a counseling student taking a licensing exam may be required to pass the exam with 60% correct to be eligible for a license; a high school student might need to achieve 70% on an exam to demonstrate proficiency and be allowed to matriculate. Criterion-referenced tests may be used to examine mastery of a knowledge base, determine the amount of knowledge understood about a particular phenomenon, or make comparisons of how much knowledge was gained within an individual or group, such as by using a pretest or baseline measure and comparing to a posttest.

Because criterion-referenced tests may be used more informally, such as by classroom teachers to assess gained knowledge of a subject area, test construction may not be adequate. These types of assessments may not be created with regard to current testing standards, so issues compromising fairness and accuracy of the test may be evident. Proper training in devising assessments is essential to ethical practice of assessment.

Consider that most exams in academic settings fall into the category of criterion-referenced tests. When a student earns 85% on an exam, the score is interpreted as the student correctly answered 85% of the material. School counselors, especially, can serve as important resources for faculty, as criterion-referenced tests are used extensively to determine grades.

Teacher-Created Examinations

Perhaps the most widely used nonstandardized examination procedure comes from educators who develop examinations to assess the extent to which individuals learned material presented to them. Although the content of courses, and even materials for a course (e.g., textbook), may be aligned with a larger curriculum, class examination occurs as an independent process. Two instructors teaching the same course may use different assessments to identify student learning. Clearly, the process of standardizing measures of achievement for teaching a variety of courses in numerous settings and various learning environments would be unfathomable. However, without a standardization procedure, how can educators and evaluators measure achievement in a fair manner? Anastasi and Urbina (1997) identified a three-step process to test development that may increase test fairness while simultaneously forgoing a formal standardization procedure: (a) test design, (b) item development, and (c) item analysis.

Test Design

Designing a test to cover appropriate content requires planning. Test developers need to make sure that the content is aligned with the material presented and that it is assessed at a variety of cognitive levels. For example, items may be developed to ascertain the degree to which test-takers recall information or may reflect higher order thinking in terms of the ability to apply or evaluate information. When designing a test, developers may wish to consider the degree to which items reflect recall, which may consist of easier items, versus items that reflect more complex cognitive tasks (e.g., analysis and evaluation). One method of identifying the complexity of an item is to create items aligned with both content presented and cognitive domains associated with Bloom's taxonomy.

Bloom (1956) identified six cognitive domains: (a) knowledge, (b) comprehension, (c) application, (d) analysis, (e) synthesis, and (f) evaluation. A team of cognitive psychologists led by Lorin Anderson revised Bloom's cognitive domains. The revised version changed the six major categories from nouns to verbs and changed some of the terminology. Most notably, creating, formerly known as synthesis, was moved to a higher level of evaluating. Thus, the ability to generate something new was seen as a more complex task than evaluating what is currently known or present. The revised taxonomy is (a) remembering, (b) understanding, (c) applying, (d) analyzing, (e) evaluating, and (f) creating (Anderson & Krathwohl, 2001).

Using the revised cognitive domain categories, test developers should consider the extent to which an item requires the examinee to employ a lower level cognitive task (e.g., remembering) versus a higher level cognitive task (e.g., evaluating). Furthermore, consideration of the development of items that measure the aforementioned cognitive domains is important. Essay exams are useful in measuring a variety of cognitive domains, but the uniformity of evaluating answers, as well as the time necessary to evaluate responses, does not always lend to this method as appropriate or useful. Multiple-choice items may be developed to assess both lower level and higher level cognitive tasks, whereas other methods, such as matching or short answer, may focus more on the lower level cognitive categories.

Such preparation should result in a blueprint for the prospective test. From this plan, test developers may ensure that (a) the appropriate content is covered and (b) a balance between lower level and higher level cognitive categories is reflected. Keep in mind that tests that are weighted toward higher level cognitive categories may be perceived as difficult, whereas tests that are weighted toward lower level cognitive categories may be perceived as easy.

Item Development

The process of creating a blueprint for the test is essential for developing test items. Test developers should align items with the appropriate content and cognitive category to be evaluated. Item type should be considered carefully. Items may be open-ended, such as short answer or essay, or they may be closed-ended, such as multiple choice.

Although multiple-choice items appear to be quite popular because of their simplicity in grading, test developers should be cautious. Creating appropriate items that are clear, content aligned, and evenly distributed among the cognitive categories being assessed is pertinent to developing a valid measure. Multiple-choice tests or items can be difficult and time-consuming to develop but can be useful in assessing a variety of cognitive domains and result in rather reliable scores.

In addition to multiple-choice items, other item types to consider in test construction include true–false items, matching, short answer, and essay tests. Although true–false items are easier to score, the items are less likely to measure a domain accurately and consistently. Scores on short-answer and essay questions may also lack consistency in scoring and/or measurement of a domain. Consider the breadth of answers for an essay question. Content may vary greatly. However, such items may be more appropriate for the cognitive domain being measured. For example, matching items may be helpful in measuring remembering, whereas essays may be more appropriate for measuring evaluating and creating. When criterion-referenced tests are used, attention to item development is essential. We advocate that users of criterion-referenced tests conduct an *item analysis*. Two prominent issues related to an item analysis include item difficulty and item discrimination.

Item Analysis

Item difficulty is simply the proportion of students who correctly answered the item. For each item on an exam, the proportion of students who answered the question correctly is calculated. Therefore, item difficulty ranges from 0.0 to 1.00, with 0.0 referring to an item that no one answered correctly correct and 1.00 referring to an item that all participants answered correctly. The formula for item difficulty can be expressed as follows:

$$P = \frac{\text{\# of correct responses}}{\text{total \# of responses}}$$

where P is the proportion of correct responses, the numerator is the number of respondents who correctly answered the item, and the denominator is the total number of respondents. Easy items are closer to 1.00; more difficult items are closer to 0.0.

Item analysis is a process by which items can be evaluated according to difficulty and discrimination. If 20 students take an exam and 8 individuals answer an item correctly, then $P = .40$ or 40% of the students answered the item correctly. Thus, a higher P indicates an easier item, and a lower P indicates a more difficult item.

Item discrimination is useful in determining the extent to which an item differentiates different levels of mastery. For example, a teacher would expect that a student who has proficiency over material to be able to answer more items correctly than a student who lacks proficiency. Not only will some items be more difficult, but students who have more knowledge of the material should be able to answer more difficult items, and students with less mastery of material may have more difficulty answering items correctly. Simply because few students answer an item correctly does not necessarily mean the item is bad, especially if the item was answered correctly by the top students. In other words, an item can discriminate between those students who have a solid understanding of material versus those who do not.

To evaluate item discrimination, participants should be divided into three groups: the upper 27% of scores, the middle 46% of scores, and the lower 27% of scores. For the purposes of calculating item discrimination, only the upper and lower groups are used. Item discrimination indices use only 54% of the participants. Similar to item difficulty, item discrimination indices need to be calculated for each item:

$$D = \left(\% \text{ of the upper group who correctly answered the item}\right) \\ - \left(\% \text{ of the lower group who correctly answered the item}\right)$$

So, if 80% of the upper group answered an item correctly and 20% of the lower group answered the same item correctly, the discrimination index would be .80 − .60 = .40.

Item discrimination indices may range from −1.00 to +1.00. When an item perfectly discriminates (+1.00), that means everyone in the upper group answered the item correctly and everyone in the lower group answered the item incorrectly. Thus, even if the difficulty index was low (i.e., a higher percentage of people missed the item), the item may still be valid, as the item helps differentiate those with more advanced knowledge with respect to this item. However, when item discrimination is low (e.g., .20), the item discriminates poorly. The closer the index is to 0.0, the less the item discriminates, and equal numbers of participants in the upper and lower groups are answering the item incorrectly. This might indicate an item in which the material was not taught well or covered adequately. Items in this category may not be good items, and test developers should consider removing them. When an item discrimination index is negative, more people in the lower group (i.e., participants with lower scores) answered the item correctly than in the upper group. This often occurs with poorly worded items or a result of guessing on the answer. Items with negative discrimination indices should be removed.

For example, say a teacher administers an exam to 28 students. From the 28 students, the top and bottom eight scores approximately will compose the upper and lower groups, respectively. In the bottom 27%, two students made the same lowest score, so nine scores were in the lower group and eight scores were in the upper group. From eight students in the upper group, six students answered the item correctly. In the lower group consisting of nine students, three students answered the item correctly. So, using the previous formula:

$$D = \frac{6}{8} - \frac{3}{9} = .42$$

Thus, 75% of individuals in the high group answered the item correctly, and 33% of individuals in the low group answered the item correctly. Generally, a discrimination index of .35 or higher is indicative of a higher quality item, whereas item discrimination below .20 is indicative of a less useful item (Hopkins, 1998). Therefore, this example is indicative of an item with rather strong discrimination. In other words, the majority of individuals in the high group know the material this item tests, but the majority of the individuals in the lower group do not.

Certainly, item difficulty can lend information about the easiness of an item and overall test. However, item difficulty alone is not sufficient in addressing whether an item should be kept and counted on an exam or removed. Evaluating item discrimination can be helpful in addressing the value of an item. Item discrimination provides for each item an index to compare how individuals who did well on the test compared to individuals who had a weaker performance on the test. Along with item difficulty, a teacher can glean some important information related to this item:

1. To some degree, this item distinguishes well between students who understand the material this item represents and students who have less understanding.
2. An item of this nature may have a higher level of difficulty (depending on how well the middle group performed, as they were not included in computing item discrimination). Simply because an item is difficult does not make it a bad item, especially if students who have learned the material perform better on this item than students who have lesser understanding of the material.
3. The teacher has feedback on which items, and possibly what material, students may struggle with in the class.

A limitation to item discrimination indices is that 46% of the participants are not included in the analysis. Counselors should carefully evaluate items on the basis of difficulty and discrimination, as neither measure should stand alone.

Key to this discussion is the need for counselors, particularly those who work in academic settings and/or serve in areas of program evaluation and training, to use proper procedures in developing test items. School counselors can provide in-services to teachers in terms of developing appropriate classroom tests and evaluating the items they use. Although item analysis is an essential component to creating tests and measuring progress, most preservice teachers are not exposed to this process in their training. Furthermore, counselors may serve as consultants and evaluators to agencies and organizations and develop proper instruments that reflect training or information related to an agency or organization.

Norm-Referenced Tests

Norm-referenced instruments use scores that compare an individual or group to a *norm group*—a group representing an estimate of the population of interest for a given phenomenon. Scores on norm-referenced tests are expressed in ways that compare the individual or group to the norm group. For example, percentile scores, such as those expressed on a standardized test, make comparisons based on how an individual's performance compares to others with similar characteristics. A student scoring in the 97th percentile has performed the same as or higher than 97% of the norm group. This could be interpreted as the individual scoring in the top 3% on a given phenomenon for individuals with similar characteristics.

Because norm-referenced tests rely on comparisons based on a norm group, also known as a *normative sample*, construction of norm-referenced tests should follow the most current guidelines in the 2014 *Standards for Educational and Psychological Testing* discussed in Chapters 4 and 5. There are many ways to express, understand, and interpret scores and comparisons made to a norm group. The following sections address the manner in which scores are expressed, known as *scales*, and various methods of understanding and interpreting test scores.

Scales of Measurement

In some cases, phenomena of interest can be directly observed. A counselor can observe a student in class and count the number of disruptive behaviors the student exhibits. A client can report the number of alcoholic beverages consumed over the past week. Scores generated from such events or occurrences are a result of some objective criteria based on direct observation. However, not all phenomena of interest can be measured through direct observation. *Constructs* are phenomena that exist but cannot be directly observed. Psychosocial variables such as depression may be observed but not objectively scored without the use of an *instrument*, a set of objective criteria designed to measure a construct. Other common constructs that are measured include intelligence, achievement, aptitude, and a wide range of psychological variables (e.g., depression, aggression, stress, life balance). Constructs can also refer to characteristics such as gender identity or multicultural competence. When an instrument is used in a study to measure a construct, the measurement may be a variable in the study. Thus, variables can be based on an objective criteria or a measured construct. To understand and communicate assessment results, counselors need to understand the types of scales that may define a variable.

A *nominal* scale refers to a variable that is classified. Examples include sex, ethnicity, religion, and so forth. Each nominal scale includes a set of categories or labels, and no label is quantitatively higher or lower than another label. Comparisons can only be based on the count for each label. For example, the Beck Depression Inventory-II (BDI-II) was normed on 500 outpatients and 120 college students. The label of *outpatients* and *college students* refer to nominal variables—categories that describe the individuals in the sample.

An *ordinal* scale denotes an order or ranking. No comparisons beyond the order or ranking can be made. For example, such rankings are often used in schools to denote valedictorians and salutatorians. The labels by themselves denote a one–two position in graduation but do not include an amount of the difference between the two categories. Only the rank is considered and not the extent to how each rank was measured. Another example may be ranking career preferences, where it may not matter by how much a client prefers one type of career over another but simply which career option was endorsed the most. In assessment, having participants rank preferences in a survey or instrument is an example of ordinal data.

An *interval* scale denotes equality between levels with no true zero. A *true zero* refers to an absence of a particular variable. Many ability tests (intelligence, aptitude, achievement) use interval scales. For example, on the ACT, the lowest score is 1 and the highest score is 36. The distance between each score is equal, and a score of zero is not possible. Interval data can be subjected to mathematical operations. In counseling research, the use of true interval scales can be questionable. Often, researchers assume choices on a scale are of equal distance, when in fact they are not. For example, the directions on the BDI-II instruct the participant to "pick out the one statement in each group that best describes the way you have been feeling" (Beck, Steer, & Brown, 1996, p. 8). Each statement references a number that can be added or subtracted to form a total score. However, the degree to which an individual believes a certain statement, such as feeling sad, is true may differ between and among individuals. So, whereas one person believes he or she experiences sadness frequently, another individual may interpret the same degree of sadness as occurring more often. Another example is often seen in Likert and Likert-type scales (pronounced "lick-urt") in which participants are asked to identify the level of agreement for a particular item similar to the following choices: (1) *strongly disagree*, (2) *disagree*, (3) *neither agree nor disagree*, (4) *agree*, and (5) *strongly agree*. The assumption is that, for each data point, the distance is equal. The distance between a 2 and a 4 is the same as the distance between a 3 and a 5. However, the extent that would lead a person to choose, for example, *strongly agree* versus *agree* differs between and among individuals. So although these items are treated as if they occur on an interval scale and are used with mathematical operations, in actuality they are not. When researchers treat such scales as interval data, the scale may be termed *quasi-interval*.

A *ratio* scale denotes equality between levels with a true zero. In this case, the absence of a measured phenomenon is possible. This could be, for example, the number of items answered correctly on a test (where zero refers to no items answered correctly), amount of income, or age. In counseling research, items related to the number of suicidal ideations a client has experienced in a given week can be a ratio variable. Because mathematical operations can be conducted on interval or ratio variables, they are often termed *continuous variables*, given the wide range of possible answers. When variables have a finite number of categories (i.e., nominal variables), they are often referred to as *discrete variables*.

One important feature of the scales of measurement is that the higher order scales can be converted to the lower order scales. For example, we can take a construct such as *the number of beers you drank over a weekend*—a naturally occurring ratio variable—and convert it to an ordinal variable or nominal variable, such as 0–2 beers, 3–4 beers, 5 or more beers, or *no drinking, a little drinking*, or *a lot of drinking*. Note that the reverse cannot be done—a variable that is nominal cannot be converted to an ordinal, interval, or ratio variable. Variables can be converted to lower scales (e.g., nominal), but lower scales cannot be converted to higher scales (e.g., ratio).

Understanding Assessment Scores: Frequency Distributions and Percentiles

There are many different methods of presenting information garnered from assessments. Frequency distributions provide a variety of important information about the nature of a set of scores. By using frequency distributions, counselors can evaluate how each individual scored and make comparisons to the whole group.

For the purposes of explaining the measurement concepts in this chapter, we use a data set consisting of 400 at-risk adolescents who were administered the Crisis Stabilization Scale (CriSS; Balkin, 2014). Clinicians who are working with adolescents in crisis (e.g., adolescents identified as a danger to self or others) can use the CriSS to establish the extent to which adolescents have met goals consistent with stabilization and present sufficient coping and plans for follow-up. The CriSS includes two scales: Coping and Commitment to Follow-Up. For this group of adolescents, we examine the Coping scale, which measures the extent to which the adolescent was committed to safety, identified problems related to the crisis (e.g., being a danger to self or others), and processed coping skills. From 400 adolescents evaluated in acute care psychiatric hospitalization, scores ranged from 23 to 71. We have arranged the scores in descending order in Table 3.1:

Frequency refers to the number of adolescents who have the exact same score on the Coping scale of the CriSS.

Percent refers to the percentage of adolescents who have the same score; it is the frequency divided by the total sample (400).

Cumulative frequency refers to the number of adolescents who are at or below the corresponding score. To obtain the cumulative frequency for a corresponding score, simply add each frequency to the cumulative frequency below the corresponding score. The first frequency and first cumulative frequency will be equal. The highest cumulative frequency will equal the total sample.

Cumulative percent refers to the percentage of adolescents who are at or below the corresponding score. To obtain the cumulative percent for a corresponding score, simply add each percent to the cumulative percent below the corresponding score. The first percentage score and first cumulative percent will be equal. The highest cumulative percent will equal 100%.

TABLE 3.1 Frequency Distribution for the Coping Scale on the CriSS ($n = 400$)

Score	Frequency	Cumulative Frequency	Percent	Cumulative Percent
71	12	400	3.00	100.00
70	7	388	1.75	97.00
69	1	381	0.25	95.25
68	1	380	0.25	95.00
67	7	379	1.75	94.75
66	3	372	0.75	93.00
65	5	369	1.25	92.25
64	10	364	2.50	91.00
63	2	354	0.50	88.50
62	5	352	1.25	88.00
61	2	347	0.50	86.75
60	11	345	2.75	86.25
59	3	334	0.75	83.50
58	32	331	8.00	82.75
57	12	299	3.00	74.75
56	13	287	3.25	71.75
55	5	274	1.25	68.50
54	5	269	1.25	67.25
53	7	264	1.75	66.00
52	7	257	1.75	64.25
51	8	250	2.00	62.50
50	11	242	2.75	60.50
49	9	231	2.25	57.75
48	6	222	1.50	55.50
47	15	216	3.75	54.00
46	12	201	3.00	50.25
45	74	189	18.50	47.25
44	11	115	2.75	28.75
43	27	104	6.75	26.00
42	10	77	2.50	19.25
41	13	67	3.25	16.75
40	15	54	3.75	13.50
39	5	39	1.25	9.75
38	5	34	1.25	8.50
37	1	29	0.25	7.25
36	5	28	1.25	7.00
35	1	23	0.25	5.75
34	3	22	0.75	5.50
33	4	19	1.00	4.75
33	2	15	0.50	3.75
32	5	13	1.25	3.25
30	4	8	1.00	2.00
29	2	4	0.50	1.00
26	1	2	0.25	0.50
23	1	1	0.25	0.25

Note: CriSS = Crisis Stabilization Scale.

Frequency distributions can also be demonstrated visually through a histogram. A histogram is a bar graph with the scores on the X-axis and the frequencies on the Y-axis. Histograms also show the shape of a distribution (see in Figure 3.1). Frequency distributions with larger sample sizes often approximate a bell-shaped distribution, which is discussed later in this chapter.

Frequency distributions may also be displayed through intervals, especially when counselors are more interested in a range of scores. There are numerous ways to create a frequency distribution using intervals. One method is demonstrated in Table 3.2. The distribution maintains the same shape, regardless of the use of intervals.

Frequency distributions provide a visual organization of the data and a method of making comparisons. An individual who achieves a particular score can easily be compared to the entire group. For example, approximately half of the participants scored 46 or below, as evidenced by the cumulative percentage of 50.25% for participants who scored 46 (see Table 3.1). On the CriSS, adolescents may be considered at risk for continued difficulties with crisis behavior for scores that are 40 or below and are generally considered unstable on a clinical scale less than 35. Based on Table 3.1, about 13.5% of the adolescents from this particular sample of 400 may be identified as having continued difficulties based on the cumulative percentage at 13.5% who scored at or below 40. By default, the rest of the sample (86.5%) is above this range.

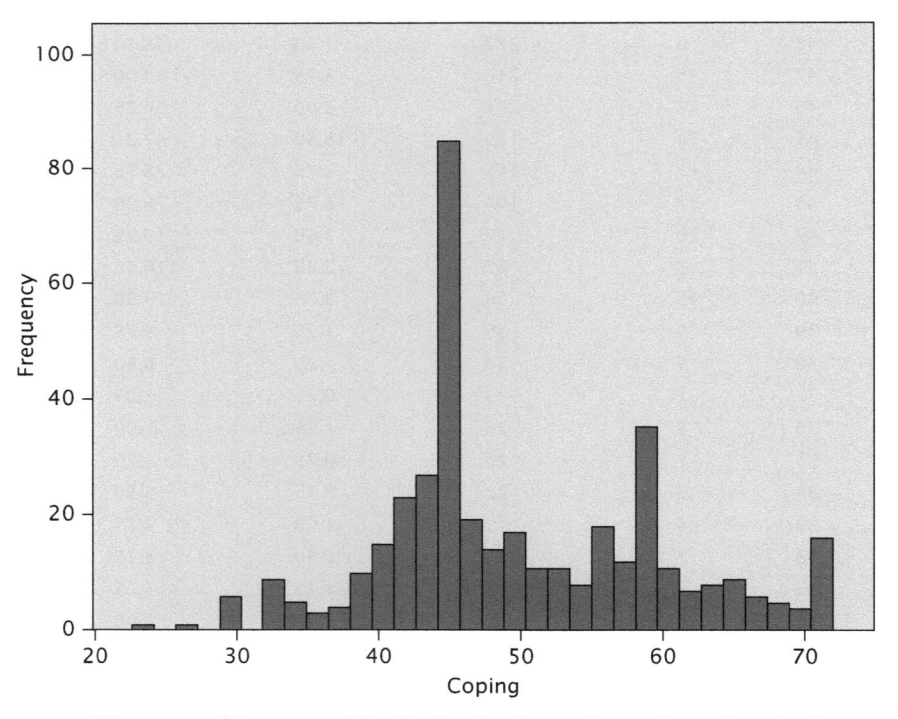

FIGURE 3.1 Histogram of Frequency Distribution for the Coping Scale on the CriSS (n = 400).

TABLE 3.2 Interval Distribution for the Coping Scale on the CriSS ($n = 400$)

Interval	Frequency	Cumulative Frequency	Percent	Cumulative Percent
71–75	12	400	3.00	100.00
66–70	19	388	4.75	97.00
61–65	24	369	6.00	92.25
56–60	71	345	17.75	86.25
51–55	32	274	8.00	68.50
46–50	53	242	13.25	60.50
41–45	135	189	33.75	47.25
36–40	31	54	7.75	13.50
31–35	15	23	3.75	5.75
26–30	7	8	1.75	2.00
21–25	1	1	0.25	0.25

Note: CriSS = Crisis Stabilization Scale.

Frequency distributions and histograms also provide a visual representation of data. By examining frequencies, common scores among a group are easily identified, and these commonalities can been seen as spikes. Table 3.1 shows scores of 45 had the highest frequency ($f = 74$) with 18.5% of the group scoring 45. This spike in the scores can be approximated in Figure 3.1 near the center of the distribution. When counselors are more interested in a range of scores, frequency distributions and histograms that use intervals (Table 3.2) may be more useful.

Measures of Central Tendency

Although frequency distributions may demonstrate how an individual fits into a group of scores, measures of central tendency indicate how a group performs on a given instrument or task. A school counselor may want to know how a group of students score on a particular assessment, such as the ACT. A mental health counselor or director may wish to ascertain the degree to which adolescents in crisis treated in an inpatient setting appear to be stable and ready for a less intensive level of care using the CriSS. To understand a particular set of scores, we must consider factors: (a) the mean, (b) the median, and (c) the mode. Each measure of central tendency is used as an indication of how a group scored on a measure. No information related to the distribution of scores is provided with the mean, median, or mode. In other words, when looking at a measure of central tendency, we will not know the extent to which individuals scored above or below the mean. We will only know a general idea of how the group scored, and with the raw data we may get an indication of the shape of the distribution as demonstrated in Figure 3.1. Put more succinctly, measures of central tendency describe a group. To explain each component of central tendency, we use a data set of 10 scores, which range from 33 to 64, on the CriSS (Table 3.3), and we have placed the scores in ascending order.

TABLE 3.3 CriSS Scores (*n* = 10)

33	43	44	46	48	49	50	50	56	64
				Middle scores		Mode			
				(48.5 = median)					

Note: CriSS = Crisis Stabilization Scale.

The Mean

Stated simply, the *mean* is an average score for a group. The mean is the most common measure of central tendency and is an integral component to research, measurement, and evaluation in the counseling profession. Most studies and statistics rely on this measure.

The mean $(\bar{x})$ is the sum (Σ) of all raw scores (x) divided by the total number of scores (n):

$$\bar{x} = \frac{\Sigma x}{n}$$

Consider the 10 scores on the CriSS as shown in Table 3.3. The sum of all of the scores is 483. Thus,

$$\bar{x} = \frac{\Sigma x}{n} = \frac{483}{10} = 48.30$$

Now take a look at the scores again, but this time in a histogram as seen in Figure 3.2. Is the mean an accurate depiction of how the group scored?

Based on the histogram and with only 10 scores, it can be hard to tell. The mean score of 48.3 is pretty close to the center of the distribution, and the most common score was 50, which lends some credibility to the mean. Keep in mind that the mean only represents an average of the group. It is not necessarily the reflection of any obtained score. Despite the mean being one of the most useful scores in statistics, when the sample size is small, as is the case here, it may not be an accurate reflection of a group. The mean may be highly influenced by extreme scores. Extreme scores are often termed *outliers*, as they represent individuals whose scores are not consistent with the rest of the group. Although extreme caution should be used when analyzing data with outliers or removing outliers, notice what happens to the distribution when the score of 64 is removed and replaced with 20. Now the mean is 43.9, and the distribution is clearly negatively skewed (see Figure 3.3). The problem with the mean is that when the sample size is small and outliers (i.e., extreme scores) are present, the mean may not be an accurate portrayal of the scores. Outliers influence the means, especially when sample sizes are small.

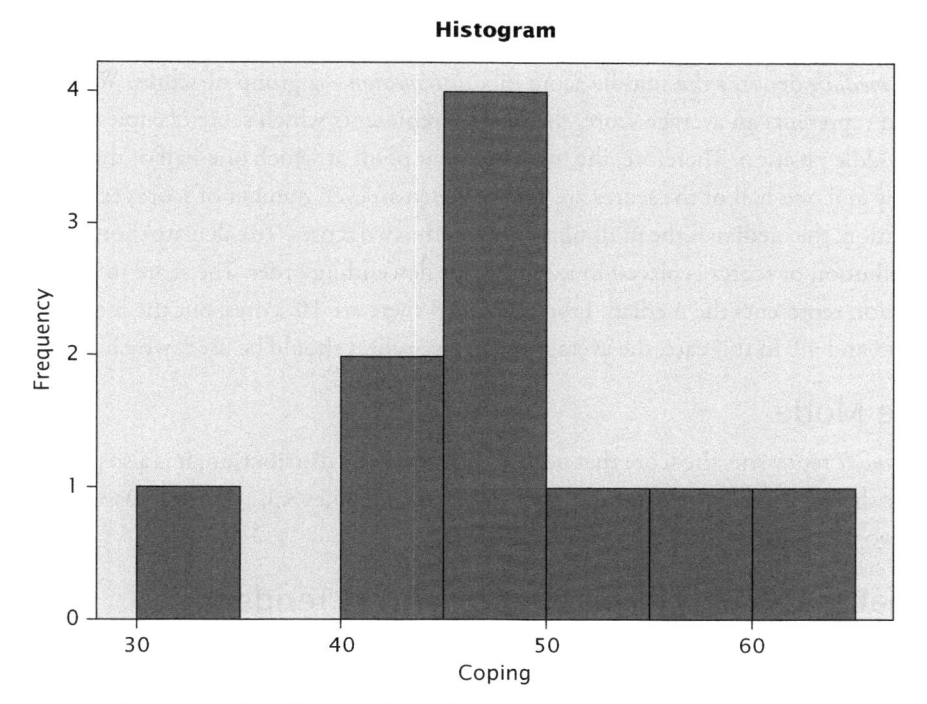

FIGURE 3.2 Histogram of CriSS scores ($n = 10$).

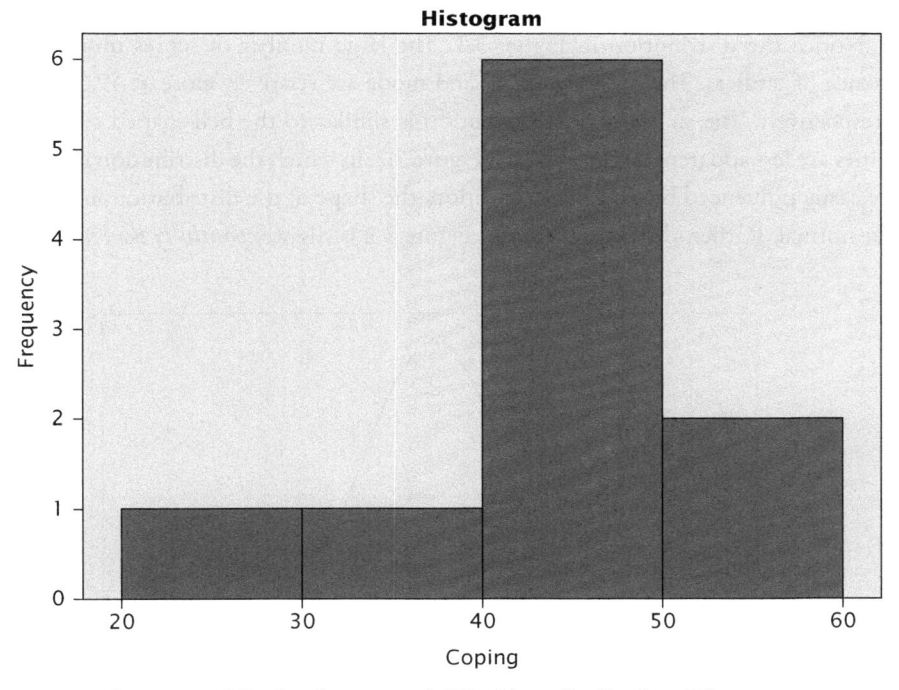

FIGURE 3.3 Histogram of Coping Scores on CriSS with an Outlier ($n = 10$).

The Median

The *median* denotes the middle score in a *distribution*—a group of scores. Whereas the mean represents an average score, the median represents which score occupies the center or middle position. Therefore, the median is that point at which one-half of the scores are below and one-half of the scores are above. When an even number of scores exist in a distribution, the median is the midpoint between the two scores. To calculate the median, the distribution of scores is placed in ascending or descending order. The score in the middle position represents the median. From Table 3.3 there are 10 scores, but the middle scores are 48 and 49. In this case, the average of the two scores should be used, which is 48.5.

The Mode

The *mode* represents the score that occurs most often in a distribution. It is also possible for more than one mode to exist. Among the 10 scores in Tables 3.3, a score of 50 was obtained by two participants. Therefore, the mode is 50.

What Is the Best Measure of Central Tendency?

The measure of central tendency that would be the most accurate for a distribution depends on many factors: (a) the number of scores in the distribution, known as *sample size;* (b) the presence of outliers; and (c) the shape of the distribution. As shown in Figure 3.4, when the mean, median, and mode are equal, the distribution of scores is said to be normal and the distribution will resemble a bell-shaped curve.

Notice the distribution in Figure 3.1. The large number of scores minimizes the influence of outliers. The mean, median, and mode are relatively close at 49.62, 46, and 45, respectively. The shape of the distribution is similar to the bell-shaped curve. These qualities are less apparent by the scores in Figure 3.2, in which the distribution is small and more easily influenced by outliers. In addition, the shape of the distribution in Figure 3.2 is not normal. Rather, the distribution in Figure 3.2 is slightly *positively skewed*, in which

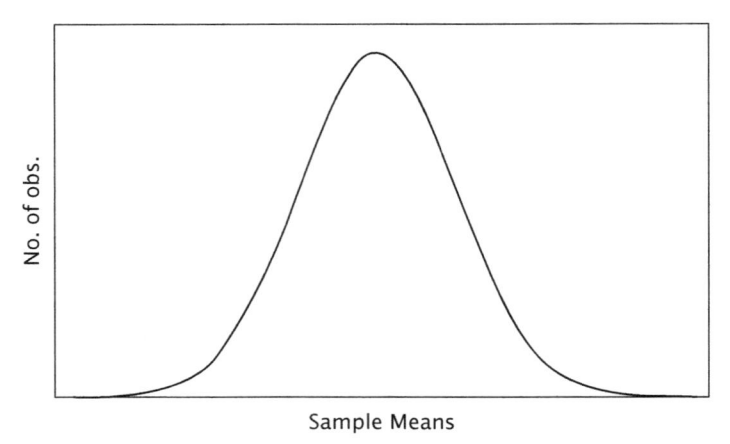

FIGURE 3.4 Normal Distribution.

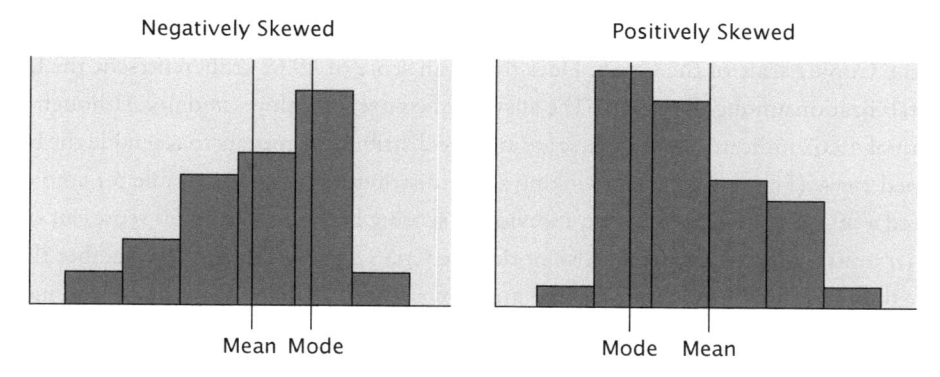

FIGURE 3.5 Negatively and Positively Skewed Distributions.

the mode is less than the mean. In a *negatively skewed distribution* (see Figure 3.3), the mode would be greater than the mean. Figure 3.5 presents a side-by-side comparison of skewed distributions. So when a distribution is normal, the mean, median, and mode are all accurate estimates, with the mean being the more preferable term because of its usefulness in statistics. However, when distributions are small, often the median or the mode represent the better measure of a distribution. In summary, the mean is an indicator of the average score; the median is the position of the center score; and the mode is the most common score.

Measures of Variability

As mentioned earlier, measures of central tendency allow counselors to evaluate the performance of an individual when compared to a group. Throughout this text, we utilize the case studies in Chapter 2 to discuss the application of various assessments. For example, using the case study of Eva Marie and reviewing her score on the Kaufman Brief Intelligence Test-2 (KBIT-2) in Chapter 9, Eva Marie obtained an IQ composite score of 119, which classifies her in the above-average range of intellectual functioning and ranks her at the 90th percentile when compared with others in the same age group. Thus, we can compare Eva Marie's score of 119 to the mean or average intelligence score of 100 and identify Eva Marie with above-average intellectual functioning. Measures of central tendency can also be used to represent the performance of a group. For example, Figure 3.1 shows the normal distribution for 400 adolescents admitted in to an inpatient psychiatric hospital on the Coping scale for the CriSS. This group has a mean of 49.62. On the CriSS, a score of 50 is considered average. Therefore, this group of adolescents appear to be near where we would expect the average adolescent to be with respect to stabilization compared to the general adolescent admitted to an inpatient acute care psychiatric program. However, when a single score is used to represent the performance of a group or population, more information is needed. An understanding of whether or not the mean is a good indicator of the group performance is necessary.

Referring back to Table 3.1, notice that 400 individuals scored between 23 and 71 on the Coping scale of the CriSS. Does the mean score of 49.62 truly represent the level of stabilization among the group? The answer, of course, is both yes and no. Although the mean of 49.62 indicates an average score and the distribution appears to resemble the bell-shaped curve (Figure 3.1), when looking at the distribution of scores (Table 3.1), no one scored a 49.62. As a matter of fact, individuals scoring between 49 and 50 represent only 5% ($n = 20$) of the distribution. Also notice the CriSS data in Table 3.3 (remember there were only 10 scores in this sample). The mean ($\bar{x} = 48.3$), median ($Md = 48.5$), and mode ($Mo = 50$) are close, which we would expect for a distribution that is approximately normal. So, when means are used to signify the performance of a group, additional information is needed to identify if the mean is truly representative of group performance. This is the rationale for measures of variability—to provide information on how much error is included in the mean or the degree of consistency (i.e., how closely participants scored to the mean) for the group. Next three measures of variability are described to address the amount of error in a distribution when using the mean to describe the performance of a group.

The Range

The range is simply a value indicating the span of scores and may be expressed as the highest value minus the lowest value:

$$(\text{highest value} - \text{lowest value})$$

In Table 3.1 of the CriSS scores, the highest value is 71 and the lowest value is 23, so the range is as follows:

$$(71 - 23) = 48$$

The purpose of the range is to provide an indication of the span of values. However, the range does not offer any indication of the relationship of scores to the mean.

The Standard Deviation and Variance

The *standard deviation* (SD) is one of the more useful terms in statistics. Although the mean indicates the average score for a distribution, the SD indicates *the average distance from the mean*. As discussed earlier, whenever a single score is used to represent an entire group, error will be present, because not everyone scores at the mean. Just how close the scores are to the mean is indicated by the SD.

The *variance* is also a measure of dispersion and is directly related to the SD. The variance is the *squared average distance from the mean*. The variance has many important properties relevant to counseling research, and in order to compute the SD, the variance is computed first. Computation of the variance and SD is discussed following a discussion of population versus sample statistics.

Estimating the Population

At times, a measure of a population is easy to determine. College entrance exams, such as the SAT and ACT, serve as an example of estimating the population. Most universities require students to take the SAT or ACT before entering college. As a result, ETS, the company that created the SAT, and ACT, Inc., collect scores for every person who takes these tests. Thus, they have a population. Each individual who takes the SAT or ACT has the scores documented by the respective company. So it is easy for ETS or ACT to make estimates on the population. We might even say that they can make an unbiased estimation, as each individual score from the respective test can be accounted for with minimal error. This of course does not include error that could occur from nonuniform testing conditions and other extraneous factors.

More often, however, counselors attempt to make generalizations about a population based upon a sample. So how do researchers make sure that the results garnered from a sample can be generalized to a population? Researchers demonstrate generalizability in two ways: (a) by describing the sample with respect to characteristics (e.g. age, ethnicity, sex) so that evidence to the appropriate population can be demonstrated and (b) by using mathematical procedures that take into account the size of the sample in order to generalize to a population. However, if mathematical adjustments are being made, how do we know that they are accurate? To discuss the nature of the mathematical formulae and proofs is beyond the scope of this book (thank goodness); we can just be glad that statisticians such as Pearson, Gosset, and Fisher created such formulae and provided the evidence so that we can apply this knowledge to the field. We next present the formulae for computing the variance and SD for both a population and a sample.

The Formula for the Variance

Recall that the variance, the squared average distance from the mean, has many important properties relevant to counseling research, and to compute the SD, the variance is computed first. The formula for the variance is represented as the sum of the squared deviation scores divided by the sample size. Let's break down this formula.

The *sum* is represented by Σ and therefore refers to the process of adding a set of values.

A *deviation score* is a raw score minus the mean. We represent the deviation score as $(x - \bar{x})$, where x is a raw score such as the scores in Table 3.4 and $\bar{x}$ is the mean, 48.3.

Sample size will vary, based on whether we are using the formula for a population or a sample. For a population, the sample size is noted as n and is the total number of participants, 10. Therefore, we say $n = 10$. For a sample, the sample size is noted as $n - 1$ and is the total number of participants minus 1 (so 9). Therefore, we say $n - 1 = 9$.

Using statistical notation for this information, the formula for the variance when using a population is

$$s^2 = \frac{\Sigma(x - \bar{x})^2}{n}$$

TABLE 3.4 CRISS Scores ($n = 10$)

x	$(x - \bar{x})$	$(x - \bar{x})^2$
33	−15.3	234.09
43	−5.3	28.09
44	−4.3	18.49
46	−2.3	5.29
48	−0.3	0.09
49	0.7	0.49
50	1.7	2.89
50	1.7	2.89
56	7.7	59.29
64	15.7	246.49
$\bar{x} = 48.3$	$\Sigma(x - \bar{x}) = 0$	$\Sigma(x - \bar{x})^2 = 598.1$

Note: CriSS = Crisis Stabilization Scale.

and for a sample is

$$s^2 = \frac{\Sigma(x - \bar{x})^2}{n - 1}$$

Computing the Variance

Using the data from Table 3.3, we next compute the variance using the population formula and the sample formula. Regardless of whether computing for a population or a sample, the numerator, $\Sigma(x - \bar{x})^2$, is computed the same. First, compute a deviation from each raw score by subtracting the mean from each raw score as shown in the second column of Table 3.4.

Notice that the deviation score can be positive or negative. Also notice that when we sum the deviation scores, we always end up with zero. This is an important point. If our eventual goal is to compute the SD, the average distance from the mean, an average cannot be computed when zero is divided by any value. So, to eventually compute the SD, we need to get rid of the zero by eliminating the negative numbers. We can do this by squaring each deviation score as shown in the third column of Table 3.4. By squaring each deviation score and summing the scores, we obtain the *sum of the squared deviations* (598.1). The next step is to compute the variance of a population and sample and obtain an average of sorts using the sum of the squared deviations. To compute the variance, simply divide by the number of cases (n) for a population or the sample size minus 1 ($n - 1$) for a sample.

Population

$$s^2 = \frac{\Sigma(x - \bar{x})^2}{n} = \frac{598.1}{10} = 59.81$$

Sample

$$s^2 = \frac{\Sigma(x-\bar{x})^2}{n-1} = \frac{598.1}{10-1} = 66.46$$

Computing the Standard Deviation

Keep in mind an average is simply a sum of scores divided by the number of scores. In the case of the variance, the deviation scores are squared, which is why the variance is the squared average of distance from the mean. To find the SD—the average distance from the mean—simply take the square root of the variance.

Population

$$s = \sqrt{\frac{\Sigma(x-\bar{x})^2}{n}} = \sqrt{\frac{598.1}{10}} = \sqrt{59.81} = 7.73$$

Sample

$$s = \sqrt{\frac{\Sigma(x-\bar{x})^2}{n-1}} = \sqrt{\frac{598.1}{10-1}} = \sqrt{66.46} = 8.15$$

So for the sample of 10 participants who completed the CriSS, the average score was 48.3, but the average amount of variation from the mean was 8.15. With a range of 31, a SD of 8.15 may seem like a large amount of variation from the mean. One reason this occurs is the small sample size. If the mean is an indication of how a group scored, the SD expresses the degree to which that mean is representative of the group. In other words, are the scores in the group consistent with the mean? With an average difference of 8.15 from the mean, the scores may not be that consistent.

In assessment, however, tests are often standardized to provide for easy interpretation of individual scores. For example, the CriSS was designed using standard scores, which we talk about later. What is important here is that an individual's score can be compared to a mean of 50 and a SD of 10. When evaluating a test, we can expect the publisher to provide information on the mean and SD, and when we receive score reports, a comparison to the mean and the corresponding percentile is often provided in a table. With this in mind, let's focus on how scores for an individual or group are interpreted and used.

The Normal Curve

The normal curve is a theoretical concept for understanding the nature of scores based on probability theory. Best and Kahn (2006) indicated that the normal curve does not actually exist, but measures of populations tend to demonstrate this distribution. The normal

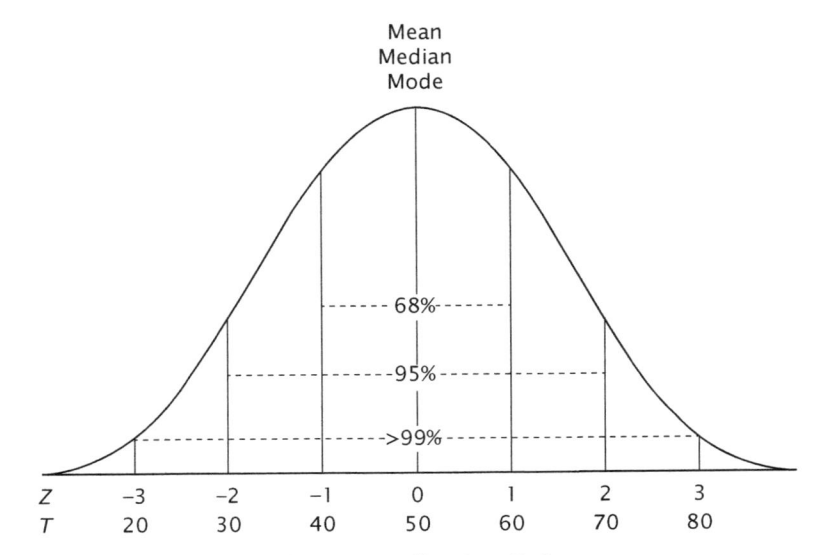

FIGURE 3.6 The Normal Curve and Corresponding Area Estimates.

curve (Figure 3.6) is symmetrical with 50% of the scores above and below the mean. The mean, median, and mode all have the same value, and the scores cluster around the center.

Although data are not usually perfectly described by the normal distribution, an independent measure taken repeatedly will eventually resemble a normal distribution. Figure 3.1 appears to demonstrate this concept, as enough data ($n = 400$) were collected to demonstrate a more normalized distribution. On the other hand, Figure 3.2, with a small sample size of 10, is less like a normal distribution. Why? The sample size is insufficient to be an accurate estimate of the population.

Confidence Intervals

One characteristic of the normal curve is that counselors can look at assessment scores and determine where an individual falls with respect to a normally distributed population. In a normally distributed population, as illustrated in Figure 3.6, 50% of the distribution lies before and after the mean. Between −1 and +1 SD units is 68% of the distribution. Between −2 and +2 SD units is 95% of the distribution. Between −3 and +3 SD units is 99% of the distribution. This is known as the *68-95-99 rule*. For the CriSS, the scales are standardized to have a mean of 50 and a standard deviation of 10. So 68% of the distribution would fall between −1 and +1 SD units (between 40 and 60); 95% of the distribution would fall between −2 and +2 SD units (between 30 and 70); 99% of the distribution would fall between −3 and +3 SD units (between 20 and 80).

We can establish *confidence intervals* (CI), estimates of where we expect scores to fall based on the mean and standard deviation. A CI expressed the range of scores that is likely to be obtained using the following formula:

$$CI = M \pm SD$$

To express a range of scores with within one standard deviation (68% confidence), we would compute as follows:

$$CI = 50 \pm 1(10)$$

$$[40, 60] = 50 \pm 10$$

To express a range of scores with within 2 SD (95% confidence), we would compute as follows:

$$CI = 50 \pm 2(10)$$

$$[30, 70] = 50 \pm 20$$

To express a range of scores with within 3 SD (99% confidence), we would compute as follows:

$$CI = 50 \pm 3(10)$$

$$[20, 80] = 50 \pm 30$$

The normal curve provides information in interpreting scores for an individual or group. To do this, we use the z table in Appendix A and the 68-95-99 rule.

Assume we wish to compare an individual's score on the CriSS to the normed population (M = 50, SD = 10). Amy, a 16-year-old female, was admitted to a crisis residence (e.g., inpatient, adolescent unit) and has been working hard in counseling. Nearing the end of her hospitalization, the counselor completed the CriSS and records a score of 64 on the Coping scale. This score would be 1.4 SD above the mean. We can use a z table in Appendix A to estimate the percentile of the group. The z table provides the amount of area (or the percentage of the distribution) that lies to the left of a score expressed in SD units, known as a *z score*. In other words, the z table provides the corresponding percentile (the percentage of participants who scored at or below a given score) for a given z score. Using the previous example, with a mean of 50 and a standard deviation of 10, Amy's score (64) is approximately 1.4 SD units above the mean or a z score of 1.4 (we discuss how a z score is computed later in the chapter, but for now we only focus on understanding Appendix A).

1. Using Appendix A, follow the left column down until you see 1.4. The row on top expresses the z score to the nearest hundredth. So you will actually use 1.4 on the left column and .00 to the top row to find the corresponding percentile for 1.40.
2. The corresponding value under 1.40 is .9192, which can be converted to a percentile, 91.92% or about the 92nd percentile.
3. In this case, a score of 64 is approximately in the 92nd percentile (.9192) of a normed population.

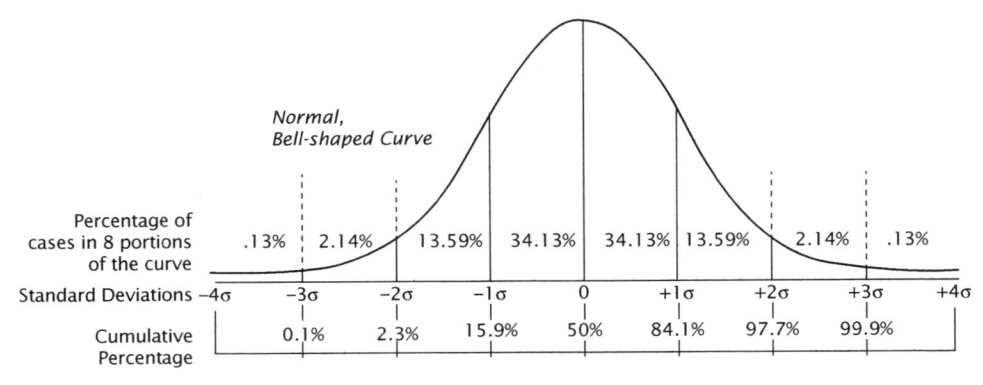

FIGURE 3.7 Estimates of Area Underneath the Normal Curve.

Percentage of cases in 8 portions of the curve: .13% | 2.14% | 13.59% | 34.13% | 34.13% | 13.59% | 2.14% | .13%

Standard Deviations: −4σ, −3σ, −2σ, −1σ, 0, +1σ, +2σ, +3σ, +4σ

Cumulative Percentage: 0.1%, 2.3%, 15.9%, 50%, 84.1%, 97.7%, 99.9%

Another way to estimate is to use the 68-95-99 rule (see Figure 3.7).

Remember, the mean of the CriSS is 50 and the SD is 10. Hence, 1 SD above the mean is 60; 1 SD below the mean is 40. We know that 50% of the distribution is before or after the mean and that 68% of the distribution is between −1 and +1 SD units. Therefore, the distance between the mean and +1 SD units (a score of 60) is 34% (one-half of 68%) plus 50% (the other half of the distribution). Therefore, the score of 64 must be above the 84th percentile (50% + 34%). Between −2 and +2 SD units is 47.5% of the distribution before and after the mean (between 30 and 70). We can add 47.5% to 50% and find that a score of 64 must be below the 98th percentile (a score of 70). Thus the value is about halfway between the 84th and the 98th percentile (1.4 SD units—around the 92nd percentile).

In summary, the normal curve can be used to determine where scores fall with respect to probability and percentiles by examining (a) the percentage of total space included between the mean and a given standard deviation, (b) the percentage of cases or n values that fall between a given mean and standard deviation, (c) the probability that an event will occur between the mean and a given standard deviation, (d) the percentile rank of scores in a normal distribution, and (e) the extent to which a distribution of scores is normalized. "The normal curve has a smooth, altogether handsome countenance—a thing of beauty" (Glass & Hopkins, 1996, p. 83).

Standard Scores

Expressing scores in SD units, as opposed to raw scores, is quite useful. When scores are expressed in SD units, we refer to them as *standard scores*. With such information, we can compare scores across different instruments that measure the same construct and provide an interpretation of raw scores. For example, an individual who scores a 21 on the ACT is approximately in the 50th percentile. Because the SAT also measures aptitude, a comparable score would be about 1550, also in the 50th percentile. Knowing the

FUNDAMENTALS OF ASSESSMENT | 71

mean and SD of each exam allows us to make comparisons when the same construct is measured. Similarly, we can take a single score and make a comparison to the normed distribution.

Z Scores

Given that raw scores may not have much meaning, z scores can be used to make comparisons of an individual or group score to a distribution by simply converting the raw score to a score expressed in SD units. A basic formula is used to convert a raw score to a z score:

$$z = \frac{x - \bar{x}}{\sigma},$$

where x is raw score;
$\bar{x}$ is the mean;
σ is the standard deviation.

From the data presented in Table 3.3, an individual we referred to earlier as Amy scored 64 on the Coping scale of the CriSS. We can convert the individual score of 64 in order to determine the percentile of the individual compared to the normative sample (M = 50, SD = 10).

$$z = \frac{x - \bar{x}}{\sigma} = \frac{64 - 50}{10} = 1.4$$

Thus, an individual scoring a 64 on the Coping scale of CriSS is 1.4 SD above the mean—the 92nd percentile (by using Appendix A). We could determine that this individual is in the top 8% in coping when compared to adolescents who are hospitalized for crisis situations. Next we do another example in which the client is below the mean, so we can see how the table works a little differently.

Derek is a 14-year-old male who was hospitalized due to severe anger outbursts, threatening his parents, running away, and oppositional behavior at school. He has struggled during his hospitalization with establishing coping behaviors. When his counselor completes the CriSS after the fifth day of hospitalization, Derek has a score of 33 on the Coping scale of the CriSS. To convert the individual score of 33 to determine the percentile of the individual compared to the normative sample (M = 50, SD = 10), we do the following:

$$z = \frac{x - \bar{x}}{\sigma} = \frac{33 - 50}{10} = -1.7$$

Thus, an individual scoring a 33 on the Coping scale of CriSS is -1.7 SD below the mean. Because only positive values are identified on the z table in Appendix A, we look at 1.7 and subtract that percentile from 1. A value of 1.70 is .9554. Since Derek's z score is -1.7, we subtract .9554 from 1.

$$1-.9554=.0446 \text{ or about the } 4.5^{th} \text{ percentile.}$$

We could determine that Derek is in the bottom 5% in coping when compared to adolescents who are hospitalized for crisis situations.

T Scores

The T score is another version of a standard score that is (a) widely used for interpreting scores on instruments, (b) converted directly from z scores, and (c) avoids the use of decimals and negative numbers. T scores have a mean of 50 and a SD of 10. So, for every unit of increase or decrease in a z score, a T score is increased or decreased by 10. A T score of 60 is 1 SD above the mean, while a T score of 30 is 2 SD below the mean. The relationship of z scores and T scores is shown in Figure 3.6. The T score is computed as follows:

$$T = 50 + 10Z$$

and rounded to the nearest whole number.

Other Types of Standard Scores

Although T scores and z scores tend to be commonly used, many instrument developers use their own methods of standard scores, such as the SAT, which uses a mean of 500 and a SD of 100, or intelligence tests with a mean of 100 and a SD of 15 (e.g., KBIT-2) For example, in the case study of Chapter 2 and information in Chapter 9, Eva Marie has a IQ composite score of 119 on the KBIT-2. A z score can easily be computed from the standard score of the KBIT-2:

$$z = \frac{x-\bar{x}}{\sigma} = \frac{119-100}{15} = 1.27$$

Both the IQ Composite score of 119 and the z score of 1.27 indicate that Eva Marie is above the mean with respect to intelligence—the 90th percentile (the top 10%) using Appendix A.

We could do the same with a score on the SAT. A student who scores 420 on the verbal section of the SAT is below the mean of 500 and therefore would have a z score in the negative range:

$$Z = \frac{x-\bar{x}}{\sigma} = \frac{420-500}{100} = -.80.$$

Using Appendix A, such as score would place the student in the 21st percentile

$$(1 - .7881 = .2119).$$

Understanding Correlation Coefficients

One of the more useful statistics in social science research is the correlation coefficient. In counseling research, it is helpful to know the relationship between variables, such as the relationship between aptitude and achievement, self-esteem and behavioral disruptions, and so forth. Correlations are also used to compare scores on instruments. For example, a strong relationship would be expected between SAT and ACT scores, because both measure aptitude. A correlation coefficient is the expression of a linear relationship between two (and only two) paired variables or data sets (Cohen et al., 2013). A correlation coefficient is most commonly expressed as r and may range from −1.00 to +1.00. Correlation coefficients are interpreted by examining two facets: (a) direction and (b) magnitude. Direction refers to the sign of the correlation, either positive (+) or negative (−). In a positive correlation, as the values in one variable increases, so do the variables in the other variable. For example, there is a positive correlation between the number of years using drugs and the severity of drug abuse. In other words, the longer someone has used drugs, the more severe the addiction is likely to be. In a negative correlation, as the values in one variable increases, the values in the other variable decreases. Such an example may be evident with exercise and depression. The more one engages in physical exercise, the fewer depressive symptoms may be evident. An illustration of positive and negative correlations is in Figure 3.8.

So while the sign of the correlation reflects direction, the number reflects magnitude. In Figure 3.8, both correlations are *perfect correlations*. A perfect correlation has a value of +1.00 or −1.00. The magnitudes are the same. In a perfect positive correlation, for every unit of *increase* in one variable, there is an equal unit of *increase* in the other variable. In a perfect negative correlation, for every unit of *increase* in one variable, there is an equal unit of *decrease* in the other variable. In counseling research, there is no perfect correlation. More likely, we will see correlations that reflect various relationships. Best and Kahn (2006) recommended the guidelines shown in Table 3.5 in interpreting correlation coefficients.

Note that the categories in Table 3.5 apply regardless of direction, as there is no difference between −.30 and +.30 in terms of magnitude. Both signify relationships as *low*.

There are two common types of correlation coefficients, although others exist as well. The most common type is the *Pearson product moment correlation coefficient*, often referred to as a *Pearson r* or just r, which indicates the relationship between two variables or data sets that contain scores at the interval or ratio level of measurement. A second common type of correlation coefficient is an adaptation of the Pearson r, known as the *Spearman rho correlation coefficient*, which computes a correlation coefficient from ordinal data.

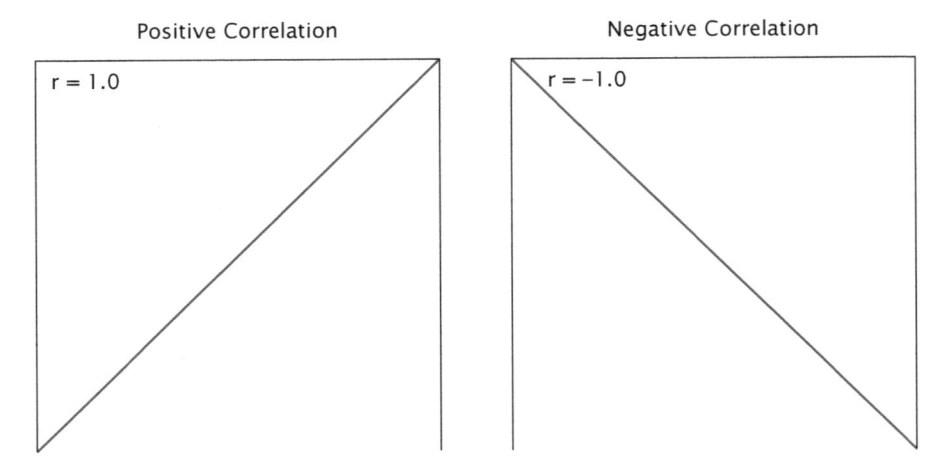

FIGURE 3.8 **Perfect Positive and Negative Correlations.**

Calculating a Pearson *r*

The most common formula for computing the Pearson *r* relies on concepts already learned for computing the variance and SD.

$$r = \frac{\Sigma xy}{\sqrt{(\Sigma x^2)(\Sigma y^2)}},$$

where

$\Sigma x^2 = \sum (X - \overline{X})^2$, the squared sum of the deviation scores for variable *x*

$\Sigma y^2 = \sum (Y - \overline{Y})^2$, the squared sum of the deviation scores for variable *y*

$\Sigma xy = \sum (X - \overline{X})(Y - \overline{Y})$, the sum of the *covariance* scores—each deviation score for *x* is multiplied by the corresponding deviation score for *y* and then summed.

Next we provide a heuristic example of data for *x* and *y* in which the computation of a Pearson *r* is illustrated. Keep in mind that variables *x* and *y* could stand for any pair of variables being measured. In this case, we use data collected on a study for exercise and depression by Balkin, Tietjen-Smith, Shen, and Caldwell (2007). Fourteen college females participated in a control group (see Table 3.6). The participants were administered the BDI-II on two occasions at six weeks apart. Because this group did not have any intervention, the expectation

TABLE 3.5 Interpretation of Correlation Coefficients

.00 to .20	Negligible
.20 to .40	Low
.40 to .60	Moderate
.60 to .80	Substantial
.80 to 1.00	High to very high

TABLE 3.6 Pretest and Posttest Scores on the BDI-II

	Pretest (x)	Posttest (y)	x	y	x^2	y^2	xy
	15	1	5.50	−6.57	30.25	43.16	−36.14
	10	6	0.50	−1.57	0.25	2.46	−0.79
	11	12	1.50	4.43	2.25	19.62	6.65
	9	11	−0.50	3.43	0.25	11.76	−1.72
	3	2	−6.50	−5.57	42.25	31.02	36.21
	0	0	−9.50	−7.57	90.25	57.30	71.92
	3	4	−6.50	−3.57	42.25	12.74	23.21
	14	12	4.50	4.43	20.25	19.62	19.94
	18	15	8.50	7.43	72.25	55.20	63.16
	5	5	−4.50	−2.57	20.25	6.60	11.57
	25	21	15.50	13.43	240.25	180.36	208.17
	8	9	−1.50	1.43	2.25	2.04	−2.15
	9	2	−0.50	−5.57	0.25	31.02	2.79
	3	6	−6.50	−1.57	42.25	2.46	10.21
Mean	9.50	7.57					
Sum					605.50	475.43	413.00

Note: BDI-II = Beck Depression Inventory-II.
Source: Balkin et al. (2007).

would be that there would be minimal change in the scores from one administration to the next. Thus, a high correlation between the two administrations was anticipated.

$$r = \frac{\Sigma xy}{\sqrt{(\Sigma x^2)(\Sigma y^2)}}$$

$$r = \frac{413}{\sqrt{(605.50)(475.43)}} = .77$$

Using Table 3.5, a correlation coefficient of .77 is indeed substantial because of the similarities in the scoring patterns.

What Types of Scores Are Reported?

Throughout the various chapters in this text, various assessment results are reported, often using standard scores. Not all tests use standard scores although, as shown in this chapter, a standard score may be obtained if the mean and SD of the norm group is used. Such information is consistently reported in test manuals for this reason. An example is the BDI-II, which simply uses a raw score to identify whether a client is mild, moderate, or severe in depressive symptoms. Moreover, by using the manual for the BDI-II, counselors can draw comparisons to clinical and nonclinical subgroups. In other words, when the counselor administers the BDI-II, standard scores may be derived by comparing the client to a clinical population, such as other clients seeking outpatient counseling, or a nonclinical population, such as undergraduate college students. A client with moderate depression, for example, may be slightly higher than the mean for the clinical population, over 1 SD above the mean when compared to the nonclinical norm group. Overall, having knowledge of standard scores and their relationship to percentiles is important to identifying the degree to which a person may be viewed with issues or concerns pertinent to counseling.

4

Current Standards for Validity

Objectives
1. Understand the historical context of validity.
2. Understand the current standards for validity.
3. Differentiate the current standards of validity with the triadic model of validity.
4. Understand the methods for demonstrating evidence of validity.
5. Identify whether test developers sufficiently address validity issues in their assessments.

Defining Validity: A Brief History

In assessment, *validity* refers to the development, administration, scoring, interpretation, and utilization of an instrument. An instrument is valid if the instrument is an actual measure of a given construct. "Validity refers to the degree to which evidence and theory support the interpretations of test scores entailed by proposed uses of tests... [and is] the most fundamental consideration in developing and evaluating tests" (American Educational Research Association [AERA], American Psychological Association (APA), & National Council of Measurement in Education [NCME], 2014, p. 11).

Validity is an evolving process. The manner in which validity was defined in the early 20th century is quite different from the current definition and criteria. Initially, validity was viewed as a fixed, stable attribute of a measure. Guilford (1946) indicated "a test is valid for anything with which it correlates" (p. 429). Thus, validity was evaluated via a correlation coefficient, which became known as a *validity coefficient*. The effect was to rely on statistics to determine evidence of validity. Issues of item content were not even considered (Reynolds & Kamphaus, 2003). Research continued to develop in this area with the definition of validity being extended to *criterion evidence* (Gulliksen, 1950), which is a relationship to a construct or phenomenon, and convergent and *discriminant* evidence (Campbell & Fiske, 1959), the extent to which items on an instrument for different scales are strongly intercorrelated (i.e., convergent evidence) or show weaker relationships (i.e., discriminant evidence). For example, an individual who endorses the item "I feel sad all of the time" on the Beck Depression Inventory-II (BDI-II) may also endorse other similar items related to depression (convergent evidence), which all could relate to depressive disorder (criterion evidence). On another note, some instruments contain more than one scale. For example, the Substance Abuse Subtle Scale Inventory-4 has scales that focus on more objective criteria related to chemical dependency, such as the amount of alcohol or drugs consumed, but it also has other scales that measure more subtle symptoms, such as feelings of guilt after using. An item measuring guilt may not correlate with objective items but could correlate with items related to feelings that occur as a result of drug or alcohol use. Both convergent and discriminant evidence would show that feelings of guilt correlate with subtle symptoms of chemical dependency (i.e., convergent evidence) and correlate less with objective symptoms of chemical dependency (i.e., discriminant evidence).

Cronbach and Meehl (1955) identified four types of validity in their seminal article, "Construct Validity in Psychological Tests": (a) predictive validity, (b) concurrent validity, (c) content validity, and (d) construct validity. The concept of criterion validity was separated into two aspects: (a) *predictive validity*, which is attained when an instrument is administered and scores are correlated to some criterion that is obtained at a later time, and (b) *concurrent validity*, which is attained when an instrument is administered while simultaneously obtaining another score on a criterion. For example, when the Strong Interest Inventory is used to guide a client to a career path, predictive evidence is demonstrated; that the Strong Interest Inventory may correlate with the interest inventory on O*NET demonstrates concurrent evidence. *Content validity* referred to the acceptance that the items of an instrument measure the intended construct. The process of evaluating content validity was quite ambiguous. According to Cronbach and Meehl (1955), "Content validity is ordinarily to be established deductively, by defining a universe of items and sampling systematically within this universe to establish the test" (p. 282). Cronbach and Meehl further elaborated that content validity was demonstrated through "*acceptance* of the ... content" (p. 282). Thus, content evidence may be demonstrated through a review of previous published research on a phenomenon of interest, expert review, or documentation of preestablished acceptance or standards. Cronbach and Meehl suggested *construct validation* be investigated when a phenomenon of interest lacked an operational definition. "Construct validity must be investigated whenever no criterion or universe of content is accepted as entirely adequate to define the quality to be measured" (p. 282). Construct validity could be established through the investigation of (a) group differences; (b) correlational procedures such as factor analysis; (c) evaluations of internal structure, such as reliability and the consistency of responses from a homogeneous sample; (d) evaluations because of changes in conditions, such as the insertion or removal of a test condition; and (e) observations of an individual performance or process of completing an instrument.

In 1966, APA et al. published the *Standards for Educational and Psychological Tests and Manuals*. Although this was not the first time these organizations had published standards for testing and measurement, it was the first joint publication for the three groups. The main change from Cronbach and Meehl's (1955) conceptualization of validity was use of the term *criterion-related validity*, which addressed specific types of predictive and concurrent evidence related to the measure (Hubley & Zumbo, 2001). The 1966 *Standards* yielded the trinity view (Goodwin & Leech, 2003; Hubley & Zumbo, 2001) of validity. Although the 1966 *Standards* related three distinct types of validity, the 1985 *Standards* identified test validity as a single concept and that content, criterion, and construct validity were merely different types of evidence for validity (AERA et al., 1985; Goodwin & Leech, 2003). Thus, a trend evolved to describe validity as a single conceptual element of evaluating instruments, in which different types of evidence may be examined to determine the extent to which an instrument meets standards of validity.

A Present View of Validity

In the 1999 *Standards for Educational and Psychological Testing* (AERA et al., 1999), validity was described as the incorporation of evidence and theory required to support the proposed interpretation and use of test scores. Validity, therefore, included not only the gathering of data to support the interpretation of scores but also how scores were used. This idea was continued in the 2014 *Standards*. For example, the use of an aptitude test to assess academic achievement and to be used as an exit exam for high school students may be contrary to the explicit definition of validity.

> The process of validation involves accumulating relevant evidence to provide a sound scientific basis for the proposed score interpretations. . . . .When test scores are used or interpreted in more than one way (e.g., both to describe a test taker's current level of the attribute being measured and to make a prediction about a future outcome), each intended interpretation must be validated. (AERA et al., 2014, p. 11)

When evaluating an instrument for use with a client, counselors should focus on the statements related to validity. Essentially, counselors should ask, "Is this the appropriate instrument for this client? Will the interpretation of test scores be used in a manner to which the instrument was designed and interpreted in a manner that is appropriate to the client?" The responsibility to evaluate validity is on both the counselor and the test developer. The developer is responsible for furnishing the evidence related to test interpretation and use; the counselor is responsible for evaluating such evidence and using the instrument, scores, and interpretation in an ethical manner (ACA, 2005; AERA et al., 2014). The 2014 *Standards for Educational and Psychological Testing* emphasized five types of evidences for test validity.

Evidence Based on Test Content

The contents of an instrument (i.e., test items) should represent the intended domain or construct being measured. "Test content refers to themes, wording, and format of the items, tasks, or questions on a test," as well as the guidelines for procedures regarding administration and scoring (AERA et al., 2014, p. 14). Evidence based on test content replaced the term *content validity* but also expanded the definition. Rather than merely focusing on what the instrument contains, evidence based on test content also incorporated procedures related to test use and interpretation. Counselors should be able to identify the extent to which scores and interpretations of an instrument are generated from the items administered and the tasks or processes placed upon the examinee. For example, administering a Wechsler Intelligence Scale for Children-V to a child with deafness may not be valid, as the processes required by the examinee involve verbal explanations of questions asked. If the examinee has difficulty responding to the questions and queries as a result of hearing impairment and not of intellectual impairment, then the measure ceases to be valid because of the inappropriate tasks and processes being placed upon the examinee. Many complications can arise that make a test invalid, such as administering a self-report inventory to an individual diagnosed with dyslexia. Counselors who use assessment instruments must consider carefully the ramifications of scoring and interpreting instruments, given the abilities of each individual client.

A term that is often confused with evidence based on test content is *face validity*, which refers to a superficial evaluation of the instrument according to how the instrument looks. In other words, an instrument would be deemed as valid if it appears valid to the individuals who decide to use it (Anastaci & Urbina, 1997). Face validity is not evidence based and therefore is not considered as sufficient evidence of validity.

How Is Evidence Based on Test Content Evaluated?

Analysis and evaluation of evidence based on test content occurs both logically and empirically (AERA et al., 2014). Test developers should document how items were derived. Relevant reviews of literature and developed theories should be cited. Often, expert opinion is cited and test developers may revise, add, or delete items according to suggestions from reviewers. In creating the Juhnke-Balkin Life Balance Inventory (JBLI), Davis, Balkin, and Juhnke (2014) engaged in the following processes to demonstrate evidence of test content:

> The items on the JBLI were developed by the authors in an attempt to assess the various domains of life balance. The authors of the JBLI consulted with eight experts during the item development phase.... The reviewers were asked to rate the relevance (i.e., highly relevant to domain [4], relevant to this domain [3], neither relevant nor irrelevant to domain [2], irrelevant to domain [1], or highly irrelevant to domain [0]) of each of the 7 question stems within the 12 domains

included in the JBLI. The domains include Mood, Stress, Physical, Exercise Health & Nutrition, Sleep, Social-Interpersonal, and Marriage-Significant Other, Sexual and Intimacy, Work-Career, Spirituality-Religious, Happiness, Hopelessness-Helplessness, and Substance Abuse-Addictions.... The JBLI domains were developed to be inclusive of the areas of work, love, and play or leisure and include assessment of substance abuse. The experts recorded their ratings on an expert reviewer form and returned them. The information from the reviewers was utilized to refine the items. (p. 183)

An empirical method for demonstrating evidence based on test content is the index of item-objective congruence, developed by Rovinelli and Hambleton (1977). In this method, a test developer identifies an objective to be measured by each item and expert raters evaluate each item and provide ratings: 1 for an item that *clearly measures the objective*, −1 for an item that *clearly does not measure the objective*, and zero for items in which the *measurement of the objective is unclear* (Turner & Carlson, 2003). Raters may have different ratings for each of the items, depending on their own subjective evaluations. An index for item-objective congruence may be computed to assess the degree to which the raters identified that an item measured a particular objective using the following formula:

$$I_{ik} = \frac{N}{2n-2}(\mu_k - \mu)$$

where I_{ik} is the index of item-objective congruence for item I on objective k, N is the number of objectives, μ_k is judges' mean rating of item I on objective k, and μ is the judges' mean rating of item I on all objectives (Crocker & Algina, 1986, p. 221).

A generally accepted value for an index score is .75 (Turner & Carlson, 2003). Although the specific computations of the index of item-objective congruence are outside the scope of this text, readers who have an interest in using the index of item-objective congruence may find more information about the measure in the cited materials. The important element of this discussion is that empirical methods of evaluating evidence based on test content may be used in test development.

Evidence Based on Response Processes

Test developers should gather evidence demonstrating that the actual responses of participants on test items is a valid operation for evaluating the construct being investigated (AERA et al., 2014). When an item appears on an instrument, the assumption is that individuals will interpret the item the same way. But this is not always true. For example, consider a common question related to substance abuse assessment, "Has drinking or taking drugs ever caused you any problems?" Such questions can be ambiguous, because individuals who use drugs or alcohol are often in denial about the problematic nature of their use/abuse. Thus, an individual who drinks only on weekends may answer "yes" while another individual who smokes marijuana every day may answer "no."

How Is Evidence Based on Response Processes Evaluated?

When developing an instrument, questioning participants regarding their understanding of the items and strategies in answering the items is important to demonstrating evidence of response processes. By examining the individual responses of examinees and even questioning examinees about their responses or how the responses were derived, test developers may gain insight to the extent to which a desired construct is being measured. There are various types of responses that can be monitored, such as the speed of the response, tasks engaged in developing a response, or physiological responses to an item. When individual differences are noted in terms of a response to an item, the test developer may wish to consider alternative formats to an item.

One aspect that is generally acknowledged in standardized testing is the issue of bias. Bias occurs when the interpretation of an instrument is different across various groups. Test developers need to be cautious when subgroups perform differently on an instrument. Investigations into ways items may be interpreted or meaning conveyed is essential so that the instrument remains relevant across a diverse population.

Evidence Based on Internal Structure

Previously labeled as *construct validity*, evidence based on internal structure refers to the interrelationships of the items and the relationships of the items to variables, constructs, or components/factors being measured. For example, when subscales are developed for an instrument, the expectation is that items on one subscale have higher correlations to each other, as they are measuring the same construct, and have lower correlations to items measuring a separate subscale, as the construct may be quite different.

The extent to which items on the same subscale have higher intercorrelations is known as *convergent evidence*; the extent to which items on one subscale have lower correlations to items on a separate subscale is known as *discriminant evidence*. Trochim (2000) identified methods for examining item correlations to establish convergent and discriminant evidence. For example, in development of the Crisis Stabilization Scale (Balkin, 2014; formerly the Goal Attainment Scale of Stabilization; Balkin, 2013; Balkin & Roland, 2007), subscales were developed to measure the extent to which adolescent clients in psychiatric hospitalization attained therapeutic goals designed around problem-solving and coping strategies and commitment to a follow-up plan upon discharge from the hospital. In this study, convergent evidence was demonstrated in the problem identification and commitment to follow-up subscales. Sample items were strongly related to items identified as measuring problem identification and less related to items measuring

TABLE 4.1 Convergent and Discriminant Evidence in the GASS

	Problem Identification			Commitment to Follow-Up		
	PI_1	PI_2	PI_3	CF_1	CF_2	CF_3
PI_1	1.00					
PI_2	**0.85**	1.00				
PI_3	**0.80**	**0.86**	1.00			
CF_1	0.40	0.41	0.37	1.00		
CF_2	0.41	0.42	0.35	**0.81**	1.00	
CF_3	0.43	0.43	0.39	**0.68**	**0.80**	1.00

Note: GASS = Goal Attainment Scale of Stabilization; PI = problem identification; CF = commitment to follow-up.

Source: Balkin & Roland, 2007.

commitment to follow-up (see Table 4.1). A similar model appears in commitment to follow-up.

Note that items in bold demonstrate strong intercorrelations. These items demonstrate convergent evidence in that items on the same subscale are more highly correlated to each other. Also note that the items not in bold are weaker correlations. These items demonstrate discriminant evidence, as items on one subscale do not correlate with items on another subscale. Each subscale measures something unique in client therapeutic goal attainment.

How Is Evidence Based on Internal Structure Evaluated?

When developing instruments, items should fit the appropriate construct of interest both theoretically (i.e., evidence based on test content) and statistically. Examining intercorrelations of items, as mentioned earlier, is one method. However, often more sophisticated methods are used to determine whether items actually measure a construct in question. Common methods include principal component analysis (PCA), exploratory factor analysis (EFA), and confirmatory factor analysis (CFA). The goal of PCA and EFA is to identify items that measure a latent trait and eliminate items that do not contribute to a measure. A *latent trait* refers to a variable or construct that is not directly observed or measured. For example, in the development of the BDI-II (Beck, Steer, & Brown, 1996), 21 items were used to measure depression. These 21 items may or may not represent the entire pool of items in which data were collected. Items that had low correlations, for instance, may have been removed. Beck et al. conducted an EFA and two latent traits emerged. Items indicating levels of sadness, agitation, loss of interest, and indecisiveness, for example, loaded on a latent trait, which was identified by the authors as Cognitive-Affective dimension. These items were indicative of cognitive or affective symptoms of depression. A second factor emerged consisting of items such as tiredness, loss of energy, and changes in appetite. These items were somatic in nature and therefore labeled as Somatic dimension. Thus, two latent traits emerged from the EFA.

An important note is that both PCA and EFA are exploratory procedures. Although a theory was in place to create items that measure depression, based on *Diagnostic and Statistical Manual of Mental Disorders* (fourth edition) criteria, the latent traits were identified through exploratory procedures. The test developers created the items and then studied the factor loadings, which were used to label the latent traits. In exploratory procedures, a theory is developed through both item content and statistical analyses. Many test developers do not run additional analyses beyond the exploratory procedures. However, CFA represents a method to statistically test a theory once the factors have been identified. CFA procedures may be more respected, because statistics are used to test a preestablished theory, as opposed to using statistics in theory development. A strong instrument is one in which both exploratory and confirmatory procedures on separate samples are used in test development.

Evidence Based on Relations to Other Variables

When developing an instrument, analyses to external variables related to the measure is pertinent to establishing evidence of test validity. Relationship to external variables may be ascertained by examining concurrent evidence and predictive evidence; similar to evaluating evidence of internal structure, convergent and discriminant evidence may also be examined with respect to external variables.

Concurrent evidence refers to an analysis of a relationship between two measures at the same time. For example, Balkin and Roland (2007) administered two instruments, the Goal Attainment Scale of Stabilization (GASS) to measure therapeutic goal attainment for adolescents at the time of discharge from psychiatric hospitalization, and the Clinician Problem Scale–Revised (CPS-R) to measure psychiatric symptoms at the time of discharge. Concurrent evidence was demonstrated on the GASS as a significant relationship was found between the GASS and CPS-R scores, indicating that increases in therapeutic goal attainment (GASS scores) were related to decreased psychiatric symptoms (CPS-R scores).

Predictive evidence is demonstrated when an instrument is related to a specific future outcome. For example, universities often use the ACT or SAT as an admission criterion because they believe that college entrance scores may be predictive of success in college. Predictive evidence, however, can be challenging to evaluate. In developing the Suicide Probability Scale (SPS), Cull and Gill (1982) attempted to demonstrate the extent to which scores on the SPS differentiated between clinical and nonclinical populations. In a clinical population, 70.8% of potential attempters were misclassified as nonsuicidal and 76.9% of nonattempters were misclassified as suicidal. In a nonclinical population, 41.5% of nonattempters were misclassified as suicidal (Golding, 1985).

Similar to evidence based on internal structure, an evaluation of convergent and discriminant evidence to external variables may provide important evidence for validity. For the purposes of evaluating relationships to other variables, stronger correlations between similar measures would be apparent in convergent evidence and weaker correlations would be apparent in discriminant evidence. For example, Beck et al. (1996) demonstrated convergent evidence by correlating scores on the BDI-II with the Hamilton Psychiatric Rating Scale for Depression. Because both instruments measure the same construct, depression, the correlation, as expected, between the two instruments was high ($r = .71$). Discriminant evidence was less evident, as the BDI-II was correlated with the Beck Anxiety Inventory (BAI). The relationship between the BDI-II and the BAI was .60. Beck et al. identified that this finding was not unexpected, as "depression and anxiety have been found to be correlated in clinical evaluations" (p. 27).

How Is Evidence Based on Relations to Other Variables Evaluated?

Correlational designs, as noted earlier, tend to be common in identifying evidence of relationships to other variables. Typically, correlations of measures and regression analyses may be used to demonstrate concurrent, predictive, convergent, and discriminant characteristics between measures. Occasionally, tests of significance between administrations of two or more measures may be analyzed to demonstrate evidence of validity. Beck et al. (1996), in their revision of the BDI–IA to the BDI-II, conducted t tests to evaluate whether scores were significantly different between the two instruments. Beck et al. identified that more items were endorsed on the BDI-II than on the BDI-IA by a sample of outpatient clients. Despite this difference, which may be used to justify the revision, correlation between the two instruments was strong (.84).

Evidence for Validity and Consequences of Testing

In a break from the triadic model, the 1999 and 2014 *Standards* emphasized the need to identify the benefits, as well as consequences, of using a measure. The benefits of using an instrument should be both stated and implied. When a test is administered, users should be able to glean information and insights that are useful and beneficial to the client and/or to society. At times, measures may be used in which either the intended construct of interest is lacking evidence of validity or the instruments measure a construct that is unrelated. A clear example of testing consequences can be examined through the advent of high-stakes testing. When No Child Left Behind was passed in 2002, accountability through the examination and demonstrated improvement of student performance was legislated, with the withholding of federal funds as a consequence for poor test scores (Thorn & Mulvenon, 2002). Hence, students are now placed under enormous pressure to achieve higher test scores. In many states, the extent to which the test measures academic progress, as well as the students' ability to work under a pressure situation, has come under scrutiny. Although no change in the present system is likely to occur, the debate about the benefits and the consequences of the test and the practice of high-stakes testing is central to obtaining evidence based on consequences of testing. AERA et al. (2014) cautioned that differentiating between social policy issues versus test validity issues may be difficult. The intent of obtaining evidence of consequences of testing is not to influence social policy but to make sure that interpretations of instruments provide the intended information. As the emphasis on consequences for testing is relatively new, Goodwin and Leech (2003) indicated that few guidelines have been established. Although the intended focus on the benefits and consequences of a test is important, test developers have not identified methods for demonstrating this aspect of validity.

What Are the Implications for Test Validity?

The *Standards for Educational and Psychological Testing* were last revised in 2014; however, neither developers nor reviewers have adhered strongly to the most recent standards. The Minnesota Multiphasic Personality Inventory-II (MMPI-II), in fact, was revised in 1989, and evidence of validity still follow the 1985 *Standards*, with emphasis on comparing norms and scales between the MMPI-II and the MMPI. Even instruments that were revised after the 2014 *Standards* tend to adhere to much older standards of validity. Modern test reviews in *Mental Measurements Yearbook* still incorporate the terms from the 1985 *Standards*.

Although the instruments in the case studies are all well established and common to the field, validity studies using the most recent standards are lacking. Counselors should be careful consumers when engaging in standardized assessment practices. Attention to reviews of instruments is essential in identifying the appropriateness of using various assessment tools. When evaluating whether the use of an instrument would be valid for a client or group of clients, counselors should consider the following issues:

1. To what extent was the instrument developed under a theoretical framework? This is essential to evidence of test content. What theory or theories were used to develop the instrument? In addition, identification of some type of review by experts is important to providing evidence that the instrument was theoretically derived.
2. To what extent do the processes involved in responding to items provide a meaningful measure of the construct in question? For example, if the instrument is a self-report inventory, is this appropriate for the client and the construct being measured? Counselors should consider the nature and type of questions that clients are

exposed to and identify if the scores obtained are likely to reflect a valid measure for the client.
3. What strategies were used to demonstrate evidence of internal structure? Most tests are validated using sophisticated statistical analyses, such as EFA and CFA. Although many master's-level counselors will not have course work covering the details of these analyses, being aware of attempts to establish factor structure is important. Counselors should ensure that the subscales in the measure are identified as part of the factor structure. The overall structure of the instrument should account for a large proportion of the variance in the model, but there are no good rules of thumb on this with some instruments as low as 40% (or possibly lower) and others much higher.
4. What measures were used to correlate to the instrument in question? Counselors should look for evidence that the instrument being evaluated was correlated with other instruments that measure a similar construct. If the instrument correlates moderately to another existing measure, that serves as evidence that the scores obtained from administration of the instrument may be valid for a particular use.
5. What are the consequences for using a test for a specific client? Counselors should be aware of the issues related to test use and abuse. The scores obtained on a particular assessment measure can help direct or guide treatment or may inadvertently label a client, which may not serve his or her best interest. Counselors should ensure that the scores obtained from a measure are going to be used appropriately.

5

Current Standards for Reliability

Objectives

1. Identify different types of reliability.
2. Define key terms related to reliability.
3. Understand the role of reliability in determining the usefulness of assessment results.
4. Interpret reliability estimates and apply them to case conceptualization.

Defining Reliability

Inherent in the practice of assessment is the repeated administration of an instrument, either to a single individual across time or across multiple individuals. An example of the former is a counselor who may wish to use the Beck Depression Inventory-II (BDI-II) to evaluate whether clients have experienced a reduction in depressive symptoms after a period of time. As an example of assessing multiple individuals, the expectation is that individuals with similar characteristics, such as adults diagnosed with depression and participating in group counseling, will demonstrate similar scoring patterns. Thus, *reliability* is the consistency of scores on a measure (American Educational Research Association [AERA], American Psychological Association, & National Council of Measurement in Education, 2014; Cohen et al., 2013). In these examples, *consistency* refers to stability over time and across populations.

When dealing with objective measures, such as an individual's weight, an individual can step on a scale, read the weight, step back on, and more than likely read the same weight. There is very little variance on the weight. Individuals of similar build will likely have similar weights, so the scale is a reliable measure of weight. However, the same cannot be said for measuring *constructs*. Not every phenomenon of interest can be directly observed. Constructs are theoretically guided phenomena that cannot be directly observed or measured. Intelligence and various mood states (e.g., depression, happiness, stress, antisocial personality) serve as constructs in the counseling profession. For example, an athlete may be labeled as brilliant for an ability to think quickly and react in creative ways, but such behavior may not translate into high scores on an intelligence test. Yet, such behavior is an act of creativity that could be recognized as a measure of intelligence. Therefore, constructs are limited by an *operational definition*, a method of explaining and limiting how a construct will be measured. Referring to the previous example of using the BDI-II, clients completing the instruments are evaluated for depression partially based on how each symptom is defined on the BDI-II. Other instruments, such as the Hamilton Rating Scale for Depression or the Suicide Probability Scale, also evaluate depression, but they do so differently. Although correlations may exist between or among the instruments, each instrument employs a separate operational definition based on having different items evaluating depression.

Reliability is a term extended from classical test theory (CTT), derived from Spearman (1904), as well as other more contemporary contributors (e.g., Guttman, Likert, Lord, Thurstone). The premise of CTT was based on two postulates:

1. the measurement of attributes of an individual that contribute to a consistent response set.
2. the measurement of attributes unrelated to the construct being measured but that affect the test scores (Gregory, 2014).

So although the first postulate relates to attributes of the construct, the second postulate is a reflection of extraneous factors that contribute to measurement error.

Although CTT is the more popular theory related to assessment and measurement, other theories are present, particularly *item response theory* (IRT), also known as latent-trait theory. IRT addresses the extent to which an item measures a particular trait (Cohen et al., 2013).

One important aspect of reliability is that reliability is a function of scores, not the scale. In other words, an instrument is never reliable. Rather, scores on the measure are accurate and consistent; the scores are the indication of reliability. In reference to the previous chapter on validity, reliability and validity complement each other, but they are separate concepts. Reliability and validity are essential to responsible test use. However, sole evaluation of reliability would be a mistake. An instrument may be reliable without being valid. For example, Lawson (2007) asserted that counselor wellness affects the quality of services clients receive. Although items that measure wellness may be consistent and accurate, would the presence of such items on a licensure exam compromise the validity of the licensure exam? So would it be appropriate for evaluating counselor competence if a licensure exam included an item such as, "How many times per week do you exercise for 30 minutes or more?" In this case, the validity of the licensure exam may be compromised even if the scores on the item were consistent across numerous test-takers. Hence, while scores on the item may be reliable, inclusion of such an item for determining whether someone is licensed as a counselor compromises the validity of the exam.

True Score

Note that the postulates of CTT indicate that an individual's responses are measures of an attribute but that unanticipated events or factors also contribute to the measurement. Therefore, measurement is fraught with error. Any score obtained from the measurement of a construct includes three elements: (a) the observed score, (b) the true score, and (c) error. If O represents an observed score, T represents a true score, and E represents error, then the following equation expresses the relationship of the observed score to the true score and error:

$$O = T + E$$

The equation is theoretical in nature. The true score is never actually known (Gregory, 2014). For example, say an aspiring college student takes the SAT and scores 510 on the quantitative section. The student decides to retake the SAT in an effort to get a higher score and obtains a 530. Which score is the true measure of the aspiring student's aptitude? According to CTT, the true score is within a range of scores in which 510 and 530 are included.

With respect to the previous equation, error can be positive or negative. Assume that the true score in the aforementioned example is 520 (again, we will never know the true score in actuality). In one administration, the error term is positive, denoting the aspiring student's aptitude to be higher than what was initially measured; whereas the error term is negative in the other administration, indicating an overestimation of aptitude.

Error

To understand the relationship of an observed score to a true score, it may be helpful to rearrange the equation:

$$T = O - E$$

Notice that in this equation, the smaller the error term, the more accurate the observed score is to the true score. If it were possible for no error to be present in a measure (i.e., $E = 0$), then the true score and the observed score would be equal. *Measurement error* is the difference between the observed score and the true score (AERA et al., 2014).

$$E = O - T$$

Measurement error occurs because of *random error*, chance, unplanned phenomena, or events that affect the measure of a construct. Stanley (1971) provided a comprehensive overview of measurement error, but the following issues were regarded as the most pertinent and likely in assessment: (a) construction of the instrument, (b) administration of the instrument, (c) scoring of the instrument, and (d) interpretation of the instrument (Cohen et al., 2013; Gregory, 2014).

Construction of the Instrument

The construct being measured by an instrument is based on a finite number of items consistent with the operational definition of the construct. With any construct of interest, there are an infinite number of possibilities for items, and the construct will ultimately be defined by a limited number of items chosen by the author(s) of the measure. For example, the BDI-II uses items that reflect one of two aspects of depression: affective symptoms and somatic symptoms. Eight items were chosen to reflect the affect (or mood) of the client and 13 items were selected to reflect somatic issues (or physical complaints). Could more of these items been created? Naturally, there are certainly many possibilities in adding to or revising the questions asked. Generally, authors of instruments seek to identify items that will provide information to measuring the construct based on the operational definition. Items that tend to elicit the same information as another item or fail to provide new information about the construct may be eliminated. Certainly, the failure to eliminate such items using statistical procedures and expert review will lead to measurement error.

Because the operational definition of a construct may lend subjectivity to the measure of the construct, instruments that measure the same construct may produce varying results. For example, an adolescent who is administered the Reynolds Adolescent Depression Scale (RADS) may score differently than if the BDI-II had been administered. That each instrument has a different item pool for measuring the same construct contributes to different results for the same construct being measured. Furthermore, each instrument may employ variations in the operational definition of depression.

When items are developed, a respondent answers each item from a subjective interpretation of the item. Any ambiguity in the interpretation or system of scoring contributes to random error. For example, the RADS uses a response pattern of four choices across 30 items to assess depressive symptoms using the following response format: 1 = *almost never*, 2 = *hardly ever*, 3 = *sometimes*, 4 = *most of the time*. Notice the subjective nature of the response format. The decision, for instance, to choose a 3 = *sometimes* versus a 4 = *most of the time* is not universal. What one person views as a 3 for a specific symptom may be viewed as a 2 or a 4 by another person. Although reliability coefficients attempt to estimate the consistency of the responses, random error affects the accuracy of these estimates.

Scaling items are similar to multiple-choice items, except that these types of items are usually used to discern a degree to which a behavior, thought, or action exists. In this case, there is no correct response but rather a response that may describe how a client thinks, feels, or behaves. One of the more common types of scales used in assessment is a Likert-type scale. In a Likert-type scale, items range from 1 to 5, in which lower scores indicate disagreement or negativity toward a construct and higher scores are indicative of agreement or affirmation toward a construct. A classic example is items in which a respondent indicates 1 = *strongly disagree*, 2 = *disagree*, 3 = *neither agree nor disagree*, 4 = *agree*, and 5 = *strongly agree*. Likert-type items may be scored reliably, but differences between the negative components (*strongly disagree* and *disagree*) or positive components (*strongly disagree* and *disagree*) may be difficult to differentiate. In addition, justifying that the measures are truly interval, that the degree of difference between two scores is universal for each respondent, is a limitation. For example, Rye et al. (2001) developed the Forgiveness Scale as part of a study involving college women who had previously been wronged in a relationship. A sample item included "I spend time thinking about ways to get back at the person who wronged me" in which the respondent indicated 1 for *strongly disagree* to 5 for *strongly agree*. Can researchers assume that respondents who indicate 4, *agree*, are the same? The extent to which an individual indicates *agree* may not be universal. A respondent who answers *agree* may experience the same degree of a construct as another respondent who answers *strongly agree*. Think of it this way—imagine going to a comedy club and the comedian tells a joke. Some in the audience laugh; others do not. Yet, each audience member was subjected to the same event. Some members may say the joke was funny; others may say the joke was very funny. The extent to which one finds a joke funny or very funny may not be the same across each individual. This is a limitation with Likert-type items, because such items are treated as interval data but are really more ordinal in nature.

Other types of common scales include Guttman scaling and Thurstone scaling (Trochim, 2000). Guttman scaling includes developing dichotomous items (*yes* or *no* responses) that build on one another to develop a cumulative measure. For example, a researcher could develop a series of items to measure religious tolerance that would be placed in a logical order:

1. I appreciate perspective from individuals of different faiths.
2. I would have no problem if my son/daughter dated an individual from a different faith.
3. I would have no problem if my son/daughter married an individual from a different faith.

Notice that each item can be answered with *yes* or *no*. In addition, an argument could be made that the items increase in intensity. The number of items in which the respondent answers *yes* could be the scale score. Usually a scale will consist of a larger series of items than the three used in this example.

The Thurstone scale is similar to the Guttman scale in that the items are dichotomous (*yes* or *no* responses; *agree* or *disagree* responses), but the development of the scale is much more complex and involves evaluating a large series of items and weighting the items to draw conclusions from respondents. Unlike the Guttman scale, the items are not necessarily presented in an ascending fashion and the scoring of the items is more involved.

Administration of the Instrument

Variability in the administration of instruments is common and can have a haphazard effect on the results. Even though instrument developers may pay careful attention to standardizing the instrument through the gathering and analyzing of scores across a chosen population, random errors related to the testing environment, the individual(s) completing the instrument, or the individual(s) administering the instrument may occur. Although items on an instrument can be evaluated for consistency, evaluation of the scores based on other factors simply does not occur on a consistent basis and is rarely considered when an instrument is scored and interpreted.

Errors within the testing environment include the variability within each testing environment. Areas may be spacious or cramped; temperatures may fluctuate; participants could be exposed to uncomfortably high or low temperatures. Rooms may be noisy or there could be disruptive activities outside of the testing area, such as construction work. Characteristics of the room in which the instrument is administered may have qualities that distract examinees, such as posters or carvings on walls or desks. Lighting in the room may be poor. Some desks may have poor writing surfaces, or perhaps issues exist with technology when computer-based instruments are administered. Older students in particular may be less adept at computer-based administrations. These attributes, as well as others, could have an effect on the participants' abilities to concentrate and be comfortable in the testing environment.

Counselors are responsible for identifying nonstandard environmental conditions or favorable testing conditions when interpreting assessment results (American Counseling Association [ACA], 2014). When nonstandard testing conditions occur, such conditions should be disclosed and reflected in the interpretation of the scores. Indeed, counselors should be cautious in the interpretation and subsequent use of test scores obtained from nonstandard testing conditions, as such conditions compromise reliability of the scores.

Individuals responsible for administering group-based assessments, such as school counselors who coordinate testing for schools, may encourage students to get adequate rest and food before the examination. However, the fact that each individual has unique characteristics related to the administration of the instrument cannot be overlooked. Students may come to the examination with varying levels of motivation, energy, and health. Some students may be overly tired or hungry; others may be ill. Issues related to test anxiety might play a role in test performance. Inadequate attention to testing protocol, such as poor time management on timed exams or mistakes made in the reading or interpretation of the items, may result in random error. Participants may mistakenly blacken the wrong oval corresponding to the item number (e.g., mistakenly mark the oval for Item 6 when answering Item 5) and thereby make the following items incongruent with the intended responses. Items may be mistakenly skipped or omitted. Such random errors can have disastrous consequences for scoring, interpreting, and even placing participants in appropriate programs or services.

Individuals administering instruments also contribute to random errors. Any accidental departure from the standardized procedures may contribute to random error. Verbal and nonverbal communications may have an impact on how participants respond to a protocol. For example, an abrupt verbal response or nod could indicate to a participant that an answer is incorrect (Gregory, 2014). In particular, any type of exam that has an oral administration, such as various intelligence tests, is highly susceptible to random errors on the part of the administrator. Cadence, rhythm, and accent in the examiner's speech may affect performance on an instrument and lend to variability from other examinees that have a different administrator for an instrument.

High-stakes testing has had a serious impact on some individuals who administer assessment instruments. Hacker (2007) documented evidence of cheating from 700 schools in Texas on the Texas Assessment of Knowledge and Skills, an achievement test used to comply with No Child Left Behind policies. In addition to teachers leaking questions out to other teachers in order to facilitate test preparation for the students, Hacker (2007) stated the following:

> In most cases, the cheating involved individual pairs or small groups of students . . . [b]ut in a few cases . . . an overwhelming number of students' answers were incredibly similar. So aside from the statistical equivalent of lightning striking the same place 10 times, those students were either all copying one source, or an adult was doctoring answer sheets. (p. 20)

The ramifications of such errors are serious. Consumers of research use test scores to make policy decisions in education. Parents use test scores to make decisions on where to send their children to school. Test scores are often used as evidence for appropriate student placement in programs for various schools, such as gifted and talented programs. Often counselors play a pivotal role in the procedures of administering various assessments, and training for administering instruments in a standardized format cannot be overlooked.

Scoring of the Instrument

Computer-based scoring may reduce random errors by increasing consistency to the scoring process. However, counselors typically use many instruments that are hand-scored or scored by scantrons. Problems may persist, especially when score sheets contain erasure marks or lightly blackened answers that may be misread by scantrons. Although instruments that rely on open-ended items, such as intelligence tests, often include substantial training to standardize scoring methods, subjectivity in scoring items may still occur, thereby compromising instrument reliability.

However, another type of scoring issue that is often overlooked when evaluating the psychometric properties of the instrument is the response format on an instrument. Forced-choice items, such as using a Guttman scale, may have less subjectivity in terms of participants understanding the item and choosing a response, yet the limited responses available may not accurately reflect the construct of interest for the participant. In contrast, Likert scale items (i.e., 5-point scales ranging from *strongly disagree* to *strongly agree*), as mentioned earlier, are often used as interval scale items, which can be summed and incorporated into mean scores. However, the response format is quite subjective, as some participants may choose *agree* while others choose *strongly agree* with no verifiable measure of whether the intensity of the construct is truly different from participant to participant. Another example would be scales that measure chronic pain. Some individuals may have a higher pain tolerance and provide lower scores yet still be in as much or more pain as someone who is endorsing higher levels of pain. Technically these items could be considered ordinal, but researchers who use these instruments treat such items as interval scales to facilitate the use of parametric statistics, many of which are included in the test manuals to support reliability of the scores and validity of the instrument. So, although the practice of quasi-interval scales is common among instrument developers, the potential for random error and subsequent effect on reliability is evident.

Interpretation of the Instrument

Many instruments provide the opportunity for counselors to use computer-generated reports once scores are tabulated. When pregenerated reports are used to communicate test results to the client, the onus of responsibility for the accuracy of the report lies with the counselor who assumes ultimate responsibility for the communication of results (ACA, 2014). In the case of using assessments for diagnostic purposes, counselors administering and creating reports are accountable for the accuracy and errors of the assessment report. However, in the case of participants contracting with testing companies to provide an assessment, such as an aptitude test, the test company assumes responsibility for the accuracy of the results.

Another source of measurement error is *systematic error*, when the instrument measures something other than the construct. In an attempt to measure commitment to safety for adolescents admitted to a crisis unit, Balkin (2004) created items that also loaded on an individual's ability to process coping skills. The end result was the reliability for scores on the scale designed to measure commitment to safety was compromised. The development of scales that consistently assess one and only one construct is improbable and compounded by the fact that systematic errors may go unnoticed. Cronin and Goodman (2008) documented the legislative approval of using the SAT to predict first-year success in college as the exit exam for high school students. In other words, an instrument designed to assess *aptitude* was implemented to assess academic *achievement*. Despite efforts from Maine counselors, the ACA, and the Association of Assessment in Counseling and Education, a major systematic error was placed into educational policy. The good intentions of legislators to boost college admissions has resulted in students being evaluated on material that may not be covered in a high school academic curriculum and therefore serves as an invalid indicator of academic achievement.

Estimating Reliability

Because of the presence of error, estimating the reliability of scores on an instrument (i.e., the consistency in which a construct is measured) can be problematic. Moreover, different methods are used, and more than one reliability estimate may be reported. Three terms are common in estimating reliability: (a) reliability coefficient, (b) standard error of measurement (SEM), and (c) reliability index.

Reliability Coefficient

To estimate reliability, a *reliability coefficient* is computed to quantify the relationship of observed scores on an instrument: r_{xx} is the correlation between two observed scores. Reliability coefficients typically range from zero to 1. A perfect correlation between observed scores is 1.0, meaning that a set of examinees will obtain the same score each time the test is administered. Consequently, a reliability coefficient of 1.0 is not likely to occur for instruments commonly used to measure psychological constructs. Scores may be similar for individuals who retake an instrument, but slight variations are expected. Ultimately, perfect reliability is difficult to obtain, even when more objective measures are used. For example, measures of blood pressure, resting heart rate, or even weight rarely show the exact values when done repeatedly in a given time frame. The reliability coefficient is the most commonly reported estimate of reliability. There are different methods of reporting the reliability coefficient, which are discussed later in the chapter.

Standard Error of Measurement

Recall that the standard deviation typically refers to the average amount of error from the mean for a given sample or population. A mean, therefore, represents the average score for a particular group and the standard deviation indicates how much each individual will differ from the group mean, on average. When administering an instrument, the standard deviation provides an indication of how a particular individual's score is similar or different from a given group, but the standard deviation is not an indication of the instrument being a consistent measure of a construct for the individual.

For example, the BDI-II for adults in outpatient settings has a mean of 22.45, a standard deviation of 12.75, and a reliability coefficient of .92 (Beck, Steer, & Brown, 1996). Beck et al. suggested the guidelines of total scores listed in Table 5.1 for diagnosing major depression.

A client who scores a 20 on the BDI-II would be classified in the moderate range for major depression according to Beck et al.'s (1996) guidelines. But how likely would the client be to get the same score on a second administration of the BDI-II if no other intervention or change in life circumstances has taken place? To answer this question, counselors use the *standard error of measurement* (SEM), which indicates the average amount of error for an individual if the instrument were to be administered repeatedly. So, although the

TABLE 5.1 Cut Scores on the Beck Depression Inventory-II

Total Scores	Range
0–13	Minimal
14–19	Mild
20–28	Moderate
29–63	Severe

standard deviation indicates variability within a group, the SEM indicates variability of a score for an individual.

The SEM can be computed with the following formula:

$$\sigma_e = \sigma\sqrt{1-r_{xx}}$$

where σ_e is the standard error of measurement, σ is the population standard deviation, and r_{xx} is the reliability coefficient. So, although an instrument has error, participants may not obtain the same score when administered an instrument repeatedly under similar conditions, and although the true score of an individual is never really known, the SEM can be computed to indicate the range in which the true score lies.

Referring back to the previous example of the BDI-II, if the test has a standard deviation of 12.75 for individuals receiving counseling services in an outpatient setting and a reliability index of .92, then the SEM for the BDI-II can be computed as follows:

$$\sigma_e = 12.75\sqrt{1-.92} = 3.61$$

Notice the attributes of the SEM. If the standard deviation remains constant and the reliability coefficient increases (moves closer to 1, demonstrating higher consistency), the SEM becomes smaller; likewise, scores on instruments that are less reliable have more error indicated by a larger SEM. For example, the reliability of the BDI-II for a college sample was .93:

$$\sigma_e = 12.75\sqrt{1-.93} = 3.37$$

When the reliability coefficient remains constant and the standard deviation decreases, the SEM once again becomes smaller and would increase if the standard deviation were to increase. When the BDI-II was administered to participants who had a previous diagnosis of a mood disorder, the mean score was 26.57 and the standard deviation was 12.15.

$$\sigma_e = 12.15\sqrt{1-.92} = 3.44$$

On any given assessment period the SEM provides information about the true score within a specific range of confidence, known as a *confidence interval*. Now, we can identify the range in which the true score lies using the information we learned in Chapter 3. Within 1 standard deviation, we can be 68% confident that the true score will lie $\pm 1\sigma_e$ of the observed score; within 2 standard deviations, we can be 95% confident that the true score will lie $\pm 2\sigma_e$ of the observed score; within 3 standard deviations, we can be 99% confident that the true score will lie $\pm 3\sigma_e$ of the observed score. The range for the true score can be expressed in the following way:

For 68% confidence, $T = O \pm 1\sigma_e$
For 95% confidence, $T = O \pm 2\sigma_e$
For 99% confidence, $T = O \pm 3\sigma_e$

In our example for the client who scored 20 on the BDI-II:

We can be 68% confident that the client's true score is between 20 ± 3.61 or between 16.39 and 23.61, inclusive.
We can be 95% confident that the client's true score is between $20 \pm (2)3.61$ or between 12.78 and 27.22, inclusive.
We can be 99% confident that the client's true score is between $20 \pm (3)3.61$ or between 9.17 and 30.83, inclusive.

Referring back to the suggested interpretative guidelines of the BDI-II, the SEM has some implications for the client, as the client may fall in between the mild to moderate range of depression, again reinforcing the importance of caution in the interpretation of assessment results.

Indeed, SEM can play a pivotal role when assessments are used. All too often educational settings overrely on scores to address placement and service issues. A student who tests in the range of borderline intellectual functioning may be refused services on the basis of the score when in fact the SEM indicates that the student may have tested in the extremely low range of intellectual functioning.

Reliability Index

The *reliability index* is the relationship between the true score and the observed score and is a less common term than the *reliability coefficient* to provide estimates of reliability. The reliability index, r_{TX}, quantifies correlation of the true score (T) to the observed score (O), as opposed to the reliability coefficient, which identifies the relationship between two forms or administrations of an instrument. The reliability index is related directly to the reliability coefficient and is computed as follows:

$$r_{TX} = \sqrt{r_{xx}}$$

As the reliability coefficient increases or decreases, the reliability index increases or decreases, respectively. A perfect reliability coefficient, 1.0, would indicate no error in consistency between administrations; therefore, a perfect reliability index, 1.0, would also be present as there would be no error in predicting the true score from the observed score.

Types of Reliability Measurement

Several methods are used to calculate reliability coefficients (r_{xx}). As r_{xx} approaches 1.0, scores on the instrument are deemed more consistent. This section addresses four different forms of computing reliability coefficients: (a) test–retest, (b) parallel/alternate forms, (c) internal consistency, and (d) interscorer reliability. When reliability estimates are reported for scores on an instrument, common practice includes the use of more than one method to demonstrate reliability.

Consistency Over Time: Test–Retest Reliability

Test–retest reliability refers to the correlation of two administrations of the same instrument. Often referred to as stability over time, reliability is evaluated by examining the relationship of the same instrument measuring the same construct at two different time periods. A Pearson product–moment correlation coefficient can be computed between the two scores to determine the relationship. This is an appropriate measure to use when the construct being measured remains stable (i.e., does not change) over time.

Psychosocial constructs, however, may change over time—even if no intervention has occurred. Balkin, Tietjen-Smith, Caldwell, and Shen (2007) studied the effect of exercise on depression for young adult women and noted a nonsignificant decrease in scores on the BDI-II for the control group (nonexercise group) when the BDI-II was administered for baseline and then six weeks later. Although depression may decrease over time when there is no intervention, that no statistically significant decrease was evident may be linked to the high test–retest reliability of the BDI-II. Beck et al. (1996) reported a test–retest reliability for the BDI-II at $r = .93$ when the BDI-II was administered twice at an interval of one week apart. Test–retest reliability is related to the amount of time between the two administrations (Trochim, 2000). Shorter time periods between administrations may yield higher reliability coefficients. A limitation in the test–retest methodology is the assumption that no meaningful changes have occurred that would alter the measurement of the construct being investigated. In addition, the presence of a *testing effect*, previous exposure to the instrument by the examinee, may alter the manner in which the examinee responds. For example, say after an initial administration of the BDI-II an examinee decides to look up symptoms of depression. In an effort to appear less depressed, the examinee could answer the items differently, because previous exposure to the items from the first administration took place.

Estimates of Equivalency: Parallel or Alternate Forms

When more than one form of the same instrument exists, the equivalency of the forms can be assessed by correlating scores on the two forms of the instrument. Although the terms *parallel* or *alternate* are used interchangeably, there is a technical difference. Parallel forms maintain the same means and variances across the various forms; alternate forms are constructed with the intention of being parallel but may not have the same descriptive information (Cohen et al., 2013).

A Pearson product–moment correlation coefficient can be computed between the two scores on each of the forms to determine the relationship. In this case, highly consistent forms will have different items that cover the same content. Instruments that measure a specific knowledge base or aptitude (e.g., SAT, ACT, Graduate Record Examination [GRE], National Counselor Examination [NCE]) should not differ across *item difficulty*, the percentage of participants answering an item correctly, or *item discrimination*, the extent to which an item distinguishes those who vary on a given construct.

The challenge in using parallel forms to evaluate the reliability of the scores on an instrument is the development of items that measure the same aspects of a construct for different forms of the instrument. A much larger item pool is necessary to develop equivalent forms. For example, a counselor who is required to take the NCE for a second time would likely encounter items that are different from the first administration but cover the same content areas. Developing items that fit the criteria for an alternate form would be much easier than developing items for a parallel form, as providing evidence for similar item difficulty and discrimination would be necessary.

Internal Consistency

Both test–retest and equivalent forms can be time-consuming methods to estimate reliability of scores, as either the instrument must be administered twice or another form of the instrument must be created. However, another way to estimate reliability may be to examine the *internal consistency* of the scores on the instrument—analyzing the relationships of the scores for each of the items on the instrument. There are several methods to evaluating the internal consistency of an instrument: (a) split-half, (b) coefficient alpha, and (c) Kuder-Richardson (K-R) formulas.

Split-Half

Assuming that all of the items measure the same construct, the instrument can be split into equivalent halves. A Pearson product–moment correlation coefficient can be computed between the two halves on each of the forms to determine the relationship or reliability coefficient. Splitting the instrument into two equivalent halves can be complicated. For example, the BDI-II may not be a good instrument with which to use this method of reliability estimation. The BDI-II has 21 items, and each item measures a distinct characteristic

TABLE 5.2 Reliability Estimates Using Split-Half and Spearman-Brown Formulas

Split-Half Reliability Coefficient	Spearman-Brown Reliability Coefficient
0.70	0.82
0.80	0.89
0.90	0.95

of depression. So identifying two equivalent halves of the instrument may not be possible. However, to use this method on the NCE may be easier, as there could be several items that measure knowledge in ethics, the helping relationship, group theory, and so forth, and these items could be equally divided between two halves of the exam.

An additional problem occurs in reliability estimation when the split-half method is used. Reliability estimates fluctuate depending on the length of the exam. An increase in items leads to an increase in reliability estimates (Gage & Damrin, 1950), and scores on shorter tests are less reliable. When an instrument is split in half, the reliability coefficient will be underestimated. The *Spearman-Brown formula* adjusts for the underestimation of the split-half method and can be computed as follows:

$$r_{sb} = \frac{2r_{hh}}{1+r_{hh}}$$

where r_{sb} is the reliability coefficient using the Spearman-Brown formula and r_{hh} is the reliability coefficient using the split-half method. Recall that the split-half method will compare two half-tests, while the Spearman-Brown adjusts for this error by providing a reliability estimate for the whole test. Using the previous formula, the adjustments found in Table 5.2 can be noted.

Because of the underestimation of the split-half method, Cohen et al. (2013) recommended that the Spearman-Brown formula always be used when estimating reliability using the split-half method.

Coefficient Alpha

As mentioned previously, test developers may have difficulty justifying how an instrument can be divided into two equivalent halves. However, there can also be many ways to divide an instrument in half. Cronbach (1951) devised a mathematical formula, *coefficient alpha* or *Cronbach's alpha*, to take into account all possible split-half methods to evaluate the internal consistency of an instrument. The formula for coefficient alpha is as follows:

$$r_\alpha = \left(\frac{n}{n-1}\right)\left(1-\frac{\Sigma\sigma_i^2}{\sigma^2}\right)$$

where r_α is coefficient alpha (this term is often referred to as α when discussing reliability estimates in published research), n is the number of items on the instrument, $\Sigma\sigma_i^2$ is the sum of the variance for each item, and σ^2 is the total variance of the instrument. Although this statistic is quite labor intensive when computed by hand, the use of computer programs has made coefficient alpha the most widely reported and preferred method for estimating reliability.

Kuder-Richardson

The coefficient alpha formula is actually an extension of an earlier formula developed to evaluate internal consistency for dichotomous items. Whereas coefficient alpha can be used to estimate reliability for items that have a range of responses (i.e., Likert scale items—*strongly agree* to *strongly disagree*), the KR-20 is used to evaluate internal consistency when items can be scored a 1 or zero (e.g., *right* or *wrong*; *relapse* or *no relapse*). The KR-20 formula is as follows:

$$r_{KR20} = \left(\frac{n}{n-1}\right)\left(1 - \frac{\Sigma pq}{\sigma^2}\right)$$

where r_{KR20} is the Kuder-Richardson reliability coefficient, n is the number of items, p is the proportion of participants who answer the item correctly or positively, q is the proportion of participants who answer the item incorrectly or negatively, and σ^2 is the total variance of the instrument. Although the KR-20 can only be used for dichotomous items, coefficient alpha will produce the same results as KR-20 for dichotomous items and can be extended to nondichotomous items as well.

Interscorer Reliability

Some measures are dependent on scoring from standardized procedures. Measures of intelligence, performance, or other subjective indicators may vary as a result of the scorers, as opposed to actual variance in the construct. For example, each year at the Olympics, a controversy ensues over scores by various judges. Sports such as figure skating, gymnastics, and boxing often experience questionable scoring procedures. These types of issues may also exist in many types of tests in which the presence or absence or pass or failure of an attribute is dependent upon a scorer's perspective. *Interscorer reliability*, often referred to as *interrater reliability* or *interrater agreement*, refers to the relationship between or among scores issued by raters. Consistency among scorers is dependent on the use and training of objective criteria to rate a construct. When low correlations exist among raters, some type of training is needed to prompt the raters to use similar criteria.

The Pearson product–moment correlation coefficient may be computed to assess the consistency between two judges. When more than two judges are being evaluated, a more sophisticated statistic, called the *intraclass correlation coefficient*, can be computed using computer programs. The intraclass correlation coefficient provides the average rating for a single judge. To account for more than one judge in the average, adjustments can be made using a Spearman-Brown correction:

$$\frac{j(icc)}{1+(j-1)icc}$$

where j is the number of judges and *icc* is the intraclass correlation coefficient. An approximation of the *icc* may be determined from the average of the Pearson product–moment correlation coefficients from all raters.

Despite the attempt to make scores or determinations from experts accurate and consistent, there are some endeavors in counseling that simply lack evidence of accuracy and consistency, and one of those is diagnosis. According to a review by Vanheule et al. (2014) that covered selected clinical field trials in 1974, 1992, 1995, and 2013, the accuracy and consistency to diagnose has not changed or improved, even though the metamorphosis of the diagnostic system from second to the fifth edition of the *Diagnostic and Statistical Manual of Mental Disorders* (DSM). In other words, although our understanding of diagnosis has changed, the ability for clinicians throughout the helping professions to accurately and consistently diagnose has not improved (Aboraya, 2007). But that has not stopped professionals from suggesting that accuracy and consistency in diagnosis has improved. Rather, what we see is that any improvement in diagnosis is due to the change of the standard and what constitutes excellence in accuracy and consistency in diagnosis. Let's explain this a little more.

Vanheule et al. (2014, p. 314) used a kappa coefficient (k), which measures the agreement of two raters between zero (*no agreement*) and 1 (*perfect agreement*) and noted the following evolution of k as it pertains to the interpretation of reliability estimates in diagnosis:

- 1974: $k \geq .90$, excellent; $k = .70 - .90$, good; $k \leq .70$, unacceptable;
- 1977: $k \geq .75$, excellent; $k = .40 - .70$, fair to good; $k \leq .40$, poor;
- 2010: $k \geq .70$, excellent; $k = .60 - .70$, good; $k = .41 - 49$, questionable; $k \leq .40$, poor;
- 2013: $k \geq .80$, excellent; $k = .60 - .79$, very good; $k = .40 - 59$, good; $k = .20 - 39$, questionable; $k \leq .20$, unacceptable.

So how does the interpretation of the k translate to the agreement between diagnosticians in clinical trials? According to Vanheule et al. (2014), a clinical field trial by Williams et al. (1992) would have used the third edition of the DSM. Based on the 1974 interpretation of the k, 72% ($n = 13$) of the interrater agreements were in *unacceptable* range, and 28% ($n = 5$) were in the *good* range. However, using the 2013 interpretation of the k of the interrater agreements, 50% were in the *good* range, 33% in the *very good* range, and 17% in the excellent range. In comparison, the more recent 2013 clinical field trial for the fifth edition of the DSM indicated that 93% (14 out of 15) of the interrater agreements would have been categorized as *questionable* or *unacceptable* in 1974, but by using the 2013 standards, only 33% ($n = 5$) are identified as *questionable* or *unacceptable* and the remaining 67% ($n = 10$) are identified as *good* or *very good*.

So what does this all mean? Essentially, the ability for experts to agree on diagnosis is a challenge that has been problematic since psychiatry attempted to standardize this process. The actual statistics of agreement on diagnoses have not changed substantially. Rather, the standards by which to judge agreement have been altered in order demonstrate improvements that do not really exist.

Interpretation of Reliability

When deciding whether or not to use a particular psychosocial instrument, the interpretation of reliability data is pertinent. Counselors should be aware of reliability estimation methods, the conditions in which reliability estimates were derived, and the description of the participants from whom the data were collected. "General statements to the effect that a test is 'reliable' or that it is 'sufficiently reliable to permit interpretations of individual scores' are rarely, if ever, acceptable" (AERA et al., 2014, p. 41).

Each method for determining reliability contains sources of error related to time, content, scoring error, and sampling variance. Test–retest is limited by time, as longer periods of time between administrations may decrease reliability estimates. Reliability estimates related to using equivalent forms may be limited by content, as alternate content may be inadvertently used because of the need to generate larger item pools. Although coefficient alpha appears to address limitation in test content that occurs with split-half methods, items that are less likely to measure the homogeneous nature of a construct will lower reliability estimates. Identifying items that measure more heterogeneous attributes of a construct may need to be eliminated. Reliability estimates, with respect to interscorer reliability, are affected by inherent biases, as well as subjective scoring procedures. Objective criteria and training may increase reliability estimates but not eliminate the error variance.

An important consideration outside of computing reliability estimates is the nature of the group in which the reliability estimates are obtained. As a rule of thumb, a heterogeneous group will provide higher reliability estimates, regardless of the method used. Imagine if a group being administered the BDI-II all scored in the severe range. There would be no way to correlate this group's depression with other characteristics, because there was no difference evident from the scores in depression—everyone scored similarly. Having a diverse sample provides evidence that attributes can be consistently measured, as they vary from person to person.

In another example, consider the construct of introversion–extroversion. There would be little relationship to any other construct, such as propensity for substance abuse or self-esteem, if each participant scored high on extroversion. Correlations would be low because of the lack of variability in the sample. With respect to interscorer reliability, if everyone obtained the highest score possible on a construct such as creativity, there would be no way to rank the participants with respect to creativity. The issue of variance in the sample underlies the importance of counselors being familiar with whom the instrument was normed.

The nature of the instrument is another important consideration. Many instruments, especially instruments geared toward measuring ability (e.g., aptitude, achievement, intelligence), rely on speed and/or power measures. *Speed measures* contain simple items that the examinee will likely answer correctly but the time limit is restricted, preventing the examinee from completing all of the items. *Power measures* provide adequate time to complete the instrument but include items of difficulty that may prevent one from obtaining a perfect score. Many instruments (ACT, SAT, GRE, Wechsler Intelligence Scale for Children–Fifth Edition) employ a combination of these measures. Because of the nature of speeded tests, traditional split-half methods, such as comparing odd and even items, may produce very high reliability estimates. A better method would be to use a test–retest method on two separately timed tests or correlate to half-tests with a Spearman-Brown formula (Gregory, 2014).

Given the limitations of reliability estimates, what constitutes adequate reliability? Hopkins (1998) indicated that standardized tests, such as those used for placement and college admission, should have reliability coefficients of .90 or higher. Yet many psychosocial instruments are used with reliability estimates near .70. Certain constructs, such as psychosis, have been difficult to measure, and reliability estimates may be lower. In the case of interrater reliability, some constructs simply lack expert agreement, as in the case of diagnosis.

Reliability estimates should not be used alone to assess the consistency of the scores. Standard error of measurement should also be considered. Although reliability estimates account for consistency of the instrument, standard error of measurement provides an indication of accuracy. Recall that the standard error of measurement incorporates two terms: a reliability coefficient and measurement error. Therefore, scores on an instrument may be consistent but could also be inaccurate.

What Are the Implications for Reliability?

Because of the many different aspects of reliability, determining whether an instrument is reliable is not a simple matter and requires a multifaceted approach. Instruments may have strong reliability evidence in one area yet be lacking in another area. Such an issue is apparent in the Child Behavior Checklist (CBCL). Although the CBCL is a popular instrument, the reliability of the scores on the instrument may be questioned in some regards. Test–retest after one week and internal consistency scores for composite scales average .80; but internal consistency scores for the subscales may be as low as .50. The attributes of the raters may also be a factor with interrater reliability averaging .66 on the parent forms (Doll, 2004). Similar to the CBCL, the Minnesota Multiphasic Personality Inventory-2 maintains strong test–retest reliability, averaging .83, but internal consistency reliability for the clinical subscales has a broader range, .34 to .87 with a median range of .63 (Matz, Altepeter, & Perlman, 1992).

Educational and cognitive tests may have higher reliability estimates because of the nature of measuring academic performance or intelligence, as opposed to psychopathology, which may be considered more diverse and complex in nature to measure. Reliability estimates for the Wechsler Adult Intelligence Scale–IV are quite adequate to strong (e.g., internal consistency estimates were .71–.96 for scores on the subtests and .97–.98 for the full scale IQ scores; Canivez, 2010). The Wechsler Intelligence Scales have a standard error of measurement of ±5 points, so this needs to be considered when applying labels and determining services for individuals. For example, if a school district employs a cut-score of 70 IQ to provide services and a student scores 72, the SEM indicates that the student could fall in the range of *borderline* to extremely low functioning.

Again, the popularity of an instrument is not a guarantee of reliable assessment results. Each of the assessments used in this sample profile are more widely known and can easily be referenced in the *Mental Measurement Yearbook* (Lincoln, NE: Buros Institute of Mental Measurements) or peer-reviewed literature. Counselors should be aware of the error related to measurement and assessment. Standardized assessments are only a tool and should never stand alone in determining treatment or diagnosis.

6

How to Choose an Assessment Instrument

> ## Objectives
> 1. Identify ethical and legal considerations in selecting an assessment instrument.
> 2. Interpret the technical quality of an instrument.
> 3. Understand the format and information in an instrument review.
> 4. Determine the appropriateness of an instrument.
> 5. Understand the factors that compromise the quality of an instrument.
> 6. Understand the limitations and strengths of a selected assessment instrument.
> 7. Identify factors that may affect performance.

Defining the Purpose of the Assessment Instrument

Counselors' decisions to use assessment instruments should be based on the construct or phenomenon to be measured, the benefit to the client, the expertise/training of the counselor, the potential to yield appropriate decisions for the client, and the cultural sensitivity of the instrument (American Counseling Association [ACA], 2014; American Educational Research Association [AERA], American Psychological Association, & National Council of Measurement in Education, 2014). When selecting an instrument, counselors should have in mind a specific purpose for which the instrument will be used. George (1997) identified three such purposes: (a) describe a client or client population, including characteristics of the client or client population; (b) identify specific needs of a client or client population; and (c) evaluate interventions and/or programs that serve clients or client populations. Ultimately, counselors need to determine the degree to which the information will be useful and contribute to timely interventions for the client or client population (Sederer, Dickey, & Eisen, 1997).

In terms of usefulness, consider the following:

1. How will the client benefit from the assessment?
2. How will the counselor use assessment results to provide best practice for the client?

In administering the assessment, both the client and the counselor will expend time, energy, and money to obtain some result. Often counselors attempt to identify problems, measure baseline behaviors, or diagnose in order to develop effective treatment plans and improve client conceptualization by the counselor. Clients might benefit by gaining insight into problem areas or identifying a particular diagnosis that helps explain the problem areas, such as a parent learning that a son or daughter has Asperger's syndrome.

As mentioned in previous chapters, counselors should consider the psychometric qualities of an instrument. "Counselors carefully consider the validity, reliability, psychometric imitations, and appropriateness of instruments when selecting assessments and, when possible, use multiple forms of assessment, data, and/or instruments in forming conclusions, diagnoses, or recommendations" (ACA, 2014, p. 121). Statements about validity and reliability should be evaluated, with indications that the instrument was evaluated with respect to content, internal structure, relationships to other variables, response processes, and consequences of testing. Rarely are all aspects of validity mentioned in manuals and reviews, and many instruments are evaluated based on the 1985 standards. Counselors should be cautious when using instruments that selectively disclose validation procedures. Also remember that instruments are not deemed reliable and/or valid. Rather, authors demonstrate evidence for validity and reliability and make a judgment or interpretation based on the estimates and evidence presented.

Beyond reliability and validity, a suitable instrument is sensitive to change (Lambert & Hawkins, 2004; Sederer, Dickey, & Eisen, 1997). For example, the Youth Outcome Questionnaire–SR 2.0 (Wells, Burlingame, & Rose, 2003) is a self-report inventory designed to measure treatment progress over time for adolescents (ages 12 to 18) receiving mental health services. As such, when clients make progress in counseling, a well-designed instrument should be able to detect such change, even if the change is somewhat limited. A well-designed instrument will also demonstrate variability between different client groups. For example, the Juhnke-Balkin Life Balance Inventory (Davis, Balkin, & Juhnke, 2014) differentiates between clinical and nonclinical subgroups. Sensitivity to change may refer to change over time or change in the extent to which clients may be classified or diagnosed. Instruments that lack sensitivity to change may be limited by broad ranges of categories or ineffective in demonstrating accountability.

The appropriateness of an assessment instrument also is determined by the qualifications/training of the counselor using the assessment instrument.

> Counselors utilize only those testing and assessment services for which they have been trained and are competent.... Counselors responsible for decisions involving individuals or policies that are based on assessment results have a thorough understanding of psychometrics. (ACA, 2014, p. 11)

However, the ethics and legality of the use of assessment instruments by counselors is also determined by test publishers and state counselor licensure laws. There are no uniform guidelines, and differences exist depending on where the instrument is published and the state in which the counselor practices.

Generally, publishing companies for assessment instruments ask for proof of training to verify qualification to use an assessment instrument. Publishing companies often print this information in their catalogues and websites. Counselors should consider their qualifications before purchasing or using an assessment instrument. Each publishing company provides their own system, and counselors must review each company's guidelines to determine qualification. A common system among publishing companies is to identify three types of qualification:

> Level A: This level includes instruments in which there is no specific training necessary to purchase the instrument.
>
> Level B: Some test companies may require test users to have a four-year degree and specific training related to use an assessment. Other companies may require a master's degree and/or specific training with an instrument. In addition, membership to a professional organization or certification/licensure may be required. Appropriate training usually includes course work in assessment ethics, administration, scoring, and interpreting of assessment instruments. Generally, counseling students graduating with a Council for Accreditation of Counseling and Related Educational Programs (CACREP) accredited master's degree in counseling qualify as Level B.
>
> Level C: To accommodate for master's-level psychologists who may not be licensed in some states, Level C often refers to people with Level B training plus licensure or certification and a doctoral degree with formal training in assessment procedures. Some companies will accept specialized training in lieu of a doctorate. In addition, a doctoral degree does not guarantee Level C qualifications. Many instruments require specialized training that is not necessarily provided in a doctoral degree (e.g., intelligence tests such as the Wechsler Intelligence Scales and diagnostic instruments such as the Minnesota Multiphasic Personality Inventory–Restructured Form).

Once a counselor decides to use an assessment instrument, he or she becomes responsible for the delivery of assessment services, including a report and an explanation to the client related to the findings and the decisions made based on the assessment results and the recommendations. "Counselors are responsible for the appropriate application, scoring, interpretation, and use of assessment instruments relevant to the needs of the client, whether they score and interpret such assessments themselves or use technology or other services" (ACA, 2014, p. 11).

Counselors who practice in assessment may receive referrals from other counselors or mental health practitioners (e.g., physicians, social workers) for assessment services. Most often counselors will develop a report related to a clinical interview, selected assessments administered with a rationale for each instrument, and a report of the findings, including standard scores, interpretations, and recommendations. If a client is referred only for assessment services, that does not relieve the counselor of the responsibility of discussing assessment results and implications with the referred client.

When selecting an assessment instrument, counselors should be aware of issues of bias. Most assessment instruments normed on a sample may lack representation from diverse groups. Assessments deemed valid may only be so for a particular group in which the assessment was normed and not across all populations (Sedlacek, 2004). In general, the idea that a measure can be developed and be fair for all groups is misguided (Sedlacek, 1994). Counselors should be wary of using assessment instruments with culturally diverse clients if no norming data are available for the group (ACA, 2014). Indeed, culture can be a factor that affects the problems clients manifest and how they cope. Thus, when using assessment to diagnose, label, or develop a treatment plan for a client, counselors should be aware of the cultural implications related to the assessment process. For example, the *Diagnostic and Statistical Manual of Mental Disorders* (fifth edition) outlines symptoms of depression to include irritability and inattentiveness, which are typical for adolescent males. Thus, counselors may miss this detail and misdiagnose a client as oppositional defiant disorder, as opposed to a depressive disorder. A culturally sensitive counselor will take the client's culture into account when engaging in the assessment process.

Counselors also need to be aware of how instruments are scored and interpreted. Many instruments may be scored by hand. However, hand-scoring can be cumbersome for some complex instruments, and computer-based scoring is available. However, counselors sometimes opt out of using computer-based scoring because of cost. At other times, however, computer-based scoring is the only scoring available. One benefit of computer-based scoring is that counselors have the ability to obtain interpretive reports. Although interpretive reports can be helpful in conceptualizing the results, counselors should use such results with extreme caution. Obviously, computerized results rely solely on the scores of the instrument. The assessment instrument, however, is merely one tool. Without the benefits of a clinical interview, other assessment tools/strategies, or previous counseling history, a computerized assessment report is lacking. Regardless of whether administration and interpretation services are used, the counselor assumes full responsibility for the administration, scoring, and interpretation of the assessment instrument (ACA, 2014).

For this reason, counselors should scrutinize computer-based interpretative results very carefully and only use the results that fit the particular aspects of the client.

Reviewing Assessment Instruments

Because of the ethical and legal implications for using assessment instruments, careful consideration of the properties of an instrument is important. Hence, counselors not only have to be aware of ethical and legal considerations of assessment but also the importance of the psychometric characteristics identified in an instrument. Using instruments that are weak in terms of psychometric quality can lead to serious consequences. Consider Golding's (1985) critique of the Suicide Probability Scale (SPS) in which 70.8% of potential attempters were misclassified as nonsuicidal and 76.9% of nonattempters were misclassified as suicidal. In a nonclinical population, 41.5% of nonattempters were misclassified as suicidal. Extant research related to the SPS continues to be limited and the instrument tends to be highly regarded (Eltz et al., 2007). As an assessment instrument designed to provide insight as to whether a client may be a danger to self or others, decisions based on this instrument could be disastrous. Not only should counselors be able to properly review an assessment instrument in order to be informed consumers, but they should also be reminded of the limitations of assessment instruments in general and never base decisions solely on the results of a single instrument. In an effort to inform counselors on reviewing assessment instruments, two databases are covered next: the *Mental Measurements Yearbook* (MMY) and test critiques from the Association for Assessment and Research Counseling (AARC).

Details of a Mental Measurements Review

The Buros Institute of Mental Measurements (BIMM) publishes the MMY. Currently, there are 19 volumes of the MMY. Not all instruments are evaluated in each volume. Rather, each volume contains selected measures for an evaluation. For a comprehensive list of all known published assessment instruments, counselors should use *Tests in Print*, which is also published by BIMM. *Tests in Print* contains bibliographic information on a published measure and the volume of MMY in which a review may be found. Not all instruments listed in *Test in Print* have a review in MMY. To determine if an assessment instrument was reviewed in MMY, see http://buros.unl.edu/buros/jsp/search.jsp. Although this website provides information related to the status of a review, users must either locate the review using a library database, use a hard copy of MMY, or purchase the review from BIMM.

MMY reviews are usually conducted by two independent reviewers with terminal degrees (i.e., PhD, PsyD, EdD) and have no conflict of interest in the test review. Each review goes through an editorial process before it is accepted, and reviews may be rejected. BIMM identified the purpose of test reviews: (a) to inform test users, (b) to encourage the development of instruments with strong psychometric properties and discourage the use of instruments with poor quality, and (c) to encourage test publishers to fully disclose the strengths, limitations, and possible misuses of assessment instruments (BIMM, 2016a).

A test review from MMY consists of 1,000- to 1,500-word document covering five areas: (a) description, (b) development, (c) technical, (d) commentary, and (e) summary. The beginning of each test review includes basic information of the test including test name, test publisher, type of scores yielded from administration, a brief statement of purpose, the intended population, the test acronym, type of administration (i.e., group or individual), instrument pricing, time to administer the instrument, and authorship. The BIMM (2016b) covers the guidelines for test reviews.

Under the test description, the purpose and intended population are covered in a brief narrative. In addition, reviews include information on test administration, scoring, and intended use of the scores. Usually a more in-depth review of the purpose and use of the scores are provided. Reviews also provide information on the procedures to administer and score the instrument. Many reviews also expand on the intended population and indicate where bias may occur and any inappropriate uses of the instrument. For example, Sandoval's (2007) review of the Draw-A-Person Intellectual Ability Test for Children, Adolescents, and Adults noted that the instrument might be inappropriate for individuals with visual or motor impairments. Such limitations are important to consider when deciding to use an assessment instrument. Other important considerations include reading level of the instrument (assuming the instrument is self-report) and the client's mastery of the language in which the instrument is administered.

A section on test development includes information on underlying theories or operational definitions of the construct measured that led to the origination or evolution of the instrument. Counselors should pay particular attention to both the theoretical underpinnings and the manner in which the construct is operationally defined. For example, the Myers-Briggs Personality Type Indicator is a popular personality instrument used in educational, clinical, career, and industrial settings. The instrument evolved from the personality theory of Carl Jung (Fleenor, 2001). Counselors not familiar with Jung's theory of psychological types may see minimal benefit to using this instrument. Recall that an operational definition is essential to measuring any construct. Be aware of how the construct is being defined for the purposes of the instrument. Such information is important to discern how the findings may be used. For example, professional athletes may be described as brilliant by the way they compete, but would this type of ability translate to scores on an achievement test? Operational definitions provide a clear purpose for what is being measured but also limit the use of the instrument to a specifically defined objective.

The technical section of an MMY review includes information on the process of standardization and the psychometric properties of the instrument. Specifically, information on the norm group is mentioned. Counselors should have an understanding of the age, gender, and cultural characteristics of the sample from which the instrument was normed. An instrument may be limited as a cross-cultural tool if variances in ethnicity, gender, disability status, and so forth were not considered. Often, strengths and limitations of the sample, specifically related to gender and ethnic differences, are identified or noted.

Psychometric considerations in the technical section include statements about the evidence of reliability and validity of the scores in the normative sample and the instrument. Counselors should keep in mind how the instrument is administered and scored when assessing reliability. For example, if the instrument is a behavioral rating scale completed by a counselor, parent, or teacher, a statement about interrater reliability of the scores in the normative sample is appropriate. Self-report inventories often include test–retest reliability on the scores of the normative sample. Tests with multiple forms, such as aptitude and achievement tests used in educational settings, should include an assessment of parallel forms to demonstrate that each version of an instrument is similar in terms of consistency. Most instruments also have a measure of internal consistency, noted by Cronbach's alpha (often referred to as coefficient alpha). Expect each measure of reliability to be separate and distinct from other reliability measures, but a good instrument will have strong reliability coefficients from scores on the normative sample. Often, reviewers provide comments on reliability estimates. For example, reliability estimates for measuring psychotic symptoms in clients tend to be low across most existing instruments. Thus, coefficients in the range of .50 are fairly typical.

With respect to reporting validity, reviewers in the MMY generally focus on the evidence that is presented in testing manuals to determine the degree to which an instrument measures what it is purported to measure. If, for example, an instrument is designed to diagnose or classify individuals or groups, then evidence related to this outcome must be presented. Generally, authors do not provide evidence of all aspects of validity as noted in the *Standards for Educational and Psychological Testing* (AERA et al., 2014). Rather, the focus is on displaying evidence that indicates that the measure provides meaningful information as outlined in the purpose of the instrument and the operational definition of the construct.

Based on the evidence presented in the previous sections, reviewers provide a summary of strengths and weaknesses of the instrument in the commentary section. Information related to the theoretical underpinnings of the instrument and the extent to which the theory is tested is presented. The reviewer may also include a statement related to the consequences (either positive or negative) of using this instrument.

A brief summary section completes an MMY review. This section includes conclusions and recommendations of the test reviewer. Explicit statements from the reviewer related to recommendations or problem areas of the instrument are common in MMY reviews. At times, reviewers may include alternative assessments that they recommend in lieu of the instrument reviewed. Although counselors should pay particular attention to the summary section, the review should be considered holistically. Attention to how the summary is or is not congruent with the evidence presented in the review should be evaluated. Taken as a whole, the MMY review is an important resource for counselors considering using an assessment instrument, as the reviews in MMY tend to be professional and free of bias.

AARC Critiques

Test reviews from the AARC are available to the public from the AARC website: http://aarc-counseling.org/test-reviewsURL. Although many of the tests reviewed on the AARC website are also reviewed by BIMM, the reviews in the MMY are only from tests that are available through test publishers. AARC test reviews may fall into the category of academic assessments and not be available through national test publishers. For example, at the time the Five Factor Wellness Inventory was reviewed by AARC in 2006, MMY had not reviewed the instrument. A review in MMY appeared in the 17th edition (2007). Thus, in addition to more established instruments, AARC may review instruments that are more avant-garde.

An AARC test review is comprised of five main areas: (a) general information, (b) purpose and nature of instrument, (c) practical evaluation, (d) technical considerations, and (e) evaluation. Much of the information in these areas is similar to the information in an MMY review. General information includes similar information in the beginning of an MMY review, including (a) title; (b) author; (c) publisher (if available); (d) date of publication (if available); (e) forms specific to various administration or populations (e.g., child, adolescent, or adult versions); (f) practical features; (g) general type—related to how the instrument is administered (e.g., self-report, rating scale); (h) cost of the instrument, forms, manuals, and so forth; (h) time required to administer; and (i) purpose of the instrument. Keep in mind the importance of the general information. A brief review of the general information provides counselors with purpose, cost, and contact information of the publisher should the counselor wish to find more information or purchase the instrument. From the general information, counselors can determine if the instrument is appropriate, cost-effective, and usable in their practice.

The section on purpose and nature of the instrument provides a more in-depth review of how the instrument is used. Beyond the stated purpose of the instrument in the previous section, this section provides information on test, item, and score descriptions. The types of items, a description of tasks to complete the instrument, and the nature of the scores are discussed. Reviews often include information on the type and number of subscales, the types of scores, and how the scores are interpreted. Unlike the MMY, which is geared toward general assessment practitioners, this section also includes specific information on the instrument relevant to counseling. Counselors may garner an understanding of how the instrument may be useful in clinical, academic, and vocational settings.

The practical evaluation covers information relevant to administering and scoring the instrument, including usefulness of the manual, adequacy of directions, qualifications of the examiner, and scoring provisions. The technical manual of an instrument often includes information about the psychometric qualities of the instrument and, without advanced course work in psychometrics, may be difficult to understand. So the practical evaluation may be helpful for practitioners in highlighting useful aspects of the manual that relate to administration, scoring, and interpretation. Often, the adequacy of the instructions is highlighted in this section, providing counselors with insight into the ease of administration. A statement regarding the qualifications of the examiner is provided, so counselors are aware of the degree to which their training prepares them to administer, score, and interpret the instrument. Scoring provisions are also covered, providing an overview of how the instrument is scored. For example, some instruments cannot be hand-scored because that option is not available. Thus, extra cost may be incurred to score the instrument or use computer-based administration and/or scoring services. Although many instruments can be hand-scored, such scoring can be timely and complex. Counselors often purchase computer-based scoring methods to save time and assist with interpretation.

The technical considerations in an AARC review are similar to the content of what is seen in an MMY review: (a) normative sample, (b) reliability, and (c) validity. Again, statements about the norming process, including descriptive information about the population, are provided. The evidence pertaining to reliability and validity is presented, so counselors can ascertain the degree to which the instrument measures what is implied in a consistent and accurate manner.

The evaluation section of an AARC review includes (a) comments of reviewers and (b) a general evaluation. In the event that the instrument is recently developed, no published reviews may be available. Otherwise, sources are cited such as reviews from MMY. The general evaluation includes comments from the reviewer based on the data and information presented. A critique is provided and an opinion may be rendered about the instrument. AARC reviews provide statements about the efficacy and application of the instrument to assessment practice.

Understanding the Technical Quality of an Instrument

As mentioned, technical manuals may be complex for counselors who do not have advanced training in psychometrics. This section provides information related to understanding the technical quality of an instrument. As noted in the discussion of MMY and AARC reviews, evidence related to representativeness of the normative sample, reliability, and validity are essential in evaluating the technical quality of an instrument.

Evaluating the Normative Sample

Before deciding to use an assessment instrument, counselors should consider the population used to develop the instrument. In other words, do the client(s) being administered this assessment fit into the normative group of the sample? For example, Beck, Steer, and Brown (1996) stated that the Beck Depression Inventory-II (BDI-II) is appropriate for measuring the severity of depression for adolescents and adults 13 years old and above.

Whether the BDI-II is truly a valid measure for this large age range is dependent on sampling groups used in developing the instrument. Beck et al. indicated in the *BDI-II Manual* that two outpatient samples were used. The first sample was a sample of 500 outpatients from four different outpatient clinics. Clients who were administered the BDI-II ranged from 13 to 86 years old with a mean age of 37.20 ($SD = 15.91$). Ninety-one percent of the sample was identified as White with the remaining 9% as African American, Asian American, or Latino/a. The second sample consisted of 120 college students from Canada with a mean age of 19.58 ($SD = 1.84$).

Based on this sample description, counselors may have difficulty discerning whether the BDI-II is appropriate for their practice. Clearly, the majority of participants were adults over the age of 18. So, without knowing how many adolescents received the BDI-II, evidence for the appropriateness of the BDI-II with clients as young as 13 years old is limited. In addition, data related to minority responses on the BDI-II are also limited. Counselors may wish to examine research articles in which the BDI-II was used with minority participants to evaluate the appropriateness of the instrument across non-White clients. Endorsement of depressive symptoms may differ across various ethnic groups. However, Carmody (2005) administered the BDI-II to 502 college students, 41% of which were ethnic minority students. Carmody concluded that the BDI-II is appropriate as a measure of depression for students of diverse ethnicity. Numerous psychometric instruments are normed using a college student population. Limitations related to the overreliance of this demographic should be noted to avoid overgeneralizing results for a client that are based on a normed sample that has little in common with the client. In addition to the technical manuals, tests reviews usually include this information, so counselors can easily ascertain whether the instrument is appropriate for a specific client or client population. Although test manuals may not be all inclusive with respect to the development of the test and the normative sample, research using well-established instruments is quite common. Counselors should actively seek out articles about an instrument when a gap in the development is apparent in order to determine if the gap was addressed.

Evaluating Reliability Evidence of an Instrument

When evaluating reliability, counselors should consider the type of reliability reported and the magnitude of the coefficients. Reliability coefficients range from zero to 1, with coefficients from .70 and above considered adequate evidence for measuring accuracy and consistency of an instrument. Reliability coefficients should be interpreted. Keep in mind the types of reliability one might expect to see in a study. The most common reliability coefficient reported is internal consistency, often reported as Cronbach's alpha or coefficient alpha. This reliability coefficient is easily computed with statistical software and is used to demonstrate that the scale meets a standard of measuring a construct consistently using multiple items. Larger sample sizes are needed to demonstrate internal consistency.

If an instrument has different forms, such as in many aptitude and achievement tests (e.g., SAT, ACT, GRE, NCE), then evidence indicating consistency over different administrations of the instrument is important. Strong reliability coefficients, in this case a positive correlation between the alternate forms (e.g., r = .80), are expected.

Recall that authors of instruments may also provide evidence of stability over time through test–retest. Essentially, a strong correlation (i.e., .70 or above) is expected when an assessment is administered and then administered again a short time later. For example, Beck et al. (1996) reported the BDI-II has a test–retest reliability coefficient of .93, indicating a very strong relationship between an administration of the BDI-II and a second administration one week later. When evaluating test–retest reliability, consider how much time lapsed between administrations. Also, understand that not all instruments may be evaluated for test–retest reliability, particularly instruments that are time sensitive.

Interrater reliability can be an important consideration for instruments that use a rating scale. Essentially, test developers want to establish a high correlation among practitioners who use the instrument. Thus, if two counselors are using a behavior rating scale to evaluate a child, an instrument with high interrater reliability will show similarity between the scores of the counselors. As with other measures of reliability, this could be ascertained through examining correlation coefficients. In this case, however, rating scales completed by multiple examiners would be correlated.

In summary, interpreting reliability is an important consideration. When reliability coefficients fall below .70, that does not mean the instrument should not be used. Rather, counselors should keep in mind what scales are prone to low reliability estimates and be careful to evaluate the client in these areas. Essentially, counselors need to ask, "Are these the scores I expect for this client?" If the answer is "no," then the counselor needs to consider whether the psychometric characteristics of the instrument are appropriate, the administration is valid, or the assessment instrument is providing new information about the client not previously considered. Keep in mind not all constructs can be measured with a high level of accuracy and consistency. Psychosis is one construct in which scores have low reliability across many different measures.

Evaluating Validity Evidence of an Instrument

As mentioned previously, rarely will all five evidences of validity (evidence of test content, response process, internal structure, relations to other variables, and consequences of testing) be discussed in a technical manual. In addition, the statistical methods used are usually quite sophisticated, which may make counselors without advanced knowledge of psychometrics and statistics feel inadequate about interpreting such information. One point to keep in mind is that nearly all of these procedures are correlational in nature. Specifically, authors of instruments tend to demonstrate five criteria:

1. There is a theoretical framework that guided the development of this instrument (evidence of test content). When reviewing the technical manual or instrument reviews, the theory driving the development of the items should be clearly explained. The author(s) identify how the tasks involved in the assessment instrument measure the intended construct.

2. The authors attempt to demonstrate that the instrument measures the theoretical structure by examining the intercorrelations of items. When an instrument has separate subscales, such as the Crisis Stabilization Scale or the Behavior Assessment System for Children, then some demonstration of how the items correlate on the subscale is in order. This is usually done through factor analysis, in which the extent of how each item loads on each subscale is reported. Generally, factor loadings of .40 for each item on a subscale are considered adequate. Sometimes we will see an item load on more than one subscale of the instrument, and then the author needs to justify the rationale for placing a particular item with a selected subscale. When this type of evidence is not reported, an instrument is likely suspect in terms of validity. Such analyses require large sample sizes, usually 5 to 10 participants per item.
3. The authors evaluate the relationship between the instrument and another instrument(s) that measures the same or similar construct. Once again, this is demonstrated through the use of correlations, in which each participant is administered two assessment instruments and the results between the instruments are correlated. Higher correlations demonstrate stronger convergent evidence, or that both instruments are measuring the same intended construct.
4. The authors evaluate the relationship between the instrument and another instrument(s) that measures a different construct. In other words, evidence is provided that the instrument is not measuring a similar yet separate construct. For example, in the development of the Crisis Stabilization Scale, a relationship between meeting goals related to coping and commitment to follow-up for adolescents in crisis and a decrease in their symptoms, as measured by the Target Symptom Rating scale, was established (Balkin, 2014; Balkin, Leicht, Sartor, & Powell, 2011).
5. Evidence related to the consequences of testing may be difficult to demonstrate. Extant literature is limited in terms of how to demonstrate such evidence (Goodwin & Leech, 2003). However, some acknowledgement of the strengths and limitations of the assessment tool is appropriate.

Although the *Standards for Educational and Psychological Testing* (2014) are explicit in terms of the types of evidence for validity, many authors who developed instruments prior to 2014 do not comply with these standards. Counselors should evaluate the type of validity evidence provided to ascertain the appropriateness of a selected assessment tool.

Understanding Factors That May Affect Performance

Even if an instrument is deemed to have strong evidence of reliability and validity, external factors may influence the performance of a client on a particular measure. Assessment may be bound by time and context. In other words, an underlying assumption in the assessment process is that the performance measured at a particular moment in time is representative of how the individual would perform generally. However, this is not always the case. An otherwise high-achieving student who takes the SAT when sick with a 102° fever may have an uncharacteristically poor performance on a rather high-stakes exam. The same problems could occur when administering other types of psychosocial instruments, such as measuring anxiety when a client has a particularly good or trying day.

Testing conditions can also be a factor. Clients often receive several instruments at one time, resulting in test fatigue. Instruments administered at the beginning of the sequence may be more accurate in measuring the desired construct than instruments at the end of the sequence. The opposite may also be true. The client could be less defensive at the end of the process than at the beginning. In addition, consider the environment in which the test is administered. Is the environment suitable for an extended period of time to complete an assessment procedure?

The client's ability to complete the tasks is an important factor to consider. Does the client possess the reading ability to understand the instructions and items? If the instrument is timed, does accommodation need to be provided? Are there any interpersonal factors (e.g., disability, medical condition) that interfere with the administration or completion of the assessment? Again, ongoing research on specific assessment instruments is often available, and counselors may need to consult the literature to identify the conditions of accommodation and alternate interpretations.

Review of Assessments in This Text

Many of the instruments referenced this text may be reviewed in MMY, and some of them can be found on the AARC website. In general, the instruments are widely established as assessment tools for measuring constructs of interest in counseling.

In our case examples throughout the text, we provide an overview of assessments that may be used with clients, such as assessments related to intelligence and ability, career, personality, substance abuse, and so forth. Keep in mind that instruments designed to measure constructs across numerous age groups throughout the lifespan may not always be appropriate. Considering the developmental gap that is covered between early adolescence to older adulthood, instruments that claim to be geared toward such a vast age range likely fall short in terms of normative sampling procedures unless careful, representative sampling methods were used, which is often the case with intelligence tests. Careful thought should go into what assessments are appropriate for a given population. We end this chapter with this final thought: an assessment instrument is a tool. When attempting to understand a client, counselors should use all of the tools available. In other words, assessment instruments should never be used as a sole basis for understanding a client. The clinical interview, ongoing counseling sessions, case notes, and counselor intuition are all important factors that should be used in addition to assessment instruments. A score on a test should never be used alone but rather as additional data and an important resource for understanding a client.

7

Conducting an Initial Interview

> ## Objectives
> 1. Identify the purpose and scope of the clinical interview.
> 2. Address the advantages of using structured interview approaches versus unstructured interviews.
> 3. Identify the elements of the CLISD-PA Model (Juhnke, 2002).
> 4. Identify essential elements of the clinical interview.
> 5. Examine specific areas of interest related to substance abuse.
> 6. Apply the concepts of the clinical interview to the case study and various clinical settings.

Purposes of the Initial Interview

Previous chapters have emphasized the standardized nature of assessment. In other words, the development and use of standardized assessment instruments quite often are regimented, with specific procedures in place to make sure that the assessment process is not compromised and accurate and meaningful information is conveyed. However, to describe the counseling process as regimented and standardized is inaccurate. Juhnke (2008) suggested assessment also implies a stochastic process, that is, understanding and preparing for random processes that occur throughout assessment in counseling. For example, the focus of this chapter is the clinical interview—a process of gathering relevant information about the client in order to conceptualize the client accurately, identify a treatment plan and/or therapeutic goals, and plan for appropriate interventions. In the midst of gathering such information, what happens if the client, say a 14 year-old female, identifies a past history of sexual abuse? Suddenly, the current process may be put on hold, as the present disclosure must be dealt with, including gathering different information, assessing client safety, and making a mandated report.

The type of information disclosed by the client may change the direction of the clinical interview.

The clinical interview most likely presents the first time the counselor meets with the client. Counseling skills are engrained in the assessment process. Although accurate intake information is essential, so is the establishment of rapport and initiation of the counseling process. Counselors often enter into an initial session with a plan to obtain specific information related to the client's presenting problem and relevant history. The type of information sought by the counselor in the initial interview often follows a general procedure, but counselors should be aware of the stochastic nature of the assessment process (Juhnke, 2008), as issues may arise that move the counselor and client in a different direction than initially anticipated. Clients may even get frustrated if the counselor's preoccupation of a specific issue is not reflective of the client's goals or desire toward further processing. Counselors should keep an open mind to the type of information presented in the counseling process. Owen (2008) found that counselors are more likely to ask questions that confirm their initial impressions about a client as opposed to questions that might contradict or disaffirm such impressions. Thus, counselors should be proactive in asking questions that challenge their initial assumptions about a client in order to identify potential issues and rule out any differential diagnostic implications. For example, if a counselor believes an adolescent male has attention deficit disorder because of the presence of low frustration tolerance, impulsivity, and inattentiveness, the counselor should also make sure there are not additional indicators of unstable mood that could indicate a mood disorder.

Scope of the Initial Interview

The initial interview can broadly be categorized into two distinct areas: the psychosocial history and the mental status exam (MSE). The purpose of the psychosocial history is to identify relevant present issues and past history. Vacc and Juhnke (1997) advocated for using a structured interview format to encourage accuracy, consistency, and meaningfulness of the information gathered. Unstructured interviews may be the least trustworthy method of gathering information because of erratic questions and various methods of gathering information, which may cause response variance—that is, a client answering a question differently based on the various ways the question is asked. For example, a client may respond differently when asked, "How often do you drink?" versus "How many drinks do you have in a given week?" In the first case, the client might respond, "I drink one or two times per week." In the latter case the client might respond, "Depending on what I am drinking, I usually drink until I feel drunk." Clearly the responses are different despite the similarities between the questions. As mentioned earlier, counselors tend to ask questions that confirm their initial impressions about a client (Owens, 2008), and this can lead to inappropriate decisions made on behalf of the client by the counselor. Counselors need to balance the stochastic nature of assessment (Juhnke, 2008) with the need to gather standard and pertinent information. According to the *Standards for Assessment in Mental Health Counseling* (Association for Assessment in Counseling and Education & American Mental Health Counselors Association, 2009):

> Mental health counselors use structured and semi-structured clinical interviews and qualitative assessment procedures (e.g., role playing, life line assessments, direct and indirect observation). Mental health counselors are able to:
> 1. Define the differences and similarities between structured and semi-structured clinical interviews.
> 2. Describe the advantages and disadvantages of structured and semi-structured clinical interviews in practice.
> 3. Use both structured and semi-structured clinical interviews as a means to develop goal setting and treatment intervention plans.
> 4. Understand the advantages and disadvantages of qualitative assessment procedures.
> 5. Apply the concepts of continuous assessment and wraparound services. (p. 1)

The clinical interview is the primary element that will lead both the counselor and the client to establishing the client problem areas, determining the need for additional assessments, and developing and implementing a treatment plan/counseling strategy. Juhnke (2002) developed a four-tiered system, referred to as the Clinical Interview, Standardized Specialty, Drug Detection, Personality Assessment (CLISD-PA) model. The first two tiers of the CLISD-PA begin with a clinical interview of the client and his or her significant other. Once the clinical interviews are concluded, additional questions or concerns may be evident. For example, perhaps after interviewing an adolescent and a parent, the counselor notes some inconsistencies between what the client self-disclosed and what the parent reported. Although a parent may report that the adolescent client is noncompliant and unruly, the adolescent client could report that the parent is rigid and unreasonable. At this point in time, additional data may be necessary.

The third tier of the CLISD-PA includes the administration of standardized specialty instruments and drug detection devices, which might be helpful in providing additional information about the client and how to weight the disclosures from the interviews. Standardized specialty instruments might include instruments that provide some additional information on a specified attribute, such as the Beck Depression Inventory-II (BDI-II), the Substance Abuse Subtle Scale Inventory-4. If during the clinical interview, the counselor identified no past history of depression and substance use but that the adolescent client recently experienced a drop in grades, appeared easily angered or frustrated, and lost interest in previously enjoyed activities, the counselor may opt to administer a BDI-II, the adolescent version of the Substance Abuse Subtle Scale Inventory (SASSI-A2), and/or the Reynolds Adolescent Adjustment Screening Inventory to evaluate areas of anger control, antisocial behavior, emotional distress, and self-concept. Such instruments may be helpful in assessing the nature of the behavioral change in an adolescent client. If the client revealed on the SASSI-A2 that he or she is using substances, then additional drug detection tests may be warranted, especially if the client is not forthcoming.

The fourth tier includes the administration of personality assessments, such as the Minnesota Multiphasic Personality Inventory-2–Restructured Form and the Millon Clinical Multiaxial Inventory-IV. Such instruments may be helpful in identifying clinical and personality disorders, respectively. Often these instruments include child and/or adolescent versions. These instruments also provide insight into personality and character traits. Such instruments can be time-consuming and expensive. Many of these instruments require specialized training or advanced course work/degrees (i.e., PhD). However, when counselors require more information about a client because of the client's divergent behavior or cognitive processes, or when the clinical interview and subsequent measures have not yielded a helpful or conclusive conceptualization of the client, personality assessments can be a valuable tool.

Essential Elements of a Psychosocial History

As evidenced from the CLISD-PA model (Juhnke, 2002), the initial session is a comprehensive process. Initial sessions, in fact, may be longer than a typical 50-minute counseling session, so counselors should plan accordingly. As mentioned previously, the clinical interview sets the stage for identifying presenting problems, obtaining relevant history, and determining if further assessments procedures are warranted. With this in mind, we turn our attention to gathering a psychosocial history. These elements include the following: (a) presenting problem, (b) relevant history, (c) mental status, (d) medical history, (e) family history/issues, (f) social support, (g) educational/occupational/economic issues, and (h) cultural/spiritual concerns.

Presenting Problem

Consider how the initiation of the counseling relationship begins. Clients may complete a standard intake form, complete with insurance information and statements about the Health Insurance Portability and Accountability Act of 1996 and confidentiality. A counselor may begin with a brief introduction and a restatement about confidentiality and safety for the client. At this point, the client may be asked any number of questions to begin the process, such as

- "What brings you here today?"
- "What would you like to get out of counseling?"
- "Where would you like to start?"
- "If you were to walk out of this session feeling better or different from when you walked in, what would be different? How would things have changed?"

The possibilities of opening the session to begin a dialogue with the client are endless, and so the counselor must choose words carefully and consider what questions will assist clients in presenting the nature of why they are seeking services, as well as fit the counselor's theoretical orientation. The nature of the presenting problem will likely guide treatment planning, therapeutic goals, and outcomes of counseling, in addition to providing justification for a diagnosis should one be necessary. Counselors should consider various methods that present the opportunity to identify and differentiate the presenting problem the client presents.

Relevant History

Although the role of past events may be weighted differently depending on the counselor's theoretical orientation, an understanding of how past events relate to present distress is pertinent, as is obtaining an accurate history of past counseling experiences. Discussion of past experiences in counseling may shed light on issues important to the client and past approaches to counseling that led to more or less meaningful experiences in the counseling process. It is always helpful to know what has worked for the client and what has not worked. In addition, counselors should be aware of informed consent processes in order to obtain documents from the client's counseling history, such as contacting previous or current providers.

Mental Status Exam

The MSE is a component of the initial interview that provides information related to client functioning. The MSE can be instrumental in identifying baseline status of the client, diagnosing, treatment planning, and justifying intervention to stakeholders and third-party payors. The MSE is a combination of objective and subjective data, based on the counselor's observations and information provided by the client (Polanski & Hinkle, 2000). Six elements are considered when assessing mental status: (a) appearance, attitude, and activity; (b) mood and affect; (c) speech and language; (d) thought process, thought content, and perception; (e) cognition; and (f) insight and judgment. These elements are addressed more specifically later in the chapter.

Medical History

Medical history may be relevant when dealing with a multitude of disorders such as depression, addiction, and disordered eating. From a diagnostic perspective, counselors need to be careful when medical issues are disclosed. Medical issues may preclude the diagnosis of many psychiatric disorders and therefore need to be considered in the assessment process.

Family History/Issues

Depending on the counselor's view of family interventions and systems theory (i.e., couples, marriage, and family counseling) and the client's presentation, family issues may be the primary presenting problem when a client initiates counseling. Family issues may pertain to significant events, such as divorce or death, as well as ongoing conflicts and sources of dysfunction (e.g., addiction, infidelity). Counselors practicing couples, marriage, and family counseling should be able to "conduct structured clinical interviews, obtain an accurate biopsychosocial history and assess intergenerational dynamics and contextual factors related to clients' family of origin (e.g., genograms)" (Association for Assessment in Counseling and Education & International Association for Marriage and Family Counselors, 2010, p. 2).

Social Support

Social support includes an assessment of the client's support system, most often outside of the home environment. Support systems may not be healthy and may be a contributing factor to the presenting problem. For example, an adolescent who engages in antisocial behavior (e.g., drug use, truancy, criminal activity) may associate with other adolescents who engage in similar behavior. Often, changes in social support are important to making overall changes to the presenting problem.

Educational/Occupational/Economic Issues

Educational, occupational, and economic issues predominate child, adolescent, and adult lifestyles. Therefore, problems in these areas often motivate individuals to seek counseling services. Adjustment problems, failure, and stress in occupational and academic settings may be presenting problems or additional issues that require intervention or processing with the client. Educational delays, past diagnoses, and testing should be noted. Economic issues may be challenging, especially when society exhibits bias toward the underprivileged and homeless. In addition, clients with limited economic resources may have difficulty obtaining necessary services, such as mental health care, medication, and medical care.

Cultural/Spiritual Concerns

In the *ACA Code of Ethics*, the American Counseling Association (ACA; 2014) included a guideline under Section E: Evaluation, Assessment, and Interpretation that "counselors recognize that culture affects the manner in which clients' problems are defined" (p. 11). Counselors have an ethical obligation to be competent with multicultural issues related to assessment and in the clinical interview. Understanding the implications of "age, color, culture, disability, ethnic group, gender, race, language preference, religion, spirituality, sexual orientation, and socioeconomic status" (ACA, 2014, p. 12) in the assessment process may affect the counselor's conceptualization of the client. As a result, counselors should employ questions that gauge clients' attitudes toward their perceptions of culture and any implications for presenting issues.

Summary

The summary includes a general statement of the overall assessment process, highlighting any issues of concern and providing a general focus of future counseling sessions. Often counseling goals and preliminary plans will be identified in the summary section, as well as a prognosis for the client.

Determining Mental Status

The MSE was adapted from psychiatry as a way to assess a client's overall level of functioning. In this respect, the MSE is, at the very least, a semi-structured component of a clinical interview. The domains represented in the MSE are well documented (Polanski & Hinkle, 2000; Trzepacz & Baker, 1993; Whiston, 2017), and although the domains may be standardized, the manner in which the counselor gathers the information is more subjective and may vary because of varying degrees of rapport established with the client. The MSE may be an integral part of the clinical interview and/or diagnostic process for clients. Establishing rapport is important to gathering information from the client, and the MSE is not an exception (Polanski & Hinkle, 2000). Third-party payors, in particular, may be interested in data collected from the MSE. Polanski and Hinkle suggested that counselors be sure to document each of the noted areas of the MSE, provide quotes from the client to support findings related to appropriate elements of the MSE (e.g., mood, language, thought content), and identify any issues in the MSE that support diagnosis.

Appearance, Attitude, and Activity

Dress, cleanliness, and overall grooming may be considered in appearance, as well as more objective traits such as health and disability status. Appearance may also be tied to development, as how clients present themselves may provide insight into their personality (e.g., disheveled, unorganized, seductive, uncaring). Appearance may relate to the manner in which a client is aware of his or her own feelings, thoughts, concept of self, and overall mood. Thus, appearance can relate to a client's diagnosis. However, counselors would be wise not to confuse appearance with other sociocultural factors such as socioeconomic status and religious identity. Notes the counselor makes related to appearance may generally be identified as objective. The counselor may identify a subjective intent of a client appearance but then support it with objective criteria. For example:

> The client is a 35-year-old White male. The client appeared disheveled. Hair was uncombed. The client did not appear clean. The client's shirt was tucked and untucked erratically, and the client sat with poor posture, legs straight out, and poor eye contact.

The attitude of a client may be assessed through observations and disclosures related to his or her motivation and understanding of counseling and the clinical interview. For adults, in particular, many of these clients approach counseling voluntarily. However, in many circumstances, adults may be court ordered, such as in court-mandated counseling (e.g., domestic violence, driving under the influence [DUI]), and therefore adults may approach counseling less willingly. Children and adolescents may show resistance as well and may either be unwilling participants or in denial of the need for services. The assessment of attitude, therefore, may be an indication of client motivation and amiability toward counseling. Counselors should remember to focus on both verbal and nonverbal behaviors when assessing attitude. For instance, a client's disclosure of a desire for counseling can be somewhat superficial when incongruent nonverbal behaviors accompany the disclosure. "Yes, I really want some help" may come across as insincere with the type of body language displayed in the previous scenario.

Activity is an indication of the client's ability to control physical movements. Activity may refer to behaviors that are purposeful (e.g., stomping feet to demonstrate anger, yelling, laughing, crying), subconscious (e.g., biting fingernails), unconscious (e.g., shaking, fidgeting), and/or involuntary (e.g. motor tics, stuttering). As with appearance and attitude, activity may have diagnostic implications (e.g., obsessive-compulsive disorder, attention deficit disorder, depression). Activity may also be relevant to features more medically related, such as traumatic brain injury, Alzheimer's, and Parkinson's. Counselors should keep in mind the broad array of activity levels, which may be overactive (e.g., mania), delayed (e.g., Alzheimer's), or nonexistent (e.g., catatonia).

Mood and Affect

Mood and affect are related terms but refer to distinct processes. Mood refers to an internal state with six categories: (a) euthymic (normal), dysphoric (dissatisfied feeling), euphoric (elated or over satisfied feeling), angry, anxious, and apathetic (Polanski & Hinkle, 2000; Trzepacz & Baker, 1993). Affect refers to an external state, in which feelings are overtly expressed. Whereas mood is assessed generally through client disclosure, affect may be observed through both verbal and nonverbal behaviors. For example, body language and overt behaviors such as laughing or crying provide an indication of affect. Generally, affect can be assessed across two dimensions: range and intensity (Polanski & Hinkle, 2000). During an interview, counselors should note if affect changes and the breadth of affect demonstrated during the session. A client may move from crying to laughing within the same session. Intensity may be evaluated by noting the degree to which a particular emotional state is demonstrated and the client's ability to function within that emotional state.

Speech and Language

Language refers to the understanding and communication of verbal and nonverbal expressions. Speech refers to the pattern or rhythm of the expressed ideas (Polanski & Hinkle, 2000). Therefore, during a MSE the counselor pays particular attention to the content and manner of expression. Polanski and Hinkle noted three areas of common deficits in speech and language:

1. Derailment, also known as loose associations, refers to the expression of unrelated ideas to the counselor, although the disconnected ideas may appear to make sense from the perspective of the client. Two common types of derailment include flight of ideas and tangential speech. In flight of ideas, the client uses a word or phrase to identify another idea that is weakly associated. For example, "I went on a date. It was Tuesday. Tuesday night is taco night. I love tacos." For tangential speech, the client may make responses to the counselor that appear unrelated to the inquiry:

    COUNSELOR: "What is your relationship like with your parents?"
    CLIENT: "I like chocolate milk."

2. Poverty of speech refers to the absence or delay of speech. Clients exhibiting poverty of speech may be more constrained. For example, clients with depression may be less likely to engage in spontaneous discourse, not because of resistance but rather because of an inability to converse resulting from delayed cognitive and/or motor processes. In addition to delayed speech, clients may also experience increased latency, an increase in response time during discourse (Polanski & Hinkle, 2000).
3. Pressured speech refers to an increased rate of verbalizations, often noted during a manic episode. Clients with pressured speech both speak and respond more rapidly, creating discourse that may seem tangential or even incoherent. However, pressured speech is specific to the rate of speech and the decreased response time during discourse, often referred to as decreased latency (Polanski & Hinkle, 2000).

Thought Process, Thought Content, and Perception

Hallucinations and delusions may result in perceptual distortions. Hallucinations refer to the presence of phenomena that are not actually being experienced. Hallucinations may be categorized as an aspect of sensory perception: auditory, visual, tactile, olfactory, and gustatory (Polanski & Hinkle, 2000). For mental health issues, auditory and visual hallucinations are more common (American Psychiatric Association, 2013). Delusions, like hallucinations, also affect perception but are characterized as only beliefs about a situation. Beliefs tend to be unrealistic and also unaltered when confronted. A client is identified as ego-dystonic when an awareness of the distorted perceptions is present; a lack of awareness of the distorted perceptions is ego-syntonic (Trzepacz & Baker, 1993).

Cognition

Assessing cognition requires the counselor to be aware of the client's clarity in thought and orientation. On a subjective level, the counselor should be able to determine if clients are thinking clearly and making sense about their situation. A more objective manner to determine cognition is to assess orientation. Orientation refers to the client's awareness of person, place, time, and situation.

Counselors should be careful about assessing orientation, as clients who are completely oriented, documented as *oriented x 4*, may find such questions as either ridiculous because they are completely lucid or frustrating because of their awareness of being unable to answer questions that they should know. For example, asking a client "What is your name? Where are you? What is the date?" may feel more like an interrogation as opposed to a therapeutic interview meant to build rapport. Rather, counselors should see if the client is able to introduce him- or herself through social cues. To see if the client is aware of his or her situation, try asking, "What brings you here today?" Keep in mind that lucid individuals frequently have to check their calendar to know the exact date, but knowing the month, day, and who the president is may be appropriate lines of questioning to assess orientation.

Insight and Judgment

Clients often have difficulty identifying how their total behavior (i.e., feelings, cognitions, actions; Glasser, 1999) leads to their current situation, which is a lack of insight. How insight or a lack thereof leads to decisions (healthy or unhealthy) is the basis for judgment. Counselors often refer to clients as having good or poor insight into their situation or problem. Often, clients may identify beliefs related to their situation or have expectations related to their behavior that are unrealistic. For example, adolescent clients may feel that it is okay to get high because they are not hurting anyone. This is known as poor reality testing—when a client identifies unrealistic expectations related to behaviors. Poor reality testing may be a result of internalizing or externalizing problems. For example, adolescents who blame their disruptive behavior in school on a teacher may be externalizing their behavior—the problems being experienced are the result of someone or something else. Clients may also accept responsibility or blame for a problem, known as internalizing, such as a child who identifies guilty feelings over a parent's drinking.

Factors Affecting Mental Status

In our discussion of mental status, focus was placed on alterations of mental status issues. Associated problems with mental status may occur as a result of such psychiatric diagnoses as mood, psychotic, and anxiety disorders or disorders normally diagnosed in childhood and adolescence. Counselors should be thorough and cautious in assuming the reason for deviations in mental status. Mental status may be compromised from substance use, mismanaged medication, or organic issues (e.g., traumatic brain injury, stroke, infections [delirium]). When evaluating a client whose mental status appears compromised, the counselor may wish to obtain consent from the client to have a family member or other significant person present to confirm history, problems, and so forth.

Clients whose mental status appears compromised may indeed be a danger to self or others. Even if the client is not identifying suicidal thoughts, he or she may not be able to engage in independent living activities (e.g., cooking, cleaning, grooming). Counselors need to carefully address the disposition of the client when mental status is compromised. Does the client require 24-hour supervision? Is the client able to function adequately and responsibly? Who is available should the client's situation further deteriorate? In cases such as this, a referral to a crisis residence and a brief in-patient hospitalization for the purposes of observation, assessment, and stabilization may be necessary.

Types of Intake Data

The clinical interview, as well as other intake information, may assume a standardized or nonstandardized format. In a nonstandardized format, counselors may gather information and focus on issues that arise at the moment. The advantage of the nonstandardized format is that the client drives the focus of the initial session more so than a prearranged questionnaire. However, the potential of missing information or failure to obtain important history or presenting issues may be problematic with a nonstandardized format. Advantages of using a standardized format include consistency of information obtained, ability to manage information across various settings, and liability protection. Vacc and Juhnke (1997) noted that nonstandardized interviews are the least trustworthy assessment procedure because of the variability in the type and quality of the information gathered. Structured interviews provide more consistency in gathering information. Counselors are less likely to omit or or skip important aspects of the client's presenting issues. Keep in mind that many third-party payors require an initial diagnosis and supporting documentation after the initial session for the client to be eligible to receive services. Many insurance companies use the right to refuse payment for services if the insurance company views the services as unnecessary. Standardized interviews help ensure that counselors collect adequate information to warrant care.

As counselors have the responsibility to employ techniques based on "rigorous research methodologies" (ACA, 2014, p. 8), standardized assessments allow for counselors to track information obtained from their clients in a manner that is consistent, comprehensive, and ethical. Consistent information allows counselors to evaluate who they treat, the types and severity of issues encountered, and the strategies that appear effective. Standardized assessments may be more useful in identifying baseline data to track client progress. For community-based mental health centers and hospitals, data may be more easily recorded and reported to stakeholders, such as state departments of health or accrediting agencies.

When counselors collect information consistently, and the information gathered is what is supported in best-practice literature, counselors protect themselves. Counselors need to be able to explain and defend why they practice in a particular manner. When the nature of the practice is ethical, thorough, and consistent, the counselor is less likely to be held liable for problems that may occur as a result of the type of services rendered.

So far, we have identified and explained the psychosocial history and MSE as primary components of the clinical interview. However, other types of data are essential in order to place information garnered from the clinical interview into proper context. Basic demographic data should be noted, including sex, age, ethnicity, and level of education. Such information provides context into present problems and development. In regard to children, for example, counselors should pay particular attention to level of education and age, as discrepancies may need to be investigated with respect to any educational delays, learning disabilities, past evaluations, and so forth.

Direct questions related to the client's living situation and past history are essential. Counselors should document with whom the client lives, past family issues (e.g., separation, divorce, remarriage), and any history of abuse, whether physical, emotional, or sexual abuse. In the case of abuse, counselors must document if a report was filed and the outcome of the report/investigation. Further follow-up from the counselor may be warranted. Essentially, counselors should assess the safety of the client's living situation.

Not only is the past psychosocial/medical history of the client important, but so is the past psychosocial/medical history of family members. Issues of suicide, abuse, addiction, and psychiatric diagnoses are important indicators of potential problems with clients. Genetic predispositions for addiction, mood, and anxiety disorders are well documented (American Psychiatric Association, 2013). In addition, such information may provide insight into the home environment. Processing coping strategies to help an adolescent avoid drugs and alcohol may be more complicated if drug and alcohol use/abuse is in the home environment.

Particular attention to problems and symptoms should be noted. The American Psychiatric Association emphasized impairment as criteria for diagnoses. The frequency, duration, and severity of symptoms should be noted, as well as the effect that such symptoms have on the client's life. In the case of substance abuse, much more information is necessary.

Substance Use/Abuse Intake

The Center for Behavioral Health Statistics and Quality (2015) reported 27 million individuals aged 12 years old and above used illicit drugs in the past month, representing 10.2% of the population. Substance use and abuse represents one of the most common diagnoses encountered by counselors. As a result, knowledge of interviewing strategies related to substance abuse and dependence is essential.

One particular area of difficulty for counselors conducting an interview in which substance abuse is apparent is the level of the client's denial. Individuals who abuse drugs/alcohol demonstrate recurrent use and often refuse to acknowledge the harmful effects or problems resulting from the substance use. Counselors may need to ask and re-ask questions in different ways in order to obtain informative or truthful responses. In particular, counselors need to avoid close-ended questions such as "Have you ever tried to quit?" and opt for more open-ended questions such as "Tell me about a time when you tried to cut down on your use."

TABLE 7.1 Substance Abuse Assessment

Current use:
Substance abuse history:

Type	Drug Name	Age Started	Duration of Use	Frequency of Use	Amount Used	Route	Last Used
Cannabis							
Cocaine							
Other stimulants							
Hallucinogenics/ narcotics							
Depressants							
Inhalants							
Alcohol							

Age of first drink:

Age of first drug use:

What problems do you have related to your drinking/using?

How have you attempted to reduce your use or quit using drugs/alcohol?

Counselors may wish to evaluate substance use by noting the types of substances used. Counselors should evaluate each type of drug, including alcohol, nicotine, opiates, amphetamines, inhalants, marijuana, hallucinogens, and prescription drugs. In noting each substance used, counselors may document the frequency of use, duration, and route (e.g. injected, smoked, snorted, swallowed). How the substances are obtained is also important. With respect to substance dependence, the time spent to acquire, use, and recover from the effects of the substance is a noted criteria for dependency (American Psychiatric Association, 2013). Counselors should note patterns of use and include a history of when the substance use began. Consequences and legal problems should be documented, keeping in mind that many clients will deny that the substance abuse plays a role in such problems. Often, clients may externalize (i.e., blame others or events) rather than accept responsibility or admit to the role substance abuse is playing in the present circumstances. Rationalization and denial of substance abuse problems are viewed as part of the nature of addiction. Table 7.1 serves as an example of a standardized form for substance abuse assessment that may be incorporated into the clinical interview.

Applying Counseling Skills to the Interview Process

Throughout the counseling process, implementation of the core conditions (i.e., unconditional positive regard, empathic understanding, congruence; Rogers, 1957) is essential, and the clinical interview is no exception. Although not every counselor may ascribe to Roger's theoretical framework, other counseling theories uphold similar frameworks. Glasser (1965) identified *involvement* as essential to the therapeutic relationship. Other theoreticians from complimentary theories (e.g., Adlerian, existentialism, cognitive-behavioral) include a collaborative relationship. Counselor–client rapport is a necessary therapeutic condition for gathering information from the client. The mere fact that a client will sit down with a complete stranger and begin to disclose highly personal information is worthy of respect for the courage and risk that accompanies this scenario.

In the traditional counseling setting, attending skills are essential to rapport building. However, the initial interview requires documentation to support the need for services, develop a treatment plan, address disposition, and establish case notes. As a result, counselors need to be able to document information, which may interfere with the traditional attending skills.

Counselors may wish to consider the assessment environment. How can the counselor communicate helpfulness, build rapport, establish comfort and confidentiality, and document the necessary details of the clinical interview? Helpful attending techniques may include sitting across from the client and writing on a note pad or clipboard, as opposed to having a desk separating the counselor and client. Although as much as possible, the counselor should maintain focus on the client, and writing can be a distraction. The counselor must strike a balance regarding the necessity of documenting what is occurring at the moment versus fully attending to the client; this may vary across settings (e.g., community mental health center, hospital, private practice, etc.). The counselor should use nonverbal, attending skills essential to building rapport and focus on using open-ended questions. More time may be needed for a clinical interview than for a regular session. The counselor should make sure that the boundaries of confidentiality and the counselor–client consent and agreement are stated upfront. An initial opening may include a brief introduction of the counselor, the nature of the counseling relationship, and a statement about confidentiality such as the following:

> I want you to know that what you say in here will stay in here. However, confidentiality may be compromised in three conditions: if you tell me you are going to hurt yourself; if you tell me you may hurt someone else; or if you disclose physical or sexual abuse or tell me you have abused a minor.

Because of the nature of the clinical interview, especially when standardized methods and models are employed, the client–counselor interaction may appear atheoretical. Keep in mind that the goal of the clinical interview is to establish rapport, gather information, assess need for services and desired interventions, and perhaps commit to future counseling sessions.

Types of Information Derived from Our Case Studies

Each of the case studies presented in Chapter 2 contains information derived from the clinical interview. Just as the clients vary in the case studies, so does the information gathered during the clinical interview. A description of some of the similarities and differences with respect to the clinical interview follows.

The cases of Eva Marie Garza, Robert Jones, and Ann Smith begin with a physical description of the client, relevant demographic information, and a description of mental status. In the authors' experience, knowledge and use of the MSE is very important but is often overlooked, particularly by novice counselors. For this reason, we point out specifically where mental status was addressed in the case studies.

For Eva Marie, five of the six elements of the mental status examination—(a) appearance, attitude, and activity; (b) mood and affect; (c) speech and language; (d) thought process, thought content, and perception; and (e) cognition—were addressed with (f) insight and judgment addressed later:

> She was oriented to person, place, time, and situation. Based on the complexity of language she used and the sophistication of the questions she asked within the session, she appeared as having above-average intelligence. Eva Marie's overall mood was anxious. Eva Marie's speech was noticeably pressured and fast. During the first 45 minutes of her initial June 7 intake, her responses to counselor-asked questions were often tangential and only loosely associated with asked questions. During that time, she was especially loquacious, and she demonstrated slight to mild psychomotor agitation. On first entering the initial intake session, Eva Marie sat in the counseling office chair. She slowly rocked back and forth as she responded to verbal questions. (Chapter 2, p. 15–17)

Similar observations were made about Robert Jones:

> He was oriented to person, place, time, and situation. He seemed of average intelligence. Although his face appeared flushed and unusually reddish, his speech was appropriate with average rate and volume. No slurring of his speech was noticed, and he had a friendly manner of interacting. Robert was appropriately dressed. He wore clean clothing, including navy blue trousers, an overly noticeable starched and pressed, white, button-down shirt; Sperry Topsider-type shoes; and no socks. His personal hygiene was appropriate and unremarkable except for the distinct and pungent aroma of Old Spice cologne mingled with the smell of alcohol and cigarettes about him. Robert presented as approximately 5 feet 10 inches tall, 175 pounds, with blue eyes and blonde hair. His appearance was trim but not gaunt. (Chapter 2, p. 15–17).

For our adolescent client Ann Smith, we noted the following:

> Ann was oriented to person, place, time, and situation. She seemed somewhat above average in cognitive intelligence and intellectual functioning. Ann was age appropriately dressed, wearing blue jeans, a red University of Arkansas Razorback t-shirt, and sandals. Ann's personal hygiene was unremarkable. No physical abnormalities were visibly noted, except scars on her left arm self-reported as a result of self-injurious behaviors: "cutting. The last time was six months ago when I was stressed." Ann's speech was appropriate with average rate, tone, and volume. Although Ann reported she is "often angry," her immediate mood appeared normal with neither psychomotor agitation nor slow behaviors. She reported her mother "made" her attend today's interview: "I don't get the point [of participating in counseling]; it won't work for me." (Chapter 2, p. 15–17).

In terms of insight and judgment, we can turn to some of the quotes by the clients. For example, Eva Marie appears to have good insight into her issues. She admits to having "'extreme anxiety' and 'complete dissatisfaction' with her life" with compromised judgment, as indicated by her statement "I don't know what to do."

In contrast to Eva Marie, Robert shows decent insight but poor judgment. Robert identifies a drinking problem, admitting, "Drinking has taken over my life," but then his poor judgment is noted when he admits, "I get a good job, swear I'll lay off the booze, but then get drunk while working." Furthermore, he consumes alcohol prior to his counseling session. Robert stated, "I drank in my car before I came inside." When asked how much alcohol Robert had consumed immediately prior to coming to session he stated, "Two bombers and two shots."

Ann could be characterized as the opposite of Robert—poor insight and decent judgment. She seems to be an unwilling participant in counseling—attending only because her mother "made" her—and has no goals related to counseling, "I don't want to be here." She disagrees with being court mandated to attend counseling: "That's totally lame." Despite her resistance to counseling, Ann does agree to the following treatment goals, demonstrating an understand of the leverage of the court and the need to participate: (a) reducing feelings of loneliness and anger; (b) stopping nonsuicidal, self-injury behaviors, (d) reducing intrusive sexual abuse memories and night terrors; and (e) reducing the frequency of her cannabis use.

In terms of addressing the presenting problem in the case studies presented, it seems that as each section of the case study is presented, additional problems may be noted. For example, Robert admits to alcohol abuse, which has impacted his relationship with his wife. Other issues may be apparent stemming from Robert's family of origin, such as his father's alcohol abuse.

For Eva Marie, the presenting problem—anxiety—addressed under "Identified Treatment Goals" is complicated by other extenuating issues addressed in subsequent areas of her case study. Eva Marie is in an unhappy marriage to a husband she describes as "absent" and "emotionless." Eva Marie is very unhappy in her current job and is also burdened with caring for her mother, whom she is quite dependent on.

From the clinical interview with Eva Marie, a counselor may feel challenged with helping Eva Marie find some alleviation for her anxiety given all of the issues that trigger stress in her life. Once again, depending on the theoretical and professional orientation of the counselor, Eva Marie's anxiety may be addressed in a multitude of ways. From a systems perspective, Eva Marie's role in the family, perspectives on marriage, and problematic relationships could receive primary consideration. Eva Marie has a long history of a dependent relationship with her mother, and her religious and cultural foundations have also played a significant role in the decisions she makes. From a mental health perspective, a long history of anxiety appears evident, and she is currently on medication to address her anxiety.

So when identifying presenting problems with Robert, where do we start? A more psychodynamically oriented counselor may wish to address Robert's relationship with his father, who drank excessively. A counselor specializing in a systems approach may wish to address Robert's relationship issues with his wife. From a mental health perspective, Robert is unlikely to make any changes if he cannot abstain from alcohol. Many of his marital and vocational issues can be tied to his drinking. For this reason, addressing issues of sobriety may be first and foremost. Even with the presence of mental health problems and diagnoses, a client who is not clean and sober will be unable to develop insight, judgment, and positive growth.

The problems presented in Ann's case study are multifaceted and not uncommon to the multiple issues adolescent clients present with in counseling. Ann is a victim of sexual abuse. Her mother is unsupportive and wrongfully blames Ann for the failure in her marriage, believing that Ann lied about the sexual abuse. Ann's cannabis use and oppositional behavior affect her peer relationships, educational achievement, and overall self-concept.

Ann's case is complicated. The conflict with her mother and lack of emotional support may impact Ann's overall disposition. In addition, as an older adolescent, Ann is at the age and stage where differentiating from her mother will be necessary for her overall well-being. An alternative placement for Ann may need to be explored to provide stability and support. When counseling with Ann, a strength-based approach may often improve counseling outcomes (Kottler & Balkin, 2017), and some of the strengths identified in the case study include the capacity to excel in school, a desire to attend postsecondary education, the potential of a positive support group, and the ability to identify relevant problems, despite frustration with the lack of support from her mother and involvement in the juvenile court.

Notice that each of the case studies concludes with diagnoses, consistent with *Diagnostic and Statistical Manual of Mental Disorders* (fifth edition) guidelines. However, the concept of providing a diagnosis after a clinical interview is controversial. On one hand, third-party payors expect, and even require, a diagnosis. On the other hand, the *ACA Code of Ethics* (2014) indicates that counselors have the right not to provide a diagnosis, particularly if the provision of a diagnosis is not in the client's best interest. Moreover, how appropriate is it to provide a diagnosis after an initial clinical interview? Keep in mind that a diagnosis can be changed. As more information is learned about the client, the need to amend treatment goals or re-evaluate the direction of counseling is important. At the early stage of a clinical interview, counselors may view diagnosis as provisional and note that it may evolve—they may even identify the need to rule out specific diagnoses. At other times, however, sufficient evidence may be presented during the clinical interview to formulate a more conclusive picture of the presenting issues, such as with Eva Marie's anxiety; Robert's alcohol dependence; and Ann's oppositional behavior, cannabis use, past trauma, and conflict with mother.

The subsequent sections that appear in a clinical interview, beyond the presenting problem, have a role in either informing the counselor about the presenting problem or addressing relevant concerns about the presenting problem, thereby lending credence to the various models of the clinical interview presented in this chapter. Thorough attention to the various components of the clinical interview provided a more comprehensive picture for each of the case studies presented. The subsequent sections provide more depth to understanding the presenting problem(s), as well as provide background information and present information on contributing factors or additional issues that may arise and be addressed through counseling.

Summary

The clinical interview is an integral component of the assessment process and pertinent to establishing treatment goals, treatment plans, and therapeutic rapport. Clinical interviews should be comprehensive. Beginning counselors should use models and standardized formats to collect relevant information and identify problem areas. Structured clinical interviews provide a framework for documentation that enable the counselor to provide ethical, evidence-based, comprehensive care. In addition, stakeholders (e.g., agencies, third-party payors) utilize information and data to ascertain that best practices are being utilized for clients. As you become more experienced with clinical interviews, they may begin to feel less formal, and you will become skilled at attending more to the client, rather than completing forms. This is not to suggest that documentation will be lessened; rather, you will simply become better at gathering the information.

A comprehensive clinical interview is atheoretical and therefore can be implemented from a variety of therapeutic approaches in a myriad of settings. From the case studies presented in Chapter 2, counselors, regardless of professional orientation and setting, can use the information from the clinical interview. Juhnke (2002) outlined a structured clinical interview format (CLISD-PA) that provides a comprehensive, atheoretical approach to the clinical interview.

8

Multicultural and Special Population Assessment Issues in Counseling

> ## Objectives
> 1. Identify issues of multicultural competence for assessment in counseling.
> 2. Identify standards and statements related to multicultural issues in assessment.
> 3. Address skills necessary to practice assessment in a multicultural world.
> 4. Identify issues of bias and perception of assessment from a multicultural perspective.

Fairness in Assessment

What makes a test fair? Certainly, much focus is placed on the development, administration, and scoring of assessments. Consider your experiences with standardized testing in school. The administration, instructions, and environment were all similar. The opportunity to prepare and/or complete the instruments must be the same for all participants, such as standardized instructions, tasks, and preparation, and all participants complete the instrument in similar conditions.

These attributes are essential to any standardized testing process. For example, schools go to great lengths to ensure the same process is provided for all students, including the reading of directions, the amount of time provided, and the similarity in the test-taking environment. Many instrument developers take time to describe the process of administering the instrument in the test manual. Scoring procedures are provided to ensure similar interpretations for all individuals being evaluated. Counselors should take time to read the manuals carefully, as scoring procedures may be different across gender, age, and grade. Intelligence, achievement, and aptitude tests often provide different norms, administration, and scoring procedures for different age and grade levels. But focus must also be on how the scores are used. As mentioned previously when discussing validity, test scores must be used and interpreted the same across all participants.

The testing process must be fair. Naturally, this step is emphasized in the standardization of testing procedures—the manner and conditions in which the test is administered and scored. But the American Educational Research Association (AERA), American Psychological Association (APA), and National Council of Measurement in Education. (2014) also addressed that sometimes flexibility in the testing process is warranted, especially if there are challenges due to "disability, cultural background, linguistic background, race, ethnicity, socioeconomic status, limitations that come with aging, or some combination of these or other factors" (p. 51). When accommodations are used, the steps toward determining and implementing accommodations should be reported in the testing report.

Bias in Assessment

Perhaps no issue in assessment is as controversial as the presence and effect of assessment bias. The existence of bias in assessment is well documented, but the reason for assessment bias is far more complex. In other words, counselors may recognize that bias exists in the assessment process but still be at a loss of what can be done about it. At times, assessment instruments may be biased, but the reason for the bias is not known. *Bias* occurs when groups or subgroups experience differences in scores or score interpretations on an instrument. *Differential item functioning* (DIF) is the result of different response patterns occurring from individuals who are of equal ability but of different group membership. When we see this occurrence over sets of items or on an instrument, it is referred to as *differential test functioning* (DTF). When such differences can be attributed to both the scores and other variables, *predictive bias* is evident (AERA et al., 2014). For example, females tend to endorse depressive symptoms more often than males (APA, 2013). Beck, Steer, and Brown (1996) noted statistically significant mean differences between males and females on the Beck Depression Inventory-II (BDI-II). Yet, cut-scores indicating mild, moderate, and severe depression are the same for both males and females, which could lead to false-positive results for females or false-negative results for males. Thus, the BDI-II may be a highly efficient and often utilized instrument; however, some gender bias may be evident, particularly with females being diagnosed with depression more often than males.

The *Standards for Educational and Psychological Testing* (AERA et al., 2014) may be the gold standard publication to which assessment and psychological tests aspire to meet, but other theories of test bias were evident in past research. DIF, DTF, and predictive bias may be seen as general categories to which other types of bias may fit. Walsh and Betz (2001) outlined several types of test biases, including internal structure, selection, slope, intercept, content, sex, and cultural bias.

Internal structure relates to the reliability and validity information of an assessment instrument. Clearly, if scores, items, or subscales lack accurate or consistent response sets or fail to measure the intended construct, biased results may be a logical consequence. Slope and intercept bias are related to predictive bias. In a slope bias, an outcome for one group is predicted differently over the same outcome for another group. Using the previous example of the BDI-II, should women be diagnosed with depression more often than men because of the tendency of women to identify depressive symptoms more often? The difference could be from social influences, rather than the development of a psychiatric disorder. Intercept bias occurs when a test overestimates or underestimates a particular group. For example, the number of ethnic minorities diagnosed with disruptive behavior disorders compared to nonminorities diagnosed with mood disorders may be an example. Although statistical biases may be data driven, they are the result of social and contextual issues related to assessment. Statistics may be useful in examining bias, but the statistics are not the problem. The problem lies in the interpretation and utilization of the information, as well as the item development of the instrument.

Content bias is a type of item bias, which occurs when the wording of an item is interpreted differently among different groups. This could result in scoring patterns that are different for one group over another. Chernin, Holden, and Chandler (1997) highlighted sex bias as an example, in which items on instruments may be biased if negative connotations or lack of references to minority groups are evident.

To be clear, test bias is an important component to test fairness. However, simply because an instrument is biased does not mean the instrument is unfair. The idea that all groups have comparable scores across an instrument defies the explicit rationale for conducting assessments. For example, in assessing wellness, should participants in a clinical setting identify different levels of wellness from participants in a nonclinical setting? In education, should students who have fewer resources have lower levels of achievement? Often, the answer to these rhetorical questions is a resounding "Yes!" Bias is expected, but instruments should be carefully evaluated when bias is found. The scores on an achievement test may vary from group to group because of unequal opportunities to learn, such as in comparing a college preparatory school with a school in a rural area of the United States.

The Achievement Gap: An Heuristic Example of Test Bias Versus Test Fairness

Tests will be biased, but to address test fairness, variables that are not being measured should not be different. Perhaps where bias and fairness become most troublesome is with disparities in scores across ethnic groups. In educational settings, comparisons across ethnic groups are commonplace at the local, state, and federal levels, with an abundance of research on the achievement gap. Addressing the achievement gap is complicated. Although the comparison of ethnic groups predominates research on the achievement gap, ethnicity does not account for the disparities in achievement. Ethnic disparities in standardized testing occur, but the reason for the disparities is unclear. To suggest that race is the mitigating factor behind scoring differences is blatantly racist. Common variables explored include socioeconomic status, parents' level of education, resiliency, culture, and so forth. The issue is multifaceted. For example, socioeconomic status can account for some differences, as the opportunity to access materials and support in the home environment may play a role in academic achievement; however, socioeconomic status cannot account for differences solely, as Asian groups typically outperform Caucasian students, despite having lower socioeconomic status (Fangzhou & Patterson, 2010).

Attempts to explain the achievement gap fall short because the variables involved are more numerous and complex to measure. Too often researchers engage in demonstrating evidence of *construct-irrelevant variance*, which refers to differences in test scores based on factors unrelated to the construct being measured (AERA et al., 2014). When researchers look for gender and racial differences in constructs such as academic achievement, they are postulating that achievement differences are from gender and/or racial differences, rather than recognizing that such factors are irrelevant to academic achievement. Racial groupings are not part of the definition of academic achievement, so why emphasize such differences when racial groupings are irrelevant to the criteria to measure academic achievement (Helms, 2006)?

Rather than focusing on irrelevant factors, Helms (2006) suggested researchers should focus on *construct underrepresentation*—when the items fail to measure the important aspects of an intended phenomenon of interest (AERA et al., 2014). In other words, maybe unintended group differences exist because of poorly constructed items or because the items do not measure the construct comprehensively.

Researchers who follow the guidelines for constructing and administering instruments should review the literature thoroughly to develop items and use a formal process of addressing whether the items address sufficient evidence of test content. Although items may be dropped because of psychometric instability (e.g., poor reliability), items are less likely to be dropped because of construct irrelevancy, as such items would not have been placed into the item pool initially. Wohlgemuth (1997) indicated that dropping items often results in decreases in accuracy, consistency, and usefulness. Care must be taken in modifying instruments.

As a result of a growing pluralistic society, instruments are commonly translated into multiple languages and re-normed according to cultural groups. Although such changes may be appropriate for instruments that measure emotional or behavioral constructs, which may be more sensitive to variations in cultural norms, instruments that assess academic achievement may be less sensitive to cultural issues. If culture does indeed play a role in predicting academic achievement, how can culture be measured and the effect of culture be accounted for in a competent, nonbiased way? Counselors must be aware that any changes to an assessment may compromise reliability and validity. In addition, the cost of norming an instrument according to specific demographic groups (e.g., sex, ethnicity, age, sexual orientation) would be an unrealistic burden on test developers because of data collection, costs, and varying interpretations (Wohlgemuth, 1997).

However, the role of culture can be acknowledged and the unique qualities of an individual's culture recognized. Sedlacek (2004) encouraged higher education institutions to use noncognitive variables, such as community involvement, preference for long-term goals, leadership experience, and realistic self-appraisal, as predictors of success in higher education, as opposed to merely focusing on high-stake testing results. An emphasis on noncognitive variables may decrease the weight of high-stakes testing in predicting performance and level the playing field for ethnic minority students who may not perform as well on high-stakes tests because of a variety of factors.

Assessment with Special Populations

An instrument becomes standardized as a result of a rigorous norming process (e.g., establishing meaningful statistics from the norm group, reliability, validity). When groups or populations are not included in that norming process, we refer to that group as a *special population*. There are reasons why groups may be excluded from the norming process.

The process involved in addressing a relevant portion of special populations is daunting, time-consuming, and improbable when taking into account sample size and the breadth of issues related to potential specialized populations (e.g., gifted, low socioeconomic status, various disabilities). For example, to obtain a sufficient amount of data to norm an instrument using more elementary methods of standardization (e.g., exploratory factor analysis), a ratio of 10 to 20 participants per item is necessary. More advanced procedures (e.g., confirmatory factor analysis) in standardization may require a separate sample of similar size as well. Thus, a 32-item instrument may require an initial norm group of 320 participants to simply get started.

Instruments often are developed with a particular population in mind. For example, the Reynolds Adolescent Adjustment Screening Inventory (RAASI) was designed to address potential problem areas faced by adolescents. Providing norming information for individuals older or younger than the adolescent age range would go against the intended design of the instrument. Thus, populations may be purposefully ignored.

The potential for an instrument to be useful among a broad range of populations is known as *generalizability*. Recall from Chapter 3 that researchers demonstrate generalizability in two ways: (a) by describing the sample with respect to characteristics (e.g., age, ethnicity, sex) so that evidence to the appropriate population can be demonstrated and (b) by using mathematical procedures that take into account the size of the sample in order to generalize to a population. Hence, when instruments are used with individuals similar to the norm group, the results may be assumed generalizable. However, when an instrument is used with individuals who may be different from the norm group, as indicated by demographic data, events, or circumstances, then the validity of the results may be called into question.

Comparing Special Populations to Normative Samples

Counselors should be cautious about using instruments in which an individual or group outside of the normative sample completes an instrument. Standardized instruments frequently lack representatives related to sociocultural demographic factors (e.g., ethnic minorities, English as a second language, low socioeconomic status) and various physical, mental, and behavioral deficits (e.g., cerebral palsy, autism, attention deficit hyperactivity disorder [ADHD]). However, as explained earlier, to expect test developers to include all potential members of various subgroups to norm an instrument is unreasonable. Individuals outside of norm groups are administered tests. Although counselors should be cautious in interpreting results, counselors should also be aware of when results may be pertinent and generalizable to an individual or group. To evaluate when an instrument may be appropriate for an individual or group from a special population, counselors should be aware of the norming process and current research related to the instrument.

Counselors should familiarize themselves with the norming process of the instrument as addressed in the test manual or relevant articles. By noting the demographic/descriptive factors of the norm group, counselors may be able to ascertain whether the instrument is an appropriate assessment tool. For example, Balkin, Miller, Ricard, Garcia, and Lancaster (2011) used the RAASI to examine influencing characteristics on recidivism for a predominately adolescent, Latino, court-referred group. However, the RAASI included a normative sample from 1,827 adolescents who were primarily Caucasian (72.1%), with only 6.4% of the group identified as Hispanic. In addition, most of the norm group lived with both parents (61.8%; Reynolds, 2001). This norm group may be quite different from the group used in the Balkin et al. study, in which the majority of participants who were administered the RAASI were Latino and from single-parent homes. So was the use of the RASSI valid in the Balkin et al. study? There may be factors, such as number of parents in the home, that may have an effect on the socialization of adolescents, and therefore the use of the RAASI with at-risk youth may have some limitations. On the other hand, counselors should be wary of construct-irrelevant variance, in which the application of variables, such as ethnicity, is inconsistent with the operational definition of the construct (i.e., adolescent adjustment) being measured. Balkin et al. (2013) conducted an evaluation of the internal structure of the RAASI using the Latino participants from single-parent homes and found a very similar factor structure. Hence, the use of the RAASI was likely valid. Despite apparent cultural differences, differences between the Latino participants in the Balkin et al. (2011, 2013) studies and the normative sample were minimal.

When using an instrument for an individual or group outside of the normative sample, counselors should review current literature to identify recent research on the instrument, particularly as the research relates to special populations. Researchers often shed light on additional generalizability issues once an instrument is published. Journals such as *Measurement and Evaluation in Counseling and Development* include articles in which established instruments are revalidated using a special population. For example, Canel-Çınarbaş, Cui, and Lauridsen (2011) examined validity of the BDI-II across a Turkish sample and compared the finding to a U.S. sample. In this case, Canel-Çınarbaş et al. were able to show how the BDI-II could be used with a special population.

Not all validated instruments come from established measures. Rye, Loiacono, Folck, Olszewski, and Madia (2001) developed the Forgiveness Scale "as part of a study involving college women who had been wronged in a romantic relationship" (p. 264). However, the authors reworded items to address any type of wrongdoing by an individual and correlated the measure to a more established instrument, the Enright Forgiveness Inventory. Thus, the instrument was revalidated with a more generalizable population and may prove useful in future research and practice related to forgiveness issues in counseling.

As shown in this example, not all instruments are published by test companies. For example, the Multicultural Awareness Knowledge and Skills Survey was used to assess multicultural competence in numerous studies (e.g., Brabeck et al., 2000; Cartwright, Daniels, & Zhang, 2008), but this instrument is not published by a testing company. When assessment instruments are published in journals, as opposed to test companies, validation across many different special populations may be easier because of access to the instrument and the inexpensive nature of conducting the research.

Counselors using assessment instruments with individuals from special populations need to assess carefully the nature of the special population, the consequences of testing and interpretation, and the relevant literature associated with the instrument. The process of validating an instrument across special populations may be just as intensive as the initial validation. When evaluating a research article or review of an instrument for use with a special population, counselors should look carefully at the methods employed in obtaining a representative sample for the special population, the reliability estimates for the special population as compared to the normative sample, and the validation procedures used, which often improve on the initial validation procedures for a given instrument.

Adapting Assessment Instruments and Procedures

Accommodations refer to processes and procedures for individuals who may be disadvantaged from a disability or condition and require a change in the processes and/or procedures of an administered assessment. Accommodations can include a multitude of measures such as additional time, verbal administration, assistance completing the instrument, and alternate response strategies. Federal guidelines, such as the Individuals with Disabilities Education Act in education and the American Disabilities Act of 1990 (ADA) for employers (see Chapter 1), require efforts to create a fair environment for individuals with disabilities. Counselors should be careful about implementing accommodations and interpreting the results. Some issues to address when considering an accommodation include legal implications, the validity of the accommodation(s), and available resources.

Counselors who work in schools, agencies, and businesses often rely on the organization for establishing protocols related to test accommodations. For example, universities often address compliance with ADA through specific services for students with disabilities, while businesses may employ professionals in human resources. In addition, school districts often include administrative personnel who oversee accommodations in testing to identify specific accommodations that are required for students, employees, and so forth. Such a procedure prevents personnel from implementing different protocols and procedures. Therefore, the decision to offer an accommodation and the type of accommodation offered may be streamlined and less subjective. For example, a student with a diagnosis of ADHD may require additional time on a test, and this accommodation may be established through an individualized education plan.

Compliance with policies and procedures for individuals with disabilities is important, and counselors should be aware that the decision to offer an accommodation should be considered carefully. Consider the implications if an organization offers an accommodation for an undocumented condition. For example, say an applicant for graduate school is administered a timed essay. However, the student has a cold that day and the administrator allows the individual more time to complete the essay. Would such an accommodation be fair? Other students who may not have felt healthy but did not ask for an accommodation may be at an unfair advantage. In addition, to what extent should an accommodation be offered? Should the student require documentation of illness? Is the illness severe enough to warrant an accommodation? The consequences may be that the process of assessing the aforementioned applicant and making comparisons to other applicants is unfair, thereby challenging the validity of the administration.

When an accommodation is offered, counselors should be aware of the validity of the accommodation and consider what conditions an accommodation may be acceptable. For example, say a high school student diagnosed with ADHD wishes to obtain an accommodation for the ACT. In this scenario, such an accommodation may be important for allowing the student the opportunity to demonstrate college preparedness. Contrast this with a scenario in which a parent requests an accommodation for a child diagnosed with a mild intellectual disability who will be administered an intelligence test. In this case, such an accommodation is invalid, as the test is designed to evaluate the construct (i.e., intelligence) that is a basis for the diagnosis. As a general rule, counselors should be aware of policies, procedures, and existing literature (test manuals, research studies) related to accommodations for a test. The following issues serve as examples of concerns related to accommodations in tests.

Speed Versus Power Tests

Speed tests refer to items or tests that are time limited. For example, many standardized tests are timed (such as performance measures in an intelligence test) or must be completed in a specific amount of time. *Power tests* include items that may increase in difficulty and therefore may not be completed or may be incorrectly answered. Many aptitude and achievement tests include this type of component. Although accommodations on a power test may be infrequent, accommodations for speed test through the allowance of increased time occur quite frequently. One factor to keep in mind is that many tests may be speed tests as an unintended consequence. Such a circumstance occurs often in educational settings. A student is administered an exam during a class and has the class period to complete the exam. Incompletion of the exam is not necessarily a result of a lack of knowledge; rather, an incomplete exam may be the result of running out of time to finish. Thus, time can be added to the exam if the properties of the exam are left intact. In this case, if the purpose of the exam is to test an understanding of information, then time is not an issue.

Language Barriers

The increase in a multicultural, diverse society results in a proliferation of individuals with English as a second language. This is an area in which failure to offer an accommodation can have deleterious effects. Consider the consequences of Henry Goddard's (1866–1957) actions of administering the Binet scale to assess intelligence of immigrants as they were arriving to Ellis Island. Not only were the individuals in poor physical condition to take a test, but the translation of the test may have been inconsistent and was certainly not normed. Thus, even when a translation of an instrument is offered, if the translation is not normed, then the use of the test is not valid. Counselors may wish to consider alternative tests that may be administered nonverbally. For example, the Test of Nonverbal Intelligence (fourth edition) tests intelligence and aptitude but does not require the use of language.

Physical Impairments

Counselors should be aware when physical impairments, such as visual, auditory, and motor disorders, interfere with the validity of an assessment. For example, Block Design is a subtest on the Wechsler Intelligence Scale for Children (fifth edition). This subtest requires the examinee to manipulate blocks in order to create a visual representation of a designated shape, and the process is timed. Clients diagnosed with motor impairments could have difficulty manipulating the blocks, which could affect their ability to complete the task in a specified time frame. Not only is time allotment a concern, but also individuals may become frustrated in attempting the task. Thus, the subtest may not be a valid measure of intelligence. When physical impairments are evident and affect the test or testing process, counselors should consider alternative measures or alternative scoring methods if the tasks cannot be completed. If an alternative scoring method is used, test manuals and existing literature should support the decision.

Cognitive Disorders

Cognitive disorders can affect the speed in which tasks are processed. Thus, a delayed reaction could alter the interpretation of a test, particularly when speed is an issue and incorporated into the score of a test, which is typical on aptitude, achievement, and intelligence tests. In addition, counselors should address the client's understanding of the tasks presented. In many tests, instructions are standardized, particularly in the areas of aptitude, intelligence, and achievement. If the instructions are not understood, an accurate measure in these areas may be compromised. The decision to alter instructions can affect how a client responds, and careful consideration of the wording, so as not to lead the client to respond in a certain way, is pertinent.

Emotional Disorders

An array of emotional disorders, such as depression, ADHD, and anxiety, may affect the processing of tasks because of reactions to the stress of the test-taking environment or delayed processing. Time accommodations are common with emotional disorders. However, counselors should be aware if the test manual or existing literature offers a rationale and empirical evidence for accommodations on a specific test. Again, consideration of the purpose of testing is essential. Time accommodations are appropriate when the purpose of the test is to investigate a construct that is not predicated on the speed of the response. Although achievement tests often do not require a timed component, evaluating the speed of a response in intelligence and aptitude testing is common practice.

Developing Multicultural Competence as an Assessment Professional

In light of the multicultural issues that emanate from assessment practices, counselors should be aware of the information garnered from the administration and scoring of an instrument and view the measure as a single tool, used in conjunction with other tools, to make appropriate recommendations to clients.

The *Multicultural and Social Justice Counseling Competencies* (Ratts, Singh, Nassar-McMillan, Butler, & McCullough (2015) addressed skills related to counselor competence:

- Acquire culturally responsive assessment skills to identify limitations and strengths when working with privileged and marginalized clients.
- Acquire assessment skills to determine how the worldviews, values, beliefs, and biases held by privileged and marginalized counselors and clients influence the counseling relationship.
- Acquire assessment skills regarding how culture, stereotypes, prejudice, discrimination, power, privilege, and oppression influence the counseling relationship with privileged and marginalized clients. (pp. 8–10)

Counselors should keep in mind that the counseling profession maintains an inclusive definition of multiculturalism: "Counselors recognize the effects of age, color, culture, disability, ethnic group, gender, race, language preference, religion, spirituality, sexual orientation, and socioeconomic status on test administration and interpretation, and they place test results in proper perspective" (American Counseling Association, 2014, p. 12). The application for multicultural competency in assessment covers a wide range of populations and special groups. Counselors need to consider carefully how the assessment process, from the type of assessment through the administration, scoring, and interpretation of the results, may be attributed to cultural issues of the client.

Sedlacek and Kim (1995) identified common misuses of assessments from a multicultural perspective that over 20 years later still apply to this day. Counselors should be aware of labeling for diverse groups. Labels have changed for various groups over the past 70 to 80 years, but the change in labels has done little to affect bias and prejudice for disenfranchised groups and populations. Although this issue can apply to various domains across the counseling profession, specific assessment issues include the creation, norming, and interpretation of assessments. Assessment instruments should be created for use among diverse populations, but many of the theories employed for the constructs that counselors measure (e.g., intelligence, achievement, depression) come from a Eurocentric worldview (Helms, 1992; Sedlacek & Kim, 1995). In addition, even if instruments are developed for use among various groups, the norm groups of many instruments often lack reflection of a diverse sample. Development of assessments overwhelmingly is dependent on college student populations of primary European American descent. As a result, assessment instruments may lack generalizability to minority groups. Counselors should then consider how an assessment instrument and the scores produced from it are a valid measure when used with a culturally diverse client. Sedlacek and Kim (1995) warned that individuals who develop instruments might lack training in multicultural issues. As a result, counselors should be cautious when using assessment instruments in which such considerations are not outlined in the manual.

Awareness of Perceptions of Counseling and Assessment among Various Cultures

Generally, the practice of counseling in the United States assumes a Western-valued process, which may be inherently biased toward persons of color. Historically, ethnic minorities are less likely to use and be satisfied with counseling services. Extant research is quite limited with respect to the role of assessment and multicultural issues. In addition, past research focused more on counselor training related to multicultural competence and less on client perceptions. Ethnic minorities are less likely to seek out counseling services. "Historically, ethnic minorities have been under-represented with respect to accessing services in the mental health system" because of disparities in the judicial system, access to private health care insurance, and increased risk of psychological and behavioral disorders (Balkin, 2006, p. 50). Jones and Markos (1997) found that the clients' attitude toward counseling is related to the clients' perception of effectiveness of counseling services. Li and Kim (2004) examined the relationship of Asian values across counselor effectiveness, counselor empathy, working alliance, session depth, and cross-cultural counseling competence. The extent to which clients adhered to Asian values was not a factor in relationship to these measures. However, Asian clients did show a preference for directive counseling methods.

can't ask for my needs

27 SOW
INTEGRATED RESILIENCE

- p 67, appendix E, Lt Col Rutherford or Maj Oldham
- ~~Music for video~~
- ~~Individual + team coaching~~
- ~~Replace pics for website~~
- Alcohol poster from internship ???
- What do I want to happen next? What do I want life too look like?

- Pesi CEUs
- ~~Call Oxford about summer textbook~~
- Make cultural presentation for Japan
- ~~AMDR slides~~
- ~~Put in battery housing request~~
- ~~CDNET~~
- ~~Call Oxford about summer textbook~~
- ~~Maintenance request~~
- Research pros vs cons of membership for website
- Look up survey monkey, google forms vs. microsoft forms
- Shame poster → pdf of manual
- ☐ Virtual activities (Play on purpose website, Training-Wheels
- ~~Discussion post~~ Japan culture presentation
- ☐ What does an app offer above + beyond microsoft
- ☐ Read scaling intimacy workbook
- ☐ slides

Take the power back!
I take care of my people
I'm striving to be the best leader I can be
walk by the office + know that she can't touch me

The need to adhere to multiculturally competent practices in the assessment process cannot be overstated, as the assessment process may indeed be the introductory step to beginning counseling for many clients. In the assessment process, culturally competent counselors take into consideration cultural values and issues of the client, avoid stereotyping the client, and continue to broaden awareness and understanding of diversity (Skiba, Knesting, & Bush, 2002). Counselors need to be aware of labels as a characteristic of the assessment process. Labels may be helpful or harmful depending on the context. The practice of labeling may contribute to overrepresentation of ethnic minorities. For example, in the school setting a disproportionate number of ethnic minorities may be labeled with a disability in order to receive special education services. Counselors, and school counselors in particular, may need to advocate for assessment strategies that identify the need for intervention and remediation, rather than eligibility for placement (Skiba et al., 2002).

The determination of ethnic differences across constructs, despite being irrelevant to the measurement of the construct, is not a practice that is likely to cease in the near future. Counselors need to be able to address ethnic differences on tests by being knowledgeable about noncognitive variables. As mentioned previously, disparities in access to academic resources and/or motivation toward counseling, treatment goals, achievement, and so forth may be evaluated independent of ethnicity and may account for variation on measured constructs.

Counselors should be aware of the norm groups for an assessment instrument. Application to a particular ethnic group or culture may be inappropriate if minorities were underrepresented in the norm group. There is a need to examine norm differences when assessment tools are used. For example, using an assessment instrument like the RAASI on Latino/a youth may require re-norming if this population was not part of the original standardization of the instrument.

Although studies on assessment training in the counseling literature may be limited, one factor that appears to increase multicultural competence for counselor trainees is clinical supervision with more non-White clients (Vereen, Hill, & McNeal, 2008). Thus, practice with non-White clients may be essential to developing multicultural counseling competence. Ultimately, counselors need to be aware of how the assessment process may feel impersonal and strive to develop therapeutic rapport and positivity toward the assessment process.

Case Study Application: Eva Marie Garza

The case of Eva Marie Garza provides an excellent opportunity to explore multicultural issues in assessment. Eva Marie is a 40-year-old Mexican American female suffering from issues related to anxiety, her marriage, and her career. A counselor working with Eva Marie may be remiss if Eva Marie's cultural issues and background were ignored. Eva Marie identified the move from Mission, Texas, to Atlanta, Georgia, as a difficult transition in her childhood. She recalled moving from a primarily Latino area of the country to being the only Latino family in the neighborhood. This, along with her father dying at an early age, may certainly be a factor related to her present-day anxiety.

Eva Marie mentioned her most important relationship is with her mother. As an individual who suffers from a rather unfulfilling marriage, counselors who are unfocused on the multicultural implications emanating from a matriarchal culture may inadvertently indicate that the most important relationship should be her marriage. Such a statement could be an ethical violation, as counselors are not to impose their values upon the client.

> Counselors are aware of—and avoid imposing—their own values, attitudes, beliefs, and behaviors. Counselors respect the diversity of clients, trainees, and research participants and seek training in areas in which they are at risk of imposing their values onto clients, especially when the counselor's values are inconsistent with the client's goals or are discriminatory in nature. (ACA, 2014, p. 5)

The value of the relationship Eva Marie has with her mother is a cultural norm and should be respected and understood.

Another aspect of Eva Marie's marriage that should be considered is her long history of remaining in an unfulfilling marriage. Such an issue should be viewed from a multicultural context in which both Eva Marie's Mexican American background and Catholic faith discourage divorce. Counselors should be aware that religious diversity is an aspect of multicultural diversity (Levitt & Balkin, 2003). Eva Marie's upbringing, her relationships as an adolescent, and her notions about family appear heavily influenced by her faith. A counselor should note that the job that Eva Marie enjoyed most was related to a position as a bookkeeper with a Catholic church. Once again, a counselor should be aware of the cultural implications related to the issues and decisions Eva Marie made regarding her marriage and understand why Eva Marie persists in a rather unhappy and unfulfilling relationship.

Ultimately, a client such as Eva Marie should be viewed within the context of her culture. The aforementioned case study contains elements related to ethnicity, Latino/a culture, religion, and spirituality that should be explored within the context of the relevant treatment issues identified by the client and counselor. Counselors working with clients like Eva Marie may need to explore cultural issues with the client but also engage in additional learning and supervision opportunities to adequately address Eva Marie's issues with a degree of multicultural competence.

9

Fundamentals of Ability Assessment

> ### Objectives
> 1. Understand historical and contemporary theories of intelligence.
> 2. Evaluate theoretical frameworks of intelligence, aptitude, and achievement and assessments instruments used to measure ability.
> 3. Identify benefits and challenges in ability assessment.
> 4. Understand the nature of assessment reports that measure ability.
> 5. Apply ability assessment to case examples.

Assessing Ability: Intelligence, Achievement and Aptitude

What do we mean by *ability assessment*? Most textbooks in counseling have independent chapters on intelligence testing, aptitude testing, and achievement testing. We have decided to present these concepts under the single construct of ability assessment.

The assessment of intelligence is intertwined with the history of assessment, as discussed in Chapter 1. The separate investigation into individual differences by Galton and Wundt led to the advent of the first intelligence test by Alfred Binet in 1905 (Gregory, 2014). Further development for intelligence testing in the United States occurred when Lewis Terman revised Binet's scale, creating the Stanford-Binet Test in 1916. Although the Stanford-Binet Test was revised in 1937, David Wechsler, who became chief psychologist at Bellevue Psychiatric Hospital, was dissatisfied with Stanford-Binet scale and developed a measure known at the time as the Wechsler-Bellevue Intelligence Test in 1939, which would later become the Wechsler Adult Intelligence Scale (WAIS).

Missing from these tests, however, was any prominent theory guiding their development. The first test of intelligence from Binet in 1905 preceded any predominant theories of intelligence. Moreover, later revisions and future tests were developed in a response to the Binet test and later the Stanford-Binet test. A famous statement associated with defining intelligence was made by the psychologist Edwin G. Boring (1923, as cited in Gregory, 2014), indicating that intelligence may be defined by whatever is being evaluated by intelligence tests. In other words, the intelligence test defines intelligence. Hence, the evolution of intelligence testing occurred without a theoretical framework for the construct being measured, which is quite a deviation from the standards of test validity used today. Thankfully, intelligence testing has evolved since the early 20th century, and many tests of intelligence may be identified with a theory. However, with multiple theories of intelligence come multiple definitions of intelligence. Today, there continues to be a lack of consensus regarding the definition of intelligence and even, perhaps, an overreliance on instruments to define intelligence. This is analogous to the tail wagging the dog. Instruments measuring intelligence are used to define the construct (Esters & Ittenbach, 1999), which results in questions of validity of these measures. We know that *intelligence* refers to a general set of mental capabilities. The numerous intelligence tests developed tend to correlate to each other, indicating that they are measuring a similar construct. However, without an operational definition, can a construct truly be measured?

Achievement testing refers to an examination over material that was learned or acquired. Unlike intelligence and aptitude tests, which are not aligned with a set of material introduced to the examinee, achievement tests are aligned with a curriculum or program. For example, states often develop their own statewide achievement tests that are aligned with the educational standards for each state, such as the Iowa Test of Basic Skills (ITBS). Other examples outside of the educational system could include state drivers' license examinations, in which participants have the option of taking a course, reading a manual, and taking the test. The key to achievement testing is that the individuals tested were exposed to the material previously. Examinees, in essence, have the opportunity to be prepared for such an examination.

Aptitude testing refers to measurement of a set or sets of abilities. In other words, aptitude should measure what individuals may be capable of achieving. Whereas achievement tests measure the acquisition of knowledge and skills in which the presentation of material was standardized or at least partially standardized, aptitude tests measure ability when the presentation of material is relatively unknown or uncontrolled. A helpful comparison may be to view achievement testing as measuring something that an individual should know and aptitude testing as predicting what an individual may be able to do (Anastasi & Urbina, 1997).

The distinction between various types of ability tests may become blurry. For example, a department of education for a given state may mandate a given curriculum for each grade level and the development of an achievement test to measure knowledge areas of the curriculum. However, the extent to which each student was exposed to the specific curricular areas and the manner in which exposure occurred might vary. Thus, educational achievement is difficult to measure given that a standardized test is employed to measure a nonstandardized procedure (i.e., teaching). The extent to which a test score is predictive of future performance may actually be tied to prior exposure to a set of materials. For instance, when taking an achievement test, an examinee is likely exposed to vocabulary words that are less familiar. However, the ability to discern the meaning of such words may be more related to the amount of reading the examinee engages in, rather than some predetermined criteria. The lack of a standardized method for enriching vocabulary may reflect more aptitude than achievement. Moreover, the antithesis is also true. When presenting more complex vocabulary on an aptitude test, such as the ACT or SAT, previous education may play a role in an examinee's ability to correctly respond to an item or scale. Anastasi and Urbina (1997) recognized the loose definitions of intelligence, achievement, and aptitude testing and advocated for the term *ability testing* as a more appropriate description of the cognitive process being measured.

The viewpoint that intelligence testing, achievement testing, and aptitude testing may be more similar than different should not be overlooked. Strong relationships have been evident among assessments related to intelligence, academic achievement (e.g., grade point average [GPA]), achievement tests, and aptitude tests (Frey & Detterman, 2004; Koenig, Frey, & Detterman, 2008; Rohde & Thompson, 2005; Schult & Sparfeldt, 2016). Recall in Chapter 5 the reference to the state of Maine, in which the state adopted the use of the SAT as an achievement measure. The issue with this decision was the use of an aptitude test to measure achievement. However, an examination of current research, along with Anastasi and Urbina's (1997) assertion of achievement testing and aptitude testing being quite similar, actually may lend credibility to Maine's decision to use the SAT as a measure of achievement. However, such a decision would only be beneficial if such aptitude tests were strong measures of future academic performance beyond GPA and standardized achievement tests.

Cimetta, D'Agostino, and Levin (2010) noted that modern aptitude tests, particularly since 1994, include more facets of educational achievement in order to give more weight to actual problem-solving, as opposed to predicting readiness for the higher education learning environment. The argument of using standardized aptitude tests for college entrance was based on the idea that a standardized aptitude test would increase fairness related to admissions to postsecondary education institutions.

> The idea of using such tests is based on the noble aim of leveling the playing field at school-leaving age so that access to higher education is not limited to those who have had access to greater educational resources during childhood. (Stringer, 2008, p. 55)

For instance, making comparisons among students with respect to GPA may be unfair because of the lack of opportunities some students had. A student who graduated from a rural school district may have less access to advanced placement courses than a student from a metropolitan school district, for instance. An argument in favor of aptitude testing is that such a test would serve as an unbiased measure of potential student achievement in higher education.

One could argue that these elements—readiness to learn and the ability to problem-solve—are synonymous. Indeed, modern aptitude tests appear quite similar to achievement tests because of the focus on knowledge-related items, and both kinds of tests appear to contribute equally to predicting first-year college GPA, approximately 6% of the variance to the model; the largest predictor to first-year college GPA was high school GPA (Cimetta et al., 2010).

Although the effort to view students without biased measures is ethical and honorable, the reality is that such tests may fall short of this goal. Tests of ability may fail to measure noncognitive variables such as study skills and motivation (Stringer, 2008), realistic self-appraisal, positive self-concept, and preference for long-term goals (Sedlacek, 2004).

Perhaps no other area of testing is more used or debated than ability testing. The mandate of high-stakes testing, required in No Child Left Behind Act (NCLB, 2002) and its successor Every Student Succeeds Act (ESSA, 2015) brought ability testing and educational accountability to the forefront in education, requiring documentation and monitoring of pass rates, educational assessment and placement of students, graduation requirements, and access to postsecondary education. Federal and state governments use ability testing to address the aforementioned requirements.

However, the role of intelligence, achievement, and aptitude testing goes beyond educational testing. Companies, state and federal agencies, the military, and other entities use achievement and aptitude tests to establish the appropriateness, skills, abilities, knowledge, and potential of applicants. The use of these tests is not without controversy, as noted in Chapter 1 relating to the New Haven, Connecticut, firefighters. The utility of ability tests, along with the interpretation, meaning, and decisions made based on these test results, may have enormous repercussions. Counselors need to be aware of the inherent strengths and weaknesses of ability testing in order to place the use of such tests in proper perspective.

So if intelligence tests, achievement tests, and aptitude tests all measure a similar construct, why are they separate and distinct in terms of utilization and practice? They are used for very distinct purposes. Intelligence tests are used to measure general cognitive ability and are helpful in diagnosing intellectual disabilities or individuals who are academically gifted. Achievement tests measure the extent to which material was learned or acquired. Similar to intelligence testing, achievement tests can be useful in identifying learning disabilities or individuals who are academically gifted. Aptitude tests are used to look at mental capabilities. These tests are often used to determine placement in higher education or job/vocational abilities. These tests could be seen as similar to counseling techniques, such as the *empty chair* technique. Empty chair is a classic Gestalt technique that may be used to help a couple process difficult emotions in couples counseling or help an individual process emotions related to a distressing event. The technique may be the same, but the reason or theory behind the use of the technique is different. Ability testing can be viewed similarly. As we dive in to each of these categories of ability testing, we discuss the theory and use of each of these tests.

Theories and Models of Intelligence

g Theory

The first theory of intelligence actually predates Boring's famous statement mentioned earlier. Charles Spearman (1904, 1927) developed the first theory of intelligence, known as *g theory*. Rather than define intelligence through the formulation of a theory, Spearman defined intelligence by correlations of numerous tests. To understand this very abstract concept, it is helpful to understand the role of factor analysis.

Keep in mind that Spearman was a pioneer in factor analysis, a statistical procedure widely used today to validate measures. Factor analysis is the process of identifying *latent variables*, variables that are not initially observed but can be identified by correlating scores on variables together to see if they have some common trait that can be identified. So, although intelligence cannot be observed, various tasks and traits can be observed (e.g., speak a foreign language, play a musical instrument, identify differences, use mathematical problem-solving). The extent to which these behaviors show a relationship and can be grouped together is deemed a factor.

Spearman, therefore, theorized that measures of intelligence converge on a unitary factor, known as a *general factor* or *g*. However, Spearman also indicated that tests might measure specific factors that relate to *g*. In other words, a test could measure a single aspect of *g*, such as response time, which is only a specific factor of *g* and may have low correlations with other factors. Intelligence, according to Spearman, was based on two factors: *g*, or general intelligence, and *s*, or specific abilities (Edwards, 1994). Louis Thurstone, a contemporary of Spearman, also used factor analysis to establish primary mental abilities. Although Thurstone identified various primary mental abilities, only some of the abilities demonstrated moderate correlations to each other and were likely to be second-order factors of *g*, thereby corroborating Spearman's theory (Gregory, 2014): (a) verbal comprehension, (b) reasoning, (c) perceptual speed, (d) numerical ability, (e) word fluency, (f) associative memory, and (g) spatial visualization (Thurstone, 1938).

Such a definition, then, lends credibility to Boring's statement—the definition of intelligence is based on the correlation of the various tests used to measure intelligence. Two of the most prominent intelligence tests used today, the Stanford-Binet Intelligence Scales (SB5)—currently in its fifth edition—and the Wechsler Scales—which include a variety of scales but most commonly refer to the Wechsler Adult Intelligence Scale-IV (WAIS-IV), the Wechsler Intelligence Scale for Children-V (WISC-V), and the Wechsler Preschool and Primary Scale of Intelligence-IV (WPPSI-IV)—were initially (i.e., in their earlier editions) developed without a theoretical framework of intelligence. The development of the Binet scale—Measuring Scale of Intelligence—was developed in France, quite far from the initial theoretical underpinnings of Charles Spearman and his study on g theory. On the other hand, the first of Wechsler's scales, developed in 1939, was Wechsler's response to his dissatisfaction with the Stanford-Binet test, which he administered to Army recruits during World War I. Wechsler noticed individuals' deviations related to the intellectual capabilities that they supposedly indicated and their performance on the Stanford-Binet (Edwards, 1994). Wechsler was sent to study with Spearman and Pearson in 1918 and had the opportunity to study under Spearman and learn firsthand Spearman's g theory, wherein he concluded that Spearman's theory was overly simplistic. In turn, Wechsler formulated his own definition of intelligence from which the subsequent Wechsler scales were all derived: intelligence is the "global capacity to act purposefully, think rationally, and deal effectively with the environment" (Edwards, 1994, p. 1135). Although the lack of a theoretical framework tied to the initial development of both the Stanford-Binet and Wechsler scales is a legitimate criticism, the wide use and contribution of these instruments cannot be disputed. The scores from these tests appear quite valid in identifying individuals with developmental needs in education, placement, and services.

Hierarchical Models

Factor analysis serves as the dominant method of devising a theory of intelligence. As noted, a legitimate criticism of this method is that the measures define the construct, as opposed to operationally defining a construct and developing a measure. This pattern of using correlated measures to define intelligence continued with Raymond Cattell (1963), but, unlike Spearman who identified a single unifying factor (g), Cattell identified two factors: fluid intelligence, known as gf, and crystallized intelligence, known as gc (Brody, 2000; Gregory, 2014). Fluid intelligence refers to the ability of an individual to adapt to new situations or environments through learning and problem-solving. Fluid abilities include flexibility, adaptability, and creative or unique approaches to problem-solving. Such skills are less likely to be influenced by formal learning, education, and culture. Crystallized intelligence, however, is more culturally and educationally dependent and refers to the completion of a task or the ability to solve problems based on formal learning, such as learning that occurred through formal education or acculturation. Crystallized abilities include information typically measured through achievement testing, such as the ability to complete a math problem or mastery of some assigned material (Hunt, 2000; Kaufman, McLean, & Kaufman, 1995). Unlike crystallized intelligence, Cattell viewed fluid intelligence as a biologically influenced component that declined during the adult lifespan (Brody, 2000; Hunt, 2000). However, later research would indicate that both gf and gc are influenced through biological and cultural factors (Davidson & Downing, 2000) and may decline with age. Crystallized ability tends to peak in middle age and decline gradually, most likely from old age, whereas fluid ability tends to peak earlier in adulthood and decline steadily throughout the adult lifespan (Kaufman & Kaufman, 2004).

Gf-gc theory, along with Thurstone's work, was important in developing intelligence theory beyond a unitary concept supported by Spearman's *g* theory. John Horn, a student of Raymond Cattell, was instrumental in expanding *gf-gc* theory. Later derivations of the *gf-gc* model included a hierarchical structure with *gf* and *gc* at the top followed by additional components such as visual and auditory processing, processing speed, short-term and long-term memory, and sensory information (Davidson & Downing, 2000; Gregory, 2014).

Different opinions pervade regarding the extent to which *gf-gc* theory links to *g*. Esters and Ittenbach (1999) indicated that *gf-gc* theory provides strong statistical evidence that intelligence is not a unitary construct. However, John Carroll developed a three-stratum theory, which combines elements of *g* and *gf-gc*. Carroll analyzed over 460 data sets and developed a hierarchical structure with three levels, structured as a pyramid. At the top stratum is *g*, followed by the middle stratum, which consists of eight factors similar to Horn's of the *gf-gc* model: (a) fluid intelligence, (b) crystallized intelligence, (c) general memory and learning, (d) broad visual perception, (e) broad auditory perception, (f) broad retrieval ability, (g) broad cognitive speediness, and (h) processing speed. The middle stratum is also hierarchical; therefore, fluid intelligence had the highest correlation to the top stratum, *g*, whereas processing speed had the smallest correlation to *g*. The bottom stratum consists of numerous specific abilities or skills (Davidson & Downing, 2000).

As mentioned, the Wechsler scales and Stanford-Binet were not developed according to a theoretical framework, but revisions of the instruments are aligned with *gf-gc* theory (Esters & Ittenbach, 1999), particularly for the fifth edition of the Stanford-Binet. For example, the nonverbal or performance measures on the tests conform to fluid ability, which relies on adaptation and flexibility to solve problems—essentially a nonverbal skill; on the other hand, vocabulary, information, and computation conform to crystallized ability, such as information learned in a formal educational environment.

Numerous intelligence tests are available and may be more theoretically derived. For example, the Kaufman Brief Intelligence Test, second edition (KBIT-2), was specifically designed to address fluid and crystallized intelligence. The KBIT provides measures based on two domains: (a) the verbal domain, which is aligned with crystallized ability, and (b) the nonverbal domain, which is aligned with fluid ability. A more comprehensive review of the KBIT-2 is presented later in this chapter.

Contemporary Models of Intelligence

Up to this point, theories of intelligence were developed post hoc, or after the fact. Existing measures were used to derive theories. More contemporary theories are less reliant on measurement principles, such as factor analysis, with the idea that theory should be used to develop measures. With this in mind, Robert Sternberg developed the triarchic theory of intelligence. Sternberg rejected the unitary concept of intelligence, g, and sought to include information processing and cognitive functioning as a component of intelligence. On the positive side, Sternberg indicated that traditional measures of intelligence do not provide a complete picture, as intelligence has numerous components that cannot be assessed by a single measure. On the negative side, empirical evidence validating Sternberg's model is limited (Davidson & Downing, 2000; Gregory, 2014).

In triarchic theory, Sternberg (1985) identified three components of intelligence. *Componential intelligence* is the first component and consists of internal processes, often associated with information processing theory. These processes include (a) metacomponents, such as processes in problem-solving (e.g., identifying a problem, defining a goal, selecting a strategy); (b) performance, which include specific processes informed by metacomponents, such as making comparisons to generate a solution or justifying a decision; and (c) knowledge acquisition, which includes the ability to learn information. *Contextual intelligence* is the second component and involves applying componential intelligence to real-world problems through adapting (i.e., fitting into an existing environment) or shaping (i.e., changing an environment to suit personal needs). Experiential intelligence is the third component and involves the ability to deal with new and/or unique situations without clear direction and quickly transition from conscious to subconscious processes, known as *automatic processing* (Davidson & Downing, 2000; Gregory, 2014).

Sternberg's model of intelligence is both complex and esoteric. As mentioned, the model is not empirically driven. However, the model is important for identifying the complex nature of intelligence and the numerous processes involved, which are quite difficult to measure.

Another contemporary model of intelligence is multiple intelligence theory, developed by Howard Gardner. Like Sternberg, Gardner rejected the unitary concept of intelligence and embraced models of intelligence that cannot be easily measured (Davidson & Downing, 2000). Another similarity to Sternberg is the absence of statistical analyses to validate the model. A distinctive aspect, however, was that Gardner established multiple intelligence theory through qualitative research, grounding theory based on the analysis of empirical data in "biology, neuropsychology, developmental psychology, and cultural anthropology" (Chen, 2004, p. 18). Gardner believed that naturalistic inquiry was the best measure of intelligence. Essentially, intelligence is best evaluated when observing real life.

According to Gardner's theory, eight intelligences were identified, with the first three representing abilities measured by traditional intelligence tests:

1. Linguistic: use language to convey meaning and recall information.
2. Logical-mathematical: use symbols to convey relationships and apply logic to evaluate concepts.
3. Spatial: discern, change, and convert visual-spatial associations.
4. Musical: comprehend and apply musical properties.

5. Bodily kinesthetic: physical skills, such as athletic abilities and coordination.
6. Intrapersonal: self-understanding of personal goals, emotions, strengths, and weaknesses.
7. Interpersonal: understanding of others' goals, feelings, and behaviors.
8. Naturalistic: understanding patterns found in natural environments (Davidson & Downing, 2000).

An important component of Gardner's multiple intelligence theory is that intelligence may be viewed in the context of an individual's strengths. For example, individuals who may struggle academically but show gifted athleticism may still be viewed as highly intelligent in specific areas related to Gardner's theory. A professional athlete, for instance, may excel in bodily kinesthetic intelligence; a musician may excel in musical intelligence. However, a major criticism of multiple intelligence theory is the lack of statistical evidence to support this model.

Emotional Intelligence

Despite the lack of statistical evidence to support multiple intelligence theory, Gardner's assertion of interpersonal and intrapersonal intelligences was a major influence in the advent of emotional intelligence (EI). EI is a controversial construct and, similar to intelligence theory, includes competing models. Thus, defining EI is not straightforward but rather is based on the model employed. Furthermore, EI is a distinct construct of intelligence discussed so far, as the focus of EI is cognitive ability, and in some cases personality characteristics, that solely relate to emotions intrapersonally and interpersonally.

The mental ability model was based on the foundational work of Jack Mayer and Peter Salovey. Mayer and Salovey (1997) identified intelligence as the model suggests, through various abilities based on (a) perceiving and expressing emotion; (b) using emotion to think and make decisions; (c) labeling, analyzing, and understanding emotions, particularly complex feeling or mixed feelings; and (d) reflecting and regulating emotions.

The mental ability model is best measured by the Mayer-Salovey-Caruso Emotional Intelligence Test (MSCEIT), which provides four scores on each of the aforementioned areas and a total score. The instruments uses emotion-based problem-solving items. For example, a respondent might be asked to identify an emotion based on a picture or identify helpful emotions to solving a problem. Two scoring systems were developed for the MSCEIT. The first was based on a normative sample of 5,000 participants. Respondents' scores are compared to a norm group. The second method of scoring is based on responses from a panel of 21 experts.

The mixed ability model was based on two prominent EI theorists, Daniel Goleman and Reuven Bar-on. Both view EI as a combination of mental ability and personality characteristics. Goleman identified five abilities/characteristics in EI: self-understanding of emotions, understanding of others' emotions, self-management, self-motivation, and relationship management. In contrast, Bar-on identified areas of interpersonal skills, intrapersonal skills, adaptability skills, stress management skills, and general mood, such as optimism and happiness (Mayer, Salovey, & Caruso, 2000). Both Goleman and Bar-on developed EI instruments that measure the respective components of their theories. Goleman developed the Emotional Competency Inventory, which measures self-awareness, self-management, social awareness, and social skills. Although the reliability estimates appear adequate, as well as the norming, validity evidence is limited (Watson, 2007). Bar-on developed the Emotional Quotient Inventory (EQ-i), which measures each of the five components of the aforementioned model and a composite score. The EQ-i uses a 5-point Likert-type scale ranging from 1 (*very seldom or not true of me*) to 5 (*very often true of me or true of me*). Cox (2001) indicated adequate psychometric characteristics, but questioned the validity of the instrument because of the controversial nature of EI.

As mentioned, the concept of EI was driven by Gardner's theory of multiple intelligences. Thus, the same problem that plagues multiple intelligence theory, the lack of statistical evidence, is a criticism in EI theory as well. Waterhouse (2006) was highly critical of both multiple intelligence theory and EI theory because of the lack of empirical evidence, conflicting multiple theories, and lack of predictive evidence. Although these instruments are popular, particularly in organizational settings, evidence is limited with respect to valid use and interpretation.

Four Common Intelligence Measures

In this section we present an overview of four common intelligence tests: the WAIS-IV, the SB5, the WISC-V, and the KBIT-2. We believe that having a conceptual understanding of these intelligence tests will provide an understanding of most intelligence you will encounter. With the exception of the KBIT-2, which has a level B qualification from Pearson and provides an excellent screening of intellectual ability but far less depth, most counselors do not conduct intelligence testing as part of their practice. The primary reasons for this include the following:

1. Competence in intelligence testing requires additional coursework, training, and supervision beyond what is usually offered in Council for Accreditation of Counseling and Related Educational Programs (CACREP) accredited counseling programs.
2. Administration, scoring, and interpretation is extremely time consuming. School districts, agencies, and organizations hire personnel to do these assessments, which easily can encompass hours of work to administer, score, and write the report.
3. Some states prohibit professional counselors from administering intelligence tests even with documented training.

The measures covered in this section have closer alignment with Carroll's expansion of *gf-gc* theory, as each provides an estimate of many of the aforementioned components of the model. Another common element is the use of subtests to estimate ability in specific types of intelligence and then to combine the scores from the scales to identify an overall measure of intelligence, commonly referred to as a Full Scale IQ (FSIQ). In each of the instruments, raw scores are transformed to standard scores consistent with the documented age of the participant. The standard scores range from 40 to 160 with a mean of 100 and standard deviation of 15. Different publishers established slightly different terminology to describe the classification ranges of intelligence. As a general rule, Table 9.1 provides classifications that may be used in score interpretation. Note that an individual who scores below 70 may have major deficits in intellectual functioning, while scores higher than 130 are indicative of individuals with very high intellectual functioning. However, as with any test, scores should never be used as a sole basis for diagnosis. For example, simply because a client scores 69 does not mean he or she should be diagnosed with a developmental disorder. Rather, further assessment is needed. An assessment of an intellectual disability should be accompanied by an assessment of adaptive behavior. For example, a score of 69 on the WISC-V may indicate the need to assess the client using the Vineland Adaptive Behavior Scale, second edition, in order to provide more data in the diagnosis of an intellectual disability.

Each of the tests measures various domains. For the SB5 and KBIT-2, the domains represent two broad categories: Verbal and Nonverbal. On the WAIS-IV, four broad categories are described. On the WISC-V, there are five categories. So when identifying a composite score (e.g., FSIQ) based on the combined subscales, individual strengths and weaknesses may influence the total score. Hence, identification of differences in the various domains or indices is important. When large enough differences occur between domains or indices, strengths and deficits in cognitive functioning may be explained, which may reflect a difference in fluid versus crystallized intelligence (Kaufman & Kaufman, 2004). The score reports on these measures, as well as the manual, provide information to compare various scores and determine whether differences between domains or indices are large enough to be of concern. When notable differences are found between scores, such differences may be deemed *statistically significant*—that is, occurring outside the realm of chance. Tests that require motor control may not be appropriate for respondents with physical disabilities, so caution must be used in making decisions about which subtests to use and how the omission or accommodations of various tests affects the scoring and interpretation.

TABLE 9.1 Classification of Intelligence Scores

Range of Standard Scores	SD Above/Below the Mean	Percentile	Category
131 or greater	+2.1 or greater	98th or higher	Upper extreme
116 to 130	+1.1 to +2	84th to 97th	Above average
85 to 115	–.9 to +1	18th to 84th	Average
70 to 84	–2 to –1	2nd to 16th	Below average
69 or below	–2 or less	less than 2nd	Lower extreme

Note: SD = standard deviation.

Another important issue to consider is the role of the standard error of measurement (SEM). Recall from Chapter 5 that the SEM accounts for error in the observed score and provides a band to which the respondent may likely score if retested. The instruments discussed in this section generally have a 4- to 5-point SEM. This becomes very pertinent when using scores for clients. In the previous example, where a client has a FSIQ of 69, given the SEM, the client may range from 64 to 74. Categories, therefore, should be interpreted with caution as, in this case, the client would be somewhere between below average and the lower extreme. How this is communicated to a client or parent is extremely important.

WAIS-IV

The Wechsler scales, which include specific instruments for adults, children, and preschool age, are among the most popular intelligence scales in the United States. Although differences may be noted between the WAIS-IV and the WISC-V, an overview of the WAIS-IV will provide a general idea of how such tests may be used. Keep in mind that with each revision of an instrument comes changes in administration and scoring. For example, previous versions of the WAIS used two subscales, Verbal and Performance. With the most recent edition of the WAIS-IV, four indices compose the FSIQ.

The WAIS-IV is a strong, highly regarded instrument. The WAIS-IV may be used for adolescents to adults from ages 16 to 90. There are 15 subtests that theoretically load (i.e., there is a lack of empirical evidence for this) four domains: Verbal Comprehension, Perceptual Reasoning, Working Memory, and Processing Speed. The normative sample included 2,200 individuals between ages 16 and 90. Reliability estimates are strong. Reliability estimates for scores among 13 age categories ranged between .71 to .96 for subtests, .87 to .98 for indices, and .97 to 98 for FSIQ. Numerous clinical studies and correlations with other measures indicate strong evidence of validity (Canivez, 2010; Schraw, 2010).

Verbal Comprehension Index

Three subtests and one supplemental subtest are included in measuring verbal comprehension. *Similarities* is a measure of verbal reasoning, which requires respondents to identify how two elements are alike. *Vocabulary* is a measure of understanding and verbal expression and requires respondents to define given words. *Information* is a measure of acquired knowledge, which is often addressed in formal education. *Comprehension* (supplemental) measures the ability to understand verbal abstractions, such as metaphors, through responses to open-ended questions. Much of what is measured in the Verbal Comprehension index may be considered as crystallized ability.

Perceptual Reasoning Index

Three subtests and two supplemental subtests are included in measuring perceptual reasoning. *Block Design* measures visual and spatial reasoning but also requires motor skills in replicating a design shown on a page with blocks that are provided to the respondent. *Matrix Reasoning* is a nonverbal test in which the respondent must identify patterns and use spatial reasoning and logic. *Visual Puzzles* is a nonverbal test in which the respondent uses pattern identification, spatial reasoning, and pattern recognition. *Picture Completion* (supplemental) measures the ability to evaluate visual elements. *Figure Weights* (supplemental) is a measure of quantitative reasoning and the ability to make logical comparisons.

Working Memory Index

Two subtests and one supplemental subtest are included in measuring working memory. *Digit Span* measures concentration and working memory by asking respondents to repeat number sequences. *Arithmetic* is a measure of concentration and quantitative reasoning, as well as the ability to comprehend and express mathematical relationships. *Letter-Number Sequencing* (supplemental) is similar to digit span and requires the respondent to sequence both numbers and letters.

Processing Speed Index

Two subtests and one supplemental subtest are included in measuring processing speed. These tests also require motor control. *Symbol Search* and *Coding* measure visual perception, motor speed, and mental speed through the identification of specified symbols and, in the case of Coding, the ability to copy the symbols quickly. *Cancellation* (supplemental) also measures visual-perceptual speed and requires respondents to mark specific symbols.

WISC-V

The WISC-V is also a strong, highly regarded instrument. The WISC-V may be used for children to adolescents from ages 6 to 16 and therefore has overlap with both the WPPSI-IV and the WAIS-IV. There are 16 subtests designed to measure five domains: Verbal Comprehension, Visual Spatial Skills, Fluid Reasoning, Working Memory, and Processing Speed. Seven indices compose the FSIQ (Similarities, Vocabulary, Block Design, Matrix Reasoning, Figure Weights, Digit Span, and Coding). There are a lot of similarities in the subtests of the WISC-V and WAIS-IV. The normative sample included 2,200 individuals between ages 6 and 16. Reliability estimates are strong. Reliability estimates for scores among 11 age categories ranged between .80 to .90 for subtests, .90 or higher for indices, and .96 to 97 for FSIQ (Keith, 2017).

Verbal Comprehension Index

This index is very similar to what is measured on the WAIS-IV. Four subtests are included in measuring verbal comprehension. *Similarities* is a measure of verbal reasoning, which requires respondents to identify how two elements are alike. *Vocabulary* is a measure of understanding and verbal expression and requires respondents to define given words. *Information* is a measure of acquired knowledge, which is often addressed in formal education. *Comprehension* measures the ability to understand verbal abstractions, such as metaphors, through responses to open-ended questions.

Visual Spatial Index

Two subtests are included in measuring visual spatial skills. *Block Design* measures visual and spatial reasoning but also requires motor skills in replicating a design shown on a page with blocks that are provided to the respondent. *Visual Puzzles* is a nonverbal test in which the respondent uses pattern identification, spatial reasoning, and pattern recognition.

Fluid Reasoning Index

Four subtests are included in measuring fluid reasoning. *Matrix Reasoning* is a nonverbal test in which the respondent must identify patterns and use spatial reasoning and logic. *Figure Weights* is a measure of quantitative reasoning and the ability to make logical comparisons. *Picture Concepts* measures the ability to evaluate visual elements by identifying pictures with a common trait from two or three rows of pictures. *Arithmetic* is a measure of concentration and quantitative reasoning, as well as the ability to comprehend and express mathematical relationships.

Working Memory Index

Three subtests are included in measuring working memory. *Digit Span* measures concentration and working memory by asking respondents to repeat number sequences. *Picture Span* requires the individual the child/adolescent to memorize pictures and identify them in order. *Letter-Number Sequencing* is similar to digit span and requires the respondent to sequence both numbers and letters.

Processing Speed Index

Three subtests are included in measuring processing speed. These tests also require motor control. *Coding* and *Symbol Search* measure visual perception, motor speed, and mental speed through the identification of specified symbols and, in the case of Coding, the ability to copy the symbols quickly. *Cancellation* also measures visual-perceptual speed and requires respondents to mark specific symbols.

SB5

The SB5, as mentioned earlier, is among the oldest and widely used intelligence instruments. The SB5 is appropriate for ages 2 to 85. Two primary domains are measured in the SB5: Verbal and Nonverbal. Within each domain are five subtests that measure a cognitive ability. The five cognitive abilities are similar in scope to what has been described earlier in this chapter: (a) Fluid Reasoning, (b) Knowledge, (c) Quantitative Reasoning, (d) Visual-Spatial Processing, and (e) Working Memory.

Because the SB5 may be used across a wide age span (2 years to 85 years), the SB5 presents six levels (1–6) that may be used, with higher levels indicating increased difficulty.

Both the Nonverbal domain and the Verbal domain begin with a routing test. Examinees may begin on Levels 1 to 5, depending on how they perform on the routing test (D'Amato, Johnson, & Kush, 2005).

For the Nonverbal domain, the routing test occurs on the Object Series/Matrices subtest, which measures fluid reasoning. Based on the performance on this subtest, the starting level on subsequent Nonverbal subtests is determined. For the rest of the Nonverbal domain, a subtest is paired with a cognitive ability. Knowledge may be measured by Picture Absurdities (Levels 4–6) and Procedural Knowledge (Levels 2–3); Quantitative Reasoning is a single scale for Levels 2–6; Visual-Spatial Processing may be measured by Form Patterns (Levels 3–6) or Form Board (Levels 1–2); Working Memory may be measured by Block Span (Levels 2–6) or Delayed Response (Level 1; D'Amato et al., 2005).

For the Verbal domain, the routing test occurs on the Vocabulary subtest, which measures knowledge. Based on the performance on this subtest, the starting level on subsequent Verbal subtests is determined. For the rest of the Verbal domain, a subtest is paired with a cognitive ability. Fluid reasoning may be measured by Verbal Analogies (Levels 5–6), Verbal Absurdities (Level 4), or Early Reasoning (Levels 2–3); Quantitative Reasoning is a single scale for Levels 2–6; Visual-Spatial Processing is a single scale titled Position and Direction for Levels 2–6; Working Memory may be measured by Last Word (Levels 4–6) or Memory for Sentences (Levels 2–3; D'Amato et al., 2005).

The raw scores on each of the subtests may be converted to a standard score with a mean of 10 and standard deviation of 3. However, as mentioned, domain scores for Verbal and Nonverbal IQ, as well as for FSIQ, are converted to standard scores with a mean of 100 and standard deviation of 15. Like the WAIS-IV, manipulatives are included in the assessment, which may require accommodations to scoring for individuals with physical disabilities. The normative sample included 4,800 individuals between the ages of 2 and 85. Reliability estimates for scores on Verbal, Nonverbal, and FSIQ domains are very high (.95 to .98) and scores on subtests range from .84 to .89. Excellent validity evidence with other established measures (i.e., correlations with other measures), such as the Wechsler scales, is indicated in the manual (Roid, 2003).

KBIT-2

Two essential issues govern the use of the Wechsler scales and SB5. The instruments are complex and take longer to administer. In addition, because of their complex nature, they are generally regarded as Class C instruments, which means assessment professionals should have a high level of expertise in test interpretation. We advocate for specific training in intelligence testing to administer either the SB5 or Wechsler scales. In contrast, the KBIT-2 is a Class B instrument, although formal training in assessment, particularly related to working with children and their parents, is required.

The KBIT-2 is a brief measure designed to provide estimates of intelligence consistent with more established measures in a short period of time. As mentioned, the KBIT-2 provides measures based on two domains: (a) Verbal domain, which is aligned with crystallized ability, and (b) Nonverbal domain, which is aligned with fluid ability.

The Verbal domain includes two subtests: Verbal Knowledge and Riddles. These subtests are designed to measure vocabulary, reasoning ability, and general information. Two types of items are evident in Verbal Knowledge, general information and vocabulary, which serve as the primary components to measuring crystallized ability (gc) in the Catell-Horn-Carroll theory (Kaufman & Kaufman, 2004). In Verbal Knowledge, the respondent is shown a series of pictures and the administrator says a word or asks a question. The respondent has to point to the picture or say the corresponding letter that either identifies what the word means or answers the question. In Riddles, a question is asked and the respondent is to provide a one-word response. For younger children (ages 4 to 6), pictures are used. The Riddles subtest evaluates knowledge of information and vocabulary. Similar to Verbal Knowledge, crystallized ability is assessed but so is reasoning and logic.

The Nonverbal domain includes one subtest—Matrices, which is designed for problem-solving that is more atypical or innovative and not necessarily taught in formal education (Kaufman & Kaufman, 2004). Hence, the Matrices subtest is more aligned with fluid ability. Matrices contain three separate sections; as the examinee moves through each section, the items become progressively more difficult. In the first section, the client is presented with a drawing in the middle of a page with a series of objects at the bottom the page. The examinee must select the object that is conceptually related to the drawing. In the second section, a pair of objects or designs is presented, with one object/design on the left and a blank on the right. The examinee is given choices to select the object/design that fits on the right. In the third section, a square array of abstract figures is presented with a blank cell in the square. The examinee must select the appropriate object/design that fits the pattern. Along with problem-solving and logic, this subtest also evaluates pattern recognition and visual-spatial ability.

A benefit of this instrument is the short administration time, compared to more intensive instruments, of 15 to 30 minutes. In our experience, the KBIT-2 can be very helpful when clients may have fallen through the system and lack any type of formal evaluation. For example, a client who has not been tested for special services from the school may be administered a KBIT-2 as a screen for intellectual functioning. Findings may be reported to the school (with consent) to build a case for more formal testing. In addition, the KBIT-2 may be useful when the counselor has concerns related to intellectual functioning because of the client's inability to adapt to new situations or understand cause and effect. Scores from the KBIT-2 may be helpful in identifying deficits in cognitive ability. Counselors should keep in mind that the KBIT-2 correlates strongly with more established measures but lacks the breadth of information as a comprehensive intelligence test like the WAIS-IV, WISC-V, or SB5.

Characteristics of Achievement Instruments

Achievement tests may be as various as the curricula intended to be measured. Achievement tests may measure a specific area, such as reading, or may be broader, encompassing many areas. Although the focus of achievement testing is on knowledge acquired or learned, achievement testing is also used to address learning proficiency (as required by NCLB) and as evidence to determine if additional educational services are needed. For example, achievements tests may serve as evidence of some type of learning disability or dyslexia if a student tests at level in mathematics but markedly lower in vocabulary.

Achievement tests may fall into different categories. Keep in mind the description of an achievement test includes the focus on material introduced in a standardized or partially standardized fashion. However, the nature of standardization is that each individual is exposed to the same conditions for learning and evaluation. So, although exposure to material may be regimented, the process of teaching the material and evaluating the acquired learning may not necessarily be standardized.

The nature and purpose of various tests may differ, and therefore so do the areas tested. The next section address common areas of achievement and aptitude testing with brief descriptions of each area. As noted previously, Cimetta et al. (2010) documented the increased similarities between modern aptitude tests and achievement tests in educational environments. Therefore, the term *ability testing* encompasses relevant aspects of both achievement and aptitude testing, as well as intelligence testing discussed previously.

Ability tests may be administered in individual and group formats, often depending on the function and purpose of the test. Group administrations may be used to gauge learning outcomes. For example, states administer achievement tests to determine accountability for a teachers, schools, and districts, as well as use scores to address placement and measure achievement of set standards aligned with the curriculum. Colleges and universities use group-administered aptitude tests in the selection process of potential students. Individual administrations, on the other hand, may be used for diagnostic purposes, such as evaluating abilities or assessing for learning disabilities. Once again, the distinction between achievement tests and aptitude tests may be blurred; what is pertinent to counselors is the nature of the assessment and the evidence of the consequences of testing. For example, using a state achievement test to evaluate for learning disabilities would be inappropriate, even though many assessment professionals use achievement tests as evidence to determine the presence of a learning disability. Essentially, counselors need to be aware of what tests were administered and how they were used in evaluating a client/student. When assessments are used for diagnostic purposes, counselors should be aware that a single measure only serves as evidence and should never be used as a sole indicator related to the presence or absence of a diagnostic condition. Finally, individual ability measures, particularly related to achievement, should be viewed with caution. Whereas a state achievement test may be created by professionals who can align the test with a state curriculum, such a feat would be impossible with individual achievement tests normed on a national basis. This begs the question: How can a person be held accountable for knowledge not included in an organized curriculum? An argument can be made that national norms were used to gauge performance on each item, thereby identifying the items as appropriate.

Rather than catalog and describe a variety of individual and group measures of ability, the following sections highlight some commonalities across widely used individual and group ability measures. Additional in-depth reviews of instruments may be found in the *Mental Measurements Yearbook* (described in Chapter 6).

Common Characteristics in Ability Assessment Instruments

Individual ability assessments use an array of subtests designed to facilitate diagnosis of learning disabilities, identification of gifted and talented students, and/or direction related to placement and planning of individuals in a variety of educational or vocational settings. These tests often include elements of verbal reasoning and mathematical reasoning.

Verbal reasoning is a term that is often used in aptitude testing but generally refers to a global process that includes reading comprehension, vocabulary, and analysis of meaning, structure, or grammar of words, sentences, and passages. Traditionally, reading comprehension referred to the ability of an individual to discern, interpret, or understand the meaning of a written passage (Harris & Hodges, 1995). However, different tests may expand the definition of reading comprehension. For example, respondents may be asked to draw conclusions about a passage, identify strengths and weaknesses, and/or establish relationships.

Sight vocabulary includes items that evaluate the respondent's ability to identify words without context or use of phonetic techniques/devices (Harris & Hodges, 1995). For example, in the Wide Range Achievement Test (WRAT-4), respondents may be asked to read a series of words in order to evaluate recognition of more easily identifiable words. *Spelling* is a common scale on many achievement tests, often measured by the test examiner saying the word and the respondent attempting to spell the word. In other tests, a word may be presented that is misspelled and the respondent is required to note the misspelling. *Writing* tests on achievement and aptitude measures are somewhat complex because of the lack of standardization in measuring writing skills. Scoring for writing tests may include raters or computer programs. Scores may be based on content, grammar, structure, and complexity. Such measures may be ascertained by sentence length and the use of different sentence structures. Although some tests include an optional writing section, other tests, particularly in areas of achievement for schools, require writing tests.

Individual ability measures like the WRAT-4 and the Wechsler Individual Achievement Test, Third Edition (WIAT-III) employ a variety of verbal reasoning measures, which, depending on the grade level of the child, may or may not be included in a verbal reasoning composite score. For example, the WRAT-4 includes three verbal reasoning subtests: Word Reading, Sentence Comprehension, and Spelling. However, only Word Reading and Sentence Comprehension were included in the Reading composite score. The WIAT-III is more complex, with up to 11 subtests used to compile five verbal reasoning composite scores: Oral Language, Total Reading, Basic Reading, Reading Comprehension and Fluency, and Written Expression.

Mathematical reasoning refers to quantitative skills in methods, analysis, deduction, and inference (Steen, 1999). Therefore, what one test references as mathematical reasoning may be quite different from how another test presents mathematical reasoning. Although the term *mathematical reasoning* may imply a subtest on an aptitude measure, scores related to mathematical reasoning may correlate with scores related to math achievement, as evidenced by the relationship of the Differential Aptitude Test (DAT) to other achievement measures (Hattrup, 1995). Essentially, mathematical reasoning may imply a variety of processes, from simple computation and procedural steps to complex tasks and applications of proofs and estimation that use more concrete skills as well as intuition. *Math calculation* refers to processes and strategies involved in computation of numerical operations. These types of items involve solving numerical problems using arithmetic operations. Some achievement tests, such as the WRAT-4, and aptitude tests, such as the Armed Services Vocational Aptitude Battery(ASVAB), time this subtest, so the evaluation may contain both speed and power elements. *Applied math skills/word problems* refer to items that require comprehension, application, and reasoning skills, which may include computation as well. In these items, examinees may be required to interpret meaning and draw inferences from what is written in order to answer the item. Hence, verbal reasoning skills are an integral component to applied math skills/word problems, so the conceptualization that verbal reasoning and mathematical reasoning are separate and distinct constructs may be unsubstantiated because of the reliance of verbal reasoning to perform many applied problems in mathematics.

What to Report

In addition to raw scores, standard score conversions, percentiles, and confidence interval measures based on standard error of measurement, score reports on achievement tests often provide information related to significant differences related to subscale scores, including grade equivalents and age equivalents. Hence, comparisons may be made in several ways: norm group (percentile rank, normal curve equivalents), age, and grade. Qualitative descriptions may accompany the scores in order to provide a perspective of how the client's score may be compared to the general population. The qualitative description is based on the percentile rank related to the standard score. As many ability tests, particularly individual achievement tests and intelligence tests, use a mean of 100 and a standard deviation of 15, a score marked as "Average" would fall between −1 and +1 standard deviation, or between 85 and 115. Scores identified as below average fall between −1 and −2 standard deviations, or between 70 and 84. Scores below 70 would therefore be at −2 standard deviations or below (see Figure 9.1). Another import facet of the summary table is the

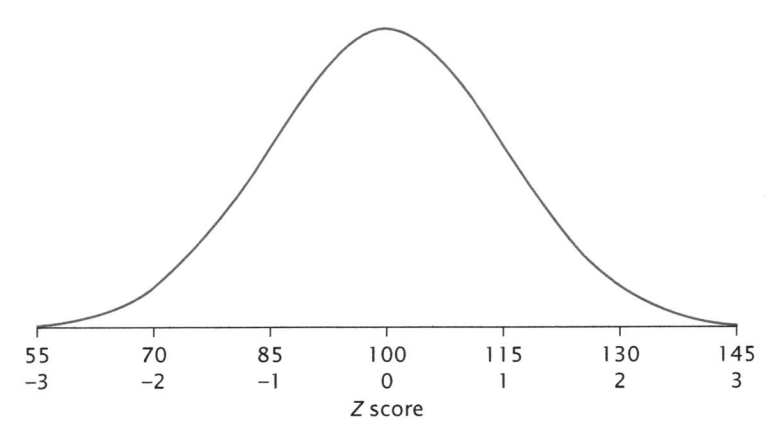

FIGURE 9.1 Interpretation of Standard Scores.

95% confidence interval (fourth column). Recall from Chapter 5 that the SEM provides a less rigid interpretation by accounting for the error in the observed score. In other words, keep in mind that the score on a test is representative of a performance at a single point in time and therefore may not be representative of the true score. The issue of the difference between the true score versus the observed score is accounted for by using a 95% confidence interval, suggesting that the true score lies somewhere within the band that includes the observed score.

Some score reports provide information related to differences between subscale scores. Once the score difference is calculated, statistical significance between the scores can be noted. Appendices in the test manual provide this information. Assessment professionals should focus on more conservative significance levels (e.g., .05, .01) for interpretation purposes. You may also be provided information on prevalence, which indicates the likelihood of such differences occurring. Noted differences between specific subscale scores, such as math reasoning and verbal reasoning, may shed light on possible learning deficits. For example, persistent differences between lower scores on word reading, sentence comprehension, and spelling when compared to math computation may indicate learning deficits with respect to verbal reasoning.

Group-Administered Ability Assessment

Group-administered ability assessments are used in a variety of settings, providing information to address accountability, understanding of preestablished standards, vocational placement, and potential. States across the country rely on standardized tests to address learning outcomes in schools. Higher education relies on group-administered ability assessments to make decisions related to placement in higher education. In addition, agencies/organizations may use ability assessments for job placement, promotion, and hiring.

High-Stakes Testing

Perhaps more than any other test, group achievement tests in education tend to be the most publicized and utilized ability assessment instrument. Although the use of group ability assessments in schools preceded ESSA (2015) and NCLB (2002), achievement testing was mandated by NCLB, thereby pushing education toward accountability and high-stakes testing. But what are the effects of such tests and testing practices in counseling? What do counseling professionals need to know about these tests and how the scores are used?

The implications of high-stakes testing—as a general practice by schools, agencies, and organizations—are serious, affecting clients, students, employees, administrators, and job seekers. High-stakes testing may be used to determine if a student, school, or school district meets a minimum standard, an employee receives a promotion, an individual meets requirements for a job, or a program receives funding. Specific to education, students may be denied a diploma or grade promotion, teachers may be denied merit, and schools/school districts may be denied funding.

In 2004, the American Counseling Association (ACA) released a position statement related to high-stakes testing. In the position statement, ACA recommended guidelines for high-stakes testing and indicated support for using high-stakes testing as a measure of accountability in education and program evaluation. "Essentially, high stakes testing should contribute to motivation and implementation of student learning, instructional effectiveness, and effective policy decisions about distribution of resources" (p. 1). ACA addressed 10 principles in the position statement: (a) alignment, (b) multiple measures, (c) impact, (d) opportunity to learn, (e) availability of remediation, (f) resources, (g) development of tests, (h) usefulness, (i) validity of scores for diverse populations, and (j) policies and applications.

The guidelines from the ACA position statement provide counselors with important information related to practical and ethical issues in high-stakes testing. Several of the principles outlined in the ACA policy statement address curriculum alignment. Alignment, as mentioned previously, refers to the extent to which the content of the exam is matched with the curriculum taught within a program. Within this alignment, examinees must have adequate and equivalent opportunities to learn the material along with the relevant resources required to address learning and, if necessary, remediation. In particular, individuals who fail to meet a minimum standard should be afforded the opportunity to remediate and rectify the situation. In addition, services should be offered to assist in remediation.

Another important element of the ACA (2004) position statement is related to validity evidence of the high-stakes testing. Recall that validity refers to the appropriateness of how test scores may be used. High-stakes testing not only uses an instrument with strong psychometric properties (e.g., reliable scores, strong internal structure and relationship to other variables, appropriate content and response processes), but the appropriateness for testing with diverse populations (e.g., disabilities, English as a second language students) should be investigated, reported, and addressed in interpretation. Test scores should be interpreted accurately in understandable terms for professionals, parents, examinees, and stakeholders.

How high-stakes testing is ultimately used should be carefully analyzed on an ongoing basis to avoid adverse ramifications toward the application of the results. Counselors should be aware that no single measure stands alone. High-stakes testing can affect individuals and large groups/organizations. Multiple measures should be used in making decisions that can influence the future standing of individuals or groups. Individuals who create policies for high-stakes testing are responsible for ensuring the consequences of the test are aligned with the stated purpose and that such policies are published and distributed to examinees and stakeholders. High-stakes testing can affect an entire system. For example, the results of high-stakes testing can have deleterious consequences for students, teachers, school administrators, and districts. Appropriate professionals and stakeholders should be involved in the formation of policies regarding high-stakes testing to ensure the use of appropriate ethical and legal processes.

Group-Administered Ability Assessments

As mentioned, the shared qualities of achievement testing, aptitude testing, and intelligence testing make differentiation between the types of tests difficult. Perhaps one theoretical distinction, however, is the supposed alignment between curriculum standards and achievement testing. Hence, achievement tests are often the tool of choice in complying with ESSA (2015) policies. States often employ or create their own measures to comply with specific standards set forth by each state's department of education. In most cases, therefore, each state adopts its own group-administered achievement measure.

Group-administered achievement tests were designed to provide teachers with data for making student-centered decisions, provide parents and students with a measure of educational progress, and evaluate student progress with a content-aligned curriculum. Most notably, these tests are used to evaluate students, schools, and districts with respect to meeting state educational standards and comply with federal guidelines. The content areas tested on group-administered achievement tests vary by level and the type of desired information. Houghton Mifflin Harcourt, which publishes the Iowa Tests of basic Skills (ITBS; grades K–9) and Iowa Tests of Educational Development (ITED; grades 9–12) at the time of this writing, provides a breakdown of the instruments, which are common among many group-administered achievement tests. The ITBS consists of three batteries listed from most extensive to least extensive: the complete battery, the core battery, and the survey battery. The entry levels (Levels 5 and 6) consist of the following areas for the complete battery: Vocabulary, Word Analysis, Listening, Mathematics, Word Reading, and Reading Comprehension. Each of these tests are untimed and read aloud by the teacher, with the exception of the reading test. In Levels 7 and 8, the complete battery consists of the following areas: Vocabulary, Word Analysis, Reading Comprehension, Listening, Language, Word Concepts, Math Problems, Math Computation, Social Studies, Science, and Sources of Information. The tests are orally administered with the exception of Vocabulary and Reading. In Levels 9 through 14, the complete battery consists of the following areas: Vocabulary, Reading Comprehension, Language, Math, Social Studies, Science, and Sources of Information (Houghton Mifflin Harcourt, 2016a). The ITED includes four levels, 15 to 18. The complete battery consists of the following areas: Vocabulary, Reading Comprehension, Language: Revising Written Materials, Spelling, Mathematics: Concepts and Problem Solving, Computation, Analysis of Social Studies Materials, Analysis of Science Materials, and Sources of Information (Houghton Mifflin Harcourt, 2016b). Similarities between individual-administered achievement measures and group-administered achievement measures, such as the ITBS and ITED, should be noted, such as areas related to mathematical and verbal reasoning in individually administered achievement tests.

Group-administered ability instruments may be designed to predict performance, identify strengths and weaknesses, and/or measure skills/abilities in key areas. These tests may be referred to as aptitude tests. Although both achievement tests and aptitude tests are ability measures that may assess strengths and weaknesses in key areas, aptitude measures are not necessarily aligned with a curriculum. Moreover, the categorization of such tests is confusing by such seminal published works like the *Mental Measurements Yearbook* (MMY). As examples of various aptitude measures follow, be aware of the MMY categorization of the measure and why confusion regarding ability measures persists.

Common measures of job performance include the DAT and the ASVAB. The DAT is for Grades 7 through 12 and adults and is designed to measure essential domains relevant to job performance based on general cognitive ability (e.g., verbal reasoning, numerical reasoning), skills (e.g., spelling, language use, perceptual speed and accuracy), and perceptual ability (abstract reasoning, mechanical reasoning, space relations). Although the publisher, Pearson Assessments, indicates that the focus of the instrument is to predict job performance, the MMY lists the DAT as an achievement test.

The ASVAB is listed as an intelligence and general aptitude measure in the MMY and administered to high school and young adult populations. The ASVAB includes eight subtests: General Science, Arithmetic Reasoning, Word Knowledge, Paragraph Comprehension, Mathematics Knowledge, Electronics Information, Auto and Shop Information, and Mechanical Comprehension. The ASVAB uses a subscale, the Armed Forces Qualifications Test, comprised of scores from word knowledge, paragraph comprehension, arithmetic reasoning, and math knowledge, to determine military service qualification.

Aptitude measures are very popular in educational settings related to college admissions (e.g., SAT, ACT) and admission to graduate studies (e.g., GRE, Law School Admission Test [LSAT], Medical College Admission Test [MCAT], Graduate Management Admission Test [GMAT]). The idea is that these tests are helpful in predicting success in postsecondary education. As a general rule, these tests emphasize verbal reasoning, mathematical reasoning, and writing. Variations do exist among the measures. For example, the SAT evaluates critical reading, mathematics, and writing. The ACT evaluates

English, mathematics, reading, and science and includes an optional writing test. Although differences may exist between the measures, the SAT and ACT both attempt to address the same issue—how might a student perform in college? Koenig, Frey, and Detterman (2008) noted that ACT composite scores were strongly correlated with SAT composite scores ($r = .87$).

The use of college and graduate entrance examinations is an ongoing debate. The noted bias of these instruments is well documented, and the need to incorporate multiple measures to address entrance into academic programs cannot be overstated (Cimetta et al., 2010; Sedlacek, 2004; Stringer, 2008). According to Cimetta et al. (2010), aptitude test scores only account for 6% of the variance in freshman year GPA. This is only slightly higher than the recommended 4% for a minimum level of practical significance (Ferguson, 2009). So more seems to be unknown about predictors of college and postgraduate success than what is actually known.

Individuals who perform well on achievement measures also tend to perform well on aptitude measures and intelligence measures. A series of studies by Frey and Detterman (2004) and Koenig, Frey, and Detterman (2008) evaluated the relationship between SAT scores and IQ scores and ACT scores and IQ scores, respectively. Relationships between aptitude measures (SAT/ACT) and various IQ tests (i.e., California Test of Mental Maturity, Otis-Lennon Mental Ability Test, Lorge-Thorndike Intelligence Test, and Henmon-Nelson Test of Mental Maturity) correlated between .55 and .82. Thus, aptitude and achievement measures not only correlate highly with each other but also correlate highly with general cognitive ability, also known as intelligence. In fact, both achievement and aptitude tests may be considered measures of crystallized ability (gc). Roberts et al. (2000) stated that the ASVAB is truly a measure of crystallized intelligence (gc), thereby measuring facets of formal education and acculturated learning. The true value of ability testing is difficult to ascertain.

Types of Information Derived from Eva Marie's Case Study

From the information presented in either of the case studies, a rationale for administering ability assessments is not readily available. In order to provide a rationale to use ability testing for a case study presented in this text, we need to add some additional information to the case study of Eva Marie Garza. Recall that Eva Marie was a good student, as evidenced by her induction in the National Honor Society in sixth grade and remaining in the National Honor Society throughout high school. Eva Marie earned an associate's degree in accounting and never considered continuing postsecondary education toward a bachelor's degree.

Previously, Eva Marie had a job as a bookkeeper, which she enjoyed immensely, but she currently works as an assistant to the chief librarian at an elementary school. At 40 years old, Eva Marie may have over 20 years to invest in a career, but she may also lack some self-efficacy with respect to going back to school to earn a four-year degree or more in order to enhance her career opportunities. Given Eva Marie's anxiety, she may feel that she lacks the capacity to succeed in additional training that would facilitate a career transition. Even with encouragement from a counselor and pointing out that her academic history was quite strong, Eva Marie may be resistant to and anxious about the idea of further education. Certainly, the pressure she places on herself to care for her mother and the unemotional relationship she has with her husband, as well as the depressive symptoms that accompany her anxiety and possible comorbid depression, Eva Marie likely engages in negative self-talk that would serve as discouragement for pursuing further education. For example, Eva Marie may tell herself, "I could never get a four-year degree at my age," "I am not that smart. I just worked hard, and I do not know if I can do that anymore," or "Even if I earned a four year degree, who would hire me?"

Often, clients like Eva Marie may benefit from a concrete, objective evaluation that could enhance her self-concept and provide information that could be used to encourage her to take some risks that may be beneficial. For this reason, the counselor may opt to administer a brief intelligence measure, such as the KBIT-2. In addition, the DAT may be helpful in assessing strengths and weaknesses that could lead to a new career path or opportunity. What follows is a score report based on an administration of the KBIT-2 and DAT to Eva Marie.

Eva Marie was administered the Kaufman Brief Intelligence Test-2 (KBIT-2) and Differential Aptitude Test (DAT) in order to provide Eva Marie general feedback about her mental capabilities. Administration of the KBIT-2 and DAT was within the guidelines of stated procedures, and results from this test may be viewed as a valid measure. The KBIT-2 is a brief measure of intelligence that may be used as a screen for intellectual functioning. The KBIT-2 correlates strongly with established measures of intelligence, such as the Wechsler Intelligence Scales. The DAT is designed to measure essential domains relevant to job performance based on general cognitive ability.

KBIT-2

Eva Marie's score report from the KBIT-2 indicated above average intellectual functioning. The following table represents Eva Marie's scores on the KBIT-2 (Table 9.2):

TABLE 9.2 Score Summary on the KBIT-2

Scale	Raw Scores	Standard Scores	90% CI (SEM)	Percentile Rank	Descriptive Category
Verbal Domain	97	112	104–119	79th	Average
Verbal Knowledge	52				
Riddles	45				
Nonverbal Domain	44	125	116–132	95th	Above average
Matrices	44				
IQ Composite[a]		119	113–124	90th	Above average

Note: KBIT-2 = Kaufman Brief Intelligence Test, second edition; CI = confidence interval; SEM = standard error of measurement.
[a] IQ composite is the sum of the standard scores (112 + 125 = 237) and then transformed to a standard score (119).

As shown in the table, Eva Marie scored in the 79th percentile of the Verbal domain, placing her in the average range of intellectual functioning. The Verbal domain is a measure of crystallized ability, which generally reflects cognitive ability associated more with formal education. Eva Marie, therefore, ranks in the average range in her ability to identify and express verbal concepts, reason, and demonstrate knowledge of general information.

Eva Marie scored in the 95th percentile of the Nonverbal domain, placing her in the above average range of intellectual functioning. The Nonverbal domain is a measure of fluid ability, which generally reflects reasoning and learning outside of acculturation and formal education. Eva Marie, therefore, shows strong ability in addressing novel problems that are not necessarily taught or trained.

Although the difference between Eva Marie's Verbal and Nonverbal scores was notable and statistically significant ($p < .05$), the difference was not large enough to be considered infrequent or unusual. Eva Marie's IQ composite is 119, also placing her in the above average range and reflective of the top 10% of intellectual functioning given her placement in the 90th percentile.

DAT

The DAT may be helpful in assessing strengths and weaknesses that could lead to a new career path or opportunity. A DAT summary report provides scale scores and percentiles based on the standard score (Table 9.3).

Eva Marie was in the average range for Verbal Reasoning, Mechanical Reasoning, Spelling, and Educational Aptitude. She was above average in Language Use and excelled in Numerical Reasoning, Abstract Reasoning, Perceptual Speed/Accuracy, and Space Relations. Eva Marie's high score in Abstract Reasoning, along with her scores in Verbal Reasoning and Educational Aptitude, are indicative of an individual

TABLE 9.3 Summary of DAT Scores for Eva Marie Garza

Scale	Percentile
Verbal Reasoning	60th
Numerical Reasoning	90th
Abstract Reasoning	95th
Perceptual Speed/Accuracy	99th
Mechanical Reasoning	55th
Space Relations	90th
Spelling	40th
Language Usage	75th
Educational Aptitude	65th

Note: DAT = Differential Aptitude Test.

who would do well in further education and training. Eva Marie shows potential for the capacity to work in more technical fields (e.g., computer programming, software engineer, science and engineering, architecture) given her high scores in abstract reasoning and space relations. In addition, her very high Numerical Reasoning and Perceptual Speed/Accuracy scores indicate why accounting and bookkeeping seemed to be natural fit. Hence, a career counselor may work with Eva Marie to either further her education and career in these areas or, given her present anxiety, assist her in finding a position more relevant to her strengths.

The purpose of these assessments was to provide Eva Marie objective information that she could use to decide whether or not she has the ability to pursue higher education at this age and stage of her life. Given Eva Marie's above average capacities, particularly as they relate to her reasoning ability and problem-solving ability with novel situations, she is likely a good candidate for further educational pursuits.

10

Fundamentals of Career Assessment

> ### Objectives
> 1. Identify various constructs related to career assessment.
> 2. View career assessment as a multifaceted assessment process, including assessment of personality, interests, values, and abilities.
> 3. Become familiar with a variety of assessment tools.
> 4. Understand Holland's RIASEC model and its relation to personality, interests, and values.
> 5. Identify how career assessment constructs can be used with clients and applied to our case studies.
> 6. Become familiar with the O*NET system.
> 7. Identify strengths and weaknesses in using technology in the career assessment process.

The purpose of this chapter is to provide an overview of assessment in career counseling. Foundations of career counseling are beyond the scope of the chapter. Rather, we focus on how career assessment may provide valuable information for guiding career counseling and overall wellness of clients served in multiple settings such as schools, agencies, organizations, and practices.

What Is Career Assessment?

The foundation of career counseling was based on career assessment. Frank Parsons, considered the founder of vocational guidance and the counseling movement, identified the assessment of traits as the primary component to selecting a career (Sharf, 2010). Examples of common career traits include personality, interests, values, and abilities. Career assessment, therefore, is a process in which counselors work with clients to gain a composite framework of personality, interests, values, and abilities to facilitate career counseling and foster a career identity. Counselors use career assessment to assist clients with career exploration, selection, and/or adjustment to new career settings.

Counselors recognize that career development begins in childhood and advocate a lifespan development approach to understanding one's career (e.g., Super, 1990). Therefore, career assessment may also begin in the formative years; yet extant research on career assessment in childhood is limited (Schultheiss & Stead, 2004). Schultheiss and Stead hypothesized that addressing career development in childhood (e.g., fourth grade) could provide information to counselors related to effective problem-solving and decision-making. The purpose in assessing career development at an early age is not to influence career choice but rather to use career assessment to promote goal-setting, achievement, and academic success.

Through matriculation of middle school and high school, career assessment may incorporate models that integrate interests, personality, abilities, and values (Armstrong & Rounds, 2010). Career assessment at this stage may influence individuals' decisions on postsecondary education, training, and vocational placements. During this phase of career assessment, individuals may explore how their interests, values, and abilities relate to goal-setting and future career choice. For example, Super (1990) encouraged younger adolescents to focus on identification of careers and awareness of one's own attributes. Older adolescents and young adults may be exposed to a wider variety of career assessment strategies that may be important to career decision-making. For example, the Armed Services Vocational Aptitude Battery (ASVAB), college entrance examinations, various state achievement tests, and potential interest, ability, and values inventories (e.g., Strong Interest Inventory, Occupational Information Network [O*NET] instruments) may be administered or made available through guidance counselors.

Throughout adulthood, career assessment may be integral for clients who wish to explore different career opportunities or options, transition between careers or within a career, identify career needs or placement opportunities, or transition because of developmental needs. Such examples may include individuals who simply wish to change careers, realizing that their current career is less satisfying, to individuals who served in the armed forces and are transitioning to civilian life, or to transition to a new phase such as semiretirement or retirement. In addition, career assessment may be helpful in identifying issues related to career satisfaction and work–life balance.

Elements of Career Assessment

Personality, interests, values, and abilities are all relevant constructs to career assessment. Each of these facets of career assessment is addressed in this chapter, along with the implications of career assessment. Previously in Chapter 9, we discussed the assessment of ability, addressing various types of instruments categories such as intelligence, achievement, and aptitude measures. Tests such as the ASVAB and Differential Aptitude Test, as well as various achievement tests, may be used to identify strengths and challenges for individuals seeking to begin, transition to, or advance in new career opportunities. Many of these tests emphasize various cognitive capacities, such as mathematical reasoning and verbal reasoning.

Evaluation of a single construct provides a limited approach to career assessment. We advocate for a multifaceted approach to career assessment that integrates abilities, interests, values, and personality in to a comprehensive profile. One extremely helpful resource discussed to greater degree in this chapter is the O*NET system. O*NET is a comprehensive assessment system funded by the U.S. Department of Labor/ Employment and Training Administration (2017a). At the time of this writing, information on the O*NET system can be found on the O*NET Resource Center website: http://www.onetcenter.org/usingOnet.html. From the website, counselors can access and facilitate a variety of career exploration tools, including assessment instruments for career exploration and various occupational support and information materials for a variety of populations.

Interests and Personality

Perhaps the most widely used personality theory tied to career assessment is Holland's model of career interest based on personality theory. For this reason, it is difficult to address issues of personality assessment and interest assessment separately when discussing career assessment. The reason is that Holland's theory incorporates issues of personality in respect to career choice. Holland believed that individuals would experience higher degrees of congruence when their personalities were matched with their occupational environment. In other words, a large degree of life satisfaction rests in the idea that an individual's personality should be aligned with the career vocation he or she chooses.

The RIASEC Model

Holland (1973, 1985, 1997) outlined a model of six personality types aligned with corresponding vocational environments in a hexagonal model that would attribute similar and dissimilar work environments for each personality type. The model incorporates six personality types, known as the RIASEC model: realistic, investigative, artistic, social, enterprising, and conventional. Figure 10.1 provides a visual representation of the model.

In Figure 10.1, personality types adjacent to each other share similar characteristics (e.g., enterprising and social), whereas personality types directly opposite (e.g., enterprising and investigative) share fewer characteristics. Next we describe each of the personality types.

Realistic

Individuals who fit this personality type often engage in hands-on activities. Such work may involve using tools or machinery in a variety of environments (e.g., forestry, farming, construction, maintenance).

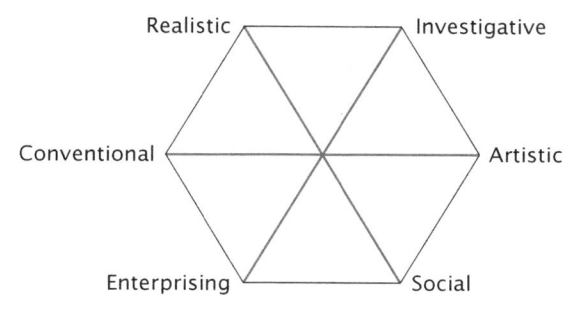

FIGURE 10.1 Holland's Code (RIASEC Model).

Investigative
Individuals who are investigative prefer careers that require problem-solving and fact-finding. Such individuals prefer to address issues mentally, rather than physically. Researchers in a variety of settings, engineers, and detectives are a few examples that fit this personality type.

Artistic
This type of individual often prefers vocations that require creative elements or expertise. Although the arts (e.g., musician, artist, writer) are a natural fit for this personality type, areas of counseling, education, and architecture also serve as examples of the artistic type. People who ascribe to this personality type may be individuals who work well with forms, patterns, and diagrams.

Social
Occupations in the social realm involve working with others in some capacity. These often include positions in the service and healthcare industries. Counselors and educators also fit this description quite well.

Enterprising
Individuals who fit this profile often prefer vocations that require leadership and decision-making. Such individuals are not adverse to risk-taking. People who enter the business professions or move into leadership within an agency or organization often fit this personality type.

Conventional
Individuals who fit this personality type may excel in working with details and prefer routines. Although this personality type often is associated with bookkeeping, other potential vocations include such jobs as accountant, pharmacist, and research analyst.

Tests that Use the RIASEC Model
Because of the prevalent nature of Holland's theory, also referred to as Holland's codes, a number of assessment batteries and career assessment resources were developed using

this theoretical framework. Common assessment batteries include the Strong Interest Inventory (SII), Self-Directed Search (SDS), and the O*NET Interest Profiler (IP).

The purpose of the SII is to match individuals across a wide range of occupations based on the individual's interests as operationally defined using Holland's codes. Hence, individuals are matched with occupations that may appear congruent to their interests (Kelly, 2010). The SII takes approximately 40 to 45 minutes to administer and is specifically geared toward ages 16 and older. Therefore, the SII is not appropriate for exploring career interests in early developmental stages. One advantage of the SII is that it may be used for group administrations, thereby making the SII an effective tool for group guidance in school settings. The psychometric properties of the instrument are sound, and the instrument has a long history with ongoing updates and renorming that encourage comprehensive, current results.

The SDS is similar to the SII in that the SDS uses the RIASEC model to facilitate career exploration. The SDS is a psychometrically sound instrument with the following added benefits:

- The SDS was developed by John Holland, who created the RIASEC model.
- The SDS was developed to comply with assessment guidelines of the National Career Development Association.
- The SDS includes multiple forms that can be used with professional-level employees, such as adults in career transition, and younger adolescents (ages 11 and above), students, and adults with limited reading levels (Brown, 2001). An advantage of the SDS is that career booklets are provided with each of the forms to assist with career exploration activities.

The O*NET IP is part of a comprehensive assessment system operated by the U.S. Department of Labor/ Employment and Training Administration described earlier in this chapter. Similar to the SII, the IP uses the RIASEC model. The IP can be accessed in two forms from the O*NET Resource Center. Individuals may download the test manual and test form to administer or self-administer. A computerized version, referred to as the CIP, is also available. The test form and computerized version are identical, containing 180 items that match occupations with career interests. The psychometric characteristics of the IP are strong; with the added flexibility of materials being accessible online and free to the user, the IP is an excellent resource for counselors to use with clients or for individuals to use the assessment forms and additional employment/vocational resources. One of the advantages to using the CIP is the wealth of resources presented at the end of the administration. Upon completing the 180 items, the user receives scores and a Holland code from the RIASEC personality types to identify potential jobs that match the user's interests. In addition, the user is asked to identify the amount of training and education he or she has at present or to search for jobs that would require some additional training. Job zones are provided for the following areas:

1. Little or no preparation.
2. Some preparation, such as previous work experience, vocational training, a high school diploma or associate's degree.
3. Medium preparation, such as on-the-job training, previous work experience, an associate's or bachelor's degree.
4. Considerable preparation, such as a bachelor's degree or two to four years' work experience.
5. Extensive preparation, such as a graduate degree and extensive training in a specific area.

One limitation of the O*NET system is the required skill needed to search through the abundance of materials in the O*NET Resource Center. Skills in using the Internet can be overwhelming for clients who have limited exposure to technology and the Internet.

Holland (1997) identified personality and interest as a unified construct. Counselors can be helpful in facilitating clients to seek out work environments that fit their personality type. Thus, through the use of assessment batteries that identify career interests according to Holland's codes (i.e., RIASEC), individuals may achieve greater career self-efficacy and self-actualization.

Other Tools

In addition to Holland's codes, other personality theories and measures are used frequently in career assessment. Specifically, the Myers-Briggs Personality Type Indicator (MBTI) and instruments related to the five-factor model of personality (e.g., NEO Personality Inventory-3, Adjective Checklist) are used frequently for career assessment.

The MBTI is a popular personality instrument used in various capacities, such as individual counseling; couples, marriage, and family counseling; and task groups in organizations. The MBTI uses Jungian theory of personality to group individuals into specified categories. Using four categorical dyads, individuals may be classified along the following:

- Introversion—Extroversion
- Sensing—Intuition
- Thinking—Feeling
- Judging—Perceiving

As a result of the multifaceted uses for the MBTI, applications to career assessment may appear to be a natural fit. Katz, Joyner, and Seaman (1999) evaluated college students and found the MBTI to be as helpful as the SII in making career decisions. Katz et al. recommended joint administration of the MBTI and SII to facilitate career choices in college students. However, correlations between MBTI personality types and the RIASEC categories are low (Pulver & Kelly, 2008), which may indicate that although the two instruments together may provide a more comprehensive profile of the individual, using the MBTI in lieu of the SII is not advisable.

The five-factor model of personality (FFM) is a well-defined, highly researched personality theory that identifies five aspects of personality: openness, conscientiousness, extraversion, agreeableness, and neuroticism. Openness refers to someone who may be receptive, accommodating, and/or amenable to new ideas and situations. Conscientiousness may refer to one who is responsible and persistent. Individuals who fit this description may plan ahead in order to achieve. Extraversion refers to individuals who are sociable, amiable, and willing to assert their thoughts and points of view to others. Agreeableness refers to individuals who may be trustworthy, cooperative, and caring. Neuroticism may refer to individuals prone to negative affective states, such as feelings of hostility, fear, depression, anxiety, or negative self-evaluation (McCrae & Costa, 1992). The personality dimensions of the FFM tend to be predictive of career self-efficacy and achievement orientation, particularly with respect to individuals who are extraverted and conscientious (Reed, Bruch, & Haase, 2004). Similar to limitations of the MBTI, the correlations between the RIASEC personality model and the FFM are not overwhelmingly strong (Nauta, 2004), thereby reiterating caution in using such personality measures in lieu of interest inventories.

An additional limitation of such personality tests that do not specifically address the RIASEC model is that career exploration tools are not inherently developed to address other personality types at this time. Instruments such as the SII and IP use the RIASEC model and include an abundant number of resources (e.g., O*NET Resource Center) that can be used to facilitate career exploration.

Values

Values within the context of career assessment refer to the subjective importance and meaningfulness of activities in work and the work environment (Smith & Campbell, 2008). Smith and Campbell further ascribed to the belief that work values are more tied to "standards or goals" (p. 41). Career interests may be viewed as means to pursue goals or objectives, which are identified through values. In this respect, career interests emanate from career values. Work values may be assessed through the identification of individuals' personal values, referred to as "person-based" assessment, or through identifying values that may be descriptive of various work environments, referred to as "occupation-based" assessment (Smith & Campbell, 2008, p. 41).

A popular person-based assessment is the Minnesota Importance Questionnaire (MIQ). The purpose of the MIQ is to evaluate adjustment toward work, operationally defined as the extent to which an individual's needs and realization of rewards are met through work (Layton, 1992). To achieve this goal, the MIQ measures 20 psychological needs across six fundamental values: (a) achievement, (b) autonomy, (c) altruism, (d) comfort, (e) safety, and (f) status. Although the MIQ exhibits adequate psychometric properties, one limitation is that the instrument is designed for individuals 16 years and older.

Therefore, the MIQ is not appropriate for evaluating work values prior to the later high school years.

Aligned with the MIQ, the Minnesota Job Description Questionnaire (MJDQ) is an occupation-based assessment. The MJDQ uses statements aligned with the 20 psychological needs of the MIQ to describe the types of reinforcement (referred to as occupational reinforcement patters) from various occupational environments (Zedeck, 1978). Counselors can use client responses on the MJDQ to address alignment with client responses on the MIQ. In this regard, the MJDQ is not an independent assessment but functions as an addition to a comprehensive assessment system with the MIQ. Similar to the MIQ, the MJDQ has strong psychometric characteristics and is appropriate for use with older adolescents and adults. An additional limitation is that counselors need to adopt the system of assessment (i.e., use the MIQ) to make use of the MJDQ.

Similar to what O*NET did with the IP, O*NET created two work values inventories based upon the MIQ and MJDQ: the Work Importance Locator (WIL) and the Work Importance Profiler (WIP). The instruments are the same, with the exception that the WIP is a computer-based administration and the WIL is a card-sort administration and hand-scored instrument (Smith & Campbell, 2008). Similar to the MIQ and MJDQ, the WIL and WIP assess six work values across 20 psychological needs. The U.S. Department of Labor/Employment and Training Administration provided the following work values and psychological needs:

1. *Achievement*—refers to individuals who value attaining results and using their strengths, resulting in feelings of accomplishment. Corresponding psychological needs are *ability utilization* and *achievement.*
2. *Independence*—refers to individuals who value making decisions and working autonomously. Corresponding psychological needs are *creativity, responsibility,* and *autonomy.*
3. *Recognition*—refers to individuals who value advancement and potential to serve as a leader. Such individuals may value positions that garner prestige. Corresponding psychological needs are *advancement, authority, recognition,* and *social status.*
4. *Relationships*—refers to individuals who value providing service to others and working with colleagues in a noncompetitive environment. Corresponding psychological needs are *coworkers, moral values,* and *social service.*
5. *Support*—refers to individuals who value management that advocates, validates, and encourages employees. Corresponding psychological needs are *company policies* and *supervision over personnel* and *technical expertise.*
6. *Working conditions*—refers to individuals who value job security and a good working environment. Corresponding psychological needs are *activity, compensation, independence, security, variety,* and *working conditions* (U.S. Department of Labor/Employment and Training Administration, 2017b; O*NET OnLine, http://www.onetonline.org/find/descriptor/browse/Work_Values/).

Both the WIL and the WIP require the individual to sort through 20 psychological needs that apply to the six corresponding values. Individuals have the option of identifying the importance of each need from a scale of 1 (*least important*) to 5 (*most important*). Only four cards can be identified under each scaled score (e.g., four needs identified as *most important* [5], four needs identified as *important* [4]). As each psychological need reflects a value, a score for each value is tallied. The top two values indicate job categories to be explored. Similar to the CIP, when the WIP is used in conjunction with the CIP, users can identify the match between their interests and values to identify jobs that are aligned with both constructs. In addition, the user can search through various job zones described earlier in the chapter to identify required training for particular jobs. Hence, training, interests, and values can all be integrated in the O*NET system to provide a comprehensive profile of the client.

O*NET offers the Ability Profiler (AP) as an additional measure. The AP measures nine job-related abilities, including (a) verbal ability, (b) arithmetic reasoning, (c) computation, (d) spatial ability, (e) form perception, (f) clerical perception, (g) motor coordination, (h) finger dexterity, and (i) manual dexterity. The AP includes components that cannot be provided online for the finger dexterity and manual dexterity subtests. In addition, the instrument requires timed tasks. An administrator with training is necessary for this instrument, and additional scoring materials need to be purchased. For these reasons, the AP is less user-friendly than other instruments offered through O*NET.

Issues in Computerized Career Assessment

Many publishing companies take advantage of technology to facilitate assessment, especially with respect to scoring and interpretation profiles. Career assessment, by comparison, includes far more resources, probably because the U.S. government dedicated significant resources to developing career assessment and exploration tools through the Department of Labor. As with any computerized assessment process, interpretations may be generated through the software and therefore lack a human element to interpretation. Hence, when counselors solely rely on computer output to evaluate clients, information garnered through clinical interviews, subsequent sessions, and/or additional assessment measures may not be reflected adequately. Career assessment may complicate this process further with the multitude of resources all individuals have access to regardless of training. For example, the O*NET system includes sophisticated measures that are not readily understood without training. Although a layperson could investigate the limited information on the RIASEC model or work values, having a theoretical understanding of how the O*NET system was developed and applied is helpful. More important is the issue of how clients will use career assessment to make decisions. Because of the amount of information presented, counselors should take considerable time to process with the client the results of various assessments. Issues that the counselor can facilitate include the amount of training the client has and is willing to obtain in order to advance or transition to a new career. Such information is important in successfully working through the O*NET system.

Counselors who use the computerized career assessments may need to provide training to clients with respect to how they can navigate through the O*NET system. We offer the following suggestions to assist counselors with using this career assessment process:

1. Counselors should become familiar with the O*NET system by self-administering the assessment instruments, particularly the CIP and WIP. Once the assessment is completed, the system produces results and provides search strategies for identifying potential career options.
2. One benefit of the O*NET system is that the client can self-administer the assessments at home. However, for the counselor to be able to process the information from the assessments, the output produced from the assessments would be helpful. Clients may need assistance in identifying important personality interests or values versus less pertinent personality interests or values.
3. Because of the opportunity to engage in career exploration after the completion of the assessment(s), administration, scoring, and subsequent career exploration activities might be best facilitated with the counselor present.
4. The scoring system for the assessment instruments, although available to the client in the user's manuals, tends to be rather technical. Ethical administration, scoring, and interpretation of measures depend on the counselor's knowledge of administration, scoring, and interpretation processes. Counselors should review the user manuals provided.
5. Clients who are less familiar with technology may find this process intimidating. Procedures to administer the instruments in the counselor's office may be necessary. In addition, use of the O*NET system requires downloading of necessary software, so a level of technology literacy is necessary.

The use of career assessment processes through the Internet provides an opportunity and accessibility for assessment tools that is unprecedented in other assessment areas. Counselors should be cautious with such technology because of the potential of unstandardized administrations. The assessment tools provided through O*NET are useful and valid when used appropriately. However, the potential for confounding results through overreliance on individual client administration is apparent and should be addressed when training the client to use the materials appropriately.

Types of Information Derived from Eva Marie's Case Study

To provide an overview of career assessment and the application of the concepts presented in this chapter, we focus on administration of the CIP and WIP with Eva Marie Garza. To facilitate interpretation of Eva Marie's career assessment profile, we present information from the user's manual of the CIP and WIP that may be accessed from the O*NET Resource Center website.

The CIP was developed to be parallel to the hand-scored administration of the IP. Recall that the goal of the CIP (and IP) is to evaluate personality interests based on the RIASEC model. The CIP includes 180 items. There are 30 items that represent each of the personality interests (realistic, investigative, artistic, social, enterprising, conventional). Each item includes a work task in which the client responds with *Like* or *Dislike*. If the client is unsure, he or she can click on a question mark as a third option. The CIP is scored through the software, and results are presented to the client. The client receives a score in each of the six areas of the RIASEC model. For each of the 30 items endorsed on a particular subscale, a point is recorded for that subscale. For example, if a client marks *Like* for an item that is matched with Conventional, then one point is recorded for Conventional. No points are scored for an item marked otherwise. So, with 30 items for each subscale, the maximum score for each subscale is 30. The top three scores represent the client's Holland code. Once a score report is produced and a Holland code is put forward, the client is presented with job zones matching the Holland code and the amount of training he or she wishes to consider for a career. Clients can search through particular vocations that match their interests.

The WIP includes two tasks. The first task is to rank work needs, described earlier as psychological needs. Five different needs are presented at one time. The client ranks each of the needs, starting with the most important to the least important. This process is repeated across 21 screens with each need appearing several times in order to compare and rank each need across all other needs. Once the client completes the 21 screens, the second task requires the client to rate work needs. On a single page, 21 statements appear and the client provides a *Yes* or *No* response to indicate whether a particular work need is important to him or her. From these two tasks, the computer generates scores for each of the six work values: (a) achievement, (b) independence, (c) recognition, (d) relationships, (e) support, and (f) working conditions. The score report may fit one of three categories. A *differentiated* score report occurs when at least one work value is positive and different from the other work values. A *negative* score report occurs when all work value scores are below zero. In this case, the client receives a notification indicating that the work values being measured on this instrument do not appear pertinent to the client. An *undifferentiated* score report occurs when no work value appears more or less important than other work values. In this case, a notification is generated to indicate this to the client. So it is possible that the results from the WIP contribute little to clients' understanding of work values and the influence on career choice. However, it is also possible that the results from the WIP can be integrated with the CIP results to provide a rather comprehensive profile of the client.

The following is a description of Eva Marie's score report on the CIP and WIP.

> Eva Marie Garza is a 40-year-old Latina female who presents with a history of anxiety and depression. Based on a clinical interview with Eva Marie, some

maladjustment is evident from dissatisfaction with her career. Eva Marie earned an associate's degree and worked previously as a bookkeeper, first for a Catholic church and then for a local drug store. Eva Marie reported being "good with numbers" and that bookkeeping gave her a "sense of purpose." Eva Marie described her previous boss at the drug store as someone who valued her work, and she took pride in her job. When Eva Marie relocated to San Antonio, she was unable to obtain a bookkeeping position and now works as an assistant to the librarian at an elementary school. Eva Marie dislikes her current position but enjoys the opportunity to make decisions.

Eva Marie was administered the Computerized Interest Profiler (CIP) and the Work Importance Profiler (WIP). Administration of the CIP and WIP was within the guidelines of stated procedures, and results from this test may be viewed as a valid measure. Eva Marie's score report from the CIP indicated a Holland code of CSA (Conventional, Social, Artistic) with the following scores:

Realistic: 0
Investigative: 0
Artistic: 3
Social: 5
Enterprising: 2
Conventional: 14

The Artistic trait was quite low and comparable to Enterprising, indicating that emphasis on job interests should focus more so on Conventional characteristics and some Social characteristics.

Eva Marie had a differentiated score report on the WIP, identifying Relationships and Achievement as her most pertinent work values as indicated in the following score report:

Achievement: 1.4
Support: 0.2
Recognition: 0.8
Relationships: 1.5
Working Conditions: 0
Independence: 0.4

The score reports from the CIP and WIP fit the information from Eva Marie's clinical interview quite well. Individuals described as Conventional tend to enjoy routines and prefer working with data and details. In addition, Eva Marie's desire to work with tasks that help people or are important to an organization fit nicely with the Social personality interest, as well as the Relationship work value. Additionally, Eva Marie's desire to feel productive and use her skills (such as working with numbers) contributes to the Achievement work value.

When exploring potential career options, Eva Marie may want to consider whether she wants to explore career options with her current training or whether she is willing to obtain additional training. Although bookkeeping was an immediate fit, given her Conventional personality interest that fit her work values, 36 potential occupations were listed from the O*NET database. Some of these diverse positions include travel agent and ticket agent, statistical assistant, emergency dispatcher, customer service representative, and municipal clerk. If Eva Marie is open to additional training, other job opportunities may include medical secretary or technician, legal secretary, city planning aide, licensing examiner and inspector, title examiner or abstractor, or court clerk. Eva Marie should be encouraged to explore both a current job that matches her interests and values as well as the potential to secure additional training/education to pursue a new career. Such a transition, while stressful, may improve her self-concept and decrease her stress, which in part stems from an unfulfilling career.

This report may accompany a psychological report or stand alone as a career assessment report. What is important is that the client obtains a sense of validation, hope, and self-efficacy from the process. In other words, if a client is experiencing maladjustment from dissatisfaction with work, the prospect of exploring new opportunities and options may be both empowering and fulfilling. Individuals may spend an inordinate amount of time in career-related activities. Thus, the importance of addressing career and assessing career satisfaction can be a major component to address the overall well-being of clients.

11

Marriage, Substance Abuse, and Suicide Assessment

> ### Objectives
> 1. Describe the Marital Satisfaction Inventory-Revised and understand how Eva Marie and her husband view their marriage, based on their scores.
> 2. Describe the Substance Abuse Subtle Screening Inventory-4, explain the instrument's scales, and provide an overview depicting Robert's scores and profile.
> 3. Describe the Suicide Probability Scales and explore how to determine if a client's scores suggest a client is at high or low risk of suicidal behaviors.
> 4. Identify the suicide SCATTT mnemonic's six phases and describe how to use the assessment with clients perceived to be at imminent risk.

Overview

Over the years, we have found the need to use many different psychological assessment instruments. Three clinical areas in which we and our supervisees frequently use assessment instruments are marital and couples counseling, addictions counseling, and suicide prevention and intervention. In an effort to enhance the readers' understanding of assessment instruments related to these important topic areas, the following instruments are described: the Marital Satisfaction Inventory–Revised (MSI-R), the Substance Abuse Subtle Screening Inventory-4 (SASSI-4), and the Suicide Probability Scale (SPS). In addition, the chapter includes the suicide SCATTT mnemonic. This mnemonic is used immediately after a client has been assessed to be at significant suicide risk. The SCATTT is intended to both protect the suicidal client and provide counselors a six-phase plan describing what to do between making the suicide assessment and moving the suicidal client to a least restrictive and protective environment. Robert Jones and Eva Marie Garza's clinical vignettes are used throughout the chapter to demonstrate the instruments.

Marital Satisfaction Inventory–Revised

We have found the MSI-R to be a user-friendly assessment instrument that has exceptional utility for counselors treating client couples. The instrument was created to help identify "the nature and extent of relationship distress with couples considering or beginning conjoint therapy" (Snyder, 1997, p. 1). The instrument can be used with traditional or nontraditional couples (Western Psychological Services [WPS], 2017). The MSI-R provides clear indications of the couples' individual and joint perceptions of their marriages, including challenges that may warrant immediate attention. These comprise 11 separate marital interaction dimensions, including Affective Communication, Role Orientation, Problem-Solving Communication, Aggression, Family History of Distress, Time Together, Dissatisfaction with Children, Disagreement about Finances, Conflict over Child Rearing, Sexual Dissatisfaction, and Global Distress (WPS, 2017). Concomitantly, the instrument provides information regarding the couples' perceptions of their children and the couples' parenting.

The MSI-R is comprised of 150 question stems with corresponding *true* and *false* response options (WPS, 2017). Childless couples complete Questions 1 through 129. Couples with children complete all 150 question stems. The last 21 questions deal specifically with perceptions related to the couple's children and parenting (e.g., disciplining, child-rearing workloads; Juhnke, 2002). A combination of 13 or more unmarked or "double-marked" responses (where the respondent endorsed both *true* and *false* responses) suggests the profile to be "unscorable" (Snyder, 1997, p. 6). According to Snyder, persons taking the instrument "should be instructed to respond to the inventory items *separately and without collaboration*" (p. 6). Thus, completing the MSI-R is not a project the couple completes together. Instead, each partner takes the instrument independently. The instrument takes approximately 25 minutes to complete and requires a sixth-grade reading level (p. 1). The MSI-R was developed for persons 16 years of age and older (D. Snyder, personal communications, September 27, 2005) and can be directly ordered from WPS (1-800-648-8857).

MSI-R Reliability and Validity

Test–retest reliability coefficients ranged between .74 and .88 with a mean coefficient of .79 (excluding the Inconsistency scale; Snyder, 1997, p. 55). These coefficients suggest the MSI-R scales appear relatively stable across time (Juhnke, 2002). Cronbach's alpha coefficients of internal consistency for all MSI-R scales except the Inconsistency scale ranged between .70 to .93 with a mean coefficient of .82 (Snyder, 1997, p. 55). Such coefficients reflect the instrument's internal consistency. Related to validity, each of the instrument's

13 scales was able to differentiate between clinical and nonclinical couples at the $p < .001$ level. Concomitantly, other research studies comparing "broad-band multidimensional measures of psychopathology and personality functioning in adults and children or adolescents" (Snyder, 1997, p. 68) suggest concurrent validity with appropriate and corresponding scales on the Minnesota Multiphasic Personality Inventory (MMPI) and the Personality Inventory for Children.

Scales

The MSI-R is comprised of 13 scales, including two validity scales and one global affective scale. The first validity scale, Inconsistency (INC), reports random or careless responses, which may also be indications of confusion or deliberate attempts at noncompliance (Snyder, 1997). High INC T scores of 66 and above suggest random scoring or a lack of investment in the assessment process. Conversely, low T scores of 54 or lower may indicate an overall investment in the testing process and potentially a more positive perception of most MSI-R relationship domains (e.g., communications, finances). The second scale, Conventionalization (CNV), reports the clients' "tendencies to distort the appraisal of their relationship in a socially desirable direction." (Snyder, 1997, p. 20). High T scores of 55 or higher on this scale suggest defensiveness and resistance to discussing conflict within the relationship. We have found couples who have been mandated into family treatment by the courts or child protective services, or legal counsel of one member of the couple has "highly encouraged" the clients to participate in family counseling before custody cases go to trial, sometimes present with highly inflated CNV T scores of 65 and above. Such scores may at first appear incongruent with the couple presenting for relationship counseling. This is because the scores initially may seem to suggest the couple is saying, "The relationship is fine. Nothing is wrong or broken." However, what they may be attempting to suggest is they "don't need help" or they are "perfect" partners or parents and warrant full custody of their children. Low CNV T scores of 40 to 45, conversely, are frequently associated with moderate overall relationship distress. Here, couples are reporting concerns within their marriages. Very low CNV T scores below 40 suggest the client is unrealistic and not acknowledging even the most basic positive features within the relationship.

The Global Distress (GDS) scale reports "overall dissatisfaction with the relationship" (Snyder, 1997, p. 21). High GDS T scores of 60 and above suggest remarkable relationship dissatisfaction that likely has existed for a significant time. Such scores are relatively common with couples when one partner struggles with addictions and the other does not, or when one partner has actively participated in long-term infidelity and the other has not. Here, the scores may reflect the nonaddicted or noncheating partner viewing the addicted or cheating partner as causing the relationship dissatisfaction. The score further indicates that the nonaddicted or noncheating partner views the other partner as critical and uncaring. Concomitantly, the chaos and dysfunction of living with an addicted or cheating partner is often strikingly apparent when the nonaddicted or noncheating partner compares his or her relationship to other relationships that are perceived as loving, caring, and void of addiction, dysfunction, or infidelity.

Another MSI-R scale is the Affective Communication (AFC) scale. The AFC scale is the "best single measure of emotional intimacy experienced" by the couple (Snyder, 1997, p. 21) and reflects dissatisfaction related to perceived partner affection and understanding. High T scores of 60 or above denote extensive dissatisfaction related to expressed love and affection within the relationship (Juhnke, 2002). On the other hand, lower T scores of 50 and below suggest the couple experiences their relationship as happy and fulfilling and their partners as loving and supportive. In couples where addiction is present for both partners, the authors have generally found these scores are more moderate than one might initially anticipate. Here, although the addicted clients' spouses may not be endorsing feelings of great affection and support, they tend to report feeling "understood" and often "accepted" by each other.

The Problem-Solving Communication (PSC) scale measures the "couple's general ineffectiveness in resolving differences and measures overt discord rather than underlying feelings of estrangement" (Snyder, 1997, p. 22). Couples scoring high on this scale with T scores at and above 60 are reporting chronic arguing within the marriage. Many times, these client couples are unable or unwilling to look at voiced partner complaints through their spouse's eyes. These clients often view their partner as intentionally mean and highly rigid. By contrast, couples presenting low T PSC scores (below 50) appear invested in their marital relationship and display behaviors or make statements suggesting they want or expect the relationship to improve. In our experience, couples endorsing moderately to significantly low PSC T scores (43 and below) are those in which either the marriage is in the early developmental stages or the identified stressor (e.g., infidelity, addictions) is perceived as being of limited consequence.

The Aggression (AGG) scale reports intimidation and physical aggression. High T scores of 60 and above on this scale denote at least moderate levels of intimidation and physical aggression (e.g., pushing, grabbing, or slapping; Snyder, 1997, p. 23). Here, at least one of the partners is endorsing perceptions of intimidating behaviors or physical aggression by his or her partner. Again, it has been our experience that when sole child custody is being sought or when one or more partners fulfill antisocial personality disorder criteria, AGG scale scores are typically higher. Conversely, lower AGG T scores (50 or below) suggest an absence of physical aggression or intimidation. It should be noted that client couples could have significant relationship struggles and stressors without having inflated AGG scale scores.

The Time Together (TTO) scale assesses "the couple's companionship as expressed in terms of the time they spend together in leisure activity" (Snyder, 1997, p. 23). Spending time as a couple is an important part of relationship development and continuance. High TTO scores with T scores above 60 suggest the couple does not spend adequate time together. Here, the partners may well be spending the majority of their waking time hours away from one another with little emotionally significant quality time together. Low TTO

T scores (below 50) suggest time together. It is important to determine if partners scoring low on this scale are actually enjoying time together or if they are "together but separate." Here, for example, the couple might report that they are spending time "together." However, one may be playing video games, Facebook hopping, and Facetiming friends while the other is in the same room but watching sporting events and talking to friends or family not in the room.

The Disagreement about Finances (FIN) scale reports relationship disharmony resulting from financial management. Most of the client couples we have counseled, even highly affluent couples, endorse at least moderate FIN scale scores. High FIN *T* scores of 60 and above indicate financial concerns, lack of confidence in the partner's money management, and frequent arguments over money within the relationship. Low FIN *T* scores of 50 and below suggest agreement in the way money is managed. In our experience, the partner earning the highest salary is often the person reporting the greatest amount of dissatisfaction on this scale.

Another scale within the MSI-R is the Sexual Dissatisfaction (SEX) scale. According to Snyder (1997), this scale "reflects the respondent's level of discontent with the frequency and quality of intercourse and other sexual activities" (p. 24). High SEX *T* scores of 60 and above suggest "extensive dissatisfaction" (p. 25) related to the sexual relationship and frequency. Low SEX *T* scores of 50 and below suggest a generally positive sexual relationship. These lower-scoring SEX individuals view their sexual relationship with their partner as being favorable. Most of the couples we have counseled and who report low SEX scale scores and favorable sexual relations report the presence of open and frequent acts of affection such as holding hands, gentle touching, and nonsexual kissing (e.g., a peck on the cheek). Thus, when both partners perceive affection within the relationship, we typically find clients score low on the MSI-R SEX scale.

The Role Orientation scale is not necessarily a scale noting marital discord. Rather, it is a scale that reflects incongruence between partners' perceptions of traditional vis-à-vis nontraditional family roles. Here, higher *T* scores of 60 and above may indicate a belief in more contemporary parenting and marital roles; lower *T* scores of 50 or below may indicate more traditional parenting and marital roles. Thus, discord can result if spouses have highly differing expectations, assumptions, and beliefs related to how one and one's spouse will participate in such roles (Juhnke, 2002; Snyder, 1997).

The Family History of Distress (FAM) scale reports "disruption of relationships within the respondent's family of origin" (Snyder, 1997, p. 25). Higher *T* scores of 55 and above on the FAM scale suggest significant family of origin conflict and dysfunction. Lower *T* scores of 45 and below suggest the endorser experienced a fairly positive family-of-origin experience.

The remaining two scales measure concerns about children and parenting. The Dissatisfaction with Children (DSC) scale measures "emotional and behavioral adjustment of their children, quality of the parent-child relationship and negative impact of child rearing demands" (Snyder, 1997, p. 25). High DSC *T* scores of 60 and above suggest "greater levels of distress in respondents' relationships with their children" (p. 26). Couples endorsing lower DSC *T* scores of 50 or below typically indicate overall satisfaction with their children.

The final scale is the Conflict over Child Rearing (CCR) scale. Unlike the parent–child relationship addressed in the DSC scale, the CCR scale measures the conflict between parents because of child-rearing practices. High CCR *T* scores of 60 and above suggest "extensive conflict in the partners' interactions regarding children" (Snyder, 1997, p. 26). In other words, there likely exists discord between partners related to the way one or both discipline or rear children in the home, as well as discord related to the distribution of child-rearing responsibilities. Low CCR *T* scores of 50 and below suggest the opposite: low scores suggest satisfaction with one's partner's child-rearing responsibilities and disciplining of the children.

Eva Marie's MSI-R

Eva Marie's MSI-R responses are described in Figure 11.1. In addition, we provide Ernest's scores. As you will remember, Ernest is Eva Marie's husband. This allows us to discuss Eva Marie and Ernest's perceptions of their marital relationship. Specifically, we use

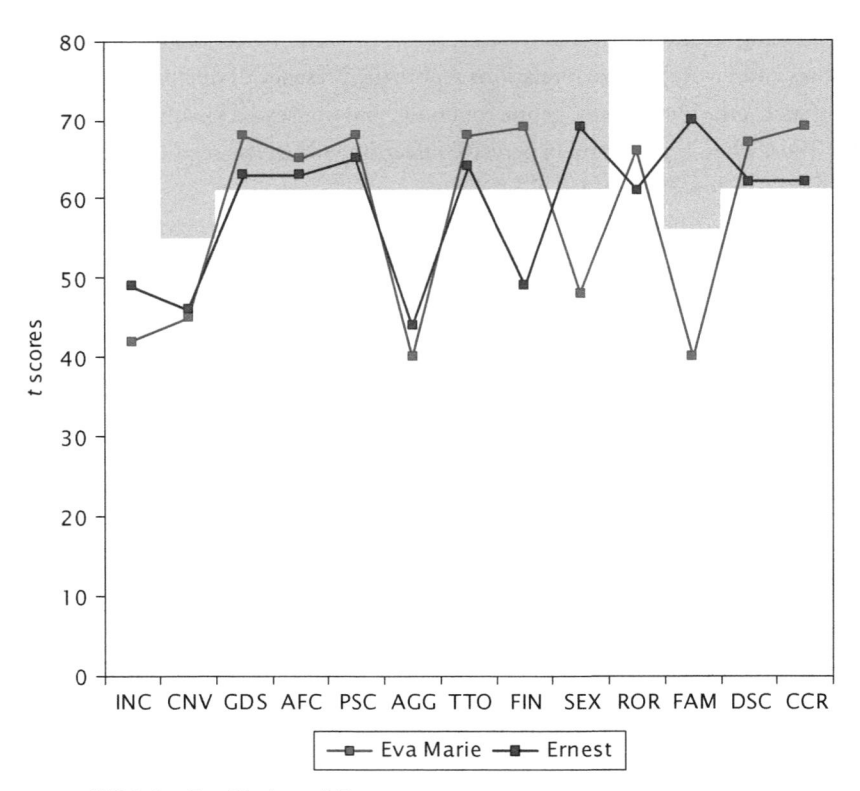

FIGURE 11.1 MSI-R for Eva Marie and Ernest.

the MSI-R scales to help identify potential areas of marital dissatisfaction and possible treatment goals.

Validity Scores

As always, we begin our review of client profiles with the client's Validity scores. Specifically, we wish to determine if the client responded in a manner that suggests she was invested in the assessment process, responded to question stems in a manner that suggested accurate or truthful endorsements, and responded in a manner that was relatively consistent.

Both Eva Marie and Ernest responded to all question stems on their respective MSI-R instruments. Examination of the couple's T scores on both the Inconsistency (Eva Marie T score of 42; Ernest T score of 49) and Conventionalization scales (Eva Maria T score of 45; Ernest T score of 46) supports further interpretation of the remaining instrument scales. In other words, both Eva Marie and Ernest appear to have endorsed the MSI-R questions stems in a manner that suggests they were at least moderately invested in the assessment process. Specifically, their Inconsistency scale T scores were noted in the low range. This suggests that both partners attended to item content but may have mixed sentiments regarding various aspects of their relationship. Neither spouse appears to report distorted appraisals of their marriage in an unrealistic, positive manner. Stated differently, both Eva Marie and Ernest admit relationship difficulties and stressors, without a blatant attempt to paint their marriage in a glowing or "perfectly heavenly" manner. In addition, Eva Marie and Ernest's low T scores on the Conventionalization scale (T scores at 45) suggest they are willing to discuss perceived conflicts within their marriage and suggest that both partners admit relationship distress and concerns.

The couple's Global Distress T scores are high. These high T scores (Eva Marie 68; Ernest 63) suggest both Eva Marie and Ernest have a predominate level of overall relationship dissatisfaction. Interestingly, Eva Marie's T score is higher than Ernest's. Thus, it is possible that Eva Marie's T score suggests she believes the relationship is in "worse shape" than Ernest believes. Given these T scores, Eva Marie and Ernest likely perceive each other as uncaring, critical, and cold and therefore as not meeting each other's perceived needs within the marriage.

Many times, we see this type of scoring in relationships where both partners are highly dissatisfied and believe the other partner's behaviors have "caused" the relationship's demise. These scores are further supported by both Eva Marie's and Ernest's Affective Communication scale T scores (Eva Marie 65; Ernest 63). Again, their high T scores on the Affective Communication scale suggest that Eva Marie and Ernest perceive a lack of affection and understanding by their partner. Given that both T scores on this scale are at such high levels, it is clear that each has extensive relationship dissatisfaction and likely feels his or her partner lacks warmth, understanding, and support. Simply stated, the couple's high T scores above 60 suggest they have mutually created what each believes is an intolerable living situation.

The couple's Problem-Solving Communications T scores (Eva Marie 68; Ernest 65) suggest the couple is ineffectively arguing with one another and unable to resolve their differences in an effective manner. Stated differently, Eva Marie and Ernest are likely openly arguing and bickering with one another without gaining mutually satisfactory responses from each other or mutually agreed-upon resolutions. Given such high T scores, their arguing appears chronic and pervasive throughout most areas of their lives. Concomitantly, both Eva Marie and Ernest likely perceive their partner as being intentionally critical, harsh, unsympathetic, and likely disparaging. In addition, it is highly unlikely that either Eva Marie or Ernest can allow him- or herself to listen to each other's concerns or even accept his or her partner's voiced concerns.

Although the earlier discussed Conventionalization scale suggested both partners would likely be willing to discuss their concerns, we have found couples presenting with such high Affective Communication scale T scores and Problem-Solving Communications scale T scores typically wish to proclaim their partner's faults and have an agenda to blame their partners for both real and perceived failures to provide affectionate and nurturing support. Thus, if given the chance, Eva Marie and Ernest would likely focus their time proclaiming his or her partner's perceived failures and lack of support rather than owning their own communication or behavior faults or limitations. Couples who reflect similar T scores like this on the Affective Communication scale and Problem-Solving Communications scale rarely take responsibility for their poor behaviors or contribute significant compromise. They also typically do not report how they could take responsibility in improving the relationship. Instead, they more often than not chose to be oblivious to their own responsibilities and prefer to verbally attack and nit-pick their partners.

Knowing Eva Marie as well as we now do, we would likely anticipate her Aggression scale T score to be low, which it is at 40. Here, Ernest's Aggression scale T score is in the low range too. (44) Thus, although the two appear to be actively arguing with one another, neither Eva Marie nor Ernest are reporting significant levels of intimidation or physical aggression, such as pushing, slapping, or hitting, within their marriage.

According to Eva Marie's and Ernest's Time Together scale T scores (Eva Marie 68; Ernest 64), the couple spends little if any time together. Thus, it is apparent that both Eva Marie and Ernest invest their energy away from one another and likely attempt to remain apart as much as possible. When forced to encounter one another, they likely interact little, and their interactions are probably guarded and argumentative. These T scores make sense given the previously noted low Affective Communication scale and Problem-Solving Communications scale T scores. Most people do not want to spend time with others they believe are argumentative and uncaring.

Based on Eva Marie's and Ernest's Disagreement About Finances scale T scores (Eva Marie 69; Ernest 49), it is evident that Eva Marie's significantly higher T score suggests she lacks confidence and is suspect of the manner in which Ernest uses the couple's money. Ernest's T score is in the low range. This suggests Ernest is generally accepting, if not supportive, of the manner in which Eva Marie manages the family's money. Clearly, however, the person with the greater concern is Eva Marie. Given that Ernest reportedly does not earn enough money to support Eva Marie and Ernest's living independently from Eva Marie's mother, we believe it is highly plausible that Eva Marie perceives Ernest as a "free loader" who is simply living at Eva Marie's mother's home and doing little to financially support Eva Marie or her aging mother. In addition, given Eva Marie's significant overall anxiety as reported in her initial clinical intake, it is likely that she is concerned about having enough money to adequately live once her mother passes. Thus, she may well be irritated that Ernest does not do more to contribute to the family's finances and perceives there is little she can do to change his lack of financial contributions.

The couple's Sexual Dissatisfaction scale T scores are interesting as well (Eva Marie, 48; Ernest 69). Given that Eva Marie has scored higher dissatisfaction on most MSI-R scales than Ernest, one might anticipate that Eva Marie would be more dissatisfied on this scale than Ernest would be. This is not the case. We suspect that Eva Marie's significant anxiety level is reflected in her low Sexual Dissatisfaction scale T score. In other words, given Eva Marie's general anxiousness and the high probability that she feels greater anxiety and discomfort being sexually intimate with a man she believes contributes little to her life and she perceives as caustic, cold, uncaring, argumentative, blaming, and unsympathetic to her emotional needs, she likely finds infrequent sexual activities quite acceptable. This clearly is not the case with Ernest. He reports clear discontent with the frequency of his sexual activities with Eva Marie, and this scale reflects this dissatisfaction.

Eva Marie's and Ernest's Role Orientation scale T scores reflect a less traditional view of typical marriage relationship roles (Eva Marie, 66; Ernest 61). Decision-making is likely predominantly made by Eva Marie due to her access and control over the couple's finances as indicated in the Disagreement About Finances scale scores. Thus, the couple's scores on the Role Orientation scale may reflect this less traditional view of Eva Marie's role—especially as money controller and administrator. Therefore, Ernest' score suggests a more contemporary marital role where he allows his wife to have greater say in in day-to-day household management.

Given what we know about both Eva Marie and remembering Eva Marie's earlier statement that Ernest grew up in an "alcoholic" family and did not want children, how might we anticipate Eva Marie and Ernest T scores will reflect their past Family History of Distress scale? As you likely may have perceived, Eva Marie's T score of 40 suggests she seems to romanticize her early life and family of origin experiences. Here, her father is painted as being perfect, and although the family struggled with being away from "The Valley" and family and friends, Eva Marie portrays a very loving and caring family of origin experience. Her low T score of 40 on the Family History of Distress scale suggests she likely experienced a very positive family of origin experience. Ernest, on the other hand, reportedly grew up in an alcoholic home. Most families that experience substance-abusing behaviors find their family of origin experiences chaotic and dysfunctional. This seems to be the case with Ernest. His Family History of Distress scale T score of 70 suggests he had significant disruption in family relationships as well as conflict and active dysfunction.

Given that Eva Marie and Ernest did not have children, the authors could not administer the Dissatisfaction with Children or Conflict over Child Rearing scales. However, for teaching purposes only, if Eva Marie and Ernest did have a 16-year-old biological son and a 14-year-old biological daughter, how might we anticipate Eva Marie and Ernest scores on these scales? Given their relationship dissatisfaction; blaming behaviors; perceptions that the other is too harsh, critical, and unsupportive; and lack of time with one another, we would anticipate elevated T scores on both scales by both Eva Marie and Ernest. In other words, Eva Marie and Ernest would likely endorse items on the Dissatisfaction with Children scale suggesting significant levels of distress in their relationships with their children.

Concomitantly, we would anticipate elevated T scores on the Conflict over Child Rearing scale. Specifically, we would anticipate T scores suggesting that Eva Marie and Ernest have significant disagreement and discord with one another's disciplining and child-rearing behaviors. In addition, it is plausible that at least Eva Marie would believe Ernest fails to invest adequate child-rearing time with the children and fails to support Eva Marie's child-rearing roles. Again, because Eva Marie and Ernest do not have children, we could not administer either the Dissatisfaction with Children or Conflict over Child Rearing scales. However, based on our knowledge of Eva Marie's clinical intake assessment and instrument scores generated thus far, we would anticipate the aforementioned scoring results.

Substance Abuse Subtle Screening Inventory-4

Another testing instrument we have found to have superior clinical utility is the SASSI-4. Over 20 years ago, we were trained to administer, score, and interpret the original SASSI. Since then, the SASSI has undergone three major revisions, and the instrument's utility has greatly increased. This is one of the most widely used substance abuse–related assessments in the mental health profession today and was identified as one of the primary specialty assessment instruments in which counselors should be trained (Dufresne, Laux, Tahani, & Juhnke, in-press; Juhnke, Vacc, Curtis, Coll, & Paredes, 2003).

The SASSI-4 (Lazowski & Geary, 2016) is the newest version of the original SASSI (Miller, 1985). The SASSI is a screening instrument designed to identify individuals with a high probability of having a substance use disorder, even if those individuals do not acknowledge substance use or symptoms associated with it (Lazowski, Kimmell, & Baker, 2016, p. 1). The SASSI-4 was developed for persons 18 years of age and older with a Lexile Framework for Reading score of 740L, which corresponds to the reading complexity for fourth- to fifth-grade students. The instrument takes approximately 15 minutes to complete (Lazowski & Geary, 2016) and is composed of 105 questions. The SASSI-4 can be ordered directly from the SASSI Institute at 1-800-726-0526 or www.sassi.com.

Side 1 of the instrument contains 74 questions to which respondents answer either *true* or *false*. Many of the questions contain subtle content that does not directly address alcohol or drug use. The second side of the instrument contains 31 face-valid items. These items are highly transparent and directly relate to alcohol and other drug (AOD) use and consequences. Responses to these items provide information regarding the extent to which the respondent acknowledges AOD use and help define the extent and nature of any identified AOD problem.

SASSI-4 Reliability and Validity

Findings from the SASSI-4 validation study (Lazowski & Geary, 2016) show test–retest reliability for the Face-Valid Alcohol scale was .99, test–retest for the Face-Valid Other Drug scale was .99, and test–retest for the various subtle subscales ranged between .78 and .97. The internal consistency coefficient omega for the entire instrument was .97 (Lazowski & Geary, 2016). These scores are high and strongly suggest both significant reliability and validity.

The SASSI-4 demonstrated positive predictive power of 97% (Lazowski & Geary, 2016). Positive predictive power indicates the ratio of true positives to test positives. In other words, 97% of the individuals who tested positive on the SASSI-4 were persons who actually had an AOD use problem. The instrument also demonstrates exceptionally high concurrent validity. For example, the SASSI-4 matched the addicted client's clinical diagnoses of the presence or absence of mild, moderate, or severe substance use disorders 92% of the time.

Scales

The SASSI-4 has 11 scales. Two of these scales are face-valid frequency scales that require clients to indicate how frequently they have experienced the alcohol or drug use consequences described. One of these scales is related to alcohol (Face-Valid Alcohol) and the other is related to all other psychoactive substances (Face-Valid Other Drug). Persons endorsing high Face-Valid Alcohol or high Face-Valid Other Drug scores are likely openly acknowledging AOD use, consequences resulting from such use, and loss of control related to their AOD use (Lazowski et al., 2016). High scores on either or both of these two scales may suggest the need for supervised detoxification (Lazowski et al., 2016).

The Symptoms scale asks clients to endorse symptoms or problems resulting from their AOD abuse (Lazowski et al., 2016). Those with high Symptoms scale scores are likely to be heavy users and be part of a social milieu (e.g., family, peers) where AOD use is prevalent. Thus, it may be difficult for these persons to perceive the negative aspects of remarkable AOD use. In other words, given that their friends and family likely use, they may consider abstinence an abnormality rather than typical.

The Obvious Attributes scale indicates the degree to which clients acknowledge characteristics typical of AOD-misusing persons (Lazowski et al., 2016). In other words, persons endorsing a high number of these scale items are indicating a high number of behaviors and characteristics typically indicated by persons who have a substance use disorder or are in recovery from their substance use. High scores suggest clients are receptive to clinical intervention (e.g., group counseling) and able to identify with the experiences of other persons with substance use disorders. Conversely, very low Obvious Attributes scores suggest clients who are reticent to acknowledge characteristics commonly associated with substance use disorders and personal flaws.

The Subtle Attributes scale identifies persons who may not recognize their behaviors as problematic or associated with AOD use (Lazowski et al., 2016). Persons who have endorsed a high number of Subtle Attributes scale items, especially when the number of these items is higher than their Obvious Attributes scale items, find it challenging to admit the degree to which AOD is prevalent and problematic within their lives.

Two other scales that directly complement one another and enrich the assessment process are the Defensiveness and Supplemental Addiction Measure scales. As is the case with all screening instruments, the scores and clinical profiles are used in conjunction with the counselor's clinical judgment to ensure appropriate assessment and intervention. The SASSI-4 Defensiveness scale identifies persons who may minimize acknowledgment of personal flaws or problems. However, the counselor must use his or her clinical judgment to determine if the defensiveness revolves around AOD abuse issues or other issues (e.g., addicted family member personality traits, immediate life circumstances). Those endorsing a high number of Defensiveness scale items are attempting to present themselves in a favorable light and minimizing acknowledgment of any signs of personal limitations and faults (Lazowski et al., 2016, p. 41). When the Defensiveness scale is used in conjunction with the Supplemental Addiction Measure scale, counselors can better assess if the client's defensiveness relates to AOD abuse or other areas. Supplemental Addiction Measure items are those items that discriminate between individuals with and without a substance use disorder when Defensiveness scores are elevated. Thus, when both the Defensiveness scale and the Supplemental Addiction Measure scale are elevated, there is increased evidence that the client's defensiveness revolves around AOD abuse. However, the counselor must weigh all evidence to make this determination and use his or her best clinical judgment when making the final clinical diagnosis.

Another important aspect of the Defensiveness scale is related to low scores at or below the 15th percentile. Such low scores may be indicative of self-abasing or overly self-critical clients. These clients may have problems related to low self-esteem and have "feelings of worthlessness and hopelessness, loss of energy, and suicidal ideation" (Lazowski et al., 2016). Given the robust correlation between feelings of hopelessness and suicide, it would be important to assess such clients for suicidal ideation and to provide appropriate intervention.

The Family vs. Control Subjects scale identifies persons who may not be AOD abusing themselves but who likely have family members or significant others who are AOD abusing (Lazowski et al., 2016). The Family scale should not be used as a codependency scale. Rather, it should be used to assess whether the client is overly focused on others and the others' needs rather than his or her own needs. Persons scoring high on this scale may benefit from counseling goals that include establishing appropriate and healthy boundaries.

The Correctional scale indicates the client's "relative risk for legal problems" (Lazowski et al., 2016, p. 44). Although the scale was not created to identify specific antisocial psychopathology, it does identify persons who, even if they discontinue their AOD abuse, may potentially require additional counseling services related to areas such as anger and impulse control. Persons scoring high on this scale may also have a checkered history of difficulties with the legal system.

The Random Answering Pattern scale is a measure of profile validity and suggests the client's scores are likely suspect or invalid if his or her score is 2 or more. Such scores may also be indicative of persons who are unable to read at the required level or who do not speak English as their primary language.

The final scale is the SASSI-4 Prescription Drug Abuse (Rx) scale. This scale identifies clients who are likely to be abusing prescription medications. In the SASSI-4 validation study (Lazowski & Geary, 2016), scores of 3 or more on the Rx scale showed a 94% overall accuracy rate in identifying persons in need for further evaluation and possible treatment for an opioid or sedative-related substance use disorder. The Rx screening outcome supplements the overall SASSI-4 screening outcome for any substance use disorder and is indicated separately on the SASSI-4 profile sheet. The Rx scale was added to the SASSI-4 to provide clinicians with a tool to detect clients' involvement in prescription drug abuse and thereby address the escalating prevalence of addiction and overdose related to nonmedical use of prescription medications.

Robert's SASSI-4

Given Robert fulfilled the *Diagnostic and Statistical Manual of Mental Disorders* (fifth edition; DSM-5) Alcohol Use Disorder (Severe) diagnosis during the clinical assessment interview and Eva Marie and Ernest did not fulfill substance use disorders, we review Robert's SASSI-4 clinical scales and profile (Figure 11.2). For the basis of this review, we report Robert's test-taking behaviors as "compliant." In other words, he has sufficiently invested himself in taking the instrument and responding in a relatively truthful manner. However, Robert has intentionally and purposefully endorsed his drinking and drugging behaviors and experiences in a manner that fails to describe the full extent of those drinking behaviors and experiences. Stated differently, he has complied with the testing

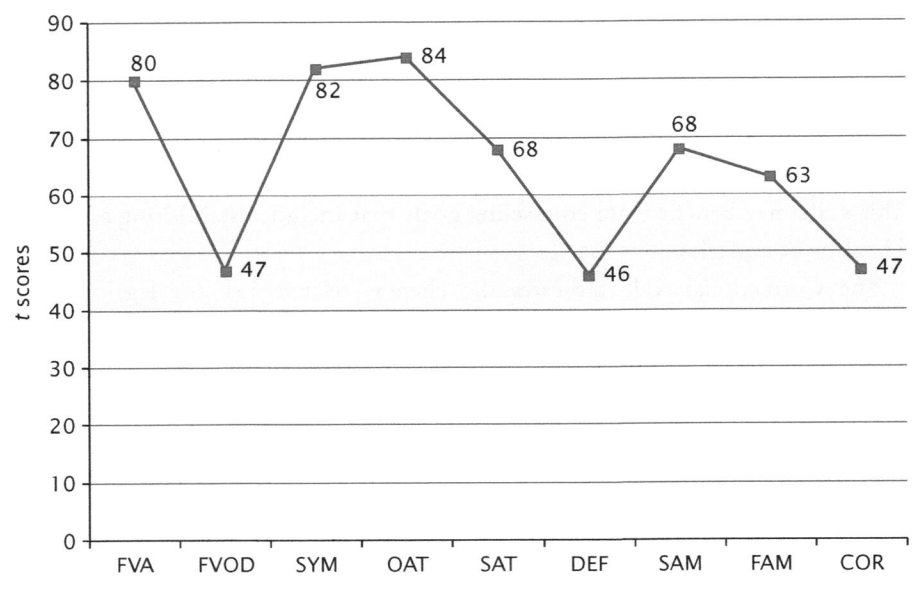

FIGURE 11.2 SASSI-4 for Robert.

experience but has purposefully attempted to present his endorsements in a more positive manner than actual reality.

Validity Scores

Robert's Random Answering Pattern (RAP) score of zero suggests he has not answered the SASSI-4 in a haphazard or random fashion. Instead, it suggests that he was invested in the test-taking experience. This perception is further supported, because Robert has responded to all screening items on the inventory. Concomitantly, when scoring the RAP, Robert did not endorse any questions suggesting prescription drug abuse. Thus, Robert did not screen positive for prescription drug abuse.

Clinical Scores

Robert's high Face-Valid Alcohol scale T score of 80 suggests Robert acknowledges extensive alcohol use with accompanying negative consequences, whereas Robert's low Face-Valid Other Drugs scale T score of 47 indicates he denies the abuse of nonalcoholic substances. These responses match Robert's verbal report that occurred during his clinical intake assessment interview. Robert's high Symptoms of Substance Misuse scale T score (82) suggests Robert acknowledges a significant pattern and history of serious substance misuse—including negative consequence of such substance misuse. His elevated Symptoms of Substance Misuse Scale score further suggests he is likely involved in an environment dominated by substance use and is aware of the social, psychological, and interpersonal consequences and pain resulting from his substance misuse. Robert's high Obvious Attributes scale T score (84) suggests Robert likely acknowledges and comprehends significant similarities between himself and other substance using people. These may include impatience, restlessness, resentment, self-pity, and feelings of being unappreciated and an outcast. Concomitantly, Robert's high Obvious Attributes scale score suggests he is likely open to feedback. His score further suggests he may respond well to addiction self-help groups, especially because he likely identifies with other group members who have substance use struggles, problems, and consequences.

Robert's Subtle Attributes scale T score (68) is congruent with his elevated Symptoms of Substance Misuse scale and Obvious Attributes scale scores and suggests Robert has characteristics of people who have a substance use disorder. Although elevated Subtle Attributes scale scores can reflect a tendency for clients to detach from their feelings and have relatively little insight into the causes of their presenting problems, Robert seems to at least verbally acknowledge that his alcohol use has resulted in his lost jobs and his current distress with his wife, Catherine. Given that clients with elevated Subtle Attributes scale scores my tend to deny the need for intensive treatment, it would be important to determine if Robert may downplay or deny the need for intensive treatment. If he does, it may be important to consider inpatient vis-à-vis intensive outpatient treatment to ensure he receives adequate care.

Robert's Defensiveness scale (DEF) T score (46) reflects someone who realistically acknowledges significant substance abuse and personal problems. Such DEF scale T scores are not necessarily uncommon for clients beginning the counseling process. However, had Robert's scores been below the 15th percentile (40), it could reflect someone who is self-critical, who may have feelings of worthlessness, hopelessness, loss of energy, and suicidal ideation. Furthermore, had Robert's DEF scale T score been high (e.g., 60 or above), the Supplemental Addiction Measure could have been used to differentiate between substance use disorder and nonsubstance use disorder diagnoses.

Robert's Family vs. Control Subjects scale T-score (63) is at the 87th percentile and suggests Robert has characteristics common among family members of people with substance use disorders. Stated differently, Robert may tend to focus on the needs of other family members such as his wife rather than focusing on his personal needs. Robert's score matches his clinical presentation and his desire to stop his alcohol consumption to save his marriage. Given Robert's score, it may be helpful to address limit setting and boundaries via the counseling process. Finally, Robert's Correctional scale T score (47) is rather unremarkable and suggests his responses are not overly similar to people with relatively extensive legal histories. In conclusion, it appears Robert's endorsed validity and clinical scale scores support Dr. Juhnke's DSM-5 Alcohol Use Disorder (Severe) diagnosis.

The Suicide Probability Scale

The SPS is a standardized suicide assessment instrument, authored by Cull and Gill (2002). It is a brief, self-report instrument designed to "aid in the assessment of suicide risk in adolescents and adults" (Cull & Gill, 2002, p. 1). The SPS was developed for persons 14 years of age and older with a minimum fourth-grade reading level. The scale takes less than 20 minutes to administer, complete, and score.

The scale is composed of 36 self-report question stems. Persons being assessed use a 4-point Likert scale (ranging from *none* to *most/all of the time*) to report the frequency of their subjective experiences (e.g., "I feel so lonely I cannot stand it") and past behaviors ("When I get mad, I throw things"; Cull & Gill, 2002, p. 2). Our clients typically report the scale to be easily understandable and "simple" to complete (Valadez et al., 2009). Although some of the question stems are relatively transparent and directly speak to the topic of suicide (e.g., "In order to punish others, I think of suicide"), many are nontransparent and subtle (e.g., "Things seem to go well for me").

SPS Reliability and Validity

Cull and Gill (2002) sought to determine the SPS's reliability and validity in an effort to demonstrate its clinical utility. They attempted this by first conducting two test–retest reliability analyses. Participants in the first test–retest consisted of "80 individuals of various ages, educational levels and ethnic backgrounds" (p. 44). The intent of using this diverse participant pool was to suggest test–retest reliability among a more generalized, heterogeneous population. Three weeks later, the same participants completed the scale a second time. The correlation of the two scale administrations was ".92 ($p < .001$), indicating a high level of test–retest reliability" (p. 44).

A second test–retest was conducted with 478 participants. Time between these two administrations was 10 days. Cull and Gill (2002) reported, "The test–retest reliability for the entire group was .94" (p. 45). Cull and Gill believe these results suggest the SPS has high test–retest reliability. According to Cull and Gill, content relevance and concurrent evidence were investigated by "correlating SPS items with an experimental MMPI scale specifically designed to measure threatened suicide" (p. 45). Participants in this study included 51 clinical patients comprised mostly of clients who had attempted suicide. The resulting correlations had a median of .27 and ranged between –.19 and .54. Correlations of .30 or greater ($p < .05$) were noted among 15 of these item questions (p. 45). Cull and Gill report, "The size and number of these correlations provide evidence that the SPS is content relevant and substantially related to an externally developed index of suicide risk" (p. 45).

Criterion-related evidence was also reportedly demonstrated by the SPS's ability to discriminate between criterion groups of "normals" ($n = 562$), psychiatric inpatients ($n = 260$), and suicide attempters ($n = 336$). This demonstration was evidenced by using "point-biserial correlations between items and criterion classifications, mean differences between groups, and cross-validated classification accuracies" (Cull & Gill, 2002, p. 48). According to Cull and Gill, "The differences between the group means for the various criterion groups were all highly significant ($p = .001$)" (p. 51).

Although there was significant consideration and discussion regarding the instrument's inclusion in this book due to potential validity, sample datedness, and sample homogeneity concerns (Cull & Gill, 2002), we ultimately believed inclusion of the SPS was warranted. The SPS is one of a limited few assessment instruments solely focused on suicide and widely used (Valadez et al., 2009). Further, based upon existing literature and our interactions with clinical supervisees and schools, agencies, and practices that exclusively use the SPS, it is clear the instrument has a dedicated following (Dufresne et al., in-press; Juhnke et al., 2003). Minimally, the SPS requires counselors to perform a thorough suicide assessment interview with their clients and investigate multiple suicide risk areas. Thus, we believe the SPS-facilitated suicide interview and assessment increases the probability that counselors using the instrument will sufficiently evaluate immediate suicide risk and create more thorough, systematic, and encompassing suicide intervention plans. Readers wishing to gain further suicide assessment instrument knowledge may also wish to consider the Columbia Suicide Severity Rating Scale (C-SSRS) as a means to augment the SPS or as a potential alternative to the SPS. The C-SSRS can be accessed at no charge at: http://cssrs.columbia.edu/the-columbia-scale-c-ssrs/about-the-scale/.

Validity Scales

The SPS authors did not create a specific Validity scale. However, Cull and Gill (2002) describe ways in which test administrators can use perceived differences and similarities between Suicide Probability scores and clinical perceptions to best ensure client clinical needs are adequately met. This might include seeking appropriate client releases of confidential information to conduct interviews with family members and friends who can provide perceptions and evidence specific to the client's past and current suicide behaviors as well as perceptions regarding the client's immediate danger to self. We believe the SPS has serious limitations that need to be understood and taken into account when using the assessment. These limitations include high rates of false positives among low-risk clients and high rates of false negatives with high-risk clients (Golding, 1985). Thus, we believe all SPS scores should be used in conjunction with multiple face-to-face clinical assessments with the client and the client's significant others. Never should a sole score on an assessment be used to ascertain the disposition of a client, and the SPS is no exception to this ethical responsibility.

Clinical Scales

The SPS is composed of four subscales and three different types of overall suicide assessment risk scores based on a total weighted score, a normalized T score, and a suicide probability score (Cull & Gill, 2002; Valadez et al., 2009).

Hopelessness

The Hopelessness subscale notes client self-reported perceptions regarding overall dissatisfaction with life and negative expectations about the future. Specifically, the subscale provides a picture of the clients' global pessimism and despair. According to Cull and Gill (2002), subscale content "reflects loneliness, hopelessness, dysphoric mood, a sense of being overburdened by circumstances, and feelings of futility about life and an inability to effect change" (p. 15). Given the strong correlations between suicidal behavior and hopelessness (Beck, Steer, Kovacs, & Garrison, 1985; Granello & Juhnke, 2009; Juhnke et al., 2010), this is a very important subscale. Persons scoring moderately high or high on this subscale are perceived as at great risk for suicidal behaviors and warrant interventions that match their degree of self-harm danger. Thus, should a client's T score on the Hopelessness subscale be at or above 70, the counselor may well wish to assess the client's reported reasons to continue living and strongly consider available least restrictive living options, especially hospitalization.

Suicidal Ideation

This subscale provides counselors a glimpse into the client's suicidal thoughts and behaviors. Individual items within this subscale can provide information regarding "the frequency of suicide ideation, the reasons for contemplating suicide . . . or whether a suicide attempt . . . is likely to be impulsive or carefully planned" (Cull & Gill, 2002, p. 15). Clients scoring high on this subscale are reporting frequent thoughts of suicide and warrant further investigation and intervention to ensure safety. Should a client present with a T score of 70 or above, we believe it is imperative to ask how the client intends to perform suicide. Again, hospitalization or another safe, least restrictive environment matching the client's presenting degree of risk should be strongly considered.

Negative Self-Evaluation

The third subscale "reflects an individual's subjective appraisal that things are not going well, that others are distant and uncaring, and that it is difficult to do anything worthwhile" (Cull & Gill, 2002, p. 15). As one can imagine, clients scoring high on this subscale may well be at higher suicide risk and therefore warrant strongly considering hospitalization and close monitoring. Thus, they warrant immediate intervention and protection from self-harm.

Hostility

This subscale "reflects a tendency to break or throw things when angry or upset, and includes a cluster of items reflecting hostility, isolation, and impulsivity" (Cull & Gill, 2002, p. 15). Again, high scores suggest someone who warrants close evaluation and potential intervention. Most persons with very high scores on this subscale frequently have enduring patterns of impulsivity and are oppositional toward others. They often use these behaviors as a means to intimidate and cope with perceived unjust demands being placed upon them.

These subscales and their clinical utility make the SPS a helpful clinical tool for most counselors. In addition, SPS subscales can be combined to create three distinct summary score types. The total weighted score is the sum of the individual items on the combined subscales. This sum can be quickly and easily translated into a normalized T score that has a mean of 50 points and a standard deviation of 10 points. Thus, according to the SPS, the pronounced risk of suicidal behaviors increases as the client's normalized T score rises above the 50-point mean. Cull and Gill (2002) write, "Although any absolute cutoff points are arbitrary, a score of 60T or above indicates the need for careful clinical evaluation of suicide" (p. 14). They further report that scores 2 or more standard deviations above the mean (i.e., 70 points or more) are "strong presumptive evidence for instituting suicide precautions" (p. 14). Stated differently, clients who score 70 points or higher should be perceived at significant suicide risk and warrant interventions that match their presenting needs. Thus, a client presenting with a normalized T score of 70 or above may well warrant hospitalization if a least restrictive environment will not provide adequate safety.

A word of warning is also noted by the test authors related to normalized T scores of 40 or less. According to Cull and Gill (2002), such scores "should alert the user to the possibility that the person has consciously or unconsciously sought to minimize his or her actual suicide potential" (p. 14). In other words, the client has most likely presented him- or herself in a favorable light void of suicidal indication. Thus, either the counselor lacked sufficient clinical judgement to correctly perceive the client's immediate suicide risk or the client consciously or unconsciously attempted to present him- or herself in a nonsuicidal manner. Should such a low score result, it is imperative the counselor seek immediate clinical supervision and, after gaining the necessary client signed releases of information, interview family and friends regarding the client's potential danger to self.

The final summary score is the suicide probability score. We have found this score exceptionally helpful when assessing clients for suicide risk. In essence, this score suggests the "statistical likelihood that an individual belongs in the population of lethal suicide attempters" (Cull & Gill, 2002, p. 14). In other words, the suicide probability score does not indicate that a client has a certain probability of suicide. Instead, the suicide probability score reports the probability that the client fits a profile of those who have made serious, highly lethal suicide attempts and is therefore at extreme risk. Such extreme risk noted by the SPS can then be explained to the client and used either to encourage participation in a least restrictive treatment setting such as intensive outpatient or partial hospitalization or, in the case of a suicidal client, support one's clinical judgment for involuntary hospitalization to the client and other mental health and insurance gatekeepers.

Eva Marie's SPS

After more than 50 years of combined clinical experience assessing clients' suicide risk, we believe hopeless clients who believe they are unloved or unlovable are at great suicide risk. Eva Marie is likely one such person. She feels unloved and unsupported by her husband and hopeless and helpless regarding her life circumstances. She has little control over finances, feels overwhelmed and burdened by her aging mother, and believes she must fulfill a marriage vow she made to God that will not allow her to escape her perceived cold,

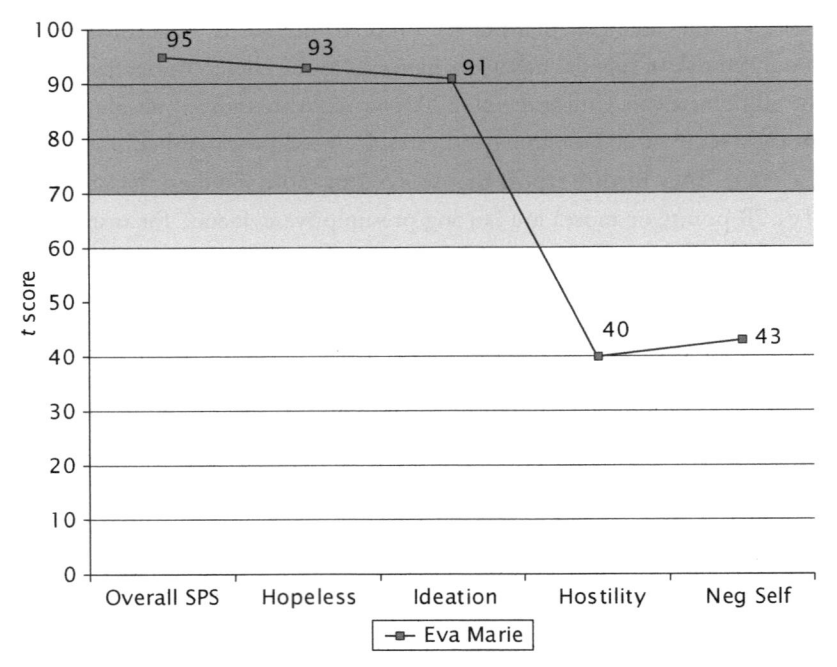

FIGURE 11.3 Eva Marie's Suicide Probability Scale.

aloof, uncaring, and using husband. Thus, for demonstration purposes, we use Eva Marie as the SPS protagonist.

Eva Marie's score on her overall suicide probability score is very high (Figure 11.3) and is more than 3 standard deviations above the mean. It suggests Eva Marie is at severe suicide risk. Eva Marie's Hopelessness subscale T score is very high as well. Likewise, this score is more than 3 standard deviations above the mean and suggests that Eva Marie has significant life dissatisfaction and negative future expectations.

Her Suicide Ideation subscale is also very high and 3 standard deviations above the mean. This indicates Eva Marie is actively thinking about suicide. Eva Marie's only two low scores are her Hostility and Negative Self-Evaluation scale scores. These low scale scores suggest Eva Marie is not impulsive but rather highly thoughtful and strategic in her behaviors, and she does not see herself in a negative fashion.

As the individual test items endorsed by Eva Marie on these subscales were reviewed with her, Eva Marie reported that she tends to isolate herself from others when she feels depressed or feels like killing herself. Her statement matches information gathered from Eva Marie's original clinical assessment intake interview and the psychological testing thus far conducted. When asked if Eva Marie was thinking about killing herself, she responded, "I want to. But I am fearful God will banish me to Hell. I can't win. I am in hell on earth with my mother and useless husband. If I escape by killing myself, I will be sent to Hell by Almighty God."

Based on Eva Marie's statements and her SPS scores, Dr. Juhnke discussed voluntary inpatient hospitalization with Eva Marie. Dr. Juhnke further indicated the hospitalization would provide Eva Marie time away from her mother and husband and allow her to consider what options are available and best for her. Eva Marie expressed relief at Dr. Juhnke's suggestion and agreed to voluntarily enter St. Michael's Psychiatric Hospital.

The Suicide SCATTT Mnemonic

Despite the existence of suicide assessment instruments like the SPS, the SAD PERSONS Scale, the Adapted-SAD PERSONS Suicide Scale, and the IS PATH WARM Scale, we have found that less experienced clinical supervisees do not fully comprehend how to immediately intervene once they determine their assessed clients are in fact suicidal and in peril of immediate suicide behaviors. Thus, the looming question for many counselors is, "What do I do now?" To answer that question, we present the suicide SCATTT mnemonic (Juhnke, Juhnke, & Hsieh, 2012). The SCATTT provides a basic, step-by-step process that can be used once it is determined that the client is suicidal and warrants a less restrictive environment. The intervention has been used by one of the authors with his clients and is reported as helpful by his supervisees (Juhnke et al., 2012).

Validity Scales

The SCATTT is a mnemonic. Therefore, it has no validity scales. As is the case with the SPS, counselors are encouraged to use a clinical assessment interview format to provide a context for the assessment.

Mnemonic Phases

The SCATTT mnemonic is an easily memorized memory aid designed to help supervisees remember the specific steps necessary when intervening with clients assessed as having immediate suicide intent and deemed suicidal by their counselor. Each mnemonic letter corresponds to a specific and required suicide intervention phase (i.e., *S*tay, *C*onsult, *A*pprise, *T*erminate, *T*runcate, and *T*ransport; Figure 11.4). SCATTT reminds entry-level counselors of six important suicide intervention plan phases that must occur when it is

> **Stay** with the client.
>
> **Consult** with supervisor(s) and professional peers.
>
> **Apprise** client of assessment findings and your professional judgement.
>
> **Terminate** threat (e.g., remove any identified suicide instrument [e.g., gun]).
>
> **Truncate** threats that cannot be terminated (e.g., remove excess medications, ensure only supervised access to cars).
>
> **Transport** to psychiatric hospital or least restrictive environment deemed best by you and your supervisors (e.g., partial hospitalization, monitored foster care).

FIGURE 11.4 The Suicide SCATTT Mnemonic.

determined via the previously completed suicide assessments that clients warrant psychiatric hospitalization or another type of least restrictive, monitored, and safe environment (e.g., monitored respite care, partial hospitalization). Supervisees are strongly encouraged to use additional intervention pieces depending on the client's specific needs. The mnemonic and each of the six intervention phases are presented next.

Phase 1: **S**tay with the Client

Whenever a client presents suicide intent, the client should never be left alone. Thus, the counselor or another mental health professional must *stay* with the client until hospitalization or an alternative safety monitoring option that corresponds with the client's degree of danger can be arranged.

Phase 2: **C**onsult

After stabilizing the immediate situation and ensuring the client's present safety, the counselor should ask another mental health professional or appropriate designee (e.g., police officer, family member) to monitor the client while the counselor *consults* her clinical supervisor. Specifically, the counselor should contact his or her clinical supervisor and report the suicide assessment findings, describe the client's immediate degree of suicide risk, and describe how the client is being monitored. Jointly, the counselor and supervisor should develop a hospital intervention or least restrictive monitoring plan that ensures the client's safety and corresponds to the client's noted degree of suicide risk. As the counselor returns to the client, and depending on the jointly agreed-upon suicide intervention plan, the supervisor or supervisor designee should begin contacting area psychiatric hospitals or other clinically appropriate options (e.g., respite care, partial hospitalization programs, psychiatric day center) to determine potential availability. Concomitantly, should it be anticipated that transportation for an involuntary or voluntary hospitalization be required, the supervisor or supervisor designee should begin to secure such transportation.

If the counselor does not have a clinical supervisor, he or she should implement the "four out of five rule." Here, the counselor consults five professional mental health peers. The professional mental health peers must have equal or greater mental health educational backgrounds (e.g., master's degrees, educational specialist degrees, or doctorates), clinical experience, and treatment licenses (e.g., licensed professional clinical counselor, licensed professional counselor). Specifically, the counselor describes the case, the findings from the suicide assessment, and the proposed clinical recommendations for hospitalization or another least restrictive and safe monitoring option to these professional peers. The counselor then solicits input from these professional peers in an effort to create the safest clinical intervention and to ensure that the proposed clinical intervention is not overlooking important intervention factors. Should four out of the five professional peers perceive the intervention as clinically appropriate, the counselor should implement the clinical intervention.

Phase 3: **A**pprise

The SCATTT further requires counselors to *apprise* clients of the suicide assessment findings and the counselor's treatment recommendations. A good way to start this phase is by praising clients for recognizing their suicide concerns and for entering counseling. Once counselors praise their clients, counselors then suggest the existence of hope and the possibility for positive change. Next, counselors apprise clients of the suicide assessment findings and treatment recommendations. Finally, if needed, counselors describe differences between voluntary and involuntary psychiatric hospitalizations and potential benefits to voluntary hospitalization.

Should clients indicate they will voluntarily admit themselves into a recommended psychiatric hospital, counselors move to the Transport phase. However, should clients refuse to voluntarily enter a psychiatric hospital, counselors explain potential differences and benefits between voluntary and involuntary hospitalization. Depending on specific state and relevant laws, clients who voluntarily admit themselves to psychiatric hospitals can often be released if the hospital staff does not perceive them as being imminent dangers to themselves. However, if clients are involuntarily hospitalized, most states require clients to remain for a minimum 72 hours monitoring period. Thus, clients will sometimes prefer to self-admit as a voluntary client with the hope that they will be quickly released vis-à-vis be admitted as an involuntary client and required to stay for a longer time.

If the suicidal client is under the age of majority and depending on the specific laws of the state where the counselor practices, the counselor will need to apprise the client's parents or legal guardians of the child's suicide risk and hospital recommendation. In general, we have found most parents to be supportive of professional recommendations for hospitalization when their children present with significant suicide risk. However, should parents refuse to allow the child to continue treatment or refuse to hospitalize a child who clearly warrants hospitalization, child protective services should be contacted. Because laws vary from state to state, legal counsel should be sought to ensure the counselor practices in a manner congruent to state laws and guidelines.

Phases 4 and 5: **T**erminate and **T**runcate the Threat

Understanding how the client plans to commit suicide is a critical component of any suicide assessment. Thus, if a client has completed the SPS and indicates she intends to shoot herself with her husband's .45 pistol that is kept in the couple's bedroom lamp stand, the counselor will ask that the gun be removed, locked, and kept in a different home or location until the client is no longer at risk of killing herself. Removing the gun is Phase 4 of the SCATTT. This terminates the suicide threat instrument (i.e., gun) by removing it from the client's availability.

Regretfully, some clients have plans that include suicide instruments where access cannot be terminated. For example, should a client's plan include overdosing on his antidepressant medications, Phase 5 of the SCATTT encourages counselors to *truncate* access to the antidepressants and other drugs. Here, the counselor should secure a release of confidential information, contact the physician prescribing the antidepressant, and inform the physician of the client's suicide plan. The counselor should request that the physician also monitor the client's safety and have the antidepressant medications dispensed in smaller quantities. Thus, instead of the client having access to a two-month antidepressant supply, the medication would be dispensed in weekly quantities. Concomitantly, the counselor should require that the client give all current medications to a trusted family member who could then secure and dispense the medications daily. Again, releases of confidential information will need to be signed by the client. The counselor would then meet with the client and the family member dispensing the medications to establish how the medications will be dispensed.

Phase 6: Transport

This final phase of the SCATTT is the Transport phase. Here, counselors must ensure that the client has safe and monitored *transport* to the hospital. Depending on the client's emotional presentation, his or her willingness to enter the hospital, and the agency's or school's transportation rules, we have found it best to have trusted client family members transport the client to the hospital. However, family transport should only be used when the client is willingly admitting him- or herself into the hospital and poses no foreseeable risk to those transporting him or her. In addition, for liability reasons and to help ensure everyone's safety, a minimum of two physically able, adult family members should make the transport. Depending on the situation and immediate needs of the client, we have found local police and emergency services workers helpful in transporting clients.

Eva Marie's SCATTT

Again, we use Eva Marie as the protagonist for the SCATTT and continue the vignette where we discontinued the SPS discussion. As you will recall, based on Eva Marie's statements and her SPS scores, Dr. Juhnke advocated that Eva Marie voluntarily enter St. Michael's Psychiatric Hospital. Thus, for this vignette, Dr. Juhnke has already apprised Eva Marie of what he thinks is best and Eva Marie has agreed to voluntarily enter the hospital. Therefore, the Appraisal phase of the SCATTT is unnecessary. Instead, at this point in the process, Dr. Juhnke needs someone to stay with Eva Marie to ensure her safety. Therefore, Dr. Juhnke tells Eva Marie he is going to introduce Eva Marie to Dr. Henderson, a female counselor who is present in the office. Eva Marie reports this would be "fine." Dr. Juhnke does not leave the room to find Dr. Henderson. Instead, he text-messages Dr. Henderson and asks if she would be willing to monitor a potentially suicidal client in Treatment Room A. Dr. Henderson, knocks on the door. Dr. Juhnke greets Dr. Henderson and introduces Eva Marie to Dr. Henderson.

DR. JUHNKE: Eva Marie, this is Dr. Henderson. She is an exceptional counselor.
DR. HENDERSON: Hello, Eva Marie.
EVA MARIE: Hello. I suppose you're here to guard me.
DR. JUHNKE: Well, Dr. Henderson is an expert in helping clients. We want to make certain you are safe, Eva Marie. Dr. Henderson will stay with you while I check to see about availability at St. Michaels.
EVA MARIE: That will be fine.
DR. HENDERSON: Eva Marie, it sounds as though you are going through a very demanding and difficult time. Your decision to enter St. Michael's is a very good decision. The clients I have referred there found St. Michael's to be very helpful, friendly, and comfortable.

Let's stop for a moment to review this process. First, and most importantly, Dr. Juhnke never leaves Eva Marie by herself. Instead, he introduces Eva Marie to a colleague. Thus, Eva Marie always has someone with her. In addition, note that Dr. Juhnke does not ask for Eva Marie's permission. He tells Eva Marie that he is introducing her to Dr. Henderson and text-messages Dr. Henderson requesting she enter the room. Although some might balk and argue that the counselor should ask permission or seek another release of confidentiality before bringing Dr. Henderson into the room with Eva Marie, Dr. Juhnke believes Eva Marie is a threat to herself and warrants immediate supervision and transport. Thus, Dr. Juhnke informs Eva Marie that she will be introduced to Dr. Henderson. Especially with anxious clients or clients with personality disorders such as borderline personality disorder, telling clients what will happen next reduces anxiety and any potential for "gaminess." Of course, readers should determine what is best for them and most ethically appropriate to comply with their state and professional ethics codes and practices rather than simply mirror Dr. Juhnke's behaviors. First and foremost, readers should follow current ethical principles and laws within their state and profession to ensure that their behaviors are legally and ethically appropriate.

Next, Dr. Juhnke introduces Eva Marie to Dr. Henderson. This is done to promote a sense of comfort and safety for Eva Marie and ensure Eva Marie's safety. Remember, Eva Marie is anxious. Simply bringing an unannounced stranger into the treatment room would likely fail to engender a sense of comfort for Eva Marie.

Also, note what Dr. Henderson does. She immediately greets Eva Marie in a friendly manner and recounts how Dr. Henderson's clients have found St. Michaels to be a friendly and comfortable place. Think of the power of Dr. Henderson's statement. She embeds the suggestion that Eva Marie will find St. Michael's helpful too. This should help quell at least some of Eva Marie's concerns and support her perception that she is making the best decision to enter St. Michaels.

If Dr. Juhnke were an entry-level clinician or working with a school district or agency with an immediate supervisor, he would consult with his superiors and provide them with up-to-date information on his intentions to hospitalize this client and the progress therein. If this were the case, he would likely contact his clinical supervisor.

DR. JUHNKE: Dr. Oldz, this is Jerry.

DR. OLDZ: Yes, Jerry, how may I help you?

DR. JUHNKE: We've been consulting about Eva Marie Garza. As you may recall, Eva Marie is a 40-year-old, married, Hispanic-American female, presenting with generalized anxiety disorder. Per your clinical supervision instructions, I administered the Suicide Probability Scale with Eva Marie. She scored quite high. When she and I reviewed her high scores, I asked if she was thinking of killing herself. She reported she was planning to kill herself with her husband's .45 caliber handgun after leaving session. The gun is located in the couple's bedroom lamp stand.

DR. OLDZ: Sounds like you did a good job. Where is Eva Marie right now?

DR. JUHNKE: She is with Dr. Henderson in Treatment Room A.

DR. OLDZ: Good Job, Jerry. Make certain she remains with someone. What is your plan from here?

DR. JUHNKE: Eva Marie has agreed to voluntarily enter St. Michael's. I wanted to consult with you and make certain that a referral would be supported by you and by the agency before I call St. Mike's.

DR. OLDZ: Seems you are making excellent decisions. St. Mike's would be good. How are you planning to transport?

DR. JUHNKE: As soon as I learn if St. Mike's has availability, I thought I would get a release of confidential information from Eva Marie so that her mother and husband could drive her over to St. Mike's.

DR. OLDZ: Sounds good. If St. Mike's doesn't have room, you may wish to contact either University Hospital or Grandover Community General Hospital. Keep me posted and let me know how things are going.

As a master's-level counselor, the second author often had this type of consultation with his supervisors. At this point, Dr. Juhnke would author a brief note recapping his supervision conversation with Dr. Oldz and include any directives in the client's case notes. Next, Dr. Juhnke would contact the intake coordinator at St. Michael's to determine availability. Typically, a hospital intake coordinator will be familiar with the counselor or counselor's agency and will need to know the type of insurance the client has as well as insurance group numbers and the insurance company's request for preauthorization telephone numbers. Often, they can secure a preauthorization from the client's insurance company for a minimum 72-hour hospital stay.

Because Dr. Juhnke had apprised Eva Marie earlier of both her SPS clinical scores as well as his clinical judgment that she would benefit by voluntarily entering the hospital to ensure her safety, the Appraise stage is not further discussed. In addition, because Eva Marie has agreed to enter the psychiatric hospital, terminating her access to the .45 caliber gun or truncating her access to medications she may have intended to overdose on, neither of these is discussed at this point. (However, before Eva Marie is released from the hospital, both of these issues should be resolved). Therefore, the next pressing issue is transporting Eva Marie to the psychiatric hospital.

In this case, the counselor will not wish to transport. Instead, he will either secure a release of confidential information from Eva Marie, allowing him to seek transportation from Eva Marie's mother and possibly her husband, a friend, a family member, or a priest, or ask that Eva Marie make the telephone calls. Remember, a minimum of two healthy adults should always transport clients.

DR. JUHNKE: Eva Marie, I just got off the telephone with Shelly. She is the intake coordinator at St. Michael's. Shelly has contacted your insurance carrier and secured a voluntary stay for you. All we need is transportation. Typically, there are two ways we transport our clients. First, we see if the client would prefer to sign a release of confidential information allowing me to contact a family member, friends, or a priest to drive him or her to St. Michaels. We need a minimum of two persons to drive you to St. Michaels. Thus, I will need at least two releases signed and two names with telephone numbers. If you prefer not to sign a release or prefer not to have your family members, friends, or priest drive you, we will contact the San Antonio Police Department and ask for a peace officer to transport you.

EVA MARIE: Why don't Dr. Henderson and you drive me to St. Michael's?

DR. JUHNKE: I am sorry, Eva Marie. I am unwilling to drive. If you wish to sign a release or contact two family members, friends, or others, we would be happy to have them transport you to St. Michael's. If that doesn't work for you, we will contact the San Antonio Police Department and have them transport you.

EVA MARIE: I certainly don't want the police to transport me; I will call my mother and husband. They will drive me over to St. Michael's.

As this vignette depicts, clients often will rather have friends or family transport them rather than the police. In this case, we do not need a release of confidential information because Eva Marie will contact her family members directly. Incidentally, some may believe it harsh to refuse to transport Eva Marie. Be aware, there are a number of reasons to refuse transporting clients. We, as inexperienced, entry-level counselors, have transported clients.

On some of those occasions the clients who originally presented as kind and endearing became belligerent and argumentative. On another occasion, a client's head lice infested the counselor's car. If these reasons are insufficient to dissuade readers from transporting clients, you should also know that some auto insurance companies may view transporting clients for business purposes outside the counselor's auto insurance policy. As entry-level counselors, we quickly learned that the best transportation options are having others transport.

Summary

This chapter has provided a general overview of the MSI-R, the SASSI-4, the SPS, and the suicide SCATTT mnemonic. Instrument reliability and validity have been reported on all instruments except the SCATTT. As well, descriptions of individual scales have been discussed. Eva Marie and Robert have been used within clinical vignettes depicting how these instruments would be used with each person. Finally, issues regarding transportation of suicidal clients have been addressed.

12

Fundamentals of Interpretation in Assessment

> **Objectives**
> 1. Understand the structure of an assessment report.
> 2. Understand the nature of assessment principles in the assessment report.
> 3. Create and interpret a score report for referrals and clients.
> 4. Develop a written assessment report.

Developing a Written Report

An assessment that is comprehensive in nature, uses structured and unstructured measures and interviews, and provides timely information regarding client disposition must be summarized in a manner that is useful to providers, stakeholders, and, most importantly, the client. One specific challenge in writing an assessment report is providing appropriate technical information essential to referring bodies and professional stakeholders (e.g., schools, other mental health providers) while simultaneously explaining such information in a manner that is helpful to the client and stakeholders outside the mental health discipline. Therefore, in this chapter we highlight what is included in an assessment report and how such a report must be structured and communicated to the client and relevant stakeholders.

The cases of Eva Marie Garza, Robert Jones, and Ann Smith presented in Chapter 2 represent comprehensive evaluations of clients in a format consistent with what is seen in many assessment reports. In addition, Chapter 7 on the clinical interview provided in-depth material on information that is relevant to case conceptualization and necessary for the assessment report. Subsequent chapters highlight the use of various types of measures that may be incorporated into an assessment report. With this in mind, we provide an outline and summary of the scope and structure of an assessment report making references, when necessary, to the aforementioned chapters.

In Chapter 7, several important features of the clinical interview were addressed, including the presenting problem, relevant history, mental status exam, medical history, family history/issues, social support, educational/occupational/economic issues, and cultural/spiritual concerns. Many of these elements are addressed in the case studies presented in Chapter 2, along with a formal diagnosis of each of the clients.

In addition, the assessment report includes a list of formal assessments administered, a brief rationale for the administration of the instruments, a statement about the validity of the administration process, a score report on each of the instruments, and an interpretation of scores, as well as how the scores fit the context provided by other information about the client. In other words, the scores of assessment instruments should never stand alone and should be used in conjunction with other information about the client. For clients who obtained scores inconsistent with their case presentation, such discrepancies should be highlighted and addressed in the assessment report.

By providing such structure and information, the diagnosis should be seen as a product, and therefore logical conclusion, from the information presented. In other words, based on the information in an assessment report, the reader, whether a stakeholder, physician, clinician, third-party payor, or other interested party, should be able to obtain a strong case conceptualization of the client.

Reporting Scores for Standardized Instruments

After providing the aforementioned information of the tests administered, rationale, and process of the administration, the counselor provides a score report for each instrument administered. This section of the assessment report requires the counselor to be aware of various aspects of the test and manual, including knowledge of the scale and any pertinent subscales, reliability estimates, and procedures that contribute to a valid administration, scoring, and interpretation of the instrument. Specifically, for each instrument administered counselors should address the following components: (a) scales and subscales, (b) raw scores, (c) standard scores, (d) percentiles, (e) standard error of measurement (SEM), and (f) category (if applicable).

The information provided may have appeal to both mental health professionals and laypeople. The information on standard scores and SEM provides important guidelines for interpretation that may be of interest to assessment professionals, whereas parents, clients, and consumers may find information related to percentiles and diagnostic indicators as more relevant to their needs. Counselors should keep in mind that the assessment report is a technical report that may be used by a variety of professionals, and therefore it needs to include a variety of information that professionals, clients,

TABLE 12.1 Score Report for Ann Smith on the Beck Depression Inventory-II

Raw Score	Standard Score	Percentile	SEM	Category
	Clinical (Nonclinical)	Clinical (Nonclinical)	Clinical (Nonclinical)	
28	.36 (1.55)	64th (94th)	3.37 [24.63, 31.37] (2.63[25.37, 30.63])	Moderate to severe

parents, and stakeholders can utilize. Throughout this chapter, we use Ann Smith's case in which she is administered the Beck Depression Inventory-II (BDI-II). Examples of how the information is processed are provided throughout the chapter. Similarly, additional implications for Robert are addressed through the administration of the Outcome Questionnaire-45.2 (OQ-45.2).

For the case of Ann Smith, a counselor would report the following:

Ann was administered the Beck Depression Inventory-II (BDI-II) to help assess the severity of the depressive symptoms that Ann exhibits. Ann displays ongoing conflict with her mother, poor relationships with peers, past trauma, and lack of an overall support system. In addition, Ann has had poor performance in school, despite a past history of strong academic grades and above average performance on her grade-level achievement tests. The BDI-II is a 21-item self-report inventory. Clients identify the extent to which they exhibit a variety of diagnostic indicators for depression on a Likert-type scale ranging from 0 (*no endorsement*) to 3 (*increased severity*) over the past two weeks. The administration of the BDI-II was under typical conditions. Results from the scores may be deemed as a valid assessment (Table 12.1).

Ann scored a 28 on the BDI-II, placing her in the 64th percentile among the clinical norm group and the 94th percentile among the nonclinical norm group. While a score of 28 places Ann in the moderate range of depression, as identified in the manual, when SEM is taken under consideration, Ann could be categorized in the severe range with respect to depressive symptoms.

Scales and Subscales

After scoring an instrument, counselors should consider the type of scores reported from the instrument. For some instruments, such as the BDI-II, this is rather self-explanatory, as only a total score is derived from the administration of the instrument. Other instruments may only provide scale scores and no total score (e.g., Minnesota Multiphasic Personality Inventory-2-Restructured Form [MMPI-2-RF]). For instruments such as the OQ-45.2, both a total score and subscale scores are derived. The purpose of the administration of the instrument and the use of the test scores are essential in determining whether total scores or subscales should be reported. For example, total scores may be used to gain a sense of overall progress or regression for clients, whereas subscale scores may be essential for identifying specific problem areas and creating goals for treatment planning.

Raw Scores

Recall that raw scores alone lack meaning. Only when scores are compared to a norm group do the scores become meaningful. However, not all instruments report scores using a standard score format. For example, instruments such as the MMPI-2-RF use the T scores to report subscale scores, but the instruments such as the BDI-II simply rely on the raw score. The problem with this practice is that raw scores will not convey any information with respect to how a client compares to the general population. Although a client may not initially see this as a problem, what he or she really wants to know is whether a score is high or low. Essentially, the client wants to know what the score means. When the counselor can say, "Compared to others who have taken the same test, your scores is in the upper (or lower) _____ percentile," then the counselor can attribute meaning to the scores. However, this ability is limited simply by reporting raw scores. What raw scores may provide, however, is a sense of how many items were endorsed, particularly on a checklist or self-report inventory, and this may have some meaningful implication for what information is garnered from the assessment and the overall acceptance the clients displays from the interpretation of the assessment.

Standard Scores

Standard scores do provide an ability to make comparisons to the norm group. However, standard scores do not provide information related to the number of items endorsed or answered in a particular manner. So assessment professionals may place more value on standard scores, whereas laypeople may not have this type of understanding. When deriving standard scores, counselors should pay particular attention to the norm group in which the comparisons are made. Quite often, more than one norm group is used in the development of a test, and the choice of which norm group is used to make comparisons can have important implications with regard to interpretation of the assessment. For example, the BDI-II has two norm groups, a group of 500 outpatient participants from various settings and age groups (13 to 86 years old) and 120 college students. Thus, the BDI-II has two categories: 500 participants representing a clinical subset of the population and 120 college students representing a nonclinical subset of the population. Researchers may argue the appropriateness of suggesting that college students are representative of a nonclinical population that is generalizable to the general population, and such an argument would have merit. Thus, there are pertinent limitations to making comparisons of the BDI-II for individual clients to the norm groups.

However, for the sake of moving this discussion forward to how comparisons are made, suppose Ann was administered the BDI-II and scored a 28, as noted earlier. In order to facilitate interpretation, the counselor converts the raw score to a standard score. The

BDI-II provides descriptive statistics for both a clinical group (outpatients) and nonclinical group (college students). In the previous example, standard scores were provided for both groups. A counselor may opt to provide scores from a single norm group.

Beck, Steer, and Brown (1996) reported means and standard deviations for outpatients ($M = 22.45$, $SD = 12.75$) and college students ($M = 12.56$, $SD = 9.93$). Applying the concepts of computing standard scores from Chapter 3, the following z scores are noted:

$$\frac{28 - 22.45}{12.75} = .36$$

for outpatients (clinical) and

$$\frac{28 - 12.56}{9.93} = 1.55$$

for college students (nonclinical).

From these computations, counselors can determine that, when compared to the clinical group, Ann scored just slightly above the mean, but when compared to the nonclinical group, Ann is over 1.5 standard deviations above the mean. By converting the raw score to standard scores, a counselor is able to explain to Ann that she is within the average range among individuals who seek counseling services for depression and well above the average range among individuals who may not be representative of individuals seeking counseling services.

Percentiles

Additional information, particularly for making comparisons and interpretations, may be ascertained from percentiles. Using the z table from Appendix A, the percentiles for the corresponding z scores are available. A z score of .36 corresponds to the 64th percentile; a z score of 1.55 corresponds to the 94th percentile. Hence, Ann is among the top 6% of individuals endorsing depressive symptoms among the nonclinical group but slightly above the middle of the group when compared to a clinical population. Based strictly on the scores from the BDI-II, Ann is like most individuals who are in outpatient counseling and administered the BDI-II but is clearly among the more depressed individuals when compared to people who may not be seeking counseling services.

SEM

A score on a test is time and context bound. Recall from Chapter 5 that SEM is used to ascertain a client's true score from the observed score that is the result of an administration of an instrument. To compute the SEM, the counselor must be aware of the test–retest reliability estimate of the instrument and the standard deviation of the norm group. Thus,

$$12.75\sqrt{1 - .93} = 3.37$$

for outpatients (clinical) and

$$9.93\sqrt{1-.93} = 2.63$$

for college students (nonclinical).

By adding and subtracting each of these values from the raw score, the range of possible scores at the 68th percent confidence interval (i.e., 1 standard deviation) are presented in the report. Counselors interested in reporting the SEM at the 95% confidence interval would simply multiple the SEM by 2, yielding the following:

$$2(3.37) = 6.74, \ [21.26, 34.74]$$

for outpatients (clinical) and

$$2(2.63) = 5.26, \ [22.74, 33.26]$$

for college students (nonclinical).

Category

Some manuals for instruments provide indicators for score interpretation. *Cut-scores* refer to scores that are used to determine classifications on a given instrument. For example, Beck et al. (1996) provided cut scores to indicate *mild, moderate*, and *severe* depression. Other instruments may establish cut-scores to indicate clinical significance (e.g., MMPI-2-RF) or diagnostic criteria (e.g., intellectual disability for IQ scores below 70). Counselors should be cautious about using categories based on scores. A score on a single instrument is not sufficient evidence to provide a label or diagnosis and to do so based on a single score is unethical. As noted in the previous example, the SEM may play a role in categorizing a client. When employing categories consistent with a particular score, counselors should demonstrate evidence based on other assessment tools to substantiate a label, indicator, and/or diagnosis.

For the purposes of evaluating Ann on the BDI-II, a score of 28 is the upper limit for moderate depression; a score of 29 is the lower limit for severe depression (Beck et al., 1996). Therefore, when considering the SEM, Ann may be in the moderate to severe level of major depressive disorder. Certainly, evidence from the clinical interview and use of additional assessments may be necessary to substantiate such a diagnosis. Based on the clinical interview, Ann also suffers from past trauma. Often, assessment measures for depression correlate with anxiety measures (Beck et al., 1996). Hence, a counselor working with Ann would need to address whether the client has posttraumatic stress disorder, depression, or comorbidity (i.e., the presence of one or more disorders).

Writing in Professional Language

From the case studies in Chapter 2 and the sample score report on Ann, professionals and laypeople alike easily understand much of the information, particularly the narrative portions in the case studies. However, the score reports are geared toward professionals. Counselors should keep in mind that the assessment report becomes part of the client's record, such as educational records, medical records, employment records, and legal records. Thus, counselors are accountable for how the assessment results are used and interpreted, particularly when such results affect the welfare of the client.

So who is the client? The request for an assessment of an individual may not come from an individual seeking services but from some other entity (e.g., court, medical professional, organization, school). Hence, the counselor conducting an assessment may be responsible to multiple parties, such as the referring professional or organization, as well as the individual assessed. We discuss ethical responsibilities to the client and stakeholders later in the chapter, but for now we focus on the fact that the assessment report must be written in a manner that pertains to multiple audiences (e.g., client, referring professional or organization).

The assessment report is not only a reflection of the client but also of the counselor conducting the assessment and providing the written report. Professionals look for evidence of a well-written report that reflects a valid administration of the test(s) and knowledgeable interpretation. In addition, multiple forms of evidence should be presented to substantiate any recommendations that are made as a result of the assessment. Writing in a professional language that communicates a logical, coherent case conceptualization is extremely pertinent, as such a report may be used to provide educational placement, medication management, vocational placement, and legal options. For example, juvenile judges often refer adolescents and families to counseling services and expect feedback and recommendations from the counselor to the court regarding the client's disposition and any recommendations. A judge may use such information to render decisions in a case. Hence, based on the counselor's recommendations, a client may be released from the juvenile court, referred for additional treatment, or even detained. In such an instance, what the judge may be looking for is evidence that supports a decision regarding the adolescent's disposition with the juvenile court. Information provided by the counselor may in fact be highly influential in rendering decisions.

Such an assessment is no less important to other professionals, such as a psychiatrist considering medication management issues, schools considering placement, and institutions considering the job placement of an individual. An example may be with the Department of Transportation (DOT), which has specific policies regarding substance abuse for professionals in the transportation industry. Counselors often provide substance abuse assessments for the DOT; the information related in such assessments may have serious ramifications on whether clients are able to continue with their jobs.

Beyond the structure of the assessment report, which has been outlined in this chapter, the manner in which information is conveyed is equally important. Because the assessment report may become part of the client's record in a variety of settings, professionalism is necessary. Counselors should avoid jargon, as professionals outside the mental health industry may need to understand the contents of the report. Although not all professionals may understand the scope of the score report, such information is necessary for those within the mental health field who may know how to interpret such information. The report should be clearly written and grammatically correct. Recommendations and the rationale for such recommendations should be easy to understand for professionals outside the mental health profession. For example, a school administrator or counselor, judge, or employer examining such a report may communicate a decision and refer to the report as a basis for such a decision.

Making Recommendations

Clients, parents/guardians, third-party payors, or other outside entities may request assessment reports. Counselors need to be aware of the intended audience for the report and what information should be communicated. Balancing the client's needs and the needs of the referring entity are important considerations. We advocate for a report that is deductive in nature—one that moves from general impressions to specific findings and recommendations. Therefore, recommendations are highlighted near the end of the report and easily distinguished from other aspects of the psychological report. Counselors should deliberate numerous considerations when making recommendations such as the data supporting the recommendations, the client's disposition, the likelihood of following the recommendations, and the scope of the recommendations.

Supporting Data

Recommendations are data driven. The reader of an assessment report should be able to follow a clear logic of how a recommendation was derived. Explicit statements connecting a recommendation to data presented in the assessment report is helpful in providing a strong rationale. For example, a statement reflecting Ann's past history of family conflict, trauma, and oppositional behavior may make her a candidate for medication management. Therefore, an assessment report may include a recommendation for a psychiatric consultation. If Ann agrees, providing information from Ann's clinical interview, subsequent sessions, and formal assessments may be helpful to a consulting psychiatrist in rendering a decision related to medication management:

Given Ann's disclosure of past trauma, family conflict, and poor support and her subsequent score on the BDI-II indicating moderate to severe depression, she may benefit from a psychiatric consultation to evaluate the appropriateness of medication management.

Thus, the statement provides a cogent recommendation based on data from the clinical interview and administration of the BDI-II.

Client Disposition

When making a recommendation, consider the client's amiability toward counseling and prognosis. *Amiability* refers to the client's receptiveness toward counseling. Is the client motivated? Is the client seeking counseling out of personal interest in self-improvement or due to a level of coercion or leverage? For example, an individual who recognizes that he or she has a substance abuse problem may be more amiable toward counseling than an individual who has been court ordered for an assessment. A client's personal motivation to be healthier may certainly facilitate the likelihood of counseling being effective when compared to the individual who attends counseling to escape or reduce logical and natural consequences of behavior.

Based on the data presented and the client's receptiveness and motivation toward counseling and/or assessment, the counselor should consider the client's prognosis. The counselor should avoid using terms that may be implied as overly predictive, such as being too positive or even fatalistic. A statement about prognosis should address the likelihood of success based on the recommendations or the potential for problems to continue. In the case Ann, the following statement may be appropriate:

Ann is a 16-year-old Caucasian female of average to above average intellectual functioning with a history of sexual abuse victim, substance use, and oppositional behavior. Symptoms of depression are evident including low self-esteem, irritability, saddened mood, and defeated outlook. Ann faces significant conflict with her mother, and Ann's mother could be characterized as nonsupportive. Without placement, Ann is at risk for regressing further to higher risk behavior problems. Placement will be pursued. Prognosis is guarded at this time pending placement.

Likelihood of Following Recommendations

Beyond the client's internal motivation toward counseling, the counselor should consider the feasibility of making recommendations. Not only should the counselor make recommendations that are supported through best practices, but the availability and accessibility to follow through with specific recommendations also is important. According to Ann's assessment report, Ann's mother is not motivated toward Ann getting help. If the counselor recommends a psychiatric consult for Ann, does Ann's mother have the necessary medical benefits to cover the consult and subsequent visits should they be necessary? If Ann is prescribed psychotropic medication, does Ann's mother possess a prescription drug plan that would cover the cost of ongoing medication?

Hence, the likelihood of a client following recommendations may be less about the client's willingness and more about the client's resources. This is especially true when counseling youth in which transportation, the ability for parents to leave work, school attendance, and financial resources can all be obstacles that interfere with the client's ability to adhere to counselor recommendations. When making a recommendation, consider the resources available and the ability of the client to take advantage of such resources.

Scope of Recommendations

The limits of the counselor with respect to an assessment report may be best described as a process in which the counselor has immense responsibility but limited authority. The counselor can make recommendations but has no authority as to whether the client will follow through. In cases where a client is referred by a judge or place of employment, the counselor may have leverage with respect to making recommendations, but follow-through on the recommendations is up to the client and the enforcement by the third party.

In addition, when working with referring professionals, agencies, or organizations, counselors should be aware of the information solicited by the referral source and the type of interventions typically used. For example, although a client may be noncompliant with counseling, the counselor does not have the authority to recommend detention or adjudication to a court. These are processes a court may employ depending on the due process of the client. Therefore, the counselor lacks the authority and knowledge to make such recommendations. Rather, the counselor should focus on making recommendations that are more factually based, once again relying on the data from the assessment process to address the client's current disposition and likely challenges and/or strengths.

Conducting an Interpretation Session with a Client

The assessment report includes a variety of technical information such as diagnosis(es), score reports, and descriptions employing language specific to mental health professionals. Therefore, a session in which the counselor provides an interpretation of the assessment report for the client is an opportunity to shed light on an otherwise complex report. According to the Wall et al. (2003):

> Conveying test results with language that the test taker, parents, teachers, clients, or general public can understand is one of the key elements in helping others understand the meaning of the test results.... The test user should indicate how the test results can be and should not be interpreted. (p. 5)

Therefore, considerable preparation and a formal interpretation session for the client is best practice. When a client has no previous contact with a counselor prior to an assessment, the client might not be invested in ongoing sessions with a counselor. Often a client will request that a report be sent to the referral source without ever scheduling an interpretation session. However, counselors should proceed cautiously with such a request. Clients have the right to know assessment results and subsequent interpretations of the information (American Counseling Association [ACA], 2014). Counselors should encourage clients to attend a subsequent session for the purposes of interpreting the assessment report.

Reviewing Informed Consent Procedures

Throughout this chapter, responsibilities to both the client and the referral source were addressed. Nevertheless, the primary responsibility of the counselor is the welfare of the client (ACA, 2014). This does not mean that the recommendations of the counselor always appear beneficial to the client's worldview. On the contrary, what is in the best interest of the client may not be what the client desires. For this reason, the counselor should spend adequate time discussing the nature of informed consent and who may obtain the contents of the assessment report before administration of any counseling assessment. Counselors have the responsibility of assuring the client that the individuals receiving the report have the qualifications to interpret the assessment report properly. Counselors must be aware of Health Insurance Portability and Accountability Act (HIPAA) guidelines when releasing information to another party. Specific forms related to releasing and obtaining information need to be signed, and the party receiving the information must be stipulated.

The counselor should be cautious about releasing information, particularly from the clinical interview. Client disclosures often are made under the pretense of confidentiality. When a counselor obtains consent to release information to a third party, the client must understand the boundaries of what information may be released. In addition, counselors should release information on a need-to-know basis. A common practice is for the counselor to obtain consent to release information from the client and then send the client file. However, this is not best practice, as first and foremost is the client's welfare and the third party's need to know. If there is information within the contents of the client's file that the third party does not require in order to render appropriate care or disposition, then such information should not be released.

Reviewing the Instruments Used

During the interpretation session with the client, the counselor will typically address information related to formal and informal assessments. The counselor may highlight information obtained from the clinical interview as well as any standardized measures that were administered. "The specific purposes for the use of such instruments are stated explicitly to the examinee" (ACA, 2005, p. 13). Counselors discuss with the client the nature of each instrument, including the purpose, rationale, and information derived from each instrument.

In the case of Ann, the counselor would review information in the assessment report related to her history, presenting problem, and relevant treatment issues, as well as highlight any formal instruments that were administered. The BDI-II was administered out of concern related to mood disturbance. Ann's score of 28 places her in the moderate to severe range of major depressive disorder and among the top 6% of individuals who may not be seeking counseling services. Compared to individuals who do seek counseling services, Ann exhibited depressive symptoms that are slightly more severe than average. A counselor making a referral for a psychiatric consultation would identify what may be gained from such a consultation and how the third party may use the information.

Summarizing the Data in Client Language

Counselors should summarize information for clients in a language they can understand. The technical information used in assessment reports is beyond most clients' understanding. Take time to address the nature of a norm group and to whom a client is being compared. In the score report for Ann, comparisons are made to both clinical and nonclinical populations. The nature of different percentiles for the same score may be confusing to a client. Ann's label of moderate to severe depression on the assessment report is easier to explain when comparing Ann to the nonclinical group, as she is in the 94th percentile. Hence, a counselor could explain that 94% of individuals in the nonclinical group scored at or below Ann's score of 28; Ann is in the top 6% when compared to this group.

Explaining Ann's score with respect to the clinical group may be a bit more confusing. How can Ann's placement in the 64th percentile, only slightly above average, be indicative of moderate to severe depression? The client would need to understand that this comparison is based on individuals who are also seeking counseling services. Even though the client may be categorized with moderate to severe depression, the fact that Ann is in the 64th percentile compared to the clinical group may help her understand that she is more like other individuals seeking counseling, which can be rather affirming.

As shown in Chapter 2, the assessment reports include a *Diagnostic and Statistical Manual of Mental Disorders* (DSM) diagnosis, which may also require explanation to the client. A diagnosis may provide information to another mental health care provider in a manner that is easily understood among clinical professionals but may be foreign to a client. Diagnoses may be necessary to obtain reimbursement from third-party payors. However, not all problems and clients require a diagnosis. "Counselors may refrain from making and/or reporting a diagnosis if they believe it would cause harm to the client or others" (ACA, 2014, p. 11). Counselors should provide clients with an explanation of a diagnosis, should one be given, and the implications, as well as treatment strategies, related to the diagnosis.

The assessment process and report may be an intimidating process for clients. Counselors should work hard to normalize the process and place the client's welfare at the forefront while not compromising objectivity. Assessment reports are forthright appraisals of a client's presenting problem(s), relevant history, disposition, and prognosis. Clients may be apprehensive about the assessment process (e.g., court-ordered clients). Counselors should make sure that the assessments are administered, scored, and reported with integrity and will be used appropriately. Such ethical intentions should be communicated to the client in order to reduce any anxiety and encourage trust in the assessment process.

Types of Information Derived from Ann's and Robert's Case Study

Presentation of Ann's case was emphasized in this chapter. An abbreviated integrative summary of Ann is in Appendix B. This type of summary could be used in a letter to a court or referral source to provide an abbreviated summary and conceptualization about the client.

Ann's case included an interpretation of the BDI-II, which is a unidimensional scale. In other words, the interpretation of the instrument is based on a single, total score. To further reiterate the points about instrument interpretation, information related to Robert's case in light of an administration of the OQ-45.2 follows.

The OQ-45.2 is a 45-item scale designed to identify problems and measure progress in three distinct areas: symptom distress, interpersonal relations, and social role. The scale may be administered repeatedly over time to demonstrate progress, stagnation, or regression in the aforementioned areas. Each of the items follows a Likert-type format identifying the frequency a symptom or behavior occurs: *never, rarely, sometimes, frequently*, or *almost always*. A completed instrument produced a Total score and three subscale scores. In addition, there are five critical items that relate to substance abuse, suicidality, and hostility toward others. Robert's primary issue is alcohol use, and his abuse of alcohol has had a significant impact on his family relationships, particularly with his wife who is threatening divorce; his employment, due to numerous lost jobs; and his legal issues, due to numerous DUIs and incarcerations.

Lambert et al. (2004) provided descriptive statistics for several norm groups, consisting of clinical and nonclinical populations. For the purposes of this assessment report, comparisons were made to the community sample (nonclinical). Descriptive statistics for the Total scale scores and subscale scores, as well as the reliability estimates (α), are in Table 12.2.

Robert is seeking counseling because of his alcohol use. Robert has had a history of abusing alcohol, which has resulted in legal problems, loss of employment, and relationship problems with his wife and family. Robert was administered the OQ-45.2 under typical conditions, and results from the scores may be deemed as a valid assessment (Table 12.3).

TABLE 12.2 Descriptive Statistics of the Community Norm Group for the Outcome Questionnaire-45.2

Scale	Mean	SD	α
Total	45.19	18.57	0.84
Symptom Distress	25.43	11.55	0.78
Interpersonal Relations	10.20	5.56	0.80
Social Role	9.56	3.87	0.82

Note: SD = standard deviation.

TABLE 12.3 Score Report for Robert Jones on the Outcome Questionnaire-45.2

Scale	Raw Score	Standard Score	Percentile	SEM (CI 68%)
Total	42	−0.17	43rd	7.43 (34.57, 49.43)
Symptom Distress	8	−1.51	7th	5.42 (2.58, 13.42)
Interpersonal Relations	20	1.76	96th	2.49 (17.51, 22.49)
Social Role	14	1.15	87th	1.64 (12.36, 15.15)

Note: SEM = standard error of measurement; CI = confidence interval.

Notice the OQ-45.2 is a multidimensional scale. The Total scale score is composed of three subscales. Also notice that if a counselor focuses solely on the Total scale score (Robert's Total score is within the average range), some very important information is missed. Robert has low scores compared to a nonclinical group in Symptom Distress. However, Robert's scores in Interpersonal Relations and Social Role are quite elevated, placing Robert in the 96th and 87th percentiles, respectively. Robert also endorsed two of the five critical items: "After heavy drinking, I need a drink the next morning to get going," and "I feel annoyed by people who criticize my drinking (or drug use)." An example of how to report Robert's scores on the OQ-45.2 follows.

Robert's Total score on the OQ-45.2, when compared to a nonclinical norm group, place him in the 43rd percentile. Robert hardly endorses any symptomatic distress, with placement in the bottom 10% (7th percentile). Robert endorsed a lot of problems with respect to Interpersonal Relations (96th percentile), which is expected given the current coercers and conflict between Robert and his wife. Robert's score in Social Role was elevated, placing him in the 87th percentile. Elevated scores in Social Role refer to higher levels of "dissatisfaction, conflict, distress, and inadequacy" in areas related to "employment, family roles, and leisure life" (Lambert et al., 2004, p. 2.). Robert endorsed items related to stress and dissatisfaction with work, likely emanating from his multiple losses of employment. In addition, Robert endorsed three of the five critical items on the OQ-45.2, which were related to substance abuse and Robert's hostility toward others in his work environment. These elevated scores and attributes fit with Robert's clinical profile of Alcohol Use Disorder, Severe. Robert's wife of over 20 years is considering divorce if he cannot quit drinking. Counseling will focus on Robert's ongoing alcohol use and providing the necessary education and support for Robert to abstain.

This score report may accompany the psychological report addressed in Chapter 2, thereby providing a comprehensive review of the client using both qualitative (e.g., session and interview information) and quantitative measures (e.g., standardized assessment instruments). Keep in mind that the client or parent/guardian may review the assessment report. In the case of Ann Smith, the counselor is acting with the client's welfare in mind. However, the counselor may defend such a report by focusing on the data collected and reminding the client and mother that addressing issues of oppositional behavior, trauma, family conflict, and peer relations is pertinent to client welfare. Thus, the counselor must maintain integrity when addressing client strengths, weaknesses, and challenges. The assessment report provided a comprehensive review and summary regarding client issues and disposition, which may affect more than the client but society as well. Whenever creating and reviewing an assessment report, keep in mind that each assessment instrument is a tool and should never be used as a sole resource in decision-making. Evaluate all of the data, such as the clinical interview, progress notes, and scores on assessment instruments, when considering the treatment and disposition of the client.

13

Assessment of Accountability in Counseling

Objectives

1. Define accountability in relation to the counseling profession.
2. Address challenges to demonstrating accountability in counseling.
3. Evaluate practices of accountability using standardized and nonstandardized measures.
4. Understand effective methods for evaluating assessment outcomes.
5. Apply assessment issues related to accountability to the case studies.

Counseling in an Era of Accountability

Counselors, regardless of specialization, operate in an era of accountability. *Accountability*, as it relates to counseling, is the use of data to validate the need for services and the outcomes related to those services. *Data* refer to quantitative or qualitative information used for the justification of services and the results for those services. Naturally, data may be generated from informal assessments, such as information generated through progress notes, or formal assessments, such as information gathered from clinical interviews, mental status examinations, and assessment instruments, rating scales, and surveys.

The demonstration of accountability is broad and ambiguous and can refer to any number of assessments. Satisfaction with services, symptom reduction, improvement in psychosocial functioning, number of clients served, or the frequency of services provided all serve as examples of assessment practices to demonstrate accountability (Balkin & Roland, 2007; Luk et al., 2001). Clearly, the difference between identifying satisfaction with services as an outcome measure versus symptom reduction is notable. An adolescent with disruptive behavior may not like coming to counseling, and perhaps even resents it, yet still makes therapeutic gains. Community mental health agencies often validate their funding by addressing points of service (e.g., number of clients seen) as opposed to providing evidence of effective treatment. Assessing accountability is multifaceted with no recognized measure or operational definition to clarify what should be assessed or measured. For the purposes of this chapter, we recognize that reporting points of service and satisfaction of services can be important components for stakeholders who fund mental health services; however, we focus more on assessing the effectiveness of counseling services in order to provide counselors with a broad range of tools to demonstrate the relevance and importance of their skills.

Accountability is an ethical mandate of the American Counseling Association (ACA). "Counselors have a responsibility to the public to engage in counseling practices that are based on rigorous research methodologies" (2014, p. 8). In addition to the ACA *Code of Ethics* (2014), three prominent areas of legislation affect the counseling profession and the mandate toward accountability: the Health Maintenance Organization (HMO) Act of 1973 (HMO), the No Child Left Behind Act of 2001 (NCLB), and Every Student Succeeds Act of 2015 (ESSA).

The 1973 HMO Act was enacted during the Nixon administration, but the effects on mental health care were not noticeable until the 1980s and beyond because of the substantial growth of managed care companies during this decade (Erickson, 2010). The HMO Act introduced managed care to mental health professionals, which influenced mental health professions in several ways. First, managed care companies required preauthorization of care from a primary care physician and quite often a case manager employed by the third-party payor to review requested services. Such a practice created a conflict of interest, as the third-party payor, often an insurance company, could increase profits by limiting and/or denying care. Hence, stated benefit packages touted by employers were often unavailable to individuals requesting access to the benefits. In addition, managed care companies instituted utilization review, in which managed care companies review services, through progress notes, formal letters, phone consultations, and so forth, to identify the necessity and benefit of requested services. For example, a client may have the benefit of mental health services but is unable to utilize those benefits if case reviewers do not believe the services are necessary. Assessment services certainly were affected by these practices. Third-party payors may limit reimbursement for assessment services and specify the monetary amount that will be covered and the number of hours that may be used and reimbursed. Often, the amount allowed was not sufficient to cover cost of materials and the time for the counselor to administer, score, interpret the instruments and develop a psychological report. Counselors have to justify the need for the assessment services, as well as the cost involved. Such procedures move decision-making from credentialed professionals onto the third-party payors, which may or may not use informed professionals in the process. Throughout the process, managed care companies could limit providers who could be in network to service clients under their plan and identify treatment strategies that are needed. Hence, managed care companies may be criticized for enforcing a one-size-fits-all approach to counseling services that disregard the unique needs of each client (Erickson, 2010).

Furthermore, managed care companies may be guilty of unfairly restricting access to mental health services. Generally, access to medical services may be attributed to socioeconomic status and obtaining private insurance. However, the opposite may be true for mental health services. Balkin (2006) found that lengths of stay for adolescents in acute care psychiatric hospitalization was shorter when the adolescent had access to private insurance, as oppose to state-funded insurance such as Medicaid. Private insurance companies are much more likely to incorporate utilization review services than state-funded insurance programs. Utilization review is an essential component to cost containment by the insurance companies and seems to affect access to services to a population that previously had more access prior to managed care.

Although managed care companies may scrutinize mental health services unfairly, an unfortunate reality is that mental health services are an easy target for cost containment. Extant research related to the effectiveness of counseling is limited, resulting in a profession that has difficulty providing evidence that counseling is beneficial. Furthermore, some of the blame for the aggressive stance of managed care toward the mental health profession must go to the mental health professionals that abused the system. Prior to managed care companies instituting utilization review, mental health practitioners had free rein with respect to the number of counseling sessions, the utilization of assessment instruments, and the use of more intensive types of treatment, such as inpatient hospitalizations with unspecified lengths of stay. The demand for accountability by counseling professionals was both reasonable and necessary.

Accountability practices were affected further by the passage of NCLB and later reinforced for states while reducing the federal government's role through ESSA. NCLB forced school districts to implement high-stakes testing practices to address accountability. School counseling services and mental health services in the schools were tied to educational goals. Hence if school counseling was to remain a viable component of the educational system, then the benefit of school counseling services should be reflected in educational achievement. The problem is that much of what the school counselor provides is not directly assessed by achievement tests. Rather, the outcomes are more indirect, such as fewer behavior problems in the classrooms, improved crisis management, and higher success in postgraduate placements (e.g., postsecondary education, career-related vocational placements). When students are pulled out of the classroom for responsive services, such as participation in counseling groups, administrators want to be assured that such interventions will be tied to improved academic performance. These types of studies, although needed, are difficult because of their complexity.

Barriers to Assessing Accountability in Counseling

Despite the role and function of assessing accountability in counseling, a dearth of outcome studies is apparent in counseling research. Part of the issue stems from training.

However, other more practical issues with respect to research design and analysis also limit the prevalence of assessing outcomes and accountability.

The training in research for counselors may be inadequate for assessing accountability in the counseling profession. Often, counselors are master's-level professionals with a single research course that focuses on traditional experimental designs used for large between- and within-subjects research. In other words, counselors receive training on understanding research methods for comparing large groups, often with an emphasis on being an intelligent consumer of research as opposed to a practitioner of research. As a result, counselors may be less comfortable assessing accountability. Furthermore, inferential statistics require a representative sample, which is not conducive to counseling practice, given that the nature of counseling practice is often centered on individuals, couples, families, and small groups. Outside the school setting, counselors do not have access to large, intact groups with sufficient numbers to make generalizable comparisons. Even in the school setting, where counselors may have access to larger groups, evaluating guidance curriculum may be easier than assessing outcomes from responsive services, which generally occur on an individual or small-group basis. Because of this barrier, we recommend counselors become adept with single-case research designs—a rather simple process of comparing a single client's progress over time without reliance on complex statistical analyses.

As mentioned earlier, addressing accountability through measuring outcomes can include a number of possibilities (e.g., satisfaction with services, symptom reduction, improvement in psychosocial functioning, points of service). Throughout the text, assessments were covered that measured operationally defined constructs. However, the notion of outcomes does not follow a singular operational definition, and it is not likely that a single measure can be developed that would adequately address the multiple outcomes necessary for clients served in counseling. For example, consider the outcomes for Eva Marie and how they differ from outcomes for Robert or Ann. Identifying a single measure that could adequately address outcomes in counseling for each of these diverse clients would be a challenge. In another example, counseling outcomes across different populations require many different measures. Outcomes for an adolescent diagnosed with anorexia nervosa indicate far different needs than an adult client diagnosed with posttraumatic stress disorder. Likewise, outcomes for families are much different than outcomes for children or adults.

Perhaps an additional challenge is the fact that because outcomes may be so diverse, third-party payors and stakeholders that desire accountability data may be nonspecific as to what exactly constitutes a valid outcome. Counselors and agencies often have some freedom to decide the type of outcomes they wish to measure. For example, a psychiatric hospital may wish to monitor the use of physical restraints, while a counselor in private practice may wish to identify whether individuals participating in a group have improved psychosocial functioning.

Outcome research can be costly. Some popular instruments do have an initial licensing cost or cost per instrument, which may be difficult to justify if the instruments are rather general and a cogent plan is lacking as to how the assessment data will be used to increase accountability and not be cost-prohibitive. Outcome instruments require time to administer, score, and interpret. Additional time may be spent inputting data to track general trends for a variety of clients. Counselors, agencies, and organizations that track outcomes may require consultants to help run the data analysis and provide feedback. Although outcome research is important to addressing accountability, careful planning is required to implement accountability research.

Finally, an important acknowledgment about counseling outcomes is that positive outcomes and success are difficult to track and even achieve. For example, in the case study, Robert has a diagnosis of alcohol use, severe. If Robert were to become invested in the counseling process and abstain from alcohol over a three-month period, would such a commitment be considered a positive outcome or success? What would happen if Robert relapsed after abstaining for three months? Does the relapse change the outcome? These are not easy questions. One could argue that Robert even committing to counseling, given his long history of alcohol abuse, is a very meaningful success. Certainly three months being clean and sober is a major accomplishment. If Robert learns from his relapse experience and continues to focus on his treatment, then perhaps the counseling outcomes are still positive. Of course, if Robert goes back to abusing alcohol then his treatment may be deemed a failure.

Although outcome instruments are more readily available for mental health counselors, outcome instruments are lacking for other types of specialization, such as career counseling, rehabilitation counseling, and couples, marriage, and family counseling. Thus, addressing accountability in these environments can be difficult, especially when the presence of formal instruments is rather limited. Often, outcomes are assessed rather subjectively, such as judging if the client has received the services he or she was expecting (e.g., client satisfaction), but such an outcome may not relate to what actually occurred in the counseling process. For example, Ann does not have a supportive living environment, and Ann's mother expressed a desire for her daughter to be in detention. If Ann is placed in an alternative home or setting, such an outcome may not be what Ann's mother wanted but may be what is best for Ann. Having Ann separated from her mother might provide a more supportive living environment. Judgments of the outcome of counseling may vary, depending on what occurred and various perspectives of the client(s), stakeholders, and counselor.

Clearly, creating lasting, personal change through the course of counseling is a tall task. Counselors need to be realistic in identifying achievable outcomes with clients. Moreover, finding outcome assessments that are useful may also be a challenge. Sederer, Dickey, and Eisen (1997) provided eight criteria to address in implementing accountability assessment: (a) the assessment is pertinent to the client in terms of being both useful and expedient; (b) the assessment is able to measure change over time; (c) the assessment is generalizable with diverse populations; (d) the assessment is easy to implement (e.g., administer and score); (e) the assessment is not cost-prohibitive; (f) the assessment is a collaborative process, involving both the client and the counselor; (g) the assessment is implemented as a standard of practice; and (h) results of the assessment can be used to address accountability standards for informing practice and presenting data to stakeholders (Lambert & Hawkins, 2004; Sederer et al., 1997). In the following section, we introduce some nonstandardized and standardized instruments that may be useful in addressing accountability in counseling.

Nonstandardized and Standardized Assessment of Accountability

Given the broad nature of tracking outcomes, counselors should consider carefully the type of accountability assessment that may be most beneficial. Nonstandardized assessments offer the advantage of being able to individualize counseling outcomes that will be assessed. However, counselors may have difficulty communicating meaning of nonstandardized assessment results, as comparisons to others are not likely. Rather, the focus is usually on the documentation of client progress when compared to the client's *baseline*, the client's symptoms and/or behavior prior to counseling intervention. The use of nonstandardized assessments requires planning, as the counselor will want to document baseline behavior or characteristics prior to beginning a specific intervention or task to address client change.

Standardized assessments, on the other hand, are often normed, which provide the opportunity to make comparisons and determine the extent to which the client's characteristics or behavior is extreme or outside the norm. However, standardized assessments may be rather generic and not address the specific problem(s) that brought the client to counseling. Often, standardized assessments are used repeatedly to ascertain client change. There are two concerns with this process. First, not all measures were designed to be repeatedly administered. For example, in order to track improvement in Ann's depression, the Beck Depression Inventory-II (BDI-II) may be administered repeatedly over time. However, the BDI-II was not developed for this purpose. The BDI-II was developed to measure the presence and severity of depression, not track client progress. Counselors should be cautious about the valid nature of the scores when using an instrument in this way. A second consideration is the presence of a *testing effect*. The repeated use of an instrument may result in the client becoming wise to what is being measured, therefore compromising the validity of the scores obtained on an administration. For example, clients may attempt to themselves in the best possible light, in order to demonstrate improvement. A client could also exacerbate symptoms in order to prolong counseling. Standardized outcome assessments are available, and these instruments were developed with the intent of being used for repeated measurement, resulting in a more valid assessment process.

Nonstandardized Assessment—Goal Attainment Scaling

Goal attainment scaling is a nonstandardized assessment in which individualized goals are measured and converted to a *T*-like score (i.e., mean of 50, standard deviation of 10). Goals are scored and can be measured against a baseline. Goal attainment scaling was first published by Kiresuk and Sherman (1968) when they presented how goals could be set, measured, and placed in a quasi-standardized format (i.e., a T score) to demonstrate progress in rehabilitation counseling. The reason the format is considered quasi-standardized is because a standard score, the T score, is used but a comparison to baseline behavior for the individual is made, as opposed to the traditional comparison to a normative sample.

Steps to Goal Attainment Scaling

Turner-Stokes (2009) outlined a five-step process to using goal attainment scaling in assessing accountability. The first step is to identify the goals. Goals for counseling often are identified from the clinical interview/initial assessment. Goals should be stated in measurable terms. We advocate for goal-setting to be a collaborative process between the counselor and client. Turner-Stokes suggested using the "SMART principle" to set goals, indicating that goals should be "specific, measurable, attainable, realistic, and timely" (p. 365). Although there is no limit to the number of goals that can be set, we encourage counselors to limit goals to three or four. Too many goals may become overwhelming to address, treat, and track.

The second step is to weight the goals. Weighting the goals allows for the client and counselor to identify both the importance and difficulty of each goal. Hence, goals that are more important or more difficult to achieve can be given more weight. To weight the goals, both the importance and the difficulty should be considered. The client is asked to identify the importance (I) of the goal and provide the following to each goal: 0 (*not at all important*), 1 (*a little important*), 2 (*moderately important*), or 3 (*very important*). A similar system is used to evaluate the difficulty (D) of each goal: 0 (*not at all difficulty*), 1 (*a little difficult*), 2 (*moderately difficult*), or 3 (*very difficult*). Using this rating system, each goal can be weighted by multiplying (I × D). For example, a goal for Robert might be to attend counseling so he can show his wife that he is serious about abstaining from alcohol. Robert may view attending counseling to be very important (3) and only a little difficult (1). Weight = I × D, or 3 × 1. Hence attending counseling would receive a weight of 3. Note that any goal that receives a zero on either importance or difficulty is eliminated from the evaluation: if a goal receives a zero on importance, then the goal should not be a focus of counseling, and if the goal receives a zero in terms of difficulty, then time may be better spent on goals that are more difficult to accomplish and more meaningful. Turner-Stokes (2009) indicated that weighting of goals should be considered an optional process, because the benefits of incorporating weighting into the goal attainment scaling may not be beneficial. When weighting is not used, all goals are weighted as 1. Perhaps a reason to avoid weighting goals might be a lack of insight on the client's behalf. A natural goal for Ann, for example, is to abstain from using marijuana. However, because of Ann's oppositional nature, Ann would be likely to view abstaining from marijuana as of little importance (1) and not difficult (0)—both of which may be untrue. So, according to the weighting formula, 1 × 0 = 0, abstaining from marijuana would be eliminated yet is still relevant if Ann is to make any progress in counseling.

The third step in goal attainment scaling is to define the expected outcome for each goal (Turner-Stokes, 2009). Once the expected outcome is defined for each goal, a measure at baseline and subsequent follow-up measures should be assessed using a 5-point scale from –2 to +2. In this scale, a zero denotes that the *expected outcome was met*. A score of –1 indicates the client was *slightly below the expected outcome*; –2 indicates the client was *much below the expected outcome*; +1 indicates the client was *slightly above expectations*; +2 indicates the client was *far above expectations*.

The fourth step is the establishment of baseline data. As noted in the previous step, both baseline data and subsequent follow-up measures use the 5-point scale from –2 to +2. For each of the goals, a baseline measure is assessed. Usually, baseline measures will be scored at a –1 or –2, thereby noting that the goal represents an area that the client needs to improve.

The fifth step is the goal attainment scoring. The client and counselor may wish to identify the frequency at which goals will be evaluated (e.g., every week, once per month). We also recommend a collaborative process when rating the goals. Once goals are rated, either at baseline or subsequent sessions, the *T* score is calculated. For the purposes of goal attainment scaling, the *T* score represents an aggregate score that can be tracked over time. As a general rule, a *T* score of 50 represents that, on average, the client is at the expected level of functioning; 60 represents the client is above the expected level of functioning; 70 represents the client is far above the expected level of functioning. Scores below 50 have the opposite effect. A *T* score of 40 represents the client is below the expected level of functioning, and 30 represents the client is far below the expected level of functioning. The *T* score is computed with the following formula:

$$T = 50 + \frac{10\Sigma(W_i X_i)}{\sqrt{[(1-p)\Sigma W_i^2 + p(\Sigma W_i)^2]}}$$

"where W_i is the weight assigned [to each goal (if equal weights, $W_i = 1$)], X_i is the numerical value achieved (between –2 to +2), and p is the expected correlation of the goal scores" (Turner-Stokes, 2009, p. 364). Turner-Stokes indicated that p might be estimated at .30, which simplifies the equation to the following:

$$T = 50 + \frac{10\Sigma(W_i X_i)}{\sqrt{[(.7\Sigma W_i^2 + .3(\Sigma W_i)^2]}}$$

Although the formula may appear a little intimidating or complex, goal attainment scale calculators, which use Excel files, are available on the Internet. A case example using goal attainment scaling follows later in the chapter.

Standardized Assessment

As noted earlier in the chapter, many standardized instruments were not developed specifically for outcome accountability assessment. Counselors should be sure to select instruments that not only measure the construct or goals of interest but also were developed for outcome measurement. Such instruments are more likely to produce reliable and valid scores over repeated measures and be sensitive to change (Lambert & Hawkins, 2004). With this in mind, we discuss some common outcome measures that meet these criteria, along with being relatively inexpensive and appropriate for master's-level counselors.

OQ and Y-OQ Instruments

The Outcome Questionnaire (OQ) and Youth Outcome Questionnaire (Y-OQ) measures are outcome questionnaires, for adults and youth, respectively, developed by OQ Measures. The OQ-45.2 is an adult measure with three subscales—Symptom Distress, Interpersonal Relationships, and Social Role—and a total score. The OQ-45.2 was highlighted in Chapter 12. To review, the scale may be administered repeatedly over time to demonstrate progress, stagnation, or regression in the aforementioned areas. Each of the items follows a Likert-type format identifying the frequency at which a symptom or behavior occurs: *never, rarely, sometimes, frequently*, or *almost always*. In addition, there are five critical items that relate to substance abuse, suicidality, and hostility toward others. Internal consistency estimates for scores on the subscales range from .78 to .82; the scores for the Total subscale have an internal consistency estimate of .84. Items on the Symptom Distress subscale tend to emphasize symptoms for anxiety and depression. Items on the Interpersonal Relationships subscale tend to emphasize the client's ability to get along with others, such as friends and family. Items on the Social Role subscale tend to emphasize the ability for the client to be purposeful and productive in essential life tasks, such as school and/or work (Hanson, 2005).

The Y-OQ includes different forms, the most comprehensive being the Y-OQ-2.0, which was developed to be completed by parents, and a self-report version for adolescents to complete, the Y-OQ-2.0 SR. The parent form and self-report form were not designed to be interchangeable or equivalent. However, both instruments have 64 items and use the same subscales. The subscales include Interpersonal Distress, Somatic, Interpersonal Relationships, Critical Items, Social Problems, and Behavior Dysfunction. A Total score is also available. Reliability estimates for scores on the YOQ-2.0 range from .74 to .93 on the subscales and .97 for the Total score (Burlingame et al., 2005); reliability estimates for scores on the YOQ-2.0 SR range from .73 to .91 on the subscales and .96 for the Total score (Wells, Burlingame, & Rose, 2003). Items on the Interpersonal Distress subscale tend to emphasize symptoms for anxiety and depression. Items on the Somatic subscale tend to emphasize somatic complaints, such as headaches, stomachaches, and dizziness. Items on the Interpersonal Relationships subscale tend to emphasize attitude and communication with adults, such as parents and teachers, as well as peers. The Critical Items subscale measures symptoms consistent with psychosis (e.g., delusions, hallucinations), suicide, and disordered eating. Items on the Social Problems subscale focus on delinquent or aggressive behavior or the tendency to break rules or social norms. Items on the Behavior Dysfunction subscale tend to be consistent with symptoms for attention deficit hyperactivity disorder, emphasizing impulsivity, inattention, and low frustration tolerance.

Despite a Total score being available on both instruments, the subscales are probably more helpful. Elevations on the subscales highlight problem areas that may be helpful in addressing issues related to treatment planning, goal-setting, and subsequent counseling sessions. The instruments developed by OQ measures tend to have strong psychometric properties and are reasonably priced, which facilitates broad use in a number of settings. Generally, individuals and organizations can purchase a license, which enables repeated use of the instrument without additional costs. More importantly, the instruments were designed for repeated use and address change over time. A practical feature of these instruments is that increases and decreases in Total scores can be tracked, which may indicate meaningful change (improvement or deterioration) that is clinically significant.

Ohio Scales

The Ohio Scales are a set of mental health outcome instruments used by the Ohio Department of Mental Health and licensed users outside of Ohio. The licensing fee for mental health providers outside of Ohio is quite reasonable, and all materials (instruments, manuals, licensing agreements) may be accessed on the Internet from the Ohio Department of Mental Health. The instruments are divided into two categories: adult outcomes instruments and youth outcomes instruments.

The adult outcomes instruments are referred to as the Ohio Mental Health Consumer Outcomes System and include two forms: a self-report inventory, known as a Consumer Form, and a Provider Form. The purpose of the Adult Consumer Form is for the client to self-report "perceptions of quality of life, effects of health on functioning, medication concerns, symptom distress, and recovery/empowerment" (Ohio Department of Mental Health, 2009, p. 5-1). The Adult Consumer Form is composed of 67 items with the last six items reflecting demographic information. Items 1 to 61 reflect four sections. The first section measures Quality of Life and includes a subscale measure on Financial Status. The second section measures Safety and Health Outcomes. The third section measures Symptom Distress. The fourth section represents Making Decisions Empowerment and includes six subscales: (a) Self-Esteem/Self-Efficacy, (b) Power/Powerlessness, (c) Community Activism and Autonomy, (d) Optimism and Control over the Future, (e) Righteous Anger, and (f) Overall Empowerment. The first three sections of the Adult Consumer Form use a Likert-type format with higher scores indicative of more severity or problematic areas. The fourth section, Making Decisions Empowerment, uses a 4-point scale ranging from *agree* to *disagree*. Once again, higher scores represent more severity or problematic areas. Initial studies on internal consistency estimates for scores on the Adult Consumer Form range from .77 to .93, indicating adequate reliability evidence.

The Provider Adult Form may be used by counselors to ascertain functioning with regard to interpersonal relationships and social roles, adult living skills, housing status, involvement in the judicial system, risk to self and others, and victimization (Ohio Department of Mental Health, 2009). The Provider Adult Form is not parallel to the Consumer Form. Two domains are measured on the Provider Adult Form. The first domain is functional status and includes items that reflect issues such as socialization and social support, housing stability, adult living skills, addictive behaviors, judicial system involvement, and aggressive behaviors. The second domain, safety and health, assesses victimization and risk of harm to self or others. The instrument uses 4- and 5-point scales, as well as a checklist format to identify areas of concern. As a general rule, lower scores indicate more areas of concern. Initial reliability estimates are adequate, with internal consistency for scores from the normative sample at .72.

Unlike the adult outcome instruments, the youth outcome instruments consist of three somewhat parallel forms to be completed by the counselor, primary caregiver (e.g., parent), and youth. The Parent and Youth forms consist of 48 items that measure four domains: (a) Problem Severity, (b) Functioning, (c) Hopefulness, and (d) Satisfaction with Behavioral Health Services. The Clinician form measures Problem Severity and Functioning and includes an additional scale on Restrictiveness of Living Environment. Each of the sections uses a 4- to 6-point response format. Problem Severity is measured by 20 items, with higher scores indicating more severity; Functioning is measured by 20 items, with higher scores indicating increased functioning, and therefore less severity; Hopefulness is measured by 4 items, with higher scores indicating more severity or decreased hopefulness; Satisfaction with Behavioral Services is measured with 4 items, with higher scores indicating decreased satisfaction. Reliability estimates for internal consistency of scores range from .65 to .97. Additional validity evidence was demonstrated through correlations to other outcome instruments, such as the Child and Adolescent Functional Assessment Scale. The benefits of the Ohio Scales are similar to the instruments published by OQ Measures. The instruments were designed for repeated use and address change over time.

Outcome Rating Scale

The Outcome Rating Scale (ORS) is a four-item measure modeled after the OQ-45.2 measuring functioning in the same domains: individual well-being, social relationships, and interpersonal relationships. The client places a mark on a 10-cm horizontal line with lower levels of functioning marked to the left and higher levels of functioning marked to the right. Reliability estimates for scores over the administrations of the ORS were strong ($\alpha = .93$) and moderately correlated ($r = .54-.69$) to scores on the OQ-45.2 (Miller, Duncan, Brown, Sparks, & Claud, 2003). Because of the abbreviated nature of the instrument, it can be used repeatedly, even after every session. However, the information is related to global outcomes and does not highlight specific issues. Use of the measure requires purchase of a license.

A practical feature of each of these instruments is that increases and decreases in scores can be tracked, which may indicate significant change (improvement or deterioration) that is clinically significant. As with any assessment, counselors should be cautious in interpreting these instruments. Although the breadth of the instruments addresses numerous issues typical in counseling, not much information may be gleaned regarding specific problem areas. For example, a client with a primary diagnosis of a substance abuse disorder or eating disorder may not find the questions on these instruments specific enough to be helpful. An assessment instrument is only valid when applied appropriately. Nevertheless, we believe that measuring and evaluating the ongoing effects of counseling can improve counseling outcomes by providing both the counselor and the client feedback related to progress. Duncan (2010) referred to this idea as *feedback effects*, indicating that assessing and providing measurable feedback to the client could enhance counseling outcomes.

Evaluating the Client–Counselor Relationship

Although the focus on accountability assessment in counseling has been on outcomes and the use of empirically supported treatments, the most valuable contribution to positive outcomes is the counseling relationship (Duncan, 2010; Kottler & Balkin, 2017; Lambert, 1986; Wampold, 2001). Yet, outside of counselor training perhaps, counselors are not asked to evaluate the counseling relationship in terms of demonstrating accountability. We believe that measuring and evaluating the nature of the counseling relationship can improve counseling outcomes by providing both the counselor and the client feedback regarding the counseling relationship and providing the opportunity for the counselor to make adjustments in the event of a therapeutic rupture or the need to further develop the relationship in order to achieve a better outcome in counseling.

Working Alliance Inventory-Short Form

The Working Alliance Inventory-Short Form (WAI-S) is a 12-item instrument aligned with Bordin's (1979) theory of the working alliance. Bordin identified three aspects of the working alliance: task, bond, and goal. Four items measure each of these aspects, but further research on the WAI-S indicated a strong correlation between Task and Goal subscales, yielding a two-factor solution: Contract (Task and Goal) and Contact (Bond; Smits, Luyckx, Smits, Stinckens, & Claes, 2015). Reliability estimates for scores on the WAI-S were strong (Contract: $\alpha = .90$; Contact: $\alpha = .81$). Smits et al. advised against using a total score for the WAI-S. There is a 36-item long form, but the short form appears to be rather interchangeable with the long form with high correlation to the long form and similar psychometric properties (Busseri & Tyler, 2003). Use of the measure requires purchase of a license.

Helping Alliance Questionnaire-II

The Helping Alliance Questionnaire-II (HAq-II) is a 19-item measure, which has versions for both the client and the counselor. The HAq-II is a unidimensional measure, producing a total score for the working alliance. Each item may be scored between 1 and 6, with 1 indicating a *weak alliance* and 6 indicating a *strong alliance*. The mean for the 19 items may be used to provide an interpretation of the scores. Reliability estimates for scores on the HAq-II were strong ($\alpha = .80$; Luborsky et al., 1996). The medical school at the University of Pennsylvania Department of Psychiatry publishes and conducts research on the HAq-II. The measure may be downloaded from its website (http://www.med.upenn.edu/cpr/instruments.html).

Session Rating Scale

The Session Rating Scale (SRS; Duncan et al., 2003) was created by the developers of the ORS. Similar to the ORS, the SRS is a four-item measure modeled after Bordin's (1979) theory related to measuring agreement between the client and counselors on tasks, bond, and goals. The client places a mark on a 10-cm horizontal line with lower levels of functioning marked to the left and higher levels of functioning marked to the right. Reliability estimates for scores over the administrations of the SRS were strong ($\alpha = .88$) and moderately correlated ($r = .48$) to scores on the HAq-II (Duncan et al., 2003). Again, because of the abbreviated nature of the instrument, it can be used repeatedly, even after every session. However, the information is related to global outcomes and does not highlight specific issues. Use of the measure requires purchase of a license.

As mentioned, measures that are brief and easy to use may be helpful in monitoring the counseling relationship, and this is a particular strength of the SRS. However, knowing how to make adjustments when the counseling relationship is not going well is extremely important, and no instrument will tell you how to do that! We maintain that assessing the working alliance on a regular basis can be helpful. When clients are not improving, counselors may often turn to a specialized theory or technique as opposed to asking the question, "How can I better connect with this client?" There is no magic pill, but monitoring of the counseling relationship and adjusting your style to better connect with the client will help produce better outcomes (Kottler & Balkin, 2017).

Evaluating Client Progress and Improvement

Both nonstandardized and standardized assessments may be used to identify accountability issues in counseling. Yet counselors should be aware that such assessment might identify client improvement or progress but not necessarily indicate that a client has made sufficient progress or is doing well. For example, an adult client may endorse a number of items indicative of symptom distress. Recall that high scores on a 5-point scale indicate increased severity. Thus, a client who endorsed *almost always* (5) at baseline for items measuring symptom distress and then endorses *frequently* (4) one month later certainly shows improvement, but the progress is not sufficient to deem the client well. When using assessment instruments to assess client outcomes, counselors need to be aware of the meaning of client responses and not simply pay attention to whether scores demonstrate improvement or deterioration. A client who indicates thoughts of self-harm *frequently*, as opposed to *almost always*, is still at risk.

To this end, goal attainment scaling may have a distinct advantage over a standardized measurement instrument when assessing client outcomes. The same limitation may apply to goal attainment scaling, in which change from *much below the expected outcome* (–2) to *slightly below the expected outcome* (–1) indicates improvement but not sufficient progress where the client has achieved a therapeutic goal. The difference, however, with goal attainment scaling is that two types of scores are provided: (a) a score on each goal ranging from –2 to +2 to indicate the extent to which a goal has been met or not met and (b) a T-like score, which serves as an aggregate score for all the goals. The T score is similar to a more global assessment for the individual, indicating more holistic progress. The disadvantage here is that a client could have made significant gain in a few areas, indicated by +2, but on one goal, the client could have –1, indicating a problem area. Because the T score is an aggregate score, high levels of progress in some areas may influence the T score, even though the client is still struggling in other areas. Hence, a T score of 60 may indicate that the client is above the expected level of therapeutic goal attainment yet he or she could still have some deficits (–1 or –2) in some areas. Looking at both the aggregate T score as well as the scores for each goal is important to determine the extent to which the client has made progress.

Applying Goal Attainment Scaling to Eva Marie

In Chapter 12, the OQ-45.2 was discussed in relation to Robert. Therefore, Chapter 12 may be useful to review how a standardized outcome assessment may be used and reported. With this in mind, we focus on using a nonstandardized outcome measure, goal attainment scaling, to address how such a measure can be used to inform practice.

From Eva Marie's case study we know that Eva Marie's presenting concern is her severe and problematic anxiety. In an effort to evade and perhaps alleviate her anxiety, Eva Marie adopts an extremely unassertive and accommodating persona, which results in many additional life stressors, such as living with her mother, staying with her husband, and maintaining a job that is relatively unsatisfying. These additional stressors not only add to her stress but also contribute to some underlying depression as well.

As part of Eva Marie's treatment plan, Eva Marie and her counselor, Dr. Juhnke, set some therapeutic goals that may also be used to measure progress. Dr. Juhnke informs Eva Marie that, with her participation and consent, they can monitor her progress collaboratively and inform Eva Marie's insurance company should additional sessions be necessary beyond what is already certified. Eva Marie agrees to this plan, and together they identify the following goals:

1. *Eva Marie will be able to identify negative thoughts that lead to irrational or unhealthy behaviors or decisions and trigger anxiety symptoms.* Because cognitive-behavioral therapies represent evidence-based practice to treating anxiety and mood disorders, Dr. Juhnke begins with a treatment goal to address cognitive distortions and/or irrational beliefs.
2. *Eva Marie will process and role-play assertiveness strategies to cope with anxiety-producing situations.* Eva Marie tends to avoid conflict, particularly with her husband and mother. However, the avoidance of conflict and the negative outcomes that continually emanate from such avoidance result in increased anxiety anyway. By addressing ways to be more assertive, Eva Marie may be better able to exert more control in her life and alleviate some of her anxiety.
3. *Eva Marie will engage in career exploration exercises.* Eva Marie's job as an assistant to a school librarian contributes to her feelings of depression and adds to her stress. Dr. Juhnke knows that 30% or more of an individual's waking hours is spent at work in a given week. Therefore, engaging in career exploration activities may lead to Eva Marie enhancing her own feelings of self-efficacy and developing future goals of finding a more satisfying career.

Several other goals could be set as well, but goals should be limited in number in order to add focus to future counseling sessions and not overwhelm the client. This does not mean that the client cannot come to counseling and process issues outside the listed goals. Rather, the purpose is to frame the client's goals and expectations for counseling.

Now that treatment goals are identified, Dr. Juhnke and Eva Marie can discuss weighting the goals with respect to importance and difficulty. Eva Marie admits that her negative thoughts tend to happen automatically and contribute to increased feelings of anxiety and sometimes depression. Furthermore, she is not always aware she is engaging in negative thinking. Although she notes that she needs to be more conscientious of her self-fulfilling prophesies, she often feels overwhelmed at home with her husband and mother and does not know how to manage those relationships. She also admits to being so frustrated and bored at her job that she comes home angry and depressed, which often results in negative interactions with her mother and husband. Clearly, the problems identified and the goals to address them have a systemic attribute (i.e., one problem affects another problem). Therefore, Dr. Juhnke and Eva Marie decide to weight the goals equally.

TABLE 13.1 Baseline and One-Month Data for Eva Marie

Goal	Weight	Score	1 Month
Negative thoughts	1	−2	−1
Assertiveness	1	−1	−1
Career exploration	1	−1	0

Note: To compute the *T* score using Goal Attainment Scaling, Dr. Juhnke applies the following computation:

Dr. Juhnke collaborates with Eva Marie to establish baseline measures. Dr. Juhnke explains the rating scale of −2 to +2 for each goal and the meaning of the *T* score. Together, Eva Marie and Dr. Juhnke identify the scores for each of the goals (Table 13.1).

$$T = 50 + \frac{10\Sigma(W_i X_i)}{\sqrt{[(.7\Sigma W_i^2) + .3(\Sigma W_i)^2]}} = 50 + \frac{10[(1)(-2)+(1)(-2)+(1)(-1)]}{\sqrt{.7(3)+.3(3^2)}}$$

$$= 50 + \frac{-50}{\sqrt{2.1+2.7}} = 50 + \frac{-50}{2.19} = 27.2$$

As expected, Eva Marie begins counseling below the expected levels of goal attainment. After four weeks of weekly counseling, some improvement is noted. Specifically, Eva Marie is able to notice some of her automatic negative thinking patterns. Although she notices her cognitive distortions and irrational beliefs, she lacks the coping skills to change her thought processes at this time. Hence, Dr. Juhnke and Eva Marie rate her as somewhat improved but still problematic with a −1. In terms of assertiveness, Eva Marie admits nothing has changed in the way she interacts with her mother and husband. Therefore, her score for assertiveness is unchanged. Eva Marie did complete the O*NET Interest Profiler and Work Importance Profiler. Eva Marie is excited about continuing to explore career options and is even considering going back to school to complete a four-year degree. Therefore, Eva Marie has met her career exploration goal. Based on her progress after four weeks, Dr. Juhnke computes her *T* score:

$$T = 50 + \frac{10\Sigma(W_i X_i)}{\sqrt{[(.7\Sigma W_i^2) + .3(\Sigma W_i)^2]}} = 50 + \frac{10[(1)(-1)+(1)(-1)+(1)(0)]}{\sqrt{.7(3)+.3(9)}} = 50 + \frac{-20}{2.19} = 40.90$$

Dr. Juhnke and Eva Marie note the progress made toward her goals, moving from a *T* score of 27 to 41. However, Dr. Juhnke reminds Eva Marie that if all goals were attained at an adequate level (e.g., all scores were zero), she would have a *T* score of 50. This serves as some objective data that encourages Eva Marie to continue in counseling. Furthermore, Dr. Juhnke has some accountability data to justify further counseling sessions.

The ability to assess clients is essential to counseling practice. Counseling outcomes are not only dependent on the services provided to the client but also the extent to which programs meet the needs of counselors who serve clients. At the beginning of this book, we noted that counselors have the opportunity to identify populations of interest and determine the scope of their practice. Assessment skills affect all areas of counseling across all populations. Assessment, therefore, is a systemic dynamic that permeates the programs and services delivered by counselors to the population at large.

APPENDIX A

Area Under the Normal Curve

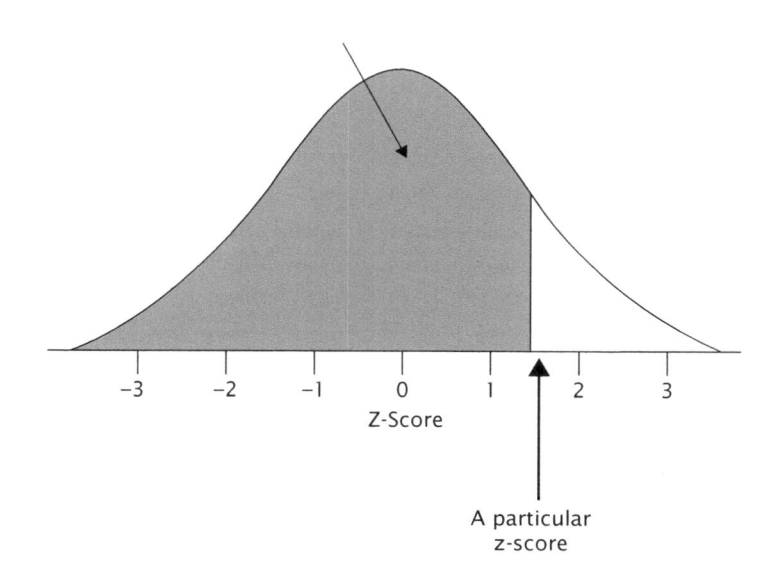

z	.00	.01	.02	.03	.04	.05	.06	.07	.08	.09
.0	.5000	.5040	.5080	.5120	.5160	.5199	.5239	.5279	.5319	.5359
.1	.5398	.5438	.5478	.5517	.5557	.5596	.5636	.5675	.5714	.5753
.2	.5793	.5832	.5871	.5910	.5948	.5987	.6026	.6064	.6103	.6141
.3	.6179	.6217	.6255	.6293	.6331	.6368	.6406	.6443	.6480	.6517
.4	.6554	.6591	.6628	.6664	.6700	.6736	.6772	.6808	.6844	.6879
.5	.6915	.6950	.6985	.7019	.7054	.7088	.7123	.7157	.7190	.7224
.6	.7257	.7291	.7324	.7357	.7389	.7422	.7454	.7486	.7517	.7549
.7	.7580	.7611	.7642	.7673	.7704	.7734	.7764	.7794	.7823	.7852
.8	.7881	.7910	.7939	.7967	.7995	.8023	.8051	.8078	.8106	.8133
.9	.8159	.8186	.8212	.8238	.8264	.8289	.8315	.8340	.8365	.8389
1.0	.8413	.8438	.8461	.8485	.8508	.8531	.8554	.8577	.8599	.8621
1.1	.8643	.8665	.8686	.8708	.8729	.8749	.8770	.8790	.8810	.8830
1.2	.8849	.8869	.8888	.8907	.8925	.8944	.8962	.8980	.8997	.9015
1.3	.9032	.9049	.9066	.9082	.9099	.9115	.9131	.9147	.9162	.9177
1.4	.9192	.9207	.9222	.9236	.9251	.9265	.9279	.9292	.9306	.9319
1.5	.9332	.9345	.9357	.9370	.9382	.9394	.9406	.9418	.9429	.9441
1.6	.9452	.9463	.9474	.9484	.9495	.9505	.9515	.9525	.9535	.9545
1.7	.9554	.9564	.9573	.9582	.9591	.9599	.9608	.9616	.9625	.9633
1.8	.9641	.9649	.9656	.9664	.9671	.9678	.9686	.9693	.9699	.9706
1.9	.9713	.9719	.9726	.9732	.9738	.9744	.9750	.9756	.9761	.9767
2.0	.9772	.9778	.9783	.9788	.9793	.9798	.9803	.9808	.9812	.9817
2.1	.9821	.9826	.9830	.9834	.9838	.9842	.9846	.9850	.9854	.9857
2.2	.9861	.9864	.9868	.9871	.9875	.9878	.9881	.9884	.9887	.9890
2.3	.9893	.9896	.9898	.9901	.9904	.9906	.9909	.9911	.9913	.9916
2.4	.9918	.9920	.9922	.9925	.9927	.9929	.9931	.9932	.9934	.9936
2.5	.9938	.9940	.9941	.9943	.9945	.9946	.9948	.9949	.9951	.9952
2.6	.9953	.9955	.9956	.9957	.9959	.9960	.9961	.9962	.9963	.9964
2.7	.9965	.9966	.9967	.9968	.9969	.9970	.9971	.9972	.9973	.9974
2.8	.9974	.9975	.9976	.9977	.9977	.9978	.9979	.9979	.9980	.9981
2.9	.9981	.9982	.9982	.9983	.9984	.9984	.9985	.9985	.9986	.9986
3.0	.9987	.9987	.9987	.9988	.9988	.9989	.9989	.9989	.9990	.9990

APPENDIX B

Integrative Summary for Ann Smith

Presenting Problem: Ann is a 16-year-old Caucasian female referred to counseling by _____ county juvenile court. Ann has a history of oppositional behavior, running away, and substance abuse. Ann tested positive on two occasions for marijuana. She was picked up by the police on two occasions for running away. She currently has charges pending a court date for selling a controlled substance on school grounds.

Relevant History: Ann has a history of sexual abuse from her biological father between the ages of four and nine. Her parents divorced when Ann was 11 years old. Ann has focused on her abuse issues in the past in outpatient counseling and tends to view her current behavior as a result of the abuse she incurred. Her mother has a history of psychiatric hospitalization. Ann's mother currently denies regular drug use but continues to drink.

Mental Status Exam
Appearance, Attitude, and Activity: Ann is a White, 16-year-old female with no physical abnormalities. The client is slightly overweight. She is dressed appropriately and does not appear to exhibit any maladaptive features related to self-care. The client has scars on her left arm from a past history of cutting but does not identify any current tendencies for self-mutilation. Ann's last occurrence was over six months ago by self-report. The client has a cynical attitude toward counseling because "it has not worked" but appears amiable to the process and responsive. No abnormal activity is noted.

Mood and Affect: Ann described feeling depressed often. She does not exhibit any sleep disturbance but indicates she generally feels unhappy. The client does not appear tearful, but she does get irritated easily with her mother and identifies frequent inattention in school. The client identifies feeling sad at school due to a lack of friends. Depressed mood does not appear abnormal given the circumstances.

Speech and Language: Speech and language appear normal. No evidence of pressured speech or poverty of speech. Ann is appropriately spontaneous in her conversations.

Thought Process, Content, and Perception: All appear within normal limits. Thoughts appear appropriately connected. No tangential associations were noted.

Cognitions: Client is oriented x 4 (person, place, time, and situation).

Insight and Judgment: Ann tends to act somewhat impulsively when angry, particularly at school or with her mother. The client demonstrates poor reality testing with respect to acknowledging logical and natural consequences. The client identifies an "I don't care" attitude when confronted, especially at home or school.

Medical History: No medical problems were identified. Ann is not on any medications currently. Ann has a history of outpatient counseling since age nine. Ann's mother indicated counseling has not been successful.

Family Issues: Ann has had no contact with her father since he was prosecuted for sexual abuse. Ann's father served time in prison. His whereabouts are unknown. Ann has ongoing conflict with her mother. Ann's mother appears to want Ann to suffer severe consequences for her behavior and is looking for relief from parenting responsibilities. Ann's mother verbalized, "I want her in detention," despite the fact that Ann's offenses do not warrant such consequences. Both Ann and her mother are open to placement for Ann outside of the home. Ann's mother does not want to participate in the counseling process and does not acknowledge how she has been harmful in her relationship with her daughter.

Social Support: Ann admits to associating with a negative peer group. Ann has recently started attending church but finds it difficult to be accepted from peers in the youth group. Ann tends to be a follower and engages in self-destructive behavior, such as getting high, due to peer pressure. Ann is not involved in any other extracurricular activities.

Educational/Occupational Issues: Ann is a "C" student, but achievement test scores indicate Ann is capable of above average work. Ann identifies a desire to go to college. Ann

TABLE AB.1 Score Report for Ann on the BDI-II

Raw Score	Standard Score Clinical	Percentile Clinical	SEM 95% Clinical	Category
28	.43	67th	3.61 [20.78, 35.22]	Moderate to Severe

Note: SEM = standard error measurement.

appears to be average to above average intellectual functioning and passes school easily when she applies herself. Ann admits to difficulty in school due to pressure from her peers.

Cultural/Spiritual Concerns: Ann's mother has not been supportive of her participation in church and has frequently grounded her from attending. Ann genuinely appears interested in church involvement and the association with a more positive peer group but struggles with her lack of acceptance from peers in the youth group.

Assessment Results and Recommendations

Ann was administered the Beck Depression Inventory-II (BDI-II) to help assess the severity of the depressive symptoms that she exhibits. The BDI-II is a 21-item self-report inventory. Clients identify the extent to which they exhibit a variety of diagnostic indicators for depression on Likert-type scale ranging from 0 (*no endorsement*) to 3 (*increased severity*) over the past two weeks. The administration of the BDI-II was under typical conditions. Results from the scores may be deemed as a valid assessment. The following table represents Ann's scores on the BDI-II (Table AB.1).

Ann scored a 28 on the BDI-II, placing her in the 67th percentile among the clinical norm group. While a score of 28 places Ann in the moderate range of depression, as identified in the manual, when standard error measurement is taken under consideration, Ann could be categorized in the severe range with respect to depressive symptoms.

Summary: Ann is a 16-year-old Caucasian female of average to above average intellectual functioning with a history of sexual abuse victim, substance use, and oppositional behavior. Symptoms of depression are evident including low self-esteem, irritability, saddened mood, and defeated outlook. Ann faces significant conflict with her mother, and Ann's mother could be characterized as nonsupportive. Without placement, Ann is at risk for regressing further to higher risk behavior problems. Placement may be pursued. Prognosis is guarded at this time.

References

Aboraya, A. (2007). The reliability of psychiatric diagnoses: Point—our psychiatric diagnoses are still unreliable. *Psychiatry, 4*(1), 22–25.

American Counseling Association. (2004). The American Counseling Association (ACA) position statement on high stakes testing. Retrieved from http://aarc-counseling.org/assets/cms/uploads/files/High_Stakes.pdf

American Counseling Association. (2014). *ACA code of ethics*. Alexandria, VA: Author.

American Educational Research Association, American Psychological Association, & National Council of Measurement in Education. (1985). *Standards for educational and psychological testing*. Washington, DC: American Psychological Association.

American Educational Research Association, American Psychological Association, & National Council of Measurement in Education. (1999). *Standards for educational and psychological testing*. Washington, DC: American Educational Research Association.

American Educational Research Association, American Psychological Association, & National Council of Measurement in Education. (2014). *Standards for educational and psychological testing*. Washington, DC: American Educational Research Association.

American Psychiatric Association. (2017). Frequently asked questions about DSM-5: Implementation-for clinicians. Retrieved from http://www.dsm5.org/Documents/FAQ%20for%20Clinicians%208-1-13.pdf

American Psychiatric Association. (2013). *Diagnostic and statistical manual of mental disorders* (5th ed.). Washington, DC: Author.

American Psychological Association, American Educational Research Association, & National Council of Measurement in Education. (1966). *Standards for educational and psychological tests and manuals*. Washington, DC: American Psychological Association.

Anastasi, A., & Urbina, S. (1997). *Psychological testing* (7th ed.). Upper Saddle River, NJ: Prentice Hall.

Anderson, L. W., & Krathwohl, D. R. (Eds.). (2001). *A taxonomy for learning, teaching and assessing: A revision of Bloom's taxonomy of educational objectives: Complete edition*. New York, NY: Longman.

Armstrong, P. I., & Rounds, J. (2010). Integrating individual differences in career assessment: The Atlas Model of Individual Differences and the Strong Ring. *The Career Development Quarterly, 59*, 143–153.

Association for Assessment and Research in Counseling. (2016). AARC mission. Retrieved from http://aarc-counseling.org/about-us

Association for Assessment in Counseling and Education, & American Mental Health Counselors Association. (2009). *Standards for assessment in mental health counseling*. Alexandria, VA: Author.

Association for Assessment in Counseling and Education, & International Association for Marriage and Family Counselors. (2010). *Marriage, couple and family counseling assessment competencies*. Alexandria, VA: Author.

Baird, B. N. (2008). *The internship, practicum, and field placement handbook: A guide for the helping professions* (5th ed.). Upper Saddle River, NJ: Pearson.

Balkin, R. S. (2004). Application of a model for adolescent acute care psychiatric programs. *Dissertation Abstracts International, 64,* 2391.

Balkin, R. S. (2006). A reexamination of trends in acute care psychiatric hospitalization for adolescents: Ethnicity, payment, and length of stay. *Journal of Professional Counseling: Practice, Theory, and Research, 34,* 49–59.

Balkin, R. S. (2014). *The Crisis Stabilization Scale manual and sampler set.* Menlo Park: CA: Mind Garden.

Balkin, R. S. (2013). Validation of the Goal Attainment Scale of Stabilization. *Measurement and Evaluation in Counseling and Development, 46,* 261–269. doi:10.1177/0748175613497040

Balkin, R. S., Cavazos J. Jr., Hernandez, A. E., Garcia, R., Dominguez, D., & Valarezo, A. (2013). Assessing at-risk youth using the Reynolds Adolescent Adjustment Screening Inventory with a Latino/a population. *Journal of Addiction and Offender Counseling,* 30–39. doi:10.1002/j.2161-1874.2013.00012.x

Balkin, R. S., Leicht, D. J., Sartor, T., & Powell, J. (2011). Assessing the relationship between therapeutic goal attainment and psychosocial characteristics for adolescents in crisis residence. *Journal of Mental Health, 20,* 32–42. http://dx.doi.org/10.3109/09638237.2010.537402

Balkin, R. S., Miller, J., Ricard, R. J., Garcia, R., & Lancaster, C. (2011). Assessing factors in adolescent adjustment as precursors to recidivism in court-referred youth. *Measurement and Evaluation in Counseling and Development, 44,* 52–59. doi:10.1177/0748175610391611

Balkin, R. S., & Roland, C. B. (2007). Reconceptualizing stabilization for counseling adolescents in brief psychiatric hospitalization: A new model. *Journal of Counseling & Development, 85,* 64–72.

Balkin, R. S., Tietjen-Smith, T., Caldwell, C., & Shen, Y. (2007). The relationship of exercise and depression among young adult women. *Adultspan Journal, 6,* 30–35.

Beck, A. T., Steer, R. A., & Brown, G. K. (1996). *BDI-II manual.* San Antonio, TX: Psychological Corporation.

Beck, A. T., Steer, R. A., Kovacs, M., & Garrison, B. (1985). Hopelessness and eventual suicide: A 10-year prospective study of patients hospitalized with suicidal ideation. *American Journal of Psychiatry, 142*(4), 559–563.

Best, J. W., & Kahn, J. V. (2006). *Research in education* (10th ed.). Boston: Allyn & Bacon.

Bloom B. S. (1956). *Taxonomy of educational objectives: Handbook I: The cognitive domain.* New York, NY: David McKay.

Bordin, E. S. (1979). The generalizability of the psychoanalytic concept of the working alliance. *Psychotherapy, 16,* 252–260.

Boring, E. G. (1923, June 6). Intelligence as the tests test it. *New Republic,* 35–37.

Brabeck, M. M., Rogers, L. A., Sirin, S., Henderson, J., Benvenuto, M., Weaver, M., & Ting, K. (2000). Increasing ethical sensitivity to racial and gender intolerance in schools: Development of the Racial Ethical Sensitivity Test. *Ethics & Behavior, 10,* 119–137. doi:10.1207/S15327019EB1002_02

Brody, N. (2000). Theories and measurements of intelligence. In R. J. Sternberg (Ed.), *Handbook of intelligence.* New York, NY: Cambridge University Press.

Brown, M. B. (2001). Test review of the Self-Directed Search. In B. S. Plake & J. C. Impara (Eds.), *The fourteenth mental measurements yearbook.* Lincoln, NE: Buros Institute of Mental Measurements.

Burlingame, G. M., Wells, M. G., Cox, J. C., Lambert, M. J., Latkowski, M., & Justice, D. (2005). *Administration and scoring manual for the Y-OQ (Youth Outcome Measures).* Salt Lake, City, UT: OQ Measures.

Buros Institute of Mental Measurements. (2016a). *Become a reviewer for the Mental Measurements Yearbook.* Retrieved from http://buros.org/become-reviewer-mental-measurements-yearbook

Buros Institute of Mental Measurements. (2016b). *Reviewers guide for the Mental Measurements Yearbook Series.* Retrieved from http://buros.org/reviewers-guide-mental-measurements-yearbook-series

Busseri, M. A., & Tyler, J. D. (2003). Interchangeability of the Working Alliance Inventory and Working Alliance Inventory, Short Form. *Psychological Assessment, 15*(2), 193–197. doi:10.1037/1040-3590.15.2.193

Butcher, J. N. (2010). Personality assessment from the nineteenth to the early twenty-first century: Past achievements and contemporary challenges. *Annual Review of Clinical Psychology, 6,* 1–20. doi:10.1146/annurev.clinpsy.121208.131420

Campbell, D. T., & Fiske, D. W. (1959). Convergent and discriminant validation by the multitrait-multimethod matrix. *Psychological Bulletin, 56*(2), 81–105. doi:10.1037/h0046016

Canel-Çınarbaş, D., Cui, Y., & Lauridsen, E. (2011). Cross-cultural validation of the Beck Depression Inventory-II across U.S. and Turkish samples. *Measurement and Evaluation in Counseling and Development, 44,* 77–91. doi:10.1177/0748175611400289

Canivez, G. L. (2010). [Test review of Wechsler Adult Intelligence Scale–Fourth Edition]. In R. A. Spies, J. F. Carlson, & K. F. Geisinger (Eds.), *The eighteenth mental measurements yearbook* (pp. 684–688). Lincoln, NE: Buros Center for Testing.

Carmody, D. (2005). Psychometric characteristics of the Beck Depression Inventory-II with college students of diverse ethnicity. *International Journal of Psychiatry in Clinical Practice, 9,* 22–28. doi:10.1080/13651500510014800

Cartwright, B. Y., Daniels, J., & Zhang, S. (2008). Assessing multicultural competence: Perceived versus demonstrated performance. *Journal of Counseling & Development, 86,* 318–322.

Cattell, R. B. (1963). Theory of fluid and crystallized intelligence: A critical experimental. *Journal of Educational Psychology, 54,* 1–22.

Center for Behavioral Health Statistics and Quality. (2015). *Behavioral health trends in the United States: Results from the 2014 National Survey on Drug Use and Health* (HHS Publication No. SMA 15-4927,NSDUH Series H-50). Retrieved from http://www.samhsa.gov/data/

Chen, J. Q. (2004). Theory of multiple intelligences: Is it a scientific theory? *Teachers College Record, 106,* 17–23.

Chernin, J., Holden, J. M., & Chandler, C. (1997). Bias in psychological assessment: Heterosexism. *Measurement and Evaluation in Counseling and Development, 30,* 68–76.

Cimetta, A. D., D'Agostino, J. V., & Levin, J. R. (2010). Can high school achievement tests serve to select college students? *Educational Measurement: Issues and Practice, 29,* 3–12.

Cohen, R. J., Swerdlik, M. E., & Sturman, E. D. (2013). *Psychological testing and assessment* (8th ed.). Boston, MA: McGraw-Hill.

Council for Accreditation of Counseling and Related Educational Programs. (2015). *2016 CACREP standards.* Alexandria, VA: Author.

Cox, A. A. (2001). Review of the Emotional Quotient Inventory. In B. S. Plake & J. C. Impara (Eds.), *The fourteenth mental measurements yearbook.* Lincoln, NE: Buros Institute of Mental Measurements.

Crocker, L., & Algina, J. (1986). *Introduction to classical modern test theory.* Orlando, FL: Harcourt Brace Jovanovich.

Cronbach, L. J. (1951). Coefficient alpha and the internal structure of tests. *Psychometrika, 16,* 297—334.

Cronbach, L. J., & Meehl, P. E. (1955). Construct validity in psychological tests. *Psychological Bulletin, 52,* 281–302.

Cronin, J. M., & Goodman, R. H. (2008). Is New England ready for P-20? *New England Journal of Higher Education, 22,* 15–17.

Cull, J. G., & Gill, W. S. (1982). *Suicide Probability Scale (SPS) manual.* Los Angeles, CA: Western Psychological Services.

Cull, J. G., & Gill, W. S. (2002). *Suicide Probability Scale (SPS) manual.* Los Angeles, CA: Western Psychological Services.

D'Amato, R. C., Johnson, J. A., & Kush, J. C. (2005). Review of the Stanford-Binet Intelligence Scales, 5th edition. In R. A. Spies & B. S. Plake (Eds.), *The sixteenth mental measurements yearbook.* Lincoln, NE: Buros Institute of Mental Measurements.

Davidson, J. E., & Downing, C. L. (2000). Contemporary model of intelligence. In R. J. Sternberg (Ed.), *Handbook of intelligence.* New York, NY: Cambridge University Press.

Davis, R. J., Balkin, R. S., & Juhnke, G. A. (2014). Validation of the Juhnke-Balkin Life Balance Inventory. *Measurement and Evaluation in Counseling & Development, 47,* 181–198. doi:10.1177/0748175614531796.

Doll, B. (2004). Test review of the Child Behavior Checklist. In J. C. Impara & B. S. Plake (Eds.), *The thirteenth mental measurements yearbook* [Electronic version]. Retrieved from the Buros Institute's Test Reviews Online website: http://www.unl.edu/buros

Duffy, M., Giordano, V. A., Farrell, J. B., Paneque, O. M., & Crump, G. B. (2008). No Child Left Behind: Values and research issues in high-stakes assessments. *Counseling and Values, 53,* 53–66.

Dufresne, R., Laux, J., Tahani, D., & Juhnke, G. A. (in press). Substance use assessment instruments: 13 years later. *Journal of Addictions & Offender Counseling.*

Duncan, B. L. (2010). *On becoming a better therapist.* Washington, DC: American Psychological Association.

Duncan, B. L., Miller, S. D., Sparks, J. A., Claud, D. A., Reynolds, L. R., Brown, J., & Johnson, L. D. (2003). The Session Rating Scale: Preliminary psychometric properties of a "working" alliance measure. *Journal of Brief Therapy, 3,* 3–12.

Edwards, A. J. (1994). Wechsler, David (1896–1981). In R. J. Sternberg (Ed.), *Encyclopedia of intelligence* (Vol. 1, pp. 1134–1136). New York, NY: Macmillan.

Eltz, M., Evans, A., Celio, M., Dyl, J., Hunt, J., Armstrong, L., & Spirito, A. (2007). Suicide Probability Scale and its utility with adolescent psychiatric patients. *Child Psychiatry & Human Development, 38,* 17–29. doi:10.1007/s10578-006-0040-7

Erard, R. E. (2004). Release of test data under the 2002 ethics code and the HIPAA privacy rule: A raw deal or just a half-baked idea? *Journal of Personality Assessment, 82,* 23–30. doi:10.1207/s15327752jpa8201_4

Erford, B. E., Basham, A., Cashwell, C. S., Juhnke, G., & Wall, J. (2003, March 22–24). *Standards for qualifications of test users* [Approved by the American Counseling Association Governing Council]. Alexandria, VA: American Counseling Association. Retrieved from http://aarc-counseling.org/assets/cms/uploads/files/standards.pdf

Erickson, G. (2010). Managed care and the mental health professions: History and effects on outpatient care. *Graduate Student Journal of Psychology, 12,* 3–7.

Esters, I. G., & Ittenbach, R. F. (1999). Contemporary theories and assessments of intelligence: A primer. *Professional School Counseling, 2,* 373–376.

Every Student Succeeds Act (ESSA). (2015). Retrieved June 25, 2017, from https://www.ed.gov/ESSA

Fangzhou, Y., & Patterson, D. (2010). Examining adolescent academic achievement: A cross-cultural review. *Family Journal, 18,* 324–327. doi:10.1177/1066480710372071.

Ferguson, C. J. (2009). An effect size primer: A guide for clinicians and researchers. *Professional Psychology: Research and Practice, 40,* 532–548. doi:10.1037/a0015808

Fleenor, J. W. (2001). [Review of the Myers-Briggs Type Indicator, Form M]. In B. S. Plake & J. C. Impara (Eds.), *The fourteenth mental measurements yearbook* (pp. 1033–1038). Lincoln, NE: Buros Institute of Mental Measurements.

Frey, M. C., & Detterman, D. K. (2004). Scholastic assessment or g?. *Psychological Science, 15*(6), 373–378. doi:10.1111/j.0956-7976.2004.00687.x

Gage, N. L., & Damrin, D. E. (1950). Reliability, homogeneity and number of choices. *Journal of Educational Psychology,* 385–404.

Geisinger, K. F., Spies, R. A., Carlson, J. F. & Plake, B. S. (2007). *The seventeenth mental measurements yearbook.* Lincoln, NE: Buros Institute of Mental Measurements.

George, L. K. (1997). Choosing among established assessment tools: Scientific demands and practical constraints. *Generations, 21,* 32–36.

Gladding, S. T. (2013). *Counseling: A comprehensive profession* (7th ed.). Upper Saddle River, NJ: Pearson.

Glass, G. V., & Hopkins, K. D. (1996). *Statistical methods in education and psychology* (3rd ed.). Boston, MA: Allyn & Bacon.

Glasser, W. (1965). Reality therapy: A new approach to psychiatry. New York, NY: Harper & Row.

Glasser, W. (1999). *Choice theory: A new psychology of personal freedom.* 1st Harper Perennial ed. New York: Harper Perennial.

Golding, S. L. (1985). Review of the Suicide Probability Scale. In J. V. Mitchell (Ed.), *The ninth mental measurements yearbook* (pp. 207–210). Lincoln, NE: Buros Institute of Mental Measurements.

Granello, P. F., & Juhnke, G. A. (2009). *Case studies in suicide: Experiences of mental health professionals.* Upper Saddle River, NJ: Merrill-Pearson.

Gregory, R. J. (2014). *Psychological testing: History, principles, and applications* (7th ed.). Upper Saddle River, NJ: Pearson.

Golding, S. L. (1985). [Review of the Supervisory Practices Inventory]. In J. V. Mitchell, Jr. (Ed.), *The ninth mental measurements yearbook.* Lincoln, NE: Buros Institute of Mental Measurements.

Goodwin, L. D., & Leech, N. L. (2003). The meaning of validity in the new Standards for Educational and Psychological Testing: Implications for measurement courses. *Measurement and Evaluation in Counseling and Development, 36,* 181–191.

Guilford, J. P. (1946). New standards for test evaluation. *Educational and Psychological Measurement, 6,* 427–438.

Gulliksen, H. (1950). *Theory of mental tests.* New York, NY: Wiley.

Hacker, H. (2007). Against the odds. *IRE Journal, 30,* 19–20.

Hanson, W. E. (2005). Review of the OQ-45.2. In R. A. Spies & B. S. Plake (Eds.), *The sixteenth mental measurements yearbook.* Lincoln, NE: Buros Institute of Mental Measurements. Retrieved from *Mental Measurements Yearbook with Tests in Print* database.

Harris, T. L., & Hodges, R. E. (1995). *The literacy dictionary: The vocabulary of reading and writing.* Newark, DE: International Reading Association.

Hattrup, K. (1995). [Review of the Differential Aptitude Tests—Fifth Edition]. In J. C. Conoley & J. C. Impara (Eds.), *The twelfth mental measurements yearbook* (pp. 1103–1104). Lincoln, NE: Buros Institute of Mental Measurements.

Health Insurance Portability and Accountability Act of 1996, 42 U.S.C. § 1320d-9 2010.

Helms, J. E. (1992). Why is there no study of cultural equivalence in standardized cognitive ability testing? *American Psychologist, 47,* 1083–1101.

Helms, J. E. (2006). Fairness is not validity or cultural bias in racial-group assessment: A quantitative perspective. *American Psychologist, 61,* 845–859. doi: 10.1037/0003-066x.61.8.845

Holland, J. L. (1973). *Making vocational choices: A theory of careers.* Englewood Cliffs, NJ: Prentice Hall.

Holland, J. L. (1985). *Making vocational choices* (2nd ed.). Englewood Cliffs, NJ: Prentice Hall.

Holland, J. L. (1997). *Making vocational choices: A theory of vocational personalities and work environments* (3rd ed.). Odessa, FL: Psychological Assessment Resources.

Hopkins, K. D. (1998). *Educational and psychological measurement and evaluation* (8th ed.). Boston, MA: Allyn & Bacon.

Houghton Mifflin Harcourt. (2016a). *Iowa Tests of Basic Skills' (ITBS') Forms A, B, and C.* Retrieved from http://www.hmhco.com/hmh-assessments/achievement/itbs

Houghton Mifflin Harcourt. (2016b). *Iowa Tests of Educational Development' (ITED') Forms A, B, and C.* Retrieved from http://www.hmhco.com/hmh-assessments/achievement/ited

Hubley, A. M., & Zumbo, B. D. (2001). A dialectic on validity: Where we have been and where we are going. *The Journal of General Psychology, 123,* 207–215.

Hunt, E. (2000). Let's hear it for crystallized intelligence. *Learning and Individual Differences, 12,* 123–129.

Jones, W. P., & Markos, P. A. (1997). Client rating of counselor effectiveness: A call for caution. *Journal of Applied Rehabilitation Counseling, 28,* 23–28.

Juhnke, G. A. (2002). *Substance abuse assessment: A handbook for mental health Professionals.* New York, NY: Brunner-Routledge.

Juhnke, G. A. (2008, March). *Utilizing stochastic processing and continuous assessment methods to produce evidenced based informed outcomes.* Paper presented at Speaker Association for Assessment in Counseling and Education, Honolulu, HI.

Juhnke, G. A., Granello, D. H., & Granello, P. F. (2010). *Suicide, self-injury, and violence in the schools: Assessment, prevention, and intervention strategies.* Hoboken, NJ: John Wiley.

Juhnke, G. A., & Hagedorn, W. B. (2006). *Counseling addicted families: An integrated assessment and treatment model.* New York, NY: Brunner-Routledge.

Juhnke, G. A., Juhnke, G. B., & Hsieh, P. (2012). *SCATTT: A suicide intervention plan mnemonic for use when clients present suicide intent.* Retrieved from http://www.counseling.org/Resources/Library/VISTAS/vistas12/Article_34.pdf

Juhnke, G. A., Vacc, N. A., Curtis, R. C., Coll, K. M., & Paredes, D. M. (2003). Assessment instruments used by addictions counselors. *Journal of Addictions & Offender Counseling, 23,* 66–72.

Katz, L., Joyner, J. W., & Seaman, N. (1999). Effects of joint interpretation of the Strong Interest Inventory and the Myers-Briggs Type Indicator in career choice. *Journal of Career Assessment, 7,* 281–297. doi:10.1177/106907279900700306

Kaufman, A. S., & Kaufman, N. L. (2004). *KBIT-2 manual: Kaufman Brief Intelligence Test, 2nd edition.* Minneapolis, MN: NCS Pearson.

Kaufman, A. S., McLean, J. F., & Kaufman, J. C. (1995). The fluid and crystallized abilities of White, Black, and Hispanic adolescents and adults, both with and without an education covariate. *Journal of Clinical Psychology, 51,* 636–647.

Keith, T. (2017). Review of the Wechsler Intelligence Scale for Children–5th edition. In J. F. Carlson, K. F. Geisinger, & J. L. Jonson (Eds.), *The twentieth mental measurements yearbook.* Lincoln, NE: Buros Institute of Mental Measurements. Retrieved from *Mental Measurements Yearbook with Tests in Print* database.

Kelly, K. R. (2010). Test review of the Strong Interest Inventory. In R. A. Spies, J. F. Carlson, & K. F. Geisinger (Eds.), *The eighteenth mental measurements yearbook.* Lincoln, NE: Buros Institute of Mental Measurements.

Kelly, V., & Juhnke, G. A. (2005). *Critical incidents in addictions counseling.* Alexandria, VA: ACA Press.

Kessler, R. C., Chiu, W. T., Demler, O., & Walters, E. E. (2005). Prevalence, severity, and comorbidity of twelve-month DSM-IV disorders in the National Comorbidity Survey Replication (NCS-R). *Archives of General Psychiatry, 62*(6), 617–627.

Kiresuk, T., & Sherman, R. (1968). Goal attainment scaling: A general method of evaluating comprehensive mental health programmes. *Community Mental Health Journal, 4,* 443–453.

Klein, A. (2016). The Every Student Succeeds Act: An ESSA overview. *Education Week*. Retrieved from https://www.edweek.org/ew/issues/every-student-succeeds-act/

Koch, L. C. (2000). Assessment and planning in the Americans with Disabilities Act era: Strategies for consumer self-advocacy and employer collaboration. *Journal of Vocational Rehabilitation, 14,* 103–108.

Koenig, K. A., Frey, M. C., & Detterman, D. K. (2008). ACT and general cognitive ability. *Intelligence, 36*(2), 153–160. doi:10.1016/j.intell.2007.03.005

Kottler, J. A., & Balkin, R. S. (2017). *Relationships in counseling and the counselor's life*. Alexandria, VA: American Counseling Association.

Lambert, M. J. (1986). Implications of psychotherapy outcome research for eclectic psychotherapy. In J. C. Norcross (Ed.), *Handbook of eclectic psychotherapy* (pp. 436–462). New York, NY: Brunner/Mazel.

Lambert, M. J., & Hawkins, E. J. (2004). Measuring outcome in professional practice: Considerations in selecting and using brief outcome instruments. *Professional Psychology: Research and Practice, 35,* 492–499.

Lambert, M. J., Morton, J. J., Hatfield, D., Harmon, C., Hamilton, S., Reid, R. C., . . . Burlingame, G. M. (2004). *Administration and scoring manual for the OQ 45.2 (Outcome Questionnaire)*. Salt Lake City, UT: OQ Measures.

Lawson, G. (2007). Counselor wellness and impairment: A national survey. *Journal of Humanistic Counseling, Education & Development, 46,* 20–34.

Layton, W. L. (1992). Test review of the Minnesota Importance Questionnaire. In J. J. Kramer & J. C. Conoley (Eds.), *The eleventh mental measurements yearbook*. Lincoln, NE: Buros Institute of Mental Measurements.

Lazowski, L. E., & Geary, B. B. (2016) Validation of the Adult Substance Abuse Subtle Screening Inventory-4 (SASSI-4). *European Journal of Psychological Assessment*. doi:10.1027/1015-5759/a000359

Lazowski, L. E., Kimmell, K. S., & Baker, S. L. (2016). *The Adult Substance Abuse Subtle Screening Inventory-4 (SASSI-4) user guide & manual*. Springville, IN: SASSI Institute.

Lazowski, L. E., Miller, F. G., Boye, M. W., & Miller, G. A. (1998). Efficacy of the Substance Abuse Subtle Screening Inventory–3 (SASSI-3) in identifying substance dependence disorders in clinical settings. *Journal of Personality Assessment, 71,* 114–128.

Leung, S. A. (2005). Review of the Mayer-Salovey-Caruso Emotional Intelligence Test. In R. A. Spies & B. S. Plake (Eds.), *The sixteenth mental measurements yearbook*. Lincoln, NE: Buros Institute of Mental Measurements.

Levitt, D. H., & Balkin, R. S. (2003). Religious diversity from a Jewish perspective. *Counseling and Values, 48,* 57–67.

Li, L. C., & Kim, B. S. K. (2004). Effects of counseling style and client adherence to Asian cultural values on counseling process with Asian American college students. *Journal of Counseling Psychology, 51,* 158–167. doi:10.1037/0022-0167.51.2.158

Luborsky, L., Barber, J. P., Siqueland, L., Johnson, S., Najavits, L. M., Frank, A., & Daley, D. (1996). The revised Helping Alliance questionnaire (HAq-II): Psychometric properties. *Journal of Psychotherapy Practice & Research, 5*(3), 260–271.

Luk, E. S. L., Staiger, P., Mathai, J., Wong, L., Birleson, P., & Adler, R. (2001). Children with persistent conduct problems who drop out of treatment. *European Child and Adolescent Psychiatry, 10,* 28–36.

Matz, P. A., Altepeter, T. S., & Perlman, B. (1992). MMPI-2: Reliability with college students. *Journal of Clinical Psychology, 48,* 330–334.

Mayer, J. D., & Salovey, P. (1997). What is emotional intelligence? In P. Salovey & D. Sluyter (Eds.), *Emotional development and emotional intelligence: Implications for educators* (pp. 3–31). New York, NY: Basic Books.

Mayer, J. D., Salovey, P., & Caruso, D. (2000). Models of emotional intelligence. In R. J. Sternberg (Ed.), *Handbook of intelligence*. New York, NY: Cambridge University Press.

McCrae, R. R., & Costa, P. T. (1992). Discriminant validity of NEO-PI-R facet scales. *Educational and Psychological Measurement, 52,* 229–237.

Miller, G. A. (1985). *The Substance Abuse Subtle Screening Inventory (SASSI) manual*. Spencer, IN: Spencer Evening World.

Miller, S. D., Duncan, B. L., Brown, J., Sparks, J. A., & Claud, D. A. (2003). The Outcome Rating Scale: A preliminary study of the reliability, validity, and feasibility of a brief visual analog measure. *Journal of Brief Therapy, 2,* 91–100.

Millon, T. (1981). *Disorders of personality: DSM-III Axis II*. New York, NY: Wiley-Interscience.

National Fair Access Coalition on Testing. (n.d.). FACT news page. Retrieved from http://www.fairaccess.org/aboutfact/factfaq

Naugle, K. A. (2009). Counseling and testing: What counselors need to know about state laws on assessment and testing. *Measurement and Evaluation in Counseling and Development, 42,* 31–45. doi:10.1177/0748175609333561

Nauta, M. M. (2004). Self-efficacy as a mediator of the relationships between personality factors and career interests. *Journal of Career Assessment, 12,* 381–394. doi:10.1177/1069072704266653

No Child Left Behind (NCLB) Act of 2001, Pub. L. No. 107-110, § 115, Stat. 1425 (2002).

O'Connor, B. P. (2008). Other personality disorders. In M. Hersen & J. Rosqvist (Eds.), *Handbook of psychological assessments, case conceptualization and treatment* (Vol. 1, pp. 438–462). Hoboken, NJ: John Wiley.

Ohio Department of Mental Health. (2009). *The Ohio mental health consumer outcomes system procedural manual* (11th ed.). Columbus, OH: Author.

Owen, J. (2008). The nature of confirmatory strategies in the initial assessment process. *Journal of Mental Health Counseling, 30,* 362–374.

Polanski, P. J., & Hinkle, J. S. (2000). The mental status examination: Its use by professional counselors. *Journal of Counseling & Development, 78,* 357–364.

Pulver, C. A., & Kelly, K. R. (2008). Incremental validity of the Myers-Briggs Type Indicator in predicting academic major selection of undecided university students. *Journal of Career Assessment, 16,* 441–455. doi:10.1177/1069072708318902

Ratts, M. J., Singh, A. A., Nassar-McMillan, S., Butler, S. K., & McCullough, J. R. (2015). *Multicultural and social justice counseling competencies.* Retrieved from http://www.multiculturalcounseling.org/index.php?option=com_content&view=article&id=205:amcd-endorses-multicultural-and-social-justice-counseling-competencies&catid=1:latest&Itemid=123

Reed, M. B., Bruch, M. A., & Haase, R. F. (2004). Five factor model of personality and career exploration. *Journal of Career Assessment, 12,* 223–238. doi:10.1177/1069072703261524

Reichenberg, L. W. (2014). *DSM-5 essentials: The savvy clinician's guide to the changes in criteria.* Hoboken, NJ: John Wiley.

Reynolds, C. R., & Kamphaus, R. W. (2003). *Handbook of psychological and educational assessment of children: Intelligence, aptitude, and achievement* (2nd ed.). New York, NY: Guilford Press.

Reynolds, W. M. (2001). *Reynolds Adolescent Adjustment Screening Inventory.* Odessa, FL: Psychological Assessment Resources.

Ricci v. DeStefano. (2012). In *Encyclopædia britannica.* Retrieved from http://www.britannica.com/EBchecked/topic/1540641/Ricci-v-DeStefano

Roberts, R. D., Goff, G. N., Anjoul, F., Kyllonen, P. C., Pallier, G., & Stankov, L. (2000). The Armed Services Vocational Aptitude Battery (ASVAB): Little more than acculturated learning (Gc)!? *Learning and Individual Differences, 12,* 81–103.

Rogers, C. (1957). The necessary and sufficient conditions of therapeutic personality change. *Journal of Consulting Psychology, 21,* 95–103.

Rohde, T. E., & Thompson, L. A. (2007). Predicting academic achievement with cognitive ability. *Intelligence, 35*(1), 83–92. doi:10.1016/j.intell.2006.05.004

Roid, G. H. (2003). *Stanford-Binet Intelligence Scale–5th edition.* Itasca, IL: Riverside. [Test battery, examiners manual, technical manual, Scoring Pro software, and interpretive manual]

Rovinelli, R. J., & Hambleton, R. K. (1977). On the use of content specialists in the assessment of criterion-references test item validity. *Dutch Journal of Educational Research, 2,* 49–60.

Rye, M. S., Loiacono, D. M., Folck, C. D., Olszewski, T. A. H., & Madia, B. P. (2001). Evaluation of the psychometric properties of two forgiveness scales. *Current Psychology: Developmental, Learning, Personality, Social, 20,* 260–277.

Sandoval, J. (2007). [Review of the Draw-A-Person Intellectual Ability Test for Children, Adolescents, and Adults]. In K. F. Geisinger, R. A. Spies, J. F. Carlson, & B. S. Plake (Eds.), *The seventeenth mental measurements yearbook* (pp. 498–502). Lincoln, NE: Buros Institute of Mental Measurements.

SASSI Institute. (2016). Adult Substance Abuse Subtle Screening Inventory-4 (SASSI-4). Retrieved from https://www.sassi.com/sassi-4-announcement/

Schraw, G. (2010). Review of the Wechsler Adult Intelligence Scale–4th edition. In R. A. Spies, K. F. Geisinger, & J. F. Carlson (Eds.), *The eighteenth mental measurements yearbook.* Lincoln, NE: Buros Institute of Mental Measurements. Retrieved from *Mental Measurements Yearbook with Tests in Print* database.

Schult, J., & Sparfeldt, J. R. (2016). Do non-*g* factors of cognitive ability tests align with specific academic achievements? A combined bifactor modeling approach. *Intelligence, 59,* 96–102. doi:10.1016/j.intell.2016.08.004

Schultheiss, D. E. P., & Stead, G. B. (2004). Childhood Career Development Scale: Scale construction and psychometric properties. *Journal of Career Assessment, 12,* 113–134. doi:10.1177/1069072703257751

Sederer, L. I., Dickey, B., & Eisen, S. V. (1997). Assessing outcomes in clinical practice. *Psychiatric Quarterly, 68,* 311–325. doi:0033-2720»7/1200-0311$12.50/0

Sedlacek, W. E. (1994). Issues in advancing diversity through assessment. *Journal of Counseling & Development, 72,* 549–553.

Sedlacek, W. E. (2004). *Beyond the big test: Noncognitive assessment in higher education.* San Francisco, CA: Jossey-Bass.

Sedlacek, W. E., & Kim, S. H. (1995). *Multicultural assessment.* ERIC Digest (ERIC Digest No.: EDO-CG-95-24).

Sharf, R. S. (2010). *Applying career development theory to counseling.* Belmont, CA: Brooks/Cole, Cengage Learning.

Shaw, M. (1997). *Charting made incredibly easy.* Springhouse, PA: Springhouse.

Skiba, R. J., Knesting, K., & Bush, L. D. (2002). Culturally competent assessment: More than non-biased tests. *Journal of Family Studies, 11,* 61–78.

Smith, T. J., & Campbell, C. (2008). The relationship between occupational interests and values. *Journal of Career Assessment, 17,* 39–-55. doi:10.1177/1069072708325740

Smits, D., Luyckx, K., Smits, D., Stinckens, N., & Claes, L. (2015). Structural characteristics and external correlates of the Working Alliance Inventory–Short Form. *Psychological Assessment, 27*(2), 545–551. doi:10.1037/pas0000066

Snyder, D. K. (1997). *Marital Satisfaction Inventory, Revised (MSI-R): Manual* (2nd ed.). Los Angeles, CA: Western Psychological Services.

Spearman, C. (1904). "General Intelligence," objectively determined and measured. *American Journal of Psychology, 15,* 201–293.

Spearman, C. (1927). *The abilities of man.* New York, NY: Macmillan.

Stanley, J. C. (1971). Reliability. In R. L. Thorndike (Ed.), *Educational measurement* (2nd ed.). Washington, DC: American Council on Education.

Steen, L. A. (1999). Twenty questions about mathematical reasoning. In L. Stiff (Ed.), *Developing mathematical reasoning in grades K-12* (pp. 270–285). Reston, VA: National Council of Teachers of Mathematics.

Sternberg, R. J. (1985). *Beyond IQ: A triarchic theory of human intelligence.* Cambridge, UK: Cambridge University Press.

Stringer, N. (2008). Aptitude tests versus school exams as selection tools for higher education and the case for assessing educational achievement in context. *Research Papers in Education, 23,* 53–68.

Super, D. E. (1990). A life-span, life-space approach to career development. In D. Brown, L. Brooks, & Associates (Eds.), *Career choice and development* (2nd ed., pp. 197–261). San Francisco, CA: Jossey-Bass.

Telzrow, C. F., & McNamara, K. (2001). New directions in assessment for students with disabilities. *Work: Journal of Prevention, Assessment & Rehabilitation, 17,* 105–116.

Thorn, A., & Mulvenon, S. (2002). High-stakes testing: An examination of elementary counselors' views and their academic preparation to meet this challenge. *Measurement & Evaluation in Counseling & Development, 35,* 195–206.

Thurstone, L. L. (1938). *Primary mental abilities.* Chicago, IL: University of Chicago Press.

Trochim, W. (2000). *The research methods knowledge base* (2nd ed.). Cincinnati, OH: Atomic Dog.

Turner, R. C., & Carlson, L. (2003). Indexes of item-objective congruence for multidimensional items. *International Journal of Testing, 3,* 163–171.

Turner-Stokes, L. (2009). Goal attainment scaling (GAS) in rehabilitation: A practical guide. *Clinical Rehabilitation, 23,* 362–370. doi:10.1177/0269215508101742

Trzepacz, P. T., & Baker, R. W. (1993). *The psychiatric mental status examination.* New York, NY: Oxford University Press.

U.S. Department of Labor/ Employment and Training Administration. (2017a). O*NET Resource Center. Retrieved from O*Net Resource Center: http://online.onetcenter.org/

U.S. Department of Labor/ Employment and Training Administration. (2017b). Work values. Retrieved from O*NET OnLine: http://www.onetonline.org/find/descriptor/browse/Work_Values/

Vacc, N. A. (1982). A conceptual framework for continuous assessment of clients. *Measurement & Evaluation in Guidance, 15*(1), 40–47.

Vacc, N. A., & Juhnke, G. A. (1997). The use of structured clinical interviews for assessment in counseling. *Journal of Counseling & Development, 75,* 470–480.

Valadez, A., Juhnke, G. A., Coll, K. M., Granello, P. F., Peters, S., & Zambrano, E. (2009). The Suicide Probability Scale: A means to assess substance abusing clients' suicide risk. *Journal of Professional Counseling: Practice, Theory, and Research, 37,* 52–65.

Vanheule, S., Desmet, M., Meganck, R., Inslegers, R., Willemsen, J., De Schryver, M., & Devisch, I. (2014). Reliability in psychiatric diagnosis with the DSM: Old wine in new barrels. *Psychotherapy and Psychosomatics, 83,* 313–314. doi:10.1159/000358809

Vereen, L. G., Hill, N. R., McNeal, D. T. (2008). Perceptions of multicultural counseling competency: Integration of the curricular and the practical. *Journal of Mental Health Counseling, 30,* 226–236.

Wall, J., Augustin, J., Eberly, C., Erford, B., Lundberg, D., & Vansickle, T. (2003). *Responsibilities of Users of Standardized Tests (RUST)* (3rd ed.). Alexandria, VA: Association for Assessment in Counseling and Education. Retrieved from http://aarc-counseling.org/assets/cms/uploads/files/rust.pdf

Walsh, W. B., & Betz, N. E. (2001). *Tests and assessment* (4th ed.). Upper Saddle River, NJ: Prentice-Hall.

Wampold, B. E. (2001). *The great psychotherapy debate: Models, methods, and findings.* Mahwah, NJ: Lawrence Erlbaum.

Waterhouse, L. (2006). Multiple intelligences, the Mozart effect, and emotional intelligence: A critical review. *Educational Psychologist, 41,* 207–225. doi:10.1207/s15326985ep4104_1

Watson, T. S. (2007). Review of the Emotional Competency Inventory. In K. F. Geisinger, R. A. Spies, J. F. Carlson, & B. S. Plake (Eds.), *The seventeenth mental measurements yearbook.* Lincoln, NE: Buros Institute of Mental Measurements.

Wells, M. G., Burlingame, G. M., & Rose, P. M. (2003). *Administration and scoring manual for the Y-OQ-SR 2.0 (Youth Outcome Questionnaire-Self Report).* Salt Lake, City, UT: OQ Measures.

Western Psychological Services (2017). (MSI-R) *Marital Satisfaction Inventory, Revised: Use the MSI-R With Any Couple – Traditional or Nontraditional.* Retrieved from https://www.wpspublish.com/store/p/2870/-(MSI%E2%84%A2-R)-Marital-Satisfaction-Inventory%E2%84%A2,-Revised

Whiston, S. C. (2017). *Principles and applications of assessment in counseling* (7th ed.). Belmont, CA: Cengage.

Williams J. B. W., et al. (1992). The structured clinical interview for DSM-III-R (SCID). II. Multisite test-retest reliability. *Archives of General Psychiatry, 49,* 630–636.

Wohlgemuth, E. A. (1997). Walking the fine line between parsimony and oversimplification: Attempting to decrease bias in assessment. *Measurement and Evaluation in Counseling and Development, 30*(2), 77–81.

World Health Organization. (2016a). Classifications: Purposes and uses. Retrieved from Paragraph 4: http://www.who.int/classifications/icd/en/

World Health Organization. (2016b) WHO Disability Assessment Schedule 2.0 (WHODAS 2.). Retrieved from http://www.who.int/classifications/icf/whodasii/en/

Zydeck, S. (1978). Test review of the Minnesota Job Description Questionnaire. In *The eighth mental measurements yearbook.* Lincoln, NE: Buros Institute of Mental Measurements.

Index

Tables and figures are indicated by an italic t and f following the page number.

AAC. *See* Association for Assessment in Counseling
AARC. *See* Association for Assessment and Research in Counseling
ability assessment, 151–77
   achievement instruments, 167–70
   group administered, 170–74
   intelligence measures, 160–66
   of O*NET, 186
   theories/models of intelligence, 155–60
ACA. *See* American Counseling Association
ACA Code of Ethics, 8–9, 12, 125, 136, 235
accommodations, 144–46, 147
accountability, 234–50
achievement, 95, 140, 185
achievement gap, 4, 140–42
achievement tests, 116, 152–54, 167–74, 254
ACT (college entrance exam), 65, 70, 73, 84, 153, 173–74
ADA. *See* Americans with Disabilities Act
addiction, 193–94
ADHD, 145
adolescents
   and Beck Depression Inventory, 115–16
   case study, 29–34, 34*t*, 134–37, 237, 238, 240–41, 253–55
   Crisis Stabilization Scale, 56, 58, 63, 71, 82
   resistance to counseling, 127
   as special population, 142
   substance use, 129, 131
affect, 91, 127, 254
affection, 194, 195, 197, 198
aggression, 194
agreeableness, 184
alcohol use, 25–29, 29*t*, 38, 43–46, 78, 81, 131–32, 132*t*, 134–37, 201–5, 231–32, 238

alignment, 171, 172
alternate forms, 100
American Counseling Association (ACA), 7, 8, 9, 10, 12, 171, 235
American Psychiatric Association, 35
Americans with Disabilities Act, 12, 144, 145
Anderson, Lorin, 50
animals, 3
anxiety, 16–24, 23*t*, 37–39, 46, 85, 135–36, 150, 175, 215, 248
appearance, 126, 134, 135, 253
applied math skills, 169
aptitude tests, 95, 116, 146, 152–54, 167, 173, 174
arithmetic, 163, 164
artistic personality type, 181
Asians, 141, 148
assessment
   of ability, 151–77, 168–69
   of accountability, 234–50
   bias in, 139–42
   definition of, 1–3
   development of counselors as professionals, 7–11
   environment, 133
   fairness in, 138–39
   fundamentals of, 48–76
   history of, 3–7
   instruments, 107–19, 148
   interpretation in, 219–33
   multicultural competence, 147–49
   nonstandardized, 3, 130, 239–41, 247
   psychosocial, 16–24
   recommendations, 226, 227–28, 229
   role in counseling, 1–14
   scores, 56–59, 68
   with special populations, 142–49

assessment (*cont.*)
  standardized, 3, 86, 120, 130, 239, 242–45
  supporting data, 226–27
  written report, 219–20
  See also career assessment; initial assessment interview
Association for Assessment and Research in Counseling, 7, 10, 111, 114–15, 119
Association for Assessment in Counseling (AAC), 7, 8
Association of Test Publishers, 11
ASVAB (Armed Services Vocational Aptitude Battery), 173, 174, 179, 180
attitude, 126–27, 253
automatic processing, 158
average. *See* mean
average distance from mean, 64

Bar-on, Reuven, 159–60
baseline data, 239, 241, 249, 249*t*
BDI-II. *See* Beck Depression Inventory-II
Beck Anxiety Inventory, 85
Beck Depression Inventory-II, 55, 98–100
  convergent evidence, 78, 85
  cut scores, 97*t*
  gender differences on, 139
  in initial interview, 122
  measuring depression, 83, 88, 89, 91, 96, 99, 104, 115–16
  measuring reliability, 88, 96, 100, 117
  norm groups, 222–23
  and Pearson *r*, 74
  pretest and posttest scores, 75*t*
  as psychological construct, 6
  raw scores, 75, 222
  Smith case study, 221–24, 221*t*, 229, 231, 239, 255, 255*t*
  with special populations, 144
  standard deviation, 96
  standard scores, 76
behavior, 127, 129
Behavior Assessment System for Children, 7, 118
beliefs, 128, 129
bell-shaped curve, 62, 62*f*, 64, 70*f*
bias, 110, 125, 139–42, 148
BIMM. *See* Buros Institute of Mental Measurements
Binet, Alfred, 5, 151–52
Binet scale, 156
Binet-Simon Intelligence Test, 5
block design, 162–63, 164
Bloom's taxonomy, 50
borderline personality disorder, 30
Boring, Edward G., 152
Buros Institute of Mental Measurements (BIMM), 111, 112

cannabis, 30, 31, 33, 132*t*, 136, 137
capitation clauses, 37
career assessment
  case study, 187–90, 248, 249, 249*t*
  computerized, 186–87
  definition of, 178–79
  elements of, 179–86
  fundamentals of, 178–90
  work values, 184–86
Carroll, John, 157, 160
case studies, 16–35
  of adolescent, 29–31, 33, 34*t*, 134–37, 237, 238, 240–41, 253–55
  of alcohol use, 25–29, 29*t*, 43–46, 203–5, 231–32, 238
  of anxiety, 17–24, 37, 38–39, 46, 150, 175, 215, 248
  of potential suicide, 214–18
  of sexual abuse, 32, 34*t*, 254
Catell-Horn-Carroll theory, 166
Cattell, James McKeen, 5
Cattell, Raymond, 156
central tendency, 59–63
change, 108
character traits, 123
cheating, 94
Child Behavior Checklist, 7, 105
children, 127, 131, 200
China, 3
CIP. *See* Computerized Interest Profiler
civil rights legislation, 12
classical test theory (CTT), 89, 90
cleanliness, 126, 134
clinical interview. *See* initial assessment interview
Clinical Interview, Standardized Specialty, Drug Detection, Personality Assessment, 122, 123, 137
Clinician Problem Scale-Revised, 84
CLISD-PA. *See* Clinical Interview, Standardized Specialty, Drug Detection, Personality Assessment
coefficient alpha, 101–2, 104, 116
cognition, 128–29, 254
cognitive disorders, 146–47
cognitive domains, 50
colleges and universities. *See* higher education
companionship, 194–95
competence, 10
componential intelligence, 158
comprehension, 162, 164
computer-based scoring, 110–11
Computerized Interest Profiler (CIP), 187–89
concurrent evidence, 84
concurrent validity, 78

confidence interval, 68–70, 98, 170, 224
confidentiality, 9, 133, 229
confirmatory factor analysis, 83–84, 87
confirmatory procedures, 84
conscientiousness, 184
consistency, 88, 102, 130
construct-irrelevant variance, 141
constructs, 2, 54, 77, 83, 86–87, 95, 152, 156
construct underrepresentation, 141
construct validity, 78, 82
content bias, 140
content evidence, 78
content validity, 78, 80
contextual intelligence, 158
continuous variables, 55
conventional personality type, 181, 189–90
convergent evidence, 78, 82, 83t, 85
Coping scale, 56, 57t, 58f, 59t, 63, 71
coping scores, 61f
correlation coefficient, 73–75, 74t, 77
Council for Accreditation of Counseling and Related Educational Programs, 3, 7
counseling
   assessment of accountability, 234–50
   client progress, 246–47
   client receptiveness, 227
   client relationship, 133, 245–46
   development for assessment professionalism, 7–11
   goals for, 240
   intake interview, 16–25, 30, 120–37
   interpretation session, 228–30
   licensing for, 10–11
   progress notes, 40–47, 234
   role of assessment in, 1–14
   satisfaction with services, 234–35
   skills in interview process, 132–33
   special populations, 138–50
   summarizing data in client language, 230
   as Western-valued practice, 148–49
covariance, 74
crisis behavior, 58
Crisis Stabilization Scale (CriSS), 56, 57t, 58–60, 58f, 59t, 60t, 61f, 63, 66t, 67–69, 70f, 82, 118
criterion evidence, 77, 78
criterion-referenced tests, 49, 51
criterion-related validity, 79
criterion validity, 78
Cronbach's alpha. *See* coefficient alpha
crystallized intelligence (*gc*), 156–57, 166, 174, 176
CTT. *See* classical test theory
cues, 2
culture, 110, 125, 141–42, 150, 255
cumulative frequency, 56, 57t, 59t
cumulative percent, 56, 57t, 58, 59t

curriculum alignment, 171, 172
cut-score, 49, 97t, 224
cutting, 30, 31, 34, 135, 253

DART notes, 42
Darwin, Charles, 3
DAT. *See* Differential Aptitude Test
data, 130–32, 226–27, 234, 241
decreased latency, 128
defensiveness, 202
delusions, 128
Department of Labor/Employment and Training Administration (U.S.), 180, 182, 185
depression
   Garza case study, 175, 247, 248
   and poverty of speech, 128
   Smith case study, 229–30, 239
   See also Beck Depression Inventory-II
derailment, 128
deviation score, 65
diagnoses
   accuracy and consistency of, 103–4, 105, 106
   in case studies, 136–37
   in cultural context, 9
   and intake data, 130
   as logical conclusions, 220
   and progress notes, 46–47
   See also Diagnostic and Statistical Manual of Mental Disorders
Diagnostic and Statistical Manual of Mental Disorders (DSM), 35–40, 43, 84, 103–4, 110, 136, 203, 230
diagnostic-related groups (DRGs), 36–37
Differential Aptitude Test (DAT), 169, 173, 175, 176, 177t, 180
differential item functioning, 139
differential test functioning, 139
direction, 73
disability, 144–45, 146, 167, 168
discrete variables, 55
discriminant evidence, 77, 78, 82–83, 83t, 85
discrimination, 12
disposition, 227
distribution, 57t, 58f, 61f, 62, 63, 64, 68, 71
Draw-a-Person Intellectual Ability Test for Children, Adolescents, and Adults, 112
DRGs. *See* diagnostic-related groups
drinking. *See* alcohol use
drug use, 29–31, 33, 34t, 78, 81, 122–23, 131–32, 132t, 201–2, 203, 240–41
DSM. *See Diagnostic and Statistical Manual of Mental Disorders*
dyslexia, 167

economic issues, 125
education, 13, 125, 140, 171, 175, 236, 254–55
ego-dystonic, 128
ego-syntonic, 128
Emotional Competency Inventory, 160
emotional disorders, 147
emotional intelligence, 159–60
emotional intimacy, 194
Emotional Quotient Inventory, 160
employment, 12, 125
empty chair technique, 155
Enright Forgiveness Inventory, 144
enterprising personality type, 181
error, 64, 65, 90–91, 95–98, 104, 162, 170
Esquirol, J.E.D., 5
ESSA. *See* Every Student Succeeds Act
ethics, 8–9, 109, 111, 125, 215
ethnicity, 4, 116, 140–42, 148–50
Every Student Succeeds Act (ESSA), 13–14, 154, 172, 235, 236
exams. *See* testing and tests
exercise, 99
exploratory factor analysis, 83–84, 87
exploratory procedures, 84
external variables, 84
extraversion, 184

face validity, 80
factor analysis, 83–84, 87, 155
Fair Access Coalition on Testing, 10–11
fairness, 138–39
family background, 124–25, 131, 195, 199–200, 203, 205, 254
Family Educational Rights and Privacy Act, 13
figure weights, 163, 164
finances, 195, 198–99
five-factor model of personality, 184
fluid intelligence (gf), 156–57, 164, 166
forced-choice items, 94
forensic evaluation, 9
Forgiveness Scale, 92
four out of five rule, 212
frequency, 56, 57t, 59t
frequency distributions, 56, 57t, 58, 58f, 59
friendship, 31
Full Scale IQ, 161, 162, 165

Galton, Sir Francis, 3–4, 151
Gardner, Howard, 158–59, 160
Garza, Eva Marie (fictional aggregate)
  anxiety, 17–24, 37–39, 46, 150, 175
  cultural issues, 149–50
  goal attainment scaling, 247–50
  initial interview, 134–37

IQ, 63, 72, 176
MSI-R, 196–200, 196f
negative thoughts, 248, 249t
outcomes for, 237
SCATT, 214–18
SPS, 209–11, 210f
GASS. *See* Goal Attainment Scale of Stabilization
gender, 139, 141
general factor. *See* g theory
generalizability, 142, 144, 148
generalized anxiety disorder, 16, 23t, 39, 46
gf-gc theory, 156–57, 160
Goal Attainment Scale of Stabilization (GASS), 83t, 84
goal attainment scaling, 239–41, 247–50
goals, 184, 240, 248–49
Goddard, Henry, 5, 146
Goleman, Daniel, 159–60
GPA (grade point average), 153, 154, 174
grooming, 126
groups, 59, 60, 63, 64, 170–74
g theory, 155, 156, 157
Guttman scale, 92, 94

hallucinations, 128
Hamilton Psychiatric Rating Scale for Depression, 85, 89
health, 35, 124, 131
healthcare legislation, 11–12
Health Insurance Portability and Accountability Act (HIPAA), 11–12, 123, 229
Health Maintenance Organization Act, 235
Helping Alliance Questionnaire-II, 246
hierarchical models, 156–57
higher education, 153–54, 170, 173–74
high-stakes testing, 171–72, 236
HIPAA. *See* Health Insurance Portability and Accountability Act
histograms, 58, 58f, 59, 60, 61f
Holland, John, 182, 183
Holland's theory/code, 180–82, 181f, 188, 189
hopelessness, 207–8, 209–10, 210f
Horn, John, 157
hostility, 208–9, 210, 210f

ICD-10 (International Statistical Classification of Diseases), 35
illness, 145
immigrants, 5–6, 146
increased latency, 128
independence, 185
Indiana, 10
individual differences, 3–4
Individuals with Disabilities Education Act, 13, 144

infidelity, 193–94
information, 162, 163, 234
informed consent, 229
initial assessment interview
   activity, 127
   affect, 127
   appearance, 126, 134, 135
   attitude, 126–27
   in case studies, 17–18, 25, 38, 134–37
   cognition, 128–29
   conducting, 120–37
   cultural concerns, 125
   economic issues, 125
   family background/issues, 124–25
   insight, 129, 135
   judgment, 129, 135
   medical history, 124, 131
   mental status, 124, 126–30, 134
   mood, 127, 134
   past counseling experiences, 124
   presenting problems, 123–24, 135–37
   purposes of, 120–21
   scope of, 121–30
   semi-structured, 122
   social support, 125
   speech/language, 127–28, 134, 135
   structured/standardized, 121–22, 130, 137
   substance use, 131–32, 132t, 134–37
   thought processes, 128
   types of data, 130–32
insight, 129, 135, 254
instrument(s), 54
   achievement, 167–68
   administration of, 93–94
   appropriateness, 171
   assessment, 107–20, 148
   construction of, 91–92
   internal consistency, 100, 101
   interpretation of, 95
   outcome, 237–38
   reliability of, 116–17
   reviewing, 229–30
   scoring, 94–95
   split-half, 100–101
   standard deviation, 96
   standardized, 220–24, 247
   strong, 84, 171
   technical quality of, 115–18
   as unreliable, 89
   validity of, 77, 79, 86–87, 117–18
   See also intelligence tests; *specific instruments*
intelligence
   of case study figures, 134, 135
   as construct, 89, 156

   contemporary modes of, 157–59
   crystallized, 156–57, 166, 174, 176
   definition of, 152, 155
   emotional, 159–60
   fluid, 156–57, 164, 166
   of immigrants, 146
   theories/models of, 155–60
intelligence tests, 5–6, 72, 153
   common measures, 160–74
   early, 151–52
   scores on, 161, 161t
   See also IQ; *specific tests*
Interest Profiler (O*NET;
   IP), 182–84, 188
interests, 180, 183, 188
internal consistency, 100–102, 105–6, 116
internal structure, 82–84, 87, 140
interrater reliability/agreement, 102, 105
interscorer reliability, 102–4
interval distributions, 58, 59t
interval scale, 55
intimidation, 194
intraclass correlation coefficient, 102–3
investigative personality type, 181
involvement, 133
Iowa Tests of Basic Skills, (ITBS), 172–73
Iowa Tests of Educational Development,
   (ITED), 172–73
IP. *See* Interest Profiler
IQ (intelligence quotient), 63, 72, 106, 174
ITBS. *See* Iowa Tests of Basic Skills
ITED. *See* Iowa Tests of Educational Development
item bias, 140
item difficulty, 51, 53, 100
item discrimination, 52–53, 100
item response theory, 89

Jones, Robert (fictional aggregate)
   case study, 25–29, 38, 43–46, 219, 231–33
   goals for, 240
   intake interview, 134–37, 219
   Outcome Questionnaire, 231–32, 231t, 232t
   outcomes for, 237, 238
   SASSI- 4, 203–5, 204f, 218
judgment, 129, 135, 254
Juhnke, Gerald, 17, 25, 29, 120, 122, 137, 210–11,
   214–17, 248–49
Juhnke-Balkin Life Balance Inventory, 80–81, 108
Jung, Carl, 112, 183

kappa coefficient, 103
Kaufman Brief Intelligence Test (KBIT- 2), 63, 72,
   157, 160, 165–66, 175–76, 176t
Kuder-Richardson formula, 102

labeling, 148, 149
language, 127–28, 134, 146, 158, 225–26, 230, 254
latent trait, 83–84
latent-trait theory. *See* item response theory
latent variables, 155
Latinos, 143, 149–50
learning disabilities, 167, 168
legal issues, 11–14, 109, 111
letter-number sequencing, 163, 164
licensing, 10–11, 109
Likert scale, 91–92, 95, 160, 206, 231
loneliness, 19, 24, 31, 207

magnitude, 73
Maine, 95, 153
managed care, 36–37, 235–36
Marital Satisfaction Inventory-Revised (MSI-R), 191–200, 196f, 218
marriage, 192–200
math calculation, 169
mathematical reasoning, 169
matrix reasoning, 163, 164
Mayer, Jack, 159
Mayer-Salovey-Caruso Emotional Intelligence Test, 159
MBTI. *See* Myers-Briggs Personality Type Indicator
mean, 59, 60, 63, 63f, 64, 67, 68, 68f, 70, 75, 96
measurement
    of central tendency, 59–63
    error, 90, 95, 105
    of intelligence, 160–66, 174
    of nonobservable processes, 4
    of outcomes, 237–38, 247
    reliability, 99–104
    scales of, 54–56
    of variability, 63–67
    See also assessment
median, 59, 60t, 62, 63, 68, 68f
mental capacities, 4
mental disorders, 35
mental health, 235–36
Mental Measurements Yearbook, 86, 106, 111–14, 119, 173
mental retardation, 4, 5
mental status exam (MSE), 121, 124, 126, 127, 134, 253
mental test, 5
Millon Clinical Multiaxial Inventory, 6, 123
Minnesota Importance Questionnaire (MIQ), 184–85
Minnesota Job Description Questionnaire, 185
Minnesota Multiphasic Personality Inventory (MMPI), 6, 86, 106, 123
minority groups. *See* ethnicity; special populations

MIQ. *See* Minnesota Importance Questionnaire
MMPI. *See* Minnesota Multiphasic Personality Inventory
MMY. *See Mental Measurements Yearbook*
mnemonic phrases, 211–14, 211f
mode, 59, 60t, 62, 63, 63f, 68, 68f
mood, 127, 134, 254
mood disorders, 16
motor control, 163
MSE. *See* mental status exam
MSI-R. *See* Marital Satisfaction Inventory-Revised
Multicultural and Social Justice Counseling Competencies (Ratts et al.), 147
multiculturalism, 147–50
multiple intelligence theory, 158–59, 160
Myers-Briggs Personality Type Indicator (MBTI), 112, 183–84

National Board of Certified Counselors, 10
National Counselor Examination, 100
NCLB. *See* No Child Left Behind Act
negative correlation, 73, 74f
negatively skewed distribution, 61f, 63, 63f
negative thoughts, 208, 210, 210f, 248, 249, 249t
NEO Personality Inventory, 6
neroticism, 184
New Haven (Ct.), 12, 154
No Child Left Behind Act (NCLB), 13, 85, 94, 154, 235, 236
nominal scale, 54–55
nominal variable, 56
nonstandardized assessment, 3, 130, 239–41, 247
normal curve, 67–70, 68f, 70f, 251f
normal distribution, 58f, 62f, 63, 68, 68f, 71
normative sample, 54, 115–16, 143–44

Obama, Barack, 13
observed score, 90, 98, 170, 223
Ohio Scales, 243–44
O*NET system, 180, 182–90, 249
openness, 184
operational definition, 2, 89
oppositional defiant disorder, 47
ordinal scale, 55
ordinal variables, 56
Outcome Questionnaire, 231–32, 231t, 232t, 242–43
Outcome Rating Scale, 244–45, 246
outcomes, 237–39, 241, 245, 247
outliers, 58f, 60, 61f, 62

parallel forms, 100
Parsons, Frank, 178
Pearson r (Pearson product-moment correlation coefficient), 73–75, 99, 100, 102, 103

pendulum, 4–5
percent, 56, 57t, 59t
percentile, 54, 223, 230
perception, 128, 254
perceptual reasoning, 162–63
perfect correlation, 73
performance, 118–19, 158
personality, 6, 39, 112, 123, 126, 180–81, 183–84, 188
physical traits, 4, 5
picture completion, 163
poor reality testing, 129
populations, 66, 68, 76
    appropriate assessments for, 119
    estimating, 65
    See also special populations
positive correlation, 73, 74f
positively skewed distribution, 61f, 62, 63f
posttraumatic stress disorder, 34t
poverty of speech, 128
power measures, 105
power tests, 145–46
predictive bias, 139, 140
predictive evidence, 84
predictive validity, 78
presenting problems, 123–24, 135–37, 253
pressured speech, 128
principal component analysis, 83–84
privacy, 11–12
problem-solving, 166, 181, 198
processing speed, 163, 164
professional writing, 225–26
progress notes, 40–47, 234
    DART notes, 42
    diagnostic-based, 43–46
    SOAP notes, 41–42
    standardized formats, 41–46
projective tests, 7
psychiatric hospital, 213–17
psychological assessment, 16
psychological testing, 8, 10
psychometrics, 108, 109, 111, 113, 114, 171
psychosocial history, 121, 123–26

quasi-interval scale, 55

RAASI. See Reynolds Adolescent Adjustment Screening Inventory
race, 141
random error, 90, 91, 93–94
range, 57t, 64
ratio scale, 55
raw score, 222
reading comprehension, 168

realistic personality type, 180
recognition, 185
relationships, 185, 192–200
reliability
    coefficient, 96, 97, 98–105, 113, 116, 117
    current standards of, 88–106
    defining, 88–95
    estimates, 96–99, 101t, 103–6, 113
    as function of scores, 89
    index, 98–99
    of instruments, 116–17
    internal consistency, 105–6, 116
    interpretation of, 104–5
    interscorer, 102–4
    test-retest, 99, 104, 106, 117
    types of measurement, 99–104
research, 237
response format, 94–95
response processes, 81–82
response time, 4–5
Responsibilities of Users of Standardized Tests (RUST; Wall et al.), 8
Reynolds Adolescent Adjustment Screening Inventory, 122, 142, 143, 149
Reynolds Adolescent Depression Scale, 91
RIASEC model, 180–84, 181f, 186, 188
Ricci v. DeStafano, 12
RUST. *See Responsibilities of Users of Standardized Tests*

Salovey, Peter, 159
sample size, 61f, 65, 67, 68
SASSI-4. *See* Substance Abuse Subtle Scale Inventory-4
SAT (college entrance exam), 65, 70, 72, 73, 84, 95, 119, 153, 173–74
SB5. *See* Stanford-Binet Intelligence Scales
scales, 91–92, 201–3, 221
    clinical, 207–9
    validity, 193–96, 207, 211
    See also specific scales
SCATT mnemonic, 191, 211–18
scores and scoring
    assessment, 56–59, 68
    computer-based, 110-11
    CriSS, 66t
    deviation, 65
    distribution, 64
    goal attainment, 241
    on intelligence tests, 161
    internal consistency, 100, 105
    meaning of, 48–49
    observed, 90, 98
    percentile, 54

scores and scoring (*cont.*)
   procedures, 138–39
   raw, 222
   reliability as function of, 89
   standard, 70–73, 76, 170*f*, 220–24
   test, 48–49, 77, 79, 86, 93, 94, 171–72
   true, 90, 98
   types reported, 75–76
   validity, 197–200, 204
   WIP (O*NET), 188
   for writing, 168
Seguin, Edouard, 5
Self-Directed Search, 182
self-report, 6, 7, 13, 86, 113
SEM. *See* standard error of measurement
Session Rating Scale, 246
sex, 195, 199
sex bias, 140
sexual abuse, 32, 34*t*, 136, 253, 254
s factor, 155
sight vocabulary, 168
SII. *See* Strong Interest Inventory
similarities, 162, 163
68-95-99 rule, 68, 69, 70*f*
slope bias, 140
SMART principle, 240
Smith, Ann (fictional aggregate)
   BDI-II, 23, 221–24, 221*t*, 226–27, 229, 231, 255, 255*t*
   case study, 29–35, 46, 219, 226, 227, 231–33
   depression, 229–30, 239
   goals for, 240–41
   intake interview, 134–37, 219
   integrative summary for, 253–55
   outcomes for, 237, 238
Smith, Carlee (fictional aggregate), 29–30
SOAP notes, 41–42
social cues, 2
social personality type, 181
social support, 125, 254
somatic symptoms, 91
Spearman, Charles, 155, 156, 157
Spearman-Brown correction, 1–3
Spearman-Brown formula, 101, 101*t*, 105
Spearman rho correlation coefficient. *See* Pearson *r*
special populations, 142–49
speech, 127–28, 134, 135, 254
speed measures, 105
speed tests, 145–46
spelling, 168
split-half instruments, 100–101, 101*t*
split-half methods, 104, 105
SPS. *See* Suicide Probability Scale
squared average distance from mean, 64, 65, 67

stability over time. *See* test-retest formula
standard deviation, 64–72, 74, 75, 96–98, 169
standard error of measurement (SEM), 96–98, 104, 162, 223–24
standardized assessment, 3, 86, 120, 130, 242–45
standardized scores, 70–73, 220–24
standardized tests, 8, 13, 67, 105, 138, 139
Standards for Assessment in Mental Health Counseling, 122
Standards for Educational and Psychological Testing, 54, 78, 79, 85, 86, 113, 118, 139
Standards for Qualifications for Test Users (Erford et al.), 8
Stanford-Binet Intelligence Scales (SB5), 155, 160, 164–65
Stanford-Binet Test, 151–52, 156, 157
statistical significance, 161
Sternberg, Robert, 157–58
stochastic process, 120, 121
Strong Interest Inventory (SII), 78, 182, 183, 184
subjectivity, 94–95
subscales, 221–22
Substance Abuse Subtle Scale Inventory-4 (SASSI-4), 78, 122–23, 191, 200–205, 204*f*, 218
substance use. *See* alcohol use; drug use
suicide, 191, 202, 205–18
Suicide Probability Scale (SPS), 84, 89, 111, 191, 205–11, 210*f*, 214–18
sum, 65
sum of squared deviations, 66
support, 125, 185, 254
systematic error, 95

Target Symptom Rating scale, 118
teacher-created exams, 49–54
Terman, Lewis, 151
testing and tests, 3
   for ability, 153–55, 167
   for achievement, 116, 152–54, 167–74
   for aptitude, 95, 116, 146, 152–54, 167, 173, 174
   conditions, 93, 119, 138
   content, 80–81
   criterion-referenced, 49, 51
   definition of, 2
   design of, 50
   for employment, 12
   essays, 50, 51
   fairness vs. bias in, 140–42
   high-stakes, 171, 236
   item analysis, 51–54
   item development, 51
   item difficulty, 51, 53, 100
   item discrimination, 52–53, 100
   mental, 5

multiple-choice, 50, 51
norm-referenced, 54
parental consent for, 13
personality, 6
projective, 7
psychological, 8, 10
publisher qualifications, 11
results, 228
scores, 48–49, 77, 79, 86, 93, 94, 171–72
speed vs. power, 145–46
standardized, 8, 13, 67, 105, 138, 139
teacher-created, 49–54
validity of, 79-87, 171
See also intelligence tests; *specific tests*
testing effect, 99, 239
Test of Nonverbal Intelligence, 146
test-retest formula, 99, 104–6, 113, 223
Tests in Print, 111
Texas, 94
thought process/content, 128, 254
Thurstone, Louis, 155, 157
Thurstone scale, 92
transportation, 214
triarchic theory of intelligence, 158
true score, 90, 98, 170, 223
true zero, 55
T score, 68f, 72, 193–200, 204–5, 240, 241, 247

validity
　current standards for, 77–87
　definition of, 77, 79
　of instruments, 86–87, 117–18
　of MSI-R, 192–93, 197–200
　present view of, 79
　scores, 197–200, 204
　of SPS, 206–7
　of testing, 79–87, 171
　types of, 78
validity coefficient. *See* correlation coefficient
variables and variability, 54, 56, 63–67, 83–85, 155
variance, 64, 65–67, 74
verbal comprehension, 162, 163–64
verbal reasoning, 168
Vineland Adaptive Behavior Scale, 161

visual puzzles, 163, 164
vocabulary, 162, 163, 165, 168

WAIS-IV. *See* Wechsler Adult Intelligence Scale
Watkins, Randal J. III, 27
Wechsler, David, 5, 151, 156
Wechsler Adult Intelligence Scale (WAIS-IV), 151, 160, 161, 162–63
Wechsler-Bellevue Intelligence Test, 151
Wechsler Individual Achievement Test, 168–69
Wechsler Intelligence Scale for Children-V (WISC-V), 146, 156, 160, 161, 163–64
Wechsler Intelligence Scales, 80, 106
Wechsler Scales, 155–56, 157, 165
wellness, 89, 140
WHO. *See* World Health Organization
WHODAS. *See* World Health Organization Disability Assessment Schedule
Wide Range Achievement Test (WRAT- 4), 168–69
WIL. *See* Work Importance Locator
WIP. *See* Work Importance Profiler
WISC-V. *See* Wechsler Intelligence Scale for Children-V
Wissler, Clark, 5
Woodworth Personality Data Sheet, 6
word problems, 169
Work Importance Locator (O*NET; WIL), 185–86
Work Importance Profiler (O*NET; WIP), 185–89
Working Alliance Inventory-Short Form, 245–46
working conditions, 185
working memory, 163, 164
work values, 184–86, 190
World Health Organization (WHO), 35, 40
World Health Organization Disability Assessment Schedule (WHODAS), 40
worry, 18, 23t
WRAT-4. *See* Wide Range Achievement Test
writing, 168, 225–26
written report, 219–20
Wundt, Wilhelm, 4, 151

Youth Outcome Questionnaire, 108, 242–43

z score, 69, 170f, 223, 251f
z table, 69

Printed in the USA/Agawam, MA
July 28, 2021